God Speaks My Language

In this very important book, Dr Aloo Mojola has traced the history of Bible translations into the languages of eastern Africa – from the earliest versions by various missionaries in the nineteenth century, to the local translation teams that collaborated to produce the versions in current use. The research for this book is vast, compiling in one volume information that would take a long time to research, collect, collate and analyze. Dr Mojola deserves commendation for packaging in one volume so much information. The book is a valuable resource for scholars interested in the history of Bible translation (as a whole and in parts) into various African languages in Eastern and Central Africa. He challenges African biblical scholars to embark on sole translations of the Bible in their respective languages, as was done in European languages at the beginning of the Reformation. Similarly, the African Reformation will enter the arena of world history when translations by African scholars become normative. He commends Professor John S. Mbiti for his pioneer translation of the New Testament into Kiikamba and challenges younger African scholars to emulate Professor Mbiti. I rejoice with both Professor Mbiti and Dr Aloo Mojola for these exemplary achievements.

Jesse N. K. Mugambi, PhD
Department of Philosophy and Religious Studies,
University of Nairobi, Kenya

The translation of the Bible into African languages has been immensely influential in the growth and development of Christianity in Africa. This book is both informative, illuminating and challenging in telling the story of Bible translation in East Africa. Scholars and students of church history in Africa will find in this book the intersection of translation, intercultural relations and mission work as it impacted the growth of the church in East Africa. They will also find the story of the growth of the church told from the perspective of a Bible translator: Bible translation was a major task for mission agencies as they endeavored to use the Bible as a text of good news of salvation, but also as a tool for teaching literacy in East Africa. Above all they will realize the significance of Bible translation in helping the mission agencies to remain alive in mission work.

This book embodies more than the story of the translation of the Bible and is a tribute to those who were engaged in the work of mission in East Africa. It is also a substantial contribution to the work of translation by both the missionaries and mission agencies, but most of all the Africans whose story has for a long time not been told. I warmly commend it.

Esther Mombo, PhD
Associate Professor of Theology,
St Paul's University, Limuru, Kenya,

That the Bible has made a statistical and linguistic home in Africa cannot be refuted. At the beginning of 2013, there were at least 748 African languages with the Bible (in full, New Testament, or portion). This is nearly 30 percent of Bible translations in the whole world. The religiously fertile African soil has now the largest indigenous settlement of the Bible on the earth. And it is thriving there!

Professor Aloo Mojola's book *God Speaks My Language: A History of Bible Translation in East Africa* articulates the beautiful story of how the Bible came to settle in Eastern Africa. Accordingly, that started in the mid-nineteenth century with the German missionary and linguist J. L. Krapf. It gained momentum in the twentieth century and continues unrelenting in our time. Thank you Dr Mojola for documenting this fascinating and unfolding outreach of the Holy Scriptures.

The book is an excellent piece of research, documentation, organization and presentation of that story. It is comprehensive, informative, up-to-date, and highly readable. It is a great compliment to the Bible and an encouraging support to its further translations and revisions.

John Mbiti, PhD
Former Emeritus Professor,
University of Bern, Switzerland

One of the pioneers of the translation of the Bible in East Africa was Alexander M. Mackay, the illustrious Scottish lay missionary with the Church Missionary Society in Uganda. He distinguished himself as a devoted and practical student of the Bible long before his missionary career commenced. It was in this vein that, while in Germany for engineering studies, he characterized the Bible as "the inexhaustible mine of pure gold" in a write-up on 14 April 1874.

Another devoted and practical student of the Bible, Prof Aloo Osotsi Mojola has painstakingly and meticulously chronicled the history of the translation of this priceless treasure – the Bible – in the larger East Africa region. In his earlier edition, he captured Bible translation endeavours in the traditional historical and political entity of East Africa as represented by Kenya, Uganda, and Tanzania. This current work, which is updated and expanded, broadens the landscape to include Rwanda and Burundi in the re-configured sphere of East Africa.

As a person, Prof Mojola is fully qualified to write the history of Bible translation in East Africa. He does not undertake this task as an armchair researcher with a shallow grasp of the field under consideration. What issues from his pen emanates from one who embodies a rare and unique ring of authenticity. The combined blend unveils one who has thoroughly immersed himself in the depth of Christian spirituality, has scaled the heights of biblical and linguistic scholarship, and is rooted in the firm ground of African identity.

The resultant product is an exquisite masterpiece of surpassing excellence. Throughout, there is ample evidence of Prof Mojola's own established Christian certitude, breadth of scholarly expertise, and genuine affinity with the subject matter. In addition to the wealth of knowledge and information on the Bible and its translation in East Africa, the book is an invaluable literary gold mine on the history, ethnography, ecclesiology, and even geography of the communities in the catchment area. In overall coverage, it is incomparable from the stand point of being comprehensive in scope, as well as detailed in content.

Rev Watson Omulokoli, PhD
Chancellor,
Africa International University, Nairobi, Kenya

In this latest version, Aloo Mojola's book on the history of Bible translation in East Africa is a work of immense importance to the field. It is detailed in its presentation of material, focused on the facts and practices of Bible translation, engaged with the agents and personalities involved, and grounded in the societies and cultures affected. Its theme is Bible translation as the signature tune of the Christian movement; its merit is the clear and lucid exposition of that theme with unflinching adherence to evidence. It is history as the Christian movement has powered and shaped it, and it shows how the purposive impetus of the indigenous discovery of the gospel is key to recognizing the inexhaustible potential of the religion. *God Speaks My Language* is a significant achievement that deserves to be celebrated.

Lamin Sanneh, PhD
Former D. Willis James Professor of Missions and World Christianity,
Yale Divinity School, New Haven, Connecticut, USA

The presence of a large and thriving Christian church in East Africa today is due in very large part to the availability of the Scriptures in the languages of the people. For this reason, the story Aloo Mojola narrates of how the Bible was translated and continues to be translated in this region, forms a very significant part of the history of the church there, and is a key factor in understanding the issues that face those churches today. Language by language and translator by translator, Mojola introduces us to the Protestant and Roman Catholic missionaries and Africans who committed themselves to the task of translating the Bible in Kenya, Tanzania, Uganda, Rwanda, Burundi and parts of the Congo. As someone who has worked with translators throughout the area, Mojola is particularly well qualified to describe and assess the linguistic, cultural and exegetical issues. His descriptions of the political and environmental obstacles they overcame make for fascinating reading and also serve as an important reminder of the great debt that today's church owes these men and women.

Philip C. Stine, PhD
Former Director for Translation, Production and Distribution Services,
United Bible Societies

God Speaks My Language

A History of Bible Translation in East Africa

Aloo Osotsi Mojola

© 2020 Aloo Osotsi Mojola

Published 2020 by HippoBooks, an imprint of ACTS and Langham Publishing.

Africa Christian Textbooks (ACTS), TCNN, PMB 2020, Bukuru 930008, Plateau State, Nigeria.
www.actsnigeria.org

Langham Publishing, PO Box 296, Carlisle, Cumbria, CA3 9WZ, UK
www.langhampublishing.org

ISBNs:
978-1-78368-544-8 Print
978-1-78368-824-1 ePub
978-1-78368-825-8 Mobi
978-1-78368-826-5 PDF

British Library Cataloguing-in-Publication Data
A catalogue record for this book is available from the British Library

ISBN: 978-1-78368-544-8

Cover & Book Design: projectluz.com

Dedication

To all Bible translators past and present,
those whose names are known and those who remain nameless, who
have worked and continue to work tirelessly and sacrificially in the East
African countries of Kenya, Uganda, and Tanzania, as well as those of
Rwanda and Burundi, in order that all who dwell in these countries may
hear God speak to each in their own language – may their memory always
be a blessing to the glory of God and the extension of his kingdom.

And to the loving memory of
my late dear mother Yunia Aluoch nyar Mindhune
– for her faith, love, joy, and labors in the Lord.

Epigraph

(Kiswahili)
Titi la mama litamu, hata likiwa la mbwa
Kiswahili naazimu, sifayo inayofumbwa
Kwa wasiokufahamu, niimbe ilivyo kubwa
Toka kama chemuchemu, furika palipozibwa
Titile mama litamu, jingine halishi hamu.

A mother's breast is sweet, even though it be a dog's.
Swahili language I am deeply indebted to your hidden wealth and
*   heritage*
For those who do not know you I will sing how great and wonderful
*   you are*
Flow forth like a spring and flood everywhere
A mother's breast is sweet, none other can satisfy.[1]

Shabaan Robert

---

1. Shabaan Robert, *Pambo la lugha* (Nairobi: Oxford University Press, 1966), 27–31. Translation author's own.

Contents

List of Figures

List of Tables

List of Maps

Foreword

The early Christian church extended across the entire width of North Africa from Alexandria in Egypt to Hippo in today's Algeria. In the second and third centuries, Christianity spread up the Nile Valley among the Coptic peoples to Upper Egypt; by the sixth century, the Nubian kingdom of Dongola was Christian; the gospel reached the kingdom of Axum as early as the fourth century, and by the sixth and seventh centuries the Scriptures were translated into Ge'ez, the national language of Ethiopia. However, it was not until the nineteenth century that the Bible reached East Africa, and when it came, it did not come overland from its African neighbors to the north, but instead it came from Europe by sea.

The origins of the Christian church in today's East African nations are found in the efforts of the first missionaries and their successors to learn local languages and to translate the Holy Scriptures; the expansion and growth of the Christian church from these early beginnings up to the present time may be identified in great part with succeeding generations of translators who translated the Bible into their own African mother tongues.

Swahili, the Bantu trade language of the East African coast, developed as a written language in the fabled cities of Lamu, Mombasa, and Zanzibar during nearly a thousand years of Islamic trade and settlement before the arrival of Christianity. Poets sang the praises of God whom they called both "Allah" according to Arabic tradition and "Mungu" in their own Swahili language; however, in conformity with Islamic practice, the Qur'an was not translated into Swahili. Christians, on the other hand, brought their Holy Book and quickly set about translating it into Swahili and into the languages of the interior of the African continent. As the Bible was rendered in one language after another, it introduced the incarnate Christ into the cultures and lives of the peoples of the East African coastlands and mainland alike.

The Kenyan theologian Jesse N. K. Mugambi asserts that, "The Bible is central to African Christianity. It is," he writes, "the most widely read book in tropical Africa. The Bible is the most widely available book in both urban and rural areas. It can be regarded as the most influential book in Africa."[1]

---

1. Mugambi, *From Liberation to Reconstruction*, 142.

The account that Aloo Mojola provides in the pages of this volume is the story of the translation of the Bible in the East African nations of Kenya, Uganda, Tanzania, Burundi, and Rwanda. It is a record that is more complex and engaging than the recital of language names and the dates that mark the undertaking of translation projects or the dedication and launching of newly published Scriptures, even though the inventory of languages in so diverse a linguistic milieu as that of these five nations makes fascinating reading in itself.

The story of translation is comprised of many elements: early mission and church policy; political, economic, and social objectives of colonial governments; world wars and independence movements; politics of new states and developing nationhood; contemporary programs for language management, literacy, and education; and of course, in today's world, mass communication, multi-media, the internet, and globalization. These factors, together with the personal vision and vicissitudes of the translators themselves, are all woven into the fabric of Scripture translation that is portrayed by the author of this book.

Since the nineteenth-century translation efforts of Johann Krapf and Johannes Rebmann in Mombasa and Bishop Edward Steere in Zanzibar, the practice of Scripture translation has been influenced by numerous trends and scientific developments. Although biblical scholarship and theological studies in their day already possessed long histories, the descriptive study of language was in its infancy. The importance of language and culture was recognized, but the scientific tools for their analysis had not yet been refined. The objective of the translators was to communicate the word of God as exactly as possible and this approach often led to what are referred to as "literal" translations. While our author acknowledges the great service rendered by these early translations in the growth of the church in East Africa, he also discusses the linguistic and anthropological findings that have led to greater emphasis on the communication of the message in today's translation of Holy Scripture.

Dr Mojola traces the history of Scripture translation from early missionary efforts with the, often unacknowledged, assistance of local-language speakers to contemporary translations that are carried out by teams of mother-tongue speakers with the technical assistance of consultants from Bible translation agencies such as the United Bible Societies and SIL International. Increasingly, Mojola notes, translations are being made from the original biblical languages instead of from other translations such as English, Arabic, and Swahili.

Translation is always an unfinished task. Calls for the revision of aging translations and eventually for altogether new translations will emerge as language adapts and renews itself to meet the needs resulting from ever-changing social conditions. Although many languages spoken today in the East African countries of this study possess Scripture translations, there are many languages that are still without any Scripture. What then are future translation needs? Which languages are growing and expanding? Which ones will die as mastery of national and international languages becomes increasingly prestigious and beneficial in the judgment of speakers of local vernaculars? With the availability of modern technology, what will be the role for translations in other than the written medium, for example, for audio and video? These are just some of the crucial questions that the author raises and discusses in the pages of this book.

On Pentecost Day, the Holy Spirit enabled travelers gathered in Jerusalem from the continents of Asia, Europe, and Africa to hear about God's great deeds in their own languages. In the nations of East Africa, it is with thanks to the labors of Bible translators that readers and listeners to the Scriptures can declare, "[we have learned] in our own languages about the great things that God has done" (Acts 2:11 GNT). Dr Mojola's work, is a monument to the translators – known and anonymous alike – who have dedicated their lives to the arduous task of engaging with the Scripture message and expressing it in their own languages.

Philip A. Noss, PhD
Former UBS Translation Services Coordinator
April 2020

Acknowledgements

This brief and general overview of the story of Bible translation in the East African countries of Kenya, Uganda, and Tanzania, together with Rwanda and Burundi, is a fruit of my work as a Bible translation consultant in each of these countries. Since May 1983 I have had the rare privilege of working with a host of Bible translation teams in a diversity of languages supported by the churches and the national Bible Societies in these beautiful countries. Needless to say, the hospitality and generosity of Bible Society staff contributed to creating an enviable learning environment that enabled me to appreciate the wealth of their historical experience in Bible translation history.

It is a joy to mention the names of Mzee Emmanuel Kibira, Rev Albert Mongi, Rev Dr Mkunga Mtingele and Rev Canon Naphtali Lusinde in Tanzania; Rt Rev Bishop Benezeri Kisembo, Mr Jeroboam Kaddu, Mr Henry Kalule, Mr Peter Mukama, Rev Father Dr Francis Mbaziira in Uganda; Rev John Ole Tompo Mpaayei, Pastor Joseph Musembi, the Rev Dr Otieno Mare Munala, Rt Rev Bishop Henry Kathii, Mrs Elizabeth Muriuki, Rev Canon Micah Amukobole, Mr Peter Munguti (BTL) in Kenya; Rev Evariste Munyabarame, Dr Tharcisse Gatwa, Rev Anasthase Kajugiro, and Mr Norbert Rutebuka in Rwanda; Mrs Marjorie Niyungeko in Burundi; and Pastor Nlandu Mukoko Thomas and Pastor Christophe Kongo Kote in the Democratic Republic of Congo (DRC).

A number of colleagues around the world in the United Bible Societies (UBS), especially those of the Africa Area, have been a strong source of support and encouragement. Special mention goes to Rev Dr Daud Soesilo of Indonesia, Dr William Mitchell of Canada and Scotland, Dr Simon Crisp of England, Dr Kees de Blois of the Netherlands, and Dr Margaret Muthwii of Kenya, my successor as the UBS Africa Area Translation Coordinator. Dr Musimbi Kanyoro introduced me to the UBS in the early 1980s and has remained a steadfast friend and encourager. I warmly acknowledge Dr Peter Masumbuko Renju of Moshi, Tanzania, Rev Dr Mikre Sellassie and Dr Haileyesus Engdashet Woldemariam of Addis Ababa, Ethiopia, and Dr Jean-Claude Loba-Mkole of the DRC for their unfailing support and counsel.

The idea for this book was given warm support and encouragement by Dr Philip A. Noss, my mentor and predecessor as the UBS Africa Area

Coordinator and later my boss as the UBS Global Translation Services Coordinator in Reading, England. His wealth of experience, advice, and unstinting support that he has freely given, has contributed enormously in enhancing the quality and shape of this book. I am extremely grateful to Phil for his friendship, kind heart, and warm generosity. As the main editor of this work, Dr Noss has painstakingly gone through it and pointed out numerous errors and inaccuracies. I am indeed most grateful to him for his commitment and generosity of spirit. I am, of course, totally responsible for any errors or inaccuracies that still remain undetected.

I cannot fail to acknowledge the special role played by the American Bible Society (ABS) and the Eugene A. Nida Institute for Biblical Scholarship in encouraging and supporting some of the research for this book and its publication. The unparalleled generosity and warm friendship of Dr Robert Hodgson Jr, the former dean of the Nida Institute has been an inspiration and a source of great encouragement. In the course of research for this study, I was privileged to visit the American Bible Society Library and Archives in New York City. It is in order to record here my heartfelt gratitude and appreciation for the kind help and generous assistance that I received from Dr Liana Lupas, Curator of the ABS Scripture collection in New York, and especially for granting me access to material pertaining to the languages of Kenya, Tanzania, Uganda, Rwanda, Burundi, and DRC from her research for the unpublished manuscript, "Book of Two Thousand Tongues." The help and assistance of Ms Jacquelyn Sapiie, Library Services Supervisor at the American Bible Society, and especially her willingness, readiness, and kindness in availing photocopies of the appropriate sections on the languages of East Africa from the ABS unpublished historical essays is gratefully appreciated. I am especially grateful to Dr Hodgson for generously hosting me in New York City for this memorable visit to the ABS for this purpose. I am equally grateful to Dr Philip Stine, one of the key leaders of the UBS in recent times for his warm and generous hospitality both at his former home in New Jersey and at his former office in New York City for initially introducing me to the ABS library. I am very grateful to him for generously offering valuable stylistic and editorial comments and suggestions on the entire work which have contributed to making this a much better and more readable text.

Special mention must be made of the help I received in England from Mrs Ingrid Roderick, the British and Foreign Bible Society (BFBS) Archivist and Senior Information Officer in Swindon, UK, who first introduced me to the Bible Society library and generously allowed me access to as much of the relevant primary documents and material as I had time for. She kindly made arrangements for me to visit the Cambridge University Library, Cambridge, where the Rev Alan Jesson and his successors as Bible Society librarians, Ms Rosemary Matthew and Mr Peter Meadows, gave me generous assistance and access to the excellent and unrivalled translation historical material at the Cambridge University Library. The time at my disposal did not do justice to the wealth of archival material relevant to my study that is found in this library. This fact helps to underline the fact that the story narrated in this study serves only as a preface to the work that waits to be done by some future church historian or missiologist.

I am equally grateful to the German Bible Society General Secretary, Herr Dr Jan Buehner, and his assistant, Frau Christel Schweitzer, for facilitating a most valuable visit to the Landesbibliothek in Stuttgart. I was especially touched by the warmth and friendship of Bible House staff, especially Herr Ruprecht Veigel, Frau Ingrid Felber-Bischof, Frau Beate Schubert, and the Executive Director Herr Dr Felix Breidenstein for a memorable tour of some of the landmarks of downtown Stuttgart. I am grateful for the generous hospitality of the Evangelisches Diakonissenanstalt Mutterhaus in downtown Stuttgart, close to the Wuerttembergische Landesbibliothek, and to Sister Ulrike Goeckelmann of the Mutterhaus for their encouragement. Special thanks go to Herr Dr Eberhard Zwink, Librarian at the Landesbibiliothek for his assistance and especially for a tour of their Africa collection in their air-conditioned safe rooms at the library. Given the political and missionary relationship between Germany and East Africa during the colonial period, the Landesbibliothek holds very valuable materials of historical interest, for example, the entire Gospel of Mark in Kikamba, translated by Johann Krapf in 1850 and printed in Tübingen, among other gems.

As indicated above, I am most fortunate on account of my work for the UBS to have visited or worked with quite a number of recent and current translation projects sponsored by the respective Bible Societies of Kenya, Uganda, Tanzania, Rwanda, Burundi, and DRC. I have been most privileged to have personally met and worked with many of the translators and translation teams mentioned in this work. I am most grateful to all of them, translators, reviewers, translation committee members, as well as church leaders from the sponsoring churches, Bible Society staff and colleagues. This has me given a unique vantage point for appreciating the intricacies and complexities of translation work, which would not have otherwise been possible. May the memory of such dedicated men and women as Miss Millie Coulton of the Alur project at Kasengu, DRC, Rev John Ole Tompo Mpaayei of the Maasai project at Ngong Hills, Kenya, Mzee Kaisi Mwamatandala of the Kinyakyusa project at Rungwe and Kyela, Mzee Jairus Asila of the Lunyole project at Kima, Kenya, Mzee Daniel Tumkou of the Pokoot project at Kapenguria, Kenya, Mzee Evan Mwavua and Daniel Kana of the Kidawida project at Wundanyi, Kenya, Ndugu Jared Mwanjala of the Swahili Habari Njema project, Sagalla Hills, Taita, Mzee Emmanuel Kibira of Dodoma and Bukoba, Tanzania, Rev Canon Naphtali Petro Lusinde and many others who toiled tirelessly that the many may have the word in languages that they understand best – may their memory always be a blessing to the praise and glory of God and his eternal word. Surely their labor in the Lord was not in vain!

A close working relationship with the Bible Societies of Kenya, Uganda, Tanzania, Rwanda, Burundi and the DRC, as well as with the Bible Translation and Literacy organization of Kenya (BTL), and with their respective general secretaries, has greatly facilitated the writing of this story. Indeed, it is the cooperation and encouragement of these wonderful colleagues and friends, together with the friendship and love of staff in their respective societies and throughout the UBS fellowship that has made this work possible. I wish I could include all their names here, as they continue to inspire me and to sustain my interest in the cause of the Bible.

The positive comments and suggestions of my good friends, Rev Prof Watson Omulokoli, professor in church history at Kenyatta University, Nairobi, and Rev Canon Micah Amukobole, former General Secretary of BTL and immediate former Chairman, Board of the Bible Society of Kenya, have contributed to improving this text. Mr Manasseh Wekunda of BTL gave many useful suggestions and special help in obtaining many of the maps included here, with the support of the BTL General Secretary, Mr Mundara Muturi, and the assistance of Mr Colin Davis of the Summer Institute of Linguistics map office in the UK. I am extremely grateful to them all.

Last, but not least, I must mention three from my immediate family circle – Namitala, Sanyu, and Bitalo – my constant joy and inspiration. *Soli Deo gloria!*

Abbreviations

AAC	African Anglican Church
AACC	All Africa Conference of Churches
ABS	American Bible Society
ACHS	African Church of the Holy Spirit
ACT	Anglican Church of Tanzania
ACK	Anglican Church of Kenya
ADRA	Adventist Relief Agency
AGC	Africa Gospel Church
AIC	Africa Inland Church
AIM	Africa Inland Mission
BCE	Before Common Era
BCMS	Bible Churchmen's Missionary Society
BEA	British East Africa
BFBS	British and Foreign Bible Society
BFBSA	British and Foreign Bible Society Archives
BHN	*Biblia Habari Njema*
BIR	*Bibiliya Ijambo Ry'Imana*
BN	*Bibiliya Ntagatifu*
BSE	Bible Society of Ethiopia
BSEA	Bible Society in East Africa
BSK	Bible Society of Kenya
BST	Bible Society of Tanzania
BSU	Bible Society of Uganda
BTL	Bible Translation and Literacy (Ltd.) Kenya
BY	*Bibiliya Yera*
CCK	Christian Council of Kenya
CCS	Christian Community Services
CEV	Contemporary English Version
CSM	Church of Scotland Mission
CTP	Central Tanganyika Press

DRC	Democratic Republic of Congo (formerly Zaire)
EAYMF	East African Yearly Meeting of Friends
ELCT	Evangelical Lutheran Church of Tanzania
EMS	Evangelical Missionary Society for German East Africa
ESV	English Standard Version
FAIM	Friends Africa Industrial Mission
FAM	Friends Africa Mission
FCBH	Faith Comes by Hearing
FCSM	Free Church of Scotland Mission
GEA	German East Africa
GEMA	Gikuyu, Embu, Meru, Akamba communities
GFF	Gospel Furthering Fellowship
GMS	Gospel Missionary Society
GNB	Good News Bible (also TEV and GNT)
GNT	Good News Translation (formerly, GNB and TEV)
GS	General Secretary
IBEA	Imperial British East Africa Company
KPCU	Kenya Planters Cooperative Union
KSFC	Kenya Students Christian Fellowship
KJV	King James Version
LBI	Living Bibles International
LMS	London Missionary Society
MMS	Methodis Missionary Society
NBSS	National Bible Society of Scotland
NCCK	National Council of Churches of Kenya
NIV	New International Version
NKJV	New King James Version
NLM	Norwegian Lutheran Mission
NRSV	New Revised Standard Version
PAEA	Pentecostal Association of East Africa
PBT	Pioneer Bible Translators
PCEA	Presbyterian Church of East Africa
PEFA	Pentecostal Evangelistic Fellowship of Africa
RC	Roman Catholic Church

RSUV	Revised Swahili Union Version
RSV	Revised Standard Version
SDA	Seventh-Day Adventist Church
SDAM	Seventh-Day Adventist Mission
SEM	Swedish Evangelical Lutheran Mission
SIL	Summer Institute of Linguistics
SIM	Sudan Interior Mission
SOAS	School of Oriental and African Studies
SPCK	Society for the Promotion of Christian Knowledge
SPG	Society for the Propagation of the Gospel
SUV	Swahili Union Version
TC	Translation Consultant
TEV	Today's English Version (also GNB and GNT)
TMP	Tabora Mission Press
UBS	United Bible Societies
UMCA	Universities Mission to Central Africa
UNESCO	United Nations Educational, Scientific and Cultural Organization
UNICEF	United Nations Children's Fund
WBT	Wycliffe Bible Translators
WBTI	Wycliffe Bible Translators International
WGM	World Gospel Mission
WO	Wycliffe Organization

1

Setting the Stage for the Story

Beginnings of Bible Translation

The message of the Judeo-Christian Scriptures is intended for everyone. In these Scriptures, the eternal God, the God of the universe, has spoken to all peoples everywhere. Although initially given in particular languages, cultures, and time, this message is intended for people of all languages and cultures across time. The God of the universe has not spoken to only one people. No, God has spoken and speaks to all peoples – of every race, tribe, nation, and language "using our own languages" (Acts 2:11 CEV), "speaking our very own languages" (Acts 2:8 CEV). Indeed, God speaks in our own languages, so that everyone can hear him speak in their own mother tongue. All the languages that humans speak are from God, all of them. And they are suitable as a sacred means for divine communication. In this respect, no language is inferior. All are equal.[1]

The original Judeo-Christian Scriptures appeared in the ancient Hebrew, Aramaic, and Greek tongues. It was only a matter of time before these would be made available to speakers of other languages. The story of Bible translation in Africa is not limited to the present period. It is as old as Bible translation itself. Its earliest beginnings go back to Egypt about 200 to 300 BCE when the Hebrew Bible, which Christians would come to call the Old Testament, was translated into Greek, the most widely spoken language or lingua franca of that time in the Middle East.

The Old Testament was originally written in ancient Hebrew. Some parts of the Old Testament such as Genesis 31:47; Jeremiah 10:11; Ezra 4:8–6:18; 7:12–26; and Daniel 2:46–7:28 were, however, written in the linguistically

---

1. For discussion of this topic see Nida and Taber, *Theory and Practice of Translation*, 3–8.

closely related language of Aramaic. The books of the New Testament, on the other hand, were all written in ancient Greek. The translation of the Hebrew Bible into Greek is usually called the *Septuaginta* (Latin word for "seventy") as it is believed by some to have been translated by seventy or seventy-two Jewish elders in the ancient city of Alexandria in Egypt. The *Septuaginta* (written briefly as LXX) later became the Old Testament used by Christians during the apostolic period and onwards. As the early church spread throughout the Mediterranean world and beyond, translations of the Bible were made from the Hebrew and Greek into some of the languages of the post-apostolic period such as Syriac, Latin, and Coptic.

The rise and hegemony of the Roman Empire and its spread on the ashes of the fallen Greek empire saw the supplanting of the Greek language and the rise of Latin as the new imperial language and lingua franca of that period. The conversion of Emperor Constantine in 312 and the establishment of Christianity as the state religion gave special status to Latin as the language of religion. The famous Latin translation of the Bible by Saint Jerome in Bethlehem in the fourth century, called the *Vulgata* (Vulgate) because it was in the vulgar or common language of the people at the time, became the major version used by the Roman Catholic Church until recent times. In Egypt, where Christianity goes back to the apostolic period, the Bible was translated in the ancient Coptic languages as early as the third century. Use of Coptic Scriptures continues in a limited way to the present time among some monks within the Egyptian Orthodox Coptic Church. An early Ethiopian translation of the Bible in the ancient language of Ge'ez goes back to the fourth century and is still in use today for liturgical purposes by the Ethiopian Orthodox church. Ge'ez was, however, overtaken by the widespread use of Amharic in Ethiopia in the centuries that followed.

Naturally, the spread of Christianity throughout the world went hand in hand with the translation of the Holy Scriptures into the languages of the receptor cultures. Thus, in the roll call of the well-known names of such luminaries as John Wycliffe and William Tyndale (England), Martin Luther (Germany), John Eliot (North America), William Carey (India), and Samuel Adjai Crowther (Nigeria), the following names, among others of both men and women, from the East African scene will surely find a place: Johann Krapf and Johannes Rebmann; John Ole Tompo Mpaayei and Joseph Kasio; Isaya and Joyce Emanikor; Stephen Houghton and David Diida; Evan Mwavua and Daniel Kana; Jared Mwanjala and Peter Renju; Emmanuel Kibira and Philip Tibaijuka; Naphtali Petro Lusinde and Oliver Timothy Cordell; Bruno Gutmann and John Mlay; Frøydis Nordbustad and Mary Bura; Edward Steere and W. P. Johnson;

Kaisi Mwamatandala and Stephini Nikodemo Nzuuli; Apolo Kivebulaya and Henry Wright Dutamaguzi (Duta) Kitaakule[2]; H. A. W. Pilkington and Harry E. Maddox; and John Kiisa and Francis Xavier Mbaziira. The list is endless and keeps growing. It includes many of the names mentioned in this survey, as well as others not mentioned.

African missionary historiography has not adequately recognized the role and place of the African players and actors in the exciting story of the Christianization of the African continent and the concomitant story of translating the Scriptures into the various languages of Africa. In this present survey a special attempt is made to give due credit wherever possible to African translators as well as to their foreign missionary colleagues.

The nineteenth and twentieth centuries are unique not only in the worldwide expansion of Christianity, but also in the accompanying wave of Bible translations in the languages of Africa as of the other continents. Christian expansion and Bible translation followed in the wake of European conquest. Just as in earlier times the rise of Christianity rode on the tide of the Greek and Roman imperial and colonial civilization, so in the nineteenth and twentieth centuries the spread of Christianity rode on the tide of European and American colonial, imperial, and postcolonial civilization. That Bible translation inevitably accompanied the Christianization of communities and peoples is part of the logic of Christianity itself. Christian teaching and practice always call for the "Book of Life" which is the basic foundation document of the Christian system.

At the heart of the message of this book is the idea of incarnation, of God becoming human, of experiencing the human condition in all its beauty as well as bestiality, in its zenith as well as its nadir. In two recent texts, Andrew Walls explores in great detail both the transmission and appropriation of faith, using the incarnation as a helpful picture of both the missionary movement and the cross-cultural process. He notes for example that "Bible translation as a process is thus both a reflection of the central act on which the Christian faith depends and a concretization of the commission which Christ gave his disciples. Perhaps no other specific activity more clearly represents the mission of the Church."[3] He notes further that, "Incarnation is translation . . . The translation of God into humanity, whereby the sense and meaning of God was transferred, was effected under very culture-specific conditions . . . The first divine act of translation into humanity thus gives rise to a constant succession of new translations. Christian

---

2. Henceforth referred to as Duta.

3. Walls, *Missionary Movement*, 28.

diversity is the necessary product of the Incarnation."[4] Incarnation is usually discussed these days in terms of such ideas as enculturation, contextualization, indigenization, and localization, among others. Any such endeavor must of necessity begin with the everyday life and concrete realities of the receptor culture, expressed in the language and thought forms of that culture. It is no accident that in the Christianization of communities and peoples it was necessary to express the message of Christianity in the everyday languages and dialects of those communities. And for the missionary, what better place to begin than in the translation of the book that is the fundamental text or foundation document of the Christian religious system?

The Gambian church historian and missiologist Lamin Sanneh has given eloquent expression to this process, which he terms vernacularization.[5] For Sanneh, "The vernacular was the magnetic field in which the attempt to transmit Christianity from Europe was primed for indigenous assimilation."[6] Sanneh sees the Christian missionary enterprise as eager "to press to its logical conclusion the premise of the universal admissibility of all cultures in the general sweep of God's 'plan of salvation,' eager to witness to God in the words and names of other people's choosing."[7] The translation of the Christian Scriptures into other languages is therefore not a one-sided process. It calls for an active encounter between cultures, meanings, symbols and their material worlds, as well as for dialogue and trans-cultural and cross-cultural interpretation and assimilation. It introduces the foreign but also allows for the domestication of the foreign in terms of the local.

Although the beginnings of Bible translation frequently coincided with the beginnings of the European colonization, in the case of East Africa, the missionary preceded the colonial settler, trader, and administrator. Johann Krapf and Johannes Rebmann, the first missionaries and translators, preceded the explorers and other imperial agents in East Africa. At the top of their agenda was Bible translation. Indeed, Krapf started translating almost before he had even mastered the languages of his translations. Obviously Krapf was on to something, the power of which he certainly had some inkling. How else to explain his foresight or his zeal and energy? David Barrett in hindsight has made the following point:

---

4. Walls, 27.

5. For a good overview on this matter, see Sanneh, *Translating the Message*; and Stine, ed., *Bible Translation*.

6. Sanneh, *Translating the Message*, 96.

7. Sanneh, "Gospel and Culture," 17.

The role of vernacular translations of the Christian Scriptures in this growth of organized Christianity has been very marked. The Scriptures have motivated the planting of Christianity in Africa at every stage; they have directly caused its expansion in countless regions; they have produced the strong and mature churches which we now observe in most parts of the continent; and they have nurtured them throughout.[8]

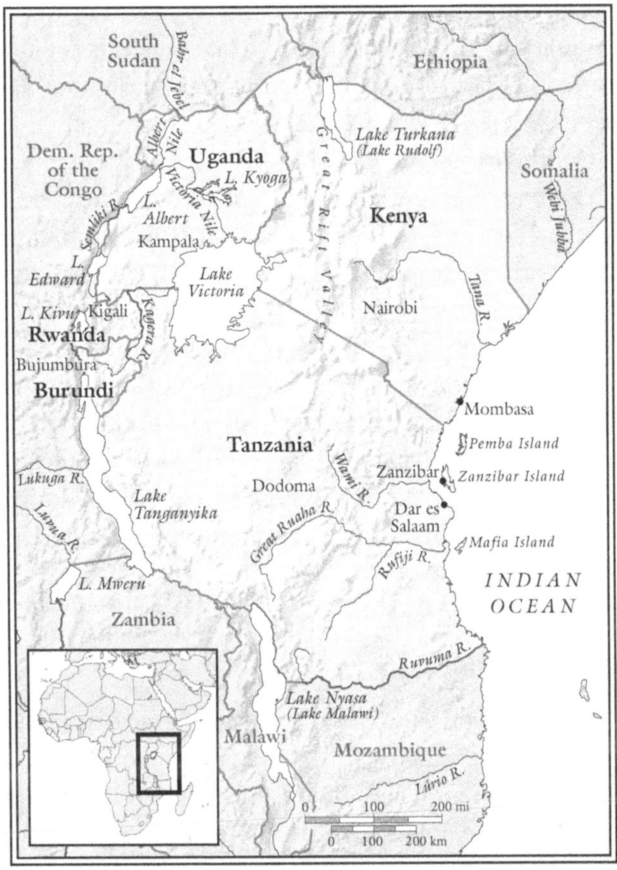

Map 1.1. Map of East Africa Today. American Bible Society Library and Archives. Used by permission.

---

8. Barrett, "Spread of the Bible," 6. See also John S. Mbiti, *Bible and Theology*. Mbiti has explored in some detail ways in which the Bible and theology have been domesticated and depend for their effective communication and relevance on the African religious, social, and cultural worlds.

In the pioneer stages of Bible translation in Africa, the missionaries tended to work in the major languages, (i.e. those that were widely spoken and used by a majority of people as trade languages or as the lingua franca of a region), hence the choice of such languages as Swahili or Luganda, and the development of so-called "union" translations. These translations were based on the rationale of using a language which would be understood across a wide area. The promotion and use of union translations in a language area comprising several dialects, deemed to be related and mutually intelligible, was intended to minimize duplication of effort by providing the Scriptures in a common version that all who spoke such related dialects could understand.

This approach or translation strategy proved unpopular and met with minimal success and has generally therefore been discontinued. The failure of the Oluluyia Union Version, for example, gave rise to alternative translations of the Bible in a number of its dialects, such as the Lubukusu, the Olulogooli, the Olunyole, the Olusamia, the Lukakamega-Lutirichi, and the Lumarama-Kisa-Wanga-Tsotso translations. The Kimeru and Kalenjin union translations achieved a measure of success but are still experiencing certain strains. The Swahili Union Version (SUV) is perhaps the best example of a successful union translation. It became the most widely read text in the region and even became the primary medium for the popularization of the standard form of the language. This was partly due to the powerful support it received from the government and from religious and missionary agencies. The Runyoro-Rutooro and the Runyankole-Rutooro union translations may also be cited as success stories in the East Africa region.

Bible Translation and Mission

Translation work was inextricably linked with literacy and education. The pioneer missionary translators not only developed writing systems or orthographies for new languages, but also developed literacy programs to teach people how to read. Obviously, the Bible in the target language would only be useful if the target audience could read and make use of it. It is not an accident that the first Christians were called "readers," (i.e. *asomi, basomi, wasomi*,[9] etc.). As Jews were identified as "People of the Book" in the Roman Empire, so Christianity in East Africa became in a real sense the religion of the Book and of readers. The readers' revolution in Buganda that was stimulated by

---

9. These Bantu words in Kikamba, Luyia, and Swahili respectively were used to mean or refer to "readers." "Readers" and "Christians" were sometimes used interchangeably.

George L. Pilkington and Duta Kitaakule's translation of the Bible in Luganda is a prime example of the influence of the Book and its readers. Other forms of education were natural outgrowths of this basic one of reading the Book. As well-known writer and novelist Ngũgĩ wa Thiong'o acknowledged, "The early African novel produced under such circumstances took its themes and moral preoccupations from the Bible," and, "I also incorporated a biblical element – the parable – because many literates would have read the [B]ible."[10] That the missionary was a pioneer of education in East Africa cannot be denied.

The Bible translation movement in East Africa, as elsewhere, was from its beginnings until contemporary times initiated and driven by Western missionary agencies and personnel. Mildred Larson[11] has categorized the movement in four stages from missionary translator to mother-tongue translator. She depicts the first stage as characterized by the missionary translator who needed mother-tongue speakers of the language as informants or assistants. The second stage is characterized by the missionary translator who was the principal translator but who needed mother-tongue speakers of the language as dependent and auxiliary translators. The third stage is characterized by the missionary advisor/exegete who is involved in the quality control of[12] the text of translation done by independent but not very well-trained translators working in their own mother tongue. The fourth stage is characterized by independent and well-trained translators working in their own languages, but receiving technical help and advice from consultants and experts.

Mildred Larson gained long and wide experience working for the Summer Institute of Linguistics International (SIL) and Wycliffe Bible Translation (WBT) agencies.[13] Consequently, the above categorization applies mainly to SIL and WBT translations but also to a lesser extent to Bible Society translations. Many of the translation projects sponsored by the Bible Societies in East Africa may be said to be mainly at the third and fourth stages. On the other hand, most of the translations of the pioneer period fell into the first or second stages. Eugene Nida of the American Bible Society noted that: "When the United Bible Societies began, fully 90% of Bible translations in the Third World were being made by missionaries with the help of informants or translation helpers. Now in 90% of the projects the translators are nationals, and missionaries have

---

10. Ngũgĩ wa Thiong'o, *Decolonising the Mind*, 69, 78.

11. Larson, "Indigenizing the Translation Process," 35.

12. Schaaf, *On Their Way Rejoicing*, 4.

13. WBT is the fundraising and personnel recruiting arm while SIL is the linguistic and scientific arm of this organization.

become the resource persons."[14] Since Nida made this statement, there have been many developments for the better. Even those agencies such as SIL that depended heavily on missionary translators are fast moving away from this strategy and encouraging the ownership of translation projects by mother-tongue speakers.

Another widely acknowledged distinction among translations is where the translators work directly from the original-language source texts and where the translators work from other translated texts or versions of the Bible in major languages. It is still a weakness of Bible translators in East Africa that very few – both in the missionary period and even in the present period – have been prepared to work directly from the primary source texts. Many of the translators have had a working knowledge of these primary source languages but not anywhere near mastery to facilitate direct and unmediated use of the source-language texts. This is certainly a major area of need. The challenge for the African translator of the new millennium is to gain control and mastery of the biblical languages so as to facilitate working directly from the primary source texts and languages.

The special role of Bible agencies worldwide has been indispensable to the challenge of making the Holy Scriptures available in the various languages of the world's peoples. The British and Foreign Bible Society (BFBS) formed in 1804, the American Bible Society (ABS) formed in 1816, the German Bible Society (GBS), as well as others which are now part of the United Bible Societies (UBS) organized in 1946 to coordinate the work of various national Bible societies in more than two-hundred countries and territories around the world, have been central in supporting, training, and equipping translators with the necessary linguistic and exegetical skills, as well as in providing primary source language texts and secondary study and reference materials.[15] In addition, these societies have provided resources and support for the publication and distribution of the Holy Scriptures by member societies worldwide. When the UBS was formed in 1946, it defined itself in its constitution as "a World Fellowship of Bible Societies united for consultation, mutual support and action in their common task of achieving the widest possible effective distribution of the Holy Scriptures."[16]

---

14. Nida, "Trends in Bible Translating," 5.

15. For an overview of the history of the UBS, see Robertson, *Taking the Word to the World.*

16. See the Mississauga World Assembly document, "50 Years: 1946–1996," *UBS Bulletin* 78, no. 179, 128.

The British and Foreign Bible Society (BFBS), now simply referred to as the Bible Society, was founded in 1804. Its origins are associated with the story of Mary Jones (1784–1864), a young Welsh girl who loved reading the Bible and desired to have a Bible of her own. She worked hard doing various odd jobs for six years and eventually saved enough money to buy one. None was, however, to be found in her neighborhood. Barely sixteen years of age, she walked on foot for over twenty-eight miles to purchase one. Her long journey ended in disappointment, as the seller, the Rev Thomas Charles, had promised the one remaining Bible to someone else. However, on hearing Mary's story, he surrendered this one remaining copy to Mary. Moved by Mary's story, Rev Charles shared it with fellow clergy and other colleagues in a meeting in London in December 1802. A proposal was made for the formation of a Society for the sole purpose of distributing the Christian Scriptures. The British and Foreign Bible Society was formed in March 1804 directly as a result of this meeting.[17] This was the world's first major Bible Society and has provided a model for those that followed. Its aim was to translate, revise, print, and distribute Bibles in England and Wales. This was extended to include worldwide work. The BFBS was founding and key member of the United Bible Societies, founded in 1946.

The American Bible Society (ABS) was formed in 1816 with the aim of translating, publishing, and distributing Bibles nationally and later globally. In 1946 the ABS was a founding member of the UBS and remains a major supporter and pillar of UBS work worldwide. The ABS spearheaded and inspired the development of translation theory and translation consultancy in the UBS, especially under the leadership of Eugene Nida. The ABS has its headquarters in New York City.

The German Bible Society (GBS) was formed in 1948 as a consolidation of Bible work which had been ongoing in the German territories since the founding of Bible work there. The Cannstein Bible Society founded in 1710 is considered the oldest modern Bible Society in the world. The GBS is a key member of the UBS family and is responsible for developing, producing, and

---

17. For an account of this meeting, see Steer, *The Story of the Bible Society*, 45–49.

> distributing critical and scholarly biblical texts for the UBS, such
> as the Biblia Hebraica, the Septuagint, the Greek New Testament,
> as well as other scholarly editions.

There is no doubt that without the great contribution of the Bible Societies to this task in Africa and East Africa in particular, the story of the plight of the amazing young girl from Wales, Mary Jones, would be multiplied many times over. As a result of the special ministry and contribution of the Bible agencies, many East Africans are able to read the Scriptures in their native tongues, and are able to procure copies at an affordable price and in accessible formats.

The trend now is for national Bible Societies to take responsibility for financing the needs of Bible translation, production, and distribution. A number of Societies are now fully self-supporting, while others are slowly moving in this direction. Both Bishop Henry Kathii and Bishop Benezeri Kisembo, former general secretaries of the Bible Society of Kenya (BSK) and Bible Society of Uganda (BSU) respectively, have expressed an urgent need for the local Bible Societies to move from dependent, supported Societies to self-supporting and supporting Societies. Bishop Kathii contributed to the successful move of the Bible Society of Kenya to its current self-supporting status. Currently the Bible Society of Kenya is one of three national Bible Societies in Africa that are fully self-supporting in financing their Scripture needs as well as their translation program. Bishop Kisembo passed on this challenge to his successor, Henry Kalule, who has also expressed confidence in eventual realization of this goal for his society. The words of Bishop Kisembo in an interview summarize this goal: "My hope is that the Bible Society can work toward sustainability and self-supporting status, through property ownership, efficient distribution and sales of what is published, support from members and churches. Like many voluntary organizations this calls for hard work and effort from those in the service of the Society."[18]

The translation task is fundamental to the life and growth of the Christian church, to the task of theology, and especially to its contextualization in new communities and cultures. Translators are indeed the first theologians in any language or community. They must grapple with how to express the ancient and eternal message of the Bible in their own languages, how to translate biblical concepts, ideas, practices, festivals, rituals, spiritual beings, cultural artifacts, metaphors, and beliefs into the local language. How to do this meaningfully,

---

18. See appendix C for the full interview as well as interviews with Bishop Henry Kathii and Henry Kalule.

accurately, and clearly, and with native genius and natural flow of language is the challenge that faces every translator. In this effort the translator is a pioneer who enters new territory, naming, demarcating, and delimiting to a great extent the nature of biblical discourse in the local language. No wonder some communities consider translation of the Bible too important to be left to translators alone! The Bible is a community document, and the community – or some of her representatives – need to participate in its creation and development, especially in the choice of theological and key terms that capture the various biblical concepts. The community needs to ensure that the language used reflects common usage and is widely understood, and that the text is accurate and faithful to the original text of the Bible and to the community interpretations of this text. The biblical text that is created is often a community product that impacts greatly on the choice of theological terminology in the language as well as on language change in the same community.

Bible Translation Methods

Every Bible translator who has been active in recent times and who has been required to read the writings of Eugene Nida and his collaborators, such as his classic texts, *Toward a Science of Translating*, *The Theory and Practice of Translation*, *Meaning Across Cultures*, and *From One Language To Another*, will be familiar with two dominant approaches to translation, namely, the formal correspondence approach and the dynamic equivalence approach, also referred to as the functional equivalence approach. The former refers to literal renderings which translate word-for-word from one language to another, emphasizing the form of the original at the expense of context, function, cultural variables, historical distance, and linguistic differences. The latter places a premium on faithfully conveying the meaning of the original text, capturing the function and purpose of the original discourse in new situations, circumstances, times, and places, and even in new media, and placing the target or receptor audience and her needs as well as the context in central focus. The latter is ready to sacrifice the form or literal words of the original on the altar of meaning.

Other approaches and variants of these two are competing widely for attention and adoption as well as application. The main focus now is on audience-centered translations – translations that take into account the language level of the audience, the cultural and historical context, as well as the intended use of the translation. In fact, with the turn of the millennium, Bible translation workers worldwide have been strongly influenced by the exciting developments in the new academic discipline of translation studies. Students of translation studies borrow insights across disciplines to deepen the understanding of translation, from philosophy and literature studies, from linguistics and anthropology – from history and sociology, from psychology and history of religions, from cultural studies, and in the case of Bible translation, from the whole range of biblical studies.[19]

Figure 1.1. Eugene Nida Teaching at the Translators' Institute, Makarere College in Kampala, Uganda. Photo used with permission.

Many of the older missionary translations were generally formally equivalent translations. Moreover, because some of these translations were by people who lacked a full mastery of the receptor or target languages and often of the original source biblical languages as well, the resulting translations had their limitations and weaknesses. Many of these translations have nonetheless served their intended communities over a long period. They are well loved and appreciated in spite of whatever faults they may have. For example, some of these translations are known to be replete with examples of entirely wrong meanings, words and phrases with no meaning at all, obscurity, ambiguity, bad grammar or style, and unnatural difficulty or complexity in numerous places in

---

19. For more on this emerging discipline, see Bassnett, *Translation Studies*; Gentzler, *Contemporary Translation Theories*; Nord, *Translating as a Purposeful Activity*.

the translation. Some of these problem areas have been misunderstood by some readers to be part of the mystery and inscrutability of Holy Scripture itself.

As the only Scriptures in their languages, many of these early versions have become as popular and as loved as the King James Version of the Bible has been for readers of English. Even where there are alternative translations, such as common language translations, these older translations are still preferred by some older readers. As a result of this preference for the older translation, rather than accepting the newer translations, many church leaders have wanted to revise and improve the quality of these older translations and thus give them a new lease on life. Examples of this are the Swahili Union Version of 1952, which has been revised and was released for circulation in 2006, the Luganda Bible of 1896, which was revised in 1968 and later in 2014, and the Kalenjin union translation of 1969, which was revised and released for circulation on 22 July 2017. It is likely that many other older translations will follow this trend.

In the past, the Bible Societies were committed to the idea of producing the Holy Scriptures "without note or comment."[20] This policy position was intended to help maintain the neutral stance of the Bible Societies, and to keep them free from denominational biases or debates, and hence free to serve all churches equally and fairly. This spirit of serving the churches fairly without denominational or doctrinal bias is still promoted. Nonetheless, the old motto "without note or comment" or its more recent formulation, "without doctrinal note and comment," is being bypassed in the interest of better serving the reader. Every effort is made to provide available helps for the reader so that they may understand the meaning of those ancient biblical texts. At the present time the Bible Societies are actively engaged in the preparation and provision of study Bibles with extensive helps for readers. This naturally makes it very hard to avoid treading on the edges of doctrinal comment, however that is defined. The preparation and provision of study Bibles highlights and brings out the limits of translation. Translation is certainly interpretation, and interpretation cannot always capture all layers of meaning behind any given text. Study Bibles make it possible to share with the ordinary reader aspects of the original source texts that cannot always be conveyed in strict translation. A pioneer project to prepare the Swahili Study Bible, *Biblia Habari Njema*, is complete and this product is in circulation. It was released in the East African Swahili market sometime at the beginning of 2011. It is proving to be a boon to Swahili Bible readers. Another study Bible project planned for Gikuyu readers, found mostly around the Mount Kenya area of Kenya, is ongoing. Portions

---

20. Burke, "Text and Context," 299–332.

of Ruth and 1 Peter have been prepared for publication in 2019. Other study Bibles in languages of East Africa are already envisaged.

The survey of Bible translation contained in this volume is an attempt to examine, in a limited way, some of the factors leading to the presence of the Bible among the peoples of East Africa. It looks at the principal actors, where and when they were active, what they achieved, and what is currently being done, with an indication of what still remains to be done. This is set against the background of the missionary enterprise and the expansion of the church in this part of the world. Some aspects of the linguistic situation of the countries of East Africa, namely, Kenya, Tanzania, and Uganda, as well as Rwanda and Burundi, which forms the backdrop of this translation program, are also looked at.

2

Krapf and Steere Set the Ball Rolling: The Beginnings of Bible Translation in East Africa and the Story of the Swahili Bible

Introducing East Africa

The nations of East Africa are of recent origin. The creation of the countries that make up East Africa – namely, Kenya, Uganda, and Tanzania with their present boundaries – is inextricably tied to the story of nineteenth-century European expansion and colonization. This region was invaded by the British and the Germans toward the last half of the nineteenth century. They divided up the territory among themselves in what historians have termed the "Scramble for Africa"[1] that followed the Berlin Conference of October 1884. This conference was attended by all major European powers and by the United States as an observer. The Berlin Conference gave formal blessing to the colonial adventure which resulted in the carving up of Africa to its present boundaries (see map 2.1). The British occupied what came to be referred to as the Kenya Colony and the Uganda Protectorate which was then referred to as British East Africa (BEA). The Germans occupied the Tanzanian mainland formerly called Tanganyika and referred to as German East Africa (GEA).

---

1. See, for example, Thomas Pakenham's book on this topic, *The Scramble for Africa.*

Map 2.1. Colonial boundaries in Africa before and after Berlin Conference of 1884. American Bible Society Library and Archives. Used by permission.

The islands of Zanzibar and Pemba had come under the effective control of Omani Arabs with the relocation of their ruler Sultan Seyyid Said to Zanzibar in 1832. The island of Mombasa fell to Omani rule from its former Mazrui Arab rulers in 1837. Many Omani Arabs moved to Zanzibar and Pemba from Muscat and the Persian Gulf area between 1700 and 1850 and settled along the East African coast. Omani rule and control were brought to an end by the British in the 1870s. After the defeat of the Germans during World War I, the British assumed control of the entire East African area. The British were, however, forced to hand over control to the nationals of these countries in the early 1960s after protracted struggles for independence. Tanganyika became independent on 9 December 1961, uniting with Zanzibar to form the United Republic of Tanzania on 22 April 1964. Uganda gained her independence from Britain on 9 October 1962, while Kenya did so on 12 December 1963.[2]

East Africa is an area of rich linguistic and cultural diversity. All the four major African language families, namely, Afro-Asiatic, Niger-Congo, Nilo-Saharan, and Khoisan are well represented in East Africa. The Afro-Asiatic language family is represented by Cushitic languages such as Borana, Somali, Iraqw, Gorwa, and Burunge. Niger-Congo is represented by Bantu languages such as Swahili,[3] Luganda, Rukiga, Runyankole, Gikuyu, Kikamba, Sukuma, Nyakyusa, Cigogo, Giriama, and Ruhaya. Nilo-Saharan is represented by both the Nilotic and Sudanic languages, that is, Nilotic languages such as Maasai, Turkana, Karamojong (Akaramojong), Kalenjin, Luo, Acoli, and Alur, and Sudanic languages such as Lugbara, Kakwa, and Madi. The click or Khoisan-type languages are represented by Sandawe and Hadza. No other region of Africa can boast of being such a microcosm of African language typology.[4]

Tanzania counts about 130 languages, Kenya around 60, and Uganda around 45, while Rwanda has 4 and Burundi 3, according to the listing in *Ethnologue*.[5] That these figures are not exact arises from the problems related to the fuzzy boundary between language and dialect. What some might count as separate languages are sometimes counted as dialects of a given language, and what are considered as independent languages are sometimes mutually intelligible with related languages or dialects. Nonetheless, these 240 or so East African languages and dialects are spoken by the various peoples or communities of these territories. In the literature they are sometimes referred to as "tribes," but they should more accurately be considered as ethnic groups.

Ethnic groups are not static social formations, but are in a constant state of flux. These East African ethnic groups have rich cultural traditions reflected in their languages, their material cultures, their religious traditions, their music, their economic life, and their political systems of organization. These peoples

---

2. For an overview of the history of these countries, see, among other works, Maxon, *East Africa*; Ogot and Kieran, *Zamani*; Sheriff and Ferguson, eds., *Zanzibar under Colonial Rule*; Sheriff, *Slaves, Spices and Ivory*; Gilbert, *Dhows and the Colonial Economy*; Ochieng, *Modern History of Kenya*; Iliffe, *Modern History of the Tanganyika*; Jørgenson, *Uganda*; Karugire, *Political History of Uganda*.

3. The form *Kiswahili* refers to the language spoken by the *Waswahili*, that is, the Swahili people. The initial prefix marks the class of the noun, and "ki" refers to the language. In this work, the convention is adopted of using "Swahili" generically without the language specific prefix.

4. See Gordon, ed., *Ethnologue*, 15th ed., online version: http://www.ethnologue.com. See also Heine and Nurse, eds., *African Languages*.

5. Gordon, *Ethnologue*.

are closely related, and they intermarry and share many things in common. The Kenyan scholar Ali Mazrui has described this diversity in terms of a "triple heritage" that, even though grounded on African cultural traditions, has been deeply penetrated and influenced by both Asiatic and European cultural traditions as well as their major religions, Christianity and Islam.[6]

The story of how these peoples came to their present locations is much older than the recent history of colonialism and political power. The origins of the human race are thought to lie somewhere in East Africa. Indeed, some of the oldest remains of our human ancestors have been traced to this area. The present Bantu-speaking peoples of East Africa are said to have migrated to this area as part of general waves of Bantu migrations originating from the vicinity of the Cross River valley near the present-day border between Nigeria and Cameroon, from where they moved both eastwards and southwards.

Bantu languages are a very large subgroup of closely related languages of the Niger-Congo family which is one of the four African language families, namely Afro-Asiatic, Nilo-Saharan, Khoisan, and Niger-Congo. Kiswahili, Lingala, Kinyarwanda, Kikongo, Makua, Xhosa, and Zulu are examples of Bantu languages with many millions of speakers. A key feature of these languages is their use of the word *mu-ntu* (singular) and *ba-ntu* (plural), or variants of these forms, to refer to human being(s). The name for these languages is derived from this word. Bantu languages are characterized by noun classes systems with concord agreement and by complex verbal structure. Most of them are tonal, Kiswahili being an exception. They are believed to be descended from an original Proto-Bantu or Ur-Bantu language.

Nilotic speakers are said to have originated from the north, in the southern parts of the present Sudan and of south-western Ethiopia, while the Cushitic speakers probably came to this area from the north-east, namely, from the territories occupied by present-day Ethiopia, Somalia, and Djibouti. The Sandawe and Hadza of Tanzania who speak click languages similar to those of the Khoi and San peoples of southern Africa are probably the oldest inhabitants of this area.[7] They have for the most part continued to maintain a hunter-gatherer life style. Their languages and way of life are under threat due to external influences. The Ogiek and Elmolo of Kenya are, like the Sandawe and Hadza, also hunter-gatherers whose original languages are thought to be

---

6. See especially Mazrui, *The Africans*; and Mazrui and Mazrui, *Power of Babel*.

7. For more on the ethnic diversity of Africa, see Newman, *Peopling of Africa*; Connah, *African Civilizations*; Ehret, *Civilizations of Africa*; Ogot and Kieran, *Zamani*; Maxon, *East Africa*.

extinct as they only speak the languages of their more dominant neighbors, the Kalenjin and Gikuyu.

Culturally, the peoples of East Africa vary from hunter-gatherers, such as the Sandawe, Hadza, Ogiek, and Elmolo, to nomadic pastoralists, such as the Turkana, Karamojong, Samburu, and Maasai, to sedentary mixed farmers, such as the Gikuyu, Sukuma, Ganda, and Haya, to fishermen, such as the Luo, and to modern urban dwellers who include representatives from all the above groups. This territory has experienced rapid cultural change that has affected virtually every area of life: religious, cultural, economic, political, educational, and technological.

Before the European period, Christianity was not part of the landscape of East Africa. The Ethiopian Orthodox church certainly existed to the north of Kenya for many centuries. It did not, however, expand southwards during the entire period of its existence. Christianity came as part of the European colonial adventure.

The Portuguese came ahead of the British and Germans. Already toward the end of the fifteenth century, Vasco da Gama anchored off Mombasa, Kenya, on 7 April 1498, and off Malindi to the north of Mombasa on 25 April. On his way back from India, he anchored off Zanzibar. A monument named after him stands on the Indian Ocean shore at Malindi to memorialize this Portuguese sailor and explorer. This monument and Fort Jesus at the old Mombasa port remind visitors of the brief Portuguese period in East Africa. It was Francesco d'Almeida with his Portuguese compatriots who is credited with landing at Mombasa on 15 August 1505, following his successful storming of Kilwa off the southern coast of Tanganyika a few weeks earlier and building Portuguese garrisons there. The construction of Fort Jesus was begun in 1593 as a means of defense against their adversaries. The Portuguese presence in East Africa was, however, short-lived. It was limited to the coast and had no impact on the local populations in the interior.[8] Apart from the crosses associated with their monuments, the Portuguese did not advance the cause of Christianity or the Bible.

Johann Krapf, Johannes Rebmann and the Beginning of the Church in East Africa

Johann Ludwig Krapf was the first serious western missionary to East Africa in the modern period. His success is closely tied to developments in the European

---

8. Strandes, *Portuguese Period in East Africa.*

world, to the rise of the evangelical movement, to the waves of exploration, and to the colonizing mission that were the order of the day during that era.

Krapf, his wife Rosine, and their baby daughter, together with his companion Johannes Rebmann, will always be remembered in any retelling of the work of the first missionaries and Bible translators in eastern Africa. Krapf's arrival on the shores of East Africa marked the beginnings of successful and effective Christian missionary activity in this part of Africa. It also heralded the European imperial and colonial project and all that came in its train. The name of Krapf stands for some of the enviable and laudable enduring values of Christian discipleship and missionary work. He was truly interconfessional at a time when the seeds of divisive and provincial denominationalism were being sown on the continent. He was a German Lutheran who chose to pioneer the cause of the British Anglican Church Missionary Society (CMS). Clearly, his concern was neither Lutheranism nor Anglicanism, but the simple gospel of Christ.

Johann Krapf was born at Derendingen near Tübingen, Germany, on 11 January 1810. His middle name Ludwig means "wrestler"[9] and hinted at what he was to become, something like Jacob in the biblical story found in Genesis 32:22–32. He joined Basel Mission College in 1827 and set out for Africa as a missionary of the Church Missionary Society (CMS) in 1837. His first assignment was to Adowa in present-day Ethiopia. Later he moved to Ankober where he developed a burning desire to evangelize the Oromo-speaking peoples. At that time the Oromo were referred to as the Galla. Krapf's Ethiopian mission was not successful despite his translation of five chapters of the Gospel of John and all of the Gospel of Mark into Oromo with the help of a person known to us as Birkius. His main objective was to convert the Oromo and to translate a complete Bible into their language. But the king of Shoa did not allow him to return to Oromo country from Malta (where he had gone to get Bibles) and from Cairo where he got married. He had married a woman from Basel, Rosine Dietrich. Krapf and his wife ventured again to the East African coast hoping to reach the Galla (Oromo) people from there. But after setting foot on East African soil, the Galla mission was overtaken by a much larger vision.

Krapf was a visionary in the pietistic tradition. His new dream and the ultimate aim of his mission was to establish a chain of Christian mission centers stretching from East Africa to West Africa. Mombasa was to be but the beginning of this enterprise. Krapf landed in Zanzibar on 7 January 1844,

---

9. Richards, *Ludwig Krapf*, 13.

and settled in Mombasa on 5 May. While there, both Krapf and his wife fell sick with malaria on 5 July. Rosine, who gave birth to a baby daughter on 6 July, died a week later on 13 July. Krapf, ill himself, "lay prostrate nearby and ignorant of whether [Rosine] was alive or not."[10] Krapf's baby daughter also succumbed to malaria and was buried on 15 July 1844, two days after her mother. Krapf the "wrestler" could have given up the struggle. Instead, he urged the CMS in London to view his tragedy as a signal that the battle for the conversion of Africa from its eastern shore had just begun. He wrote to his superiors at CMS London as follows:

> Tell our friends at home that there is on the East African coast a lonely grave. This is a sign that you have commenced the struggle . . . As the victories of the Church are gained by stepping over the graves of her members, you may be the more convinced that the hour is at hand when you are summoned to the conversion of Africa from its eastern shore.[11]

Without wasting any time, Krapf made several journeys to the interior of present-day Kenya and Tanzania. He devoted himself to "continuous study of the Swahili and Nyika languages, of which there were then no grammars or dictionaries. In his study he had the help of some of the Wanyika chiefs and Arab sheikhs, and his own knowledge of Arabic greatly helped him."[12]

His journeys took him as far as the country of the Kamba people where he met and befriended their leader Chief Kivoi at Kitui and also saw Mount Kenya for the first time. His missionary compatriot Johannes Rebmann joined him on 10 June 1846.

Both Krapf and Rebmann settled at Rabai Mpya, a village of about twenty-five huts standing in the middle of a coconut plantation not far from Mombasa. This became their work station or missionary base with the full assent of the villagers.[13] From this base the two German Anglican missionaries traveled far into the interior. Rebmann went to the Taita Hills in Kenya and three times to the Kilimanjaro and Chagga country in Tanganyika, while Krapf went to the Usambara Mountains in Tanganyika and to Ukambani in Kenya. In the course of these journeys the two men reported sighting snow-capped mountains on the equator, namely, Mounts Kenya and Kilimanjaro. Rebmann sighted Mount

---

10. Richards, 10.

11. Omulokoli, "Historical Development of the Anglican Church," 34.

12. Richards, *Ludwig Krapf*, 16.

13. Richards, 20.

Kilimanjaro for the first time on 11 May 1848, and Krapf Mount Kenya for the first time on 10 November 1849. The unbelieving scientific community back in their homeland was not convinced that snow could exist on the equator. The two men documented carefully these journeys. Krapf's *Reisen in Ostafrika* (1858) translated into English as *Travels, Researches and Missionary Labours in East Africa* (1860) provides a good record of his discovery.[14]

What is striking about Krapf's missionary labors is his indefatigable preoccupation with matters relating to the languages and cultures of the people with whom he worked. In his short sojourn at Rabai Mpya, which lasted only from 1844 to 1853, his linguistic and Scripture translation output was staggering. Krapf's reported accomplishment in learning many of the languages of the area was considerable, given how long it usually takes to learn any language to a satisfactory level for basic communication purposes. However, it is unlikely that in that short time he actually mastered these languages well enough to be able to translate the Scriptures in them by himself. It is very likely that he accomplished this task through the help of informants and local scribes.

Although Roland Oliver, in his evaluation of Krapf's and Rebmann's contributions, observes that these "sad and other-worldly men achieved no great evangelistic success," he acknowledges that it was they "who set in motion the missionary invasion of East Africa."[15] Their pioneering linguistic research and publications as well as their work in Bible translation laid a lasting foundation for subsequent work. As an example, Krapf's translation of the New Testament in Kimvita Swahili completed in 1846 followed by his translation of Genesis published in 1847 were a basis for future work in Swahili. Nevertheless, Kimvita Swahili, of which Krapf and later CMS missionaries at Mombasa on the Kenyan coast were champions, lost the battle for hegemony as the standard and official form of the language, despite having an older written literary tradition as well as Krapf's monumental dictionary and groundbreaking grammar. Likewise, Krapf's visit to the kingdom of Usambara under Chief Kimweri, and Rebmann's visit to Kilimanjaro and his encounter with Chagga Chief Mankinga of Machame led to no immediate success.

Thus, despite their pioneering missionary efforts, Krapf's and Rebmann's ultimate impact on Kenya and Tanganyika was rather limited in terms of real accomplishment on the ground. They nonetheless laid a solid and lasting foundation for the work that followed. Roland Oliver's claim that "it was

---

14. A more recent edition was published under the title *Travels, Researches and Missionary Labours During an Eighteen Years' Residence in Eastern Africa.*

15. Oliver, *Missionary Factor,* 6.

Livingstone the individual, and not the CMS missionaries with their twelve years' start and their powerful society behind them, who set in motion the missionary invasion of East Africa"[16] is only partly true. David Livingstone's contribution to this enterprise was more on the media and campaign trail. He gave this enterprise enormous publicity and aroused widespread interest and enthusiasm. Indeed, it was Livingstone's campaign against the Arab slave-trade and his call for the Christianization, civilization, and commercialization of Africa that opened the gate for the coming of the first wave of missionaries and other Westerners to East Africa. Among these pioneers were the men and women of the Universities' Mission to Central Africa (UMCA), whose linguistic work and contribution to Bible translation is discussed below. Others were the Methodists, the Lutherans, the Catholic Benedictines, and the Africa Inland Mission.

Krapf's Pioneering Contributions to Bible Translation

Krapf's understanding of the centrality and pivotal role of Scripture translation or indeed of vernacular Scriptures in the missionary enterprise is apparent. The University of Tübingen in Germany awarded him a doctorate in recognition of his scholarly contribution to linguistic study and Bible translation both in Ethiopia and East Africa. His translation work underlined the indispensable need of the missionary to work in the vernacular language and to use vernacular Scriptures in the fulfillment of the missionary task. Clearly the description of Krapf as a visionary who had tenacity and boundless courage is evident from the abundance of his activities.[17] He was a trail-blazer for those who came after him, a source of inspiration to many generations of missionaries. Yet it is also true that Krapf was in many respects an impractical man. He was eager to do everything at once. His actual work was rather hurriedly done and short-lived.

Immediately after settling in Mombasa in May 1844, Krapf started translating Genesis into Swahili. The vocabulary and much of the orthography in Krapf's translation reflects the Kimvita dialect and is substantially different from contemporary Swahili orthography and usage. The first three chapters

---

16. Oliver, 7.

17. Oliver, 6.

of Genesis were published, but these constitute the only published Scriptures in Swahili that were translated by Krapf.[18]

Krapf was busy not only with Swahili but with other languages as well. In 1848 the Gospel of Luke translated by Krapf in Kiduruma (or Kinyika Rabai) was published in Bombay by the American Mission Press. In 1850 the Gospel of Mark translated by Krapf in Kamba was published in Tübingen, Germany, by L. F. Fues. His New Testament in Kimvita Swahili was completed, but has never been published. His Kamba Gospel and his other translations were never used in a real church context. This is understandable since during these early days Krapf did not meet much success in the area of church planting.

Regarding Krapf's linguistic capacity, Ype Schaaf makes the unconvincing claim that, "By October 1844 he [Krapf] had completed not only a Swahili grammar and dictionary, but also the New Testament and Genesis."[19] Considering that Krapf settled in Mombasa in May of that year, this kind of output seems unlikely. It does not seem possible that someone could master a language and produce a reliable and acceptable or authoritative work in that short a time. W. B. Anderson allows for more time and is probably closer to the truth when he writes, "By 1846 when his colleague Johann Rebmann arrived, Krapf had translated most of the New Testament into Swahili."[20]

Ype Schaaf writes that Krapf's translation "proved not to be usable, because it was the Swahili of the Arabs and not that of the Africans."[21] This may be due to the fact that Krapf did not rely on first-language speakers for his knowledge of Swahili but on Ali bin Mohedin, a Muslim *kadhi* or judge. It may also be that Krapf's mastery of Swahili was limited. It is, however, interesting to note that Krapf did not use the Muslim name for God, *Allah*, in his Swahili translation. He used rather the Bantu name, *Mungu*, qualified as *Mwenyezi* "Almighty." This choice cannot be credited to Krapf. It is more likely that Muslim usage had already adopted and established *Mungu* as the name for God, a tradition that is accepted and still continues to this day among Swahili Muslims.

Krapf's New Testament in Kimvita Swahili was the first New Testament to be translated into Swahili. After retirement in Germany he continued reworking and improving his Swahili NT, but it never saw the light of day. All

---

18. They were published in the *Journal of the American Oriental Society*, vol. 1 (1849): 261–274, produced in Bombay, India. A copy of this journal can be viewed at the London School of Oriental and African Studies library. A copy of Krapf's translation of Genesis 1:1–5 are included in Anglican Church of Kenya's Rabai to Mumias (Nairobi: Uzima Press, 1994), 5–6.

19. Schaaf, *On Their Way Rejoicing*, 75.

20. Anderson, *Church in East Africa*, 2.

21. Schaaf, *On Their Way Rejoicing*, 76.

was not lost, however. Krapf was able to pass his NT to Bishop Edward Steere, the pioneer and leading translator of the Bible in Kiunguja Swahili. Steere's Swahili Bible, the first in East Africa, shows Krapf's influence as he had been the first to exercise his mind on translating biblical concepts and metaphors into Swahili, as well as into related coastal Bantu languages. Interestingly, the Gospel of Luke in Kiunguja Swahili translated by Rebmann and revised by Krapf was published by the British and Foreign Bible Society (BFBS) in 1876 and in a revised form in 1881.

Even though Krapf did not do any serious sociolinguistic survey of Kenyan coastal Swahili, his choice of Kimvita was well founded. He intuitively understood the pivotal importance of Swahili in this part of Africa and moreover understood well the need for standardizing both the language and the orthography. In the introduction to his classic dictionary, he formulated the problem as follows: "What confusion must arise, if the University Mission at Zanzibar, the Church Missionary Society's agents at Frere Town and in Uganda, the Free Methodists at Ribe, the Scotch Mission near Lake Nyasa and the London Society near Lake Tanganyika, would have their separate orthography!"[22]

Other Swahili dialects along the Kenyan coast such as Kitikuu (Kibajuni), Kisiyu, Kipate, Kiamu, Kishirazi (or Chichifundi) and Kivumba (or Kivanga)[23] were not as widely spoken as Kimvita. Perhaps the only possible rival for a place of prominence might have been the Kiamu dialect of Lamu by virtue of its high number of speakers as well as its long history of Swahili poetic texts in Arabic script.

Krapf's pioneering Swahili research provided a significant and lasting contribution to Swahili lexicography and linguistics.[24] His Swahili publications and writings provide useful data for diachronic studies of the Kimvita dialect of Swahili spoken around Mombasa. These examples together with those in the Kiamu dialect of Swahili spoken on the island of Lamu provide us with around four centuries of written Swahili text.[25]

---

22. Krapf, *Dictionary of the Swahili Language*, x, quoted in Whiteley, *Swahili: The Rise of a National Language*, 80.

23. These together with Kimvita are part of the Swahili dialect cluster usually included in Guthrie's Group G40 and which includes the dialects spoken on the Tanzania coast from Tanga to Mtwara on the Zanzibar archipelago, as well as on the Comoro Islands. See Maho, "Classification of the Bantu Languages," 639–651.

24. For example, his *A Dictionary of the Swahili Language* as well as *his Outline of the Elements of the Ki-Suaheli Language: With Special Reference to the Kinika Dialect* (1850) are indispensable tools to any historical study of this language.

25. Knappert, *Four Centuries of Swahili Verse*.

The Bible into Kimvita Swahili

It is unfortunate that Krapf's translation of the New Testament into Kimvita Swahili was never published. Krapf's colleague and co-laborer Johannes Rebmann, while not as gifted or prolific as Krapf, also attempted to translate into Kimvita Swahili. He had the Gospel of Luke ready by 1859. A review of this Gospel translation reveals that it is generally good, except for a few typographical and grammatical problems. However, Rebmann's translations into Kimvita Swahili were also destined to fall by the wayside, never resulting in a published New Testament or Bible. The book of Jonah published by the United Methodist Free Church at Ribe, Kenya, in 1878 was the first full book of the Old Testament to be published in Kimvita Swahili.

It was the work of Canon W. E. Taylor, an Anglican priest and missionary from the Church Missionary Society, that eventually resulted in the first Bible in Kimvita Swahili. Taylor's concerns and interests were essentially liturgical, so the first translation from his pen was of the Psalms, published in 1883 by the Society for Promoting Christian Knowledge (SPCK). Taylor's primary concern was to have the Anglican liturgy in Kimvita. Thus, the Psalms were immediately followed by the Book of Common Prayer and selections from the Gospels and Epistles. Thereafter, Taylor collaborated with H. K. Binns, also of CMS, to have the entire Bible translated into Kimvita Swahili.

Although Taylor played a central role in the translation into Kimvita, it was Binns who saw to the completion of the work. The table below (table 2.1) shows the publications from 1889 to 1909 when the entire New Testament was published. Five years later, in 1914, a preliminary translation of the Old Testament was published.

Table 2.1. Scriptures published in Kimvita Swahili, 1889–1914

1889	Deuteronomy and 2 Chronicles published by CMS at Kisauni
1892	Tentative translation of Luke in diglot with Giriama translation
1894	Luke published in Arabic script
1897	Test portion of the John published; also released in Arabic script
1901	Complete Gospels
1904	Revised and corrected edition of Psalms
1909	Complete New Testament
1914	Tentative translation of Old Testament published

Table 2.2. Sample titles of Kimvita Swahili Scriptures

Old Testament Titles
Hichi ni Chuo Kitakatifu cha Mwenyiezi Mngu kiitwacho Maagano ya Kale, Maneno ya Kisawahili *This is the Holy Book of Almighty God Called The Old Covenant, in Swahili Words*
Chuo cha Kwanza cha Musa Ghalibu huitwa Genesis au Mwanzo wa Mwenyiezi Mngu Kuumba *The First Book of Moses Also Called Genesis or The Beginning of Almighty God's Creating*
Chuo cha Pili cha Musa kiitwacho Ghalibu Exodus au Kutoka *The Second Book of Moses Also Called Exodus or the Exit*
Chuo cha Tatu cha Musa ghalibu huitwa Leviticus au Mambo ya Walawi *The Third Book of Moses Also Called Leviticus or The Matters Relating to the Levites*
Chuo cha-ne cha Musa ghalibu huitwa Numbers au Hisabu *The Fourth Book of Moses Also Called Numbers or Counting*
Chuo cha Tano cha Musa ghalibu huitwa Deuteronomy au Marejezo *The Fifth Book of Moses Also Called Deuteronomy or Recollections*
New Testament Titles
Chuo cha Maagano mapya ya Bwana wetu Jesu Masihi Mwokozi wetu, Maneno ya Kisawahili *The Book of the New Covenant of Our Lord Jesus Messiah, Our Savior, in Swahili Words*
Injili Takatifu maana ni Habari Njema kama alikvyoileta Mathayo [Mariko, Luka, Johana] *The Holy Gospel which is the Good News as it was Brought by Matthew [Mark, Luke, John]*
Vitendo vya Mitume *The Acts of the Apostles*

However, even though Kimvita was the most prestigious dialect for Swahili poetry since it was the language of Muyaka bin Haji (1776–1840), one of the most celebrated nationalist poets of the East African coast,[26] the future did not

---

26. Abdulaziz's *Muyaka: 19th Century Swahili Poetry*, is a fine study of Muyaka bin Mwinyi Haji. Muyaka bin Haji's poetry in Kimvita Swahili has been described as "resistance poetry" and was crafted to defend the interests of his home city of Mombasa during the Mazrui period over against the interests of Zanzibar and her Busaidi Omani rulers. Casco describes *Muyaka*

lie with these translations in Kimvita Swahili. As will be seen below, the future would lie with the Kiunguja Swahili of Zanzibar.

Pioneering Efforts of the UMCA

David Livingstone's visit to the elite universities of Oxford, Cambridge, and Edinburgh championing Africa's cause is best remembered by his famous and moving address delivered at the University of Cambridge, on 4 December 1857. The conclusion to this lecture, an often-quoted sound bite, was delivered, so writes historian Stephen Neill, "in a shout which electrified his audience."[27] Livingstone's challenge to the learned men and women of this university was as follows:

> I beg to direct your attention to Africa. I know that in a few years I shall be cut off in that country which is now open. Do not let it be shut again! I go to Africa to make an open path for commerce and Christianity. *Do you carry out the work which I have begun? I leave it with you.*[28]

This challenge was answered by the creation of an elite missionary group called the Universities' Mission to Central Africa (UMCA) with chapters at Cambridge (1858) and Oxford (1859). This group was theologically of the Anglican High Church variety and hence close to the Roman Catholic tradition. The first group of UMCA pioneers who obeyed this call to Africa was led by Bishop Charles Frederick Mackenzie. They first traveled to Cape Town from where they hoped to travel overland to East Africa. Mackenzie was consecrated first Bishop of the UMCA on 1 January 1861, at Cape Town. Unfortunately, this group of UMCA pioneers never made it to East Africa. Many of the team members perished along the way due to the hardships and challenges of the difficult and long route. Bishop Neill writes:

> The mission was ill served by its intermediaries. Without anyone to guide them as to African realities, the missionaries too soon became engaged in the complex business of freeing slaves (sometimes at the cost of violence) and in the internecine conflicts

---

as "a fervent partisan of the Mazrui regime in its fight against the Busaidi's efforts to incorporate Mombasa into their dependencies," see Casco, *Utenzi, War Poems*, 63.

27. Neill, *History of Christian Missions*, 267.

28. Neill, 267, emphasis added.

of local politics. In less than a year Mackenzie was dead, to be soon followed by others of the party.[29]

The one chosen to succeed Bishop Mackenzie was Bishop George Tozer of St John's College, Oxford. He relocated the UMCA base from Central Africa to Zanzibar in East Africa. He arrived on the island on 31 August 1864, in the company of Dr Edward Steere. Steere, like Johann Krapf in Mombasa, immediately immersed himself in learning and mastering the language of Zanzibar, namely, Kiunguja Swahili. He set up the mission printing press at Zanzibar from which by 1865 the first parts of his celebrated *Handbook of the Swahili Language as Spoken in Zanzibar* (1865) started coming out.[30] Steere's ultimate goal was to make the Holy Scriptures available in Kiunguja Swahili.

It was under Dr Steere, who was consecrated in Westminster Abbey as third Bishop of the UMCA on 24 August 1874, that the famous Zanzibar landmark, Christ Church Cathedral, was erected. Bishop Steere himself designed and supervised the construction of this cathedral, apparently, as it is reported, on the very spot where the Zanzibar slave market had been, or alternatively, at the site of the old whipping post for slaves. This famous cathedral took six years to complete from Christmas Day, 1873, when the foundation stone was laid, to Christmas Day, 1879, when it was officially opened.

UMCA in Zanzibar founded as part of its "civilizing mission" a Christian village at Mbweni, Zanzibar, on the model of the Bagamoyo Christian village that had been started in 1868 by missionaries from the Roman Catholic Holy Ghost Fathers Congregation. Also in 1868, the UMCA missionaries founded St Andrew's College at Kiungani, Zanzibar, also called Kiinua Mguu. It was better known in the UMCA community as the "School of the Prophets." St Andrew's College was the first educational institution of its type in East Africa and was intended for the training of some of the new converts as teachers or preachers. Many of the early students of St Andrew's College were ex-slaves. It is said that the best educated Tanganyikans at the beginning and during the first half of the twentieth century were graduates of St Andrews.

After initial exploratory visits in 1867 by the Rev Charles Argentine Alington and in 1868 by Bishop Tozer, UMCA finally established their work in the Usambara Mountains in the territory of Chief Kimweri in 1875. A mission center was opened at Magila not far from Tanga. The next move was to the southern parts of Tanganyika in 1876. This eventually led to the

---

29. Neill, 323.

30. Steere, *Handbook of the Swahili Language*, was published in full in 1870 with a recent edition published by Asian Educational Services, New Delhi, 1999.

establishment of mission centers at Masasi among the Yao and Makhuwa and at Newala among the Makonde in present-day Mtwara Region. These UMCA centers were intended to be nuclei for the promotion of commerce and for the Christianization and civilization of the native communities. They were in this respect similar to those at Freretown, Rabai, and Ribe on the Kenyan coast near Mombasa. They were all intended to be beacons of light and models of Christian values and lifestyle. They also served their role as centers for the catechetical formation and training of indigenous Christians. Despite innumerable difficulties and shortcomings, there is no doubt that the success of these pioneer efforts in Christian mission cannot be judged by the disappointment that strikes the present-day visitor to the ruins of the former St Andrew's College, Kiungani, Zanzibar.

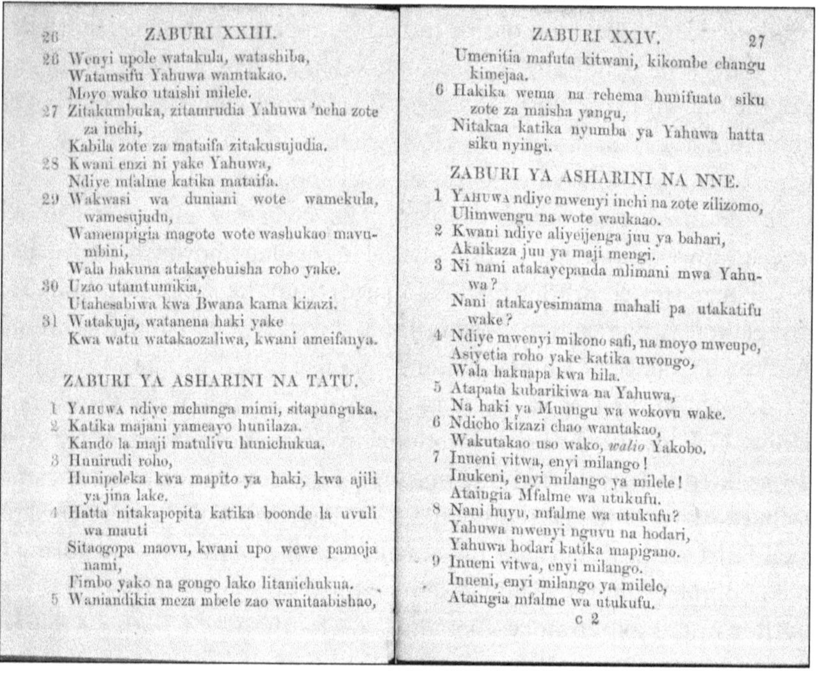

Figure 2.1. Psalm 23 in Kiswahili, 1871. American Bible Society Library and Archives. Used by permission.

Beginnings of Bible Translation in Zanzibar and the First Bible in East Africa

From the start, Bishop Edward Steere was involved in research, writing a Swahili grammar and lexicon, and in Bible translation, together with his other numerous duties as bishop, which included the supervision of the building of Christ Church Cathedral, as already mentioned. The first books of the Bible in Kiunguja Swahili to come off the UMCA Mission Press in Zanzibar were the Old Testament books of Ruth and Jonah in 1868. The table below (table 2.3) shows the subsequent publications by the BFBS and the Mission Press in Zanzibar from 1868 until the New Testament was published in 1879. The Gospel of Luke, published in 1872 by the Missionary Press, had originally been translated by Abd al Aziz, a Zanzibar sheikh, together with the missionary Richard L. Pennell.

Table 2.3. Scriptures published in Kiunguja Swahili, 1868–1879

1868	Ruth and Jonah, UMCA Mission Press, Zanzibar
1869	Gospel of Matthew, BFBS, London
1871	Psalms, BFBS, London
1872	Gospel of Luke, UMCA Mission Press, Zanzibar
1875	1 and 2 Kings, UMCA Mission Press, Zanzibar Gospel of John, BFBS, London
1876	Revised edition of the Gospel of Matthew, BFBS, London Ephesians and Philippians, UMCA Mission Press, Zanzibar
1878	Acts, Romans, 1 and 2 Corinthians, James, 1 John, UMCA Mission Press, Zanzibar
1879	Genesis, Galatians, Colossians–2 Peter, 2 John–Jude, Revelation, UMCA Mission Press, Zanzibar Mark and a revised edition of John, BFBS, London New Testament, BFBS, London

The BFBS record of translation work in the report of 1879 noted:

Bishop Steere has been working hard on the translation of the New Testament which he prints in portions at Zanzibar, with a view to having them reprinted in England in one volume. The translation of the New Testament is now completed – the Apocalypse is in the press, and the Gospel of Mark alone remains in manuscript. The Rev W. P. Johnson is translating the Pentateuch from the Hebrew.[31]

The complete Swahili NT was published in 1879, as was the complete liturgy. The following year the Mission Press released copies of Exodus and in 1882 published 1 and 2 Kings, Isaiah, and a revised edition of Acts.

A revision of the NT appeared the following year in 1883, published by BFBS in London. Five thousand copies of this NT were produced.[32] This was the result mainly of Bishop Steere's labors, together with those of some of his UMCA colleagues, namely, Chauncey Maples, Herbert Geldart, Arthur C. Madan, and Mary A. H. Allen. T. H. Sparshott of the CMS also participated in this effort. On 27 August 1882, Bishop Steere entered into rest and was interred inside Christ Church Cathedral behind its High Altar, at Mkunazini, Zanzibar.

Figure 2.2. Bishop Edward Steere's tombstone, Christ Church Cathedral, Zanzibar. Photo © Aloo Osotsi Mojola

As already noted, this splendid work did not stop with Bishop Steere's death. Others continued the translation effort where he left off. Already in 1882, the year he died, the book of Daniel came off the Mission Press in Zanzibar. The table below (table 2.4) shows the output of Old Testament books by the BFBS and the Mission Press in Zanzibar in the nine years from 1882 to 1891. The main translators of this Old Testament were Francis Roger Hodgson and his wife Jessie Hodgson.

---

31. BFBS record of translation work: 1855–1876, 381.

32. BFBS record of translation work: 1855–1876, 381.

Table 2.4. Old Testament books in Kiunguja Swahili, 1882–1891

1882	Daniel, UMCA Mission Press, Zanzibar
1883	Judges, UMCA Mission Press, Zanzibar
1884	Genesis and Joshua, BFBS, London
1886	Proverbs, UMCA Mission Press, Zanzibar
1886	Exodus, BFBS, London
1886–1887	Numbers, 1 and 2 Samuel, Ecclesiastes, Song of Solomon, Jeremiah–Ezekiel, Hosea–Obadiah, and Micah–Malachi, UMCA Mission Press, Zanzibar
1889–1891	Exodus–2 Samuel, 1 Chronicles–Malachi, BFBS London

During this period, Mary A. H. Allen prepared an Arabic transliteration of the Gospel of John, which was published in 1888, and Petro Limo did the same for the Gospel of Matthew, published in 1891. Arthur C. Madan and Percy L. Jones-Bateman revised the NT that was published by BFBS London in 1892. A BFBS report in 1893 noted that, "The New Testament revised by Mr. A.C. Madan was found to be unsatisfactory to the people and the synod of the Universities Mission appointed a Committee under the presidency of the late Bishop Smythies assisted by Christian natives to revise the revision. The book has now been published by the Mission Press at Zanzibar."[33]

The BFBS report does not, however, provide the grounds for this action. It is possible that usage of these Scriptures by local Christians brought out weaknesses in the translation, highlighting issues of unnaturalness, lack of clarity, or unintelligibility in the translation in addition perhaps to other inconsistencies and inaccuracies in the revised translation. A further revision was prepared by Percy L. Jones-Bateman and Herbert W. Woodward, assisted by Petro Limo and Cecil Majaliwa, and printed at the Zanzibar Mission Press. A revision of the OT was prepared by Francis Hodgson and published by BFBS, London, in 1895. A final revision of this Zanzibar Bible was undertaken by Godfrey Dale and Frank Weston, both of the UMCA. Their efforts saw the publication of the NT in 1921, Psalms and Proverbs in 1925, and Isaiah–Malachi in 1930 by BFBS, London. The continuous revision of this translation is to be commended, as it reflected a desire to make available a Swahili Bible that was not only satisfactory to users, but also reliable and intelligible. The involvement of local Christians such as Cecil Majaliwa and Petro Limo in

---

33. BFBS record of translation work: 1855–1876, 395.

the revision is also to be highly commended. Their participation no doubt contributed to the acceptability of the translation by Swahili speakers.

Roman Catholic Initiatives

The White Fathers Congregation of the Roman Catholic Church arrived at Zanzibar in April, 1878. The first Roman Catholic attempt at translating the Scriptures in Kiunguja Swahili was led by one of their members, Emile Brutel. His translation of the four Gospels and Acts was published by the Société des Missionaires d'Afrique, Algiers, in 1913. Further editions were published in 1923 and 1929. Unfortunately, Brutel's work did not receive the wide circulation it deserved, as it was part and parcel of the first-rate research and immense contribution of the French Holy Ghost Fathers to Swahili studies.[34] This is a legacy that is widely known through the enviable work of Father Charles Sacleux whose research and publications in Swahili dialectology and grammar in 1909, as well as his voluminous Swahili lexicon of 1939–1941, are still widely respected and consulted. From 1893 onward Father Sacleux lent his linguistic proficiency and accomplishments to the translation in Swahili of the Roman Catholic catechism and the Thomas à Kempis classic devotional work, *The Imitation of Christ.* He also translated a number of OT and NT selections, and his translation of the NT into Kiunguja Swahili was published in 1937 at Grasse by the Maison Spiritaine, the same year as Karl Roehl's Bible in Swahili, as will be discussed shortly.

There have been a number of other Roman Catholic translation efforts as well. Alfons Loogman, also of the Holy Ghost Fathers of the Morogoro Catholic Mission, published his translation of the Gospels and Acts in 1947 at Morogoro. This was followed by his translation of the complete NT in Swahili, which was also published by the Morogoro Catholic Mission in 1958 and later reprinted by Duquesne University Press (Pittsburgh, USA), in 1965. Another Catholic priest, Father Alkuin Bundschuh, had his translation of the Swahili New Testament published at the Ndanda Catholic Mission Press in 1986.[35] He benefited from the support and help of Father Filipo Mrope. Unfortunately,

---

34. The earliest Swahili translation by the Holy Ghost Fathers was by Father Etienne Baur in Zanzibar in 1867, consisting of lectionary readings from the Gospels and Epistles. See Rijks, *Guide to Catholic Bible Translations*, vol. 2, 415.

35. It was published by the Benedictine Publications, Ndanda Peramiho, Tanzania in 1986 with an imprimatur from Bishop Maurus Libaba of Mtwara, Tanzania. For a comprehensive record of Catholic translations, see Rijks, *Guide to Catholic Bible Translations*, vol. 2. For Swahili publications, see pp. 415–420.

these Catholic translations did not meet with wide acceptability or popularity, and are consequently mostly out of print and unavailable. One possible reason may be that they were efforts of individual persons without the involvement or participation of various churches, or in their case, of the Roman Catholic Church in Tanzania. But it is impossible to determine the reasons for their lack of popularity without researching more thoroughly the reasons that these translations have not proved competitive with the existing Swahili Union Version or the contemporary *Habari Njema* translation.

Karl Roehl's Translation and the Beginnings of Swahili Standardization

Dr Karl Roehl's translation of the Bible into Swahili represented a new stage in the writing of Swahili. Roehl aimed not only at fully utilizing Kiunguja Swahili as spoken in Zanzibar as a base, but also attempted to go beyond it in capturing its expanded use and function inland. He aimed at minimizing its Arabic lexical borrowings while at the same time maximizing the use of its Bantu lexical roots as reflected by usage in the interior of mainland Tanganyika.

Karl Roehl was a missionary of the Bethel Mission of the German Lutheran church who, together with Ernst W. Johanssen and Paul Wohlrab of the same German mission to East Africa between 1901 and 1908, translated the New Testament into Kishambala, a language spoken in the Usambara Mountains of northeastern Tanganyika. Roehl was supported by the Berlin Missionary Society in the translation of a new Swahili Bible. This translation was carried out on behalf of four German missionary societies, namely, the Berlin Mission, the Bielefeld Mission, the Leipzig Mission, and the Moravian Mission. At meetings held in August and October 1914, representatives of these missions resolved to make "a new translation, of the scriptures in Swahili suitable for use throughout German East Africa" and whose "main object was to purify Swahili as a Bantu language, by eliminating the majority of the Zanzibar Arabic words, which are either not used, or only imperfectly understood, by the natives on the coast, and are quite unintelligible to those in the interior."[36]

Martin Klamroth of the Berlin Missionary Society, with the help of some of his colleagues, and with some linguistic assistance and advice from Prof Carl Meinhof of the University of Hamburg, completed the NT in 1914, but the outbreak of World War I made its publication impossible. After the war,

---

36. BFBS East African languages Correspondence files (E3/3/629/48); see also the BFBS – ESC minutes cards, vol. 7.

in the mid-1920s, Roehl commenced working on the revision of the Klamroth translation at Dar es Salaam. Roehl's NT was thus essentially a revision of the earlier translation by Martin Klamroth. It was reported by Professor Diedrich Westermann, also of the University of Hamburg (and later Berlin), in 1926 that this translation was, "especially adapted to the Swahili as spoken in the interior. Many Arab words have been replaced by authentic Swahili words. It is written in the orthography officially adopted by the Government."[37]

It is interesting that when the Roehl NT first appeared in 1930 it was entitled *Agano Jipya la Bwana na Mwokozi wetu Yesu Kristo katika msemo wa Kiswahili cha bara* (The New Testament of our Lord and Savior Jesus Christ in the Swahili language of the inland), while the inside cover page referred to it as "The New Testament in Swahili (Zanzibar) as spoken in the inland."[38] Attempts by BFBS to enlist the help of the Germans and Dr Roehl in launching a common union translation in standard Swahili for the whole of East Africa proved unsuccessful.

Roehl did not do his translation work singlehandedly. He was assisted by Pastor Martin Nganisya and Mwalimu[39] Andrea Ndekeja. His version in Swahili of the complete Bible containing both the Old and New Testaments was published in 1937 by the Württemberg Bible Society in Stuttgart, Germany, for which the Swahili text reads, *Chama cha Wuerttemberg kitoacho vitabu vya Neno la Mungu* (The Society of Wuerttemberg which produces God's Word). A second edition soon followed in 1939. The complete Bible has as its title, *Biblia ndio Maandiko Matakatifu yote ya Agano la Kale nayo ya Agano Jipya katika msemo wa Swahili* (The Bible which is the Holy Scriptures including the Old Testament and the New Testament in the Swahili language).

Representatives of the Bible Society in Stuttgart made this observation: "Our Swahili Bible is, as far as we know, the first edition of the Bible in a standardized Swahili written in the standardized orthography."[40] This Bible had as its target audience "all the Christian people in the whole East and Central Africa."[41] Rev Heinrich Scholten, the Secretary of the Tanganyika Missionary

---

37. Quote taken from the BFBS East African languages correspondence files.

38. See the Roehl New Testament of 1930, for example, at the Wuerttembergische Landesbibliothek, Stuttgart, Germany (Ref. B Afrika 193001).

39. *Mwalimu* means "teacher," but is used as a title of respect. Julius Nyerere, first president of Tanzania, was respectfully addressed by this term.

40. BFBS East African languages Correspondence files (E3/3/629/48); see also the BFBS – ESC minutes cards, vol. 7.

41. BFBS East African languages Correspondence files (E3/3/629/48); see also the BFBS – ESC minutes cards, vol. 7.

Council, writing about this translation and the new Swahili Union Version (SUV), observed, "I still regret that two translations of the Swahili Bible will follow each other in short periods, but I do think that Dr. Roehl has done a great piece of work. I hardly doubt that his version of the Old Testament will be easily surpassed."[42]

The fate of the Roehl Bible was short-lived even though it was considered a first-class translation. With the fall of the Germans after World War II and the establishment of British hegemony in East Africa, the Roehl Bible did not receive much support and was reprinted only once during the British period, and then some years later in 1961. The Roehl Bible soon went out of print and most of its champions were gone. The influence of BFBS in East Africa saw to it that the Roehl Bible did not supplant the Swahili Union Version translated by British Anglican missionaries and published by the BFBS in 1952. Some observers attribute the support of the SUV by the establishment to its strong endorsement by the two main British Anglican missions, namely, the CMS and the UMCA, as well as to its promotion by its publisher, the BFBS.

However, the arrival in 1990 of a new General Secretary at the Bible Society of Tanzania, an ardent supporter of the Roehl translation, changed the situation. He vigorously campaigned for a new edition, which was printed in 1995 with a reprint in 1999. Nevertheless, although the Roehl Bible had the support of the numerically stronger Tanzanian Lutheran church, it lacked the requisite support from other institutions. In the era of British control in the East African dependencies, Roehl's open agenda of de-Arabizing Swahili was not popular in church politics. This agenda has been bypassed by recent developments in the use, growth, and standardization of contemporary Swahili in East Africa.

The Move to Standard Swahili

The Swahili of Zanzibar gained favor over other varieties as Zanzibar became Sultan Seyyid Said's power base in the early nineteenth century, as well as the political and religious center of the East African region. Here was the biggest slave market on the whole East African coast. This was also the base for the first translation of the complete Bible and the first printed NT in any East African language. The choice of Kiunguja (Zanzibar Swahili) in preference to Kimvita (Mombasa Swahili) led to conflict and bitter feelings between scholars and missionaries from these two areas. Wilfred Whiteley observes:

---

42. BFBS East African languages Correspondence files (E3/3/629/48); see also the BFBS – ESC minutes cards, vol. 7.

This was doubly unfortunate: the richness of the historical and literary traditions of Mombasa and the northern coast, together with their links with Islam, seemed to offer little of relevance to the rest of Kenya, which tended to look towards the Swahili of Tanganyika; but the south lacked any such traditions, and their absence from school syllabuses in both Tanganyika and Kenya certainly impoverished the Swahili Courses of several generations of students. Against this, however, the adoption of a variety closely akin to varieties of the language already spoken over large areas of inland Tanganyika contributed powerfully to its rapid acceptance.[43]

Eventually a standard form of Swahili emerged. The statement found in the *Bulletin of the East African Interterritorial Language (Swahili) Committee* of 1934 in which a committee member expresses the following view on the new standard Swahili is of interest:

We have standardized Swahili and in the process Swahili seems to have become a new language. While, doubtless, all are ready to admit that Swahili, like any other language is bound to develop and grow, in form, idiom and vocabulary, as a result of the impact of the civilizations of the immigrant communities, yet surely the development must come from the Swahili mind, and must not be superimposed on them from without. But that is just what we have tried, and are still trying to do, with the result that we are in the somewhat ludicrous position of teaching Swahilis their own language through the medium of books, many of which are not Swahili in form or content, and whose language has but little resemblance to the spoken tongue. We are perhaps too apt to overlook the fact that the people themselves are not only capable of adapting their language to modern needs, but are doing so with amazing rapidity.[44]

Without going into the details of this question of standardization and some of its problems, it is noteworthy that Bible translation played no little part in this process.[45]

---

43. Whiteley, *Swahili*, 81.

44. Quoted in Whiteley, *Swahili*, 85.

45. For a detailed discussion of the standardization of Swahili, a good starting point is Angogo, "Standard Swahili," (1978), or Mbaabu, *Historia ya Usanifishaji wa Kiswahili* (1991). It is noteworthy that many of those who played a leading role in the standardization of Swahili were missionaries and missionary-translators of the Swahili Bible, among them: Rev Canon

The Swahili Union Version and the Standardization of Swahili[46]

Already, in 1928, a number of scholars and institutions were considering the possibility of a common Swahili Bible in "standard Swahili" bringing together Mombasa and Zanzibar with their Kimvita and Kiunguja versions as well as their UMCA and CMS traditions. The Conferences on the Standardization of Swahili held at Dar es Salaam in October 1925 and at Mombasa in June 1928, as well as the government's promotion of a new common Swahili orthography, gave impetus to this effort. These conferences had resolved to create a standard Swahili that adopted the "Zanzibar dialect with such modifications as may be required . . . as the Standard form of Swahili."[47] Resolution No. 2 was of some interest to the debate which was to follow. It read: "That in deciding on the modifications Bantu words be employed wherever possible, but due regard should be paid to Arabic words which are established and have become part and parcel of the Swahili language."[48]

The BFBS took an active part in encouraging the UMCA and CMS missions to explore the possibility of this new joint union translation in standard Swahili and standard orthography. The first meeting held in London at Bible House on 3 June 1937, to discuss this matter included Professor Westermann (University of Berlin, Germany), Dr Roehl (Bethel Mission), Dr Diehl (Bible Society, Stuttgart), Dr Broomfield (UMCA), Canon Hubert J. Butcher (CMS), the Rev Pittway (CMS), and the Rev Wilkinson (BFBS), and was chaired by E. W. Smith (BFBS). This meeting affirmed the acceptance of the Zanzibar NT as the basis of a new translation, with the Mombasa and Roehl versions being consulted in the course of preparation. For the OT, they agreed to accept Roehl's version as the basis, with reference being made to the Mombasa and Zanzibar versions. It was also agreed at this meeting that the translation would be shared between German and British Swahili scholars and that a Committee of Reference, which was to include competent Africans, be formed. The Rules of BFBS on translation were expected to be followed, each translator being furnished with a copy.

Broomfield, Rev Canon Hellier, Rev Canon Dale, Rev B. J. Ratcliffe, Rev Karl Roehl, Rev Dr. Reusch, and Rev F. Gleiss. See also Frederick Johnson Preface to *A Standard Swahili-English Dictionary*, ix.

46. Some material in this section was first printed in Aloo Mojola, "Postcolonial Tranlation Theory and the Swahili Bible," in *Postcoloniality, Translation, and the Bible in Africa*, ed. Musa W. Dube and R. S. Wafula (Eugene, OR: Wipf & Stock, 2017), 26–56.

47. This was Resolution No. 1 of the *Report of the Committee for the Standardisation of the Swahili Language.*

48. *Report of the Committee for the Standardisation*, 8.

It was noted that Dr Roehl disagreed with his colleagues on the proportion of Arabic words to be admitted in the translation. His idea was to substitute Bantu words wherever possible for Arabic words. The British members were of the view that "this limits the possibility of bringing out the meaning of the sacred text, especially if words which have been for a long time in use are replaced by less meaningful words."[49] It seems that Dr Roehl did not receive complete support from Professor Westermann, the German professor and linguistic expert, or from Dr Diehl, Secretary of the Stuttgart Bible Society, who, the report notes:

> [s]eemed to be chiefly concerned with safeguarding the financial interests of his Society as they were about to issue a complete Bible as translated by Dr Roehl. This will include a Revised New Testament (which incidentally will contain more Arabic words than the previous edition), and Dr Diehl seemed to be anxious that nothing should be done to prejudice the sale of this version.[50]

A first tentative edition of the proposed joint union version had been translated by Godfrey Dale (UMCA, Zanzibar) and revised by G. Pittway and Hubert J. Butcher (CMS, Mombasa), and published by BFBS in 1934. This test portion had been presented as a possible model, but Dr Roehl rejected it on the grounds that it contained "so many Arabic words."[51]

In the end, cooperation between Dr Roehl and the Stuttgart Society proved unworkable. Canon Hellier (UMCA, Muheza, Tanganyika) was welcomed as the chief translator and was assisted by Canon Butcher (CMS, Mombasa, Kenya) as his chief collaborator. Dr Rickard Reusch (Lutheran, Marangu, Tanganyika) and others were invited to be reviewers for this translation. By 1945 tentative editions of the Gospels of Matthew, Mark, and John were published by the CMS in Nairobi. In 1949 the book of Psalms was printed. The NT in this new Union Version appeared in 1950 and the OT appeared in 1952, published by the BFBS, London.

This task required a lot of patience, and give-and-take, as well as mutual respect. Surviving correspondence, however, reveals that such good intentions were sometimes not easily achieved. At one point, for example, Canon Hellier

---

49. BFBS East African language files—ESC Minutes of June 16, 1937, p. 20 (BSA/E3/3/545/5).

50. BFBS East African language files—ESC Minutes of June 16, 1937, p. 20 (BSA/E3/3/545/5).

51. BFBS East African language files—ESC Minutes of 6.11.35, p. 38; see also 16.6.37, pp. 20–21 (BSA/E3/3/545/5).

wrote to Canon Coleman: "Nobody can produce agreement between us on such a point . . ."[52] Butcher wrote to Coleman: "The position with regard to these Psalms is a bit complicated as they are almost solely Canon Hellier's work."[53] Meanwhile, Canon Broomfield, UMCA Secretary, writing to A. Wilkinson, BFBS General Secretary, observed: "I feel that final decisions should rest with Hellier. After all, he is a scholar, and I do not think Messrs. Butcher and Pittway for instance would make that claim for themselves. At one of our meetings to discuss NT translation they admitted that they knew practically no Greek."[54] Earlier, writing to E. W. Smith of BFBS, Broomfield complained: "[A]s far as Swahili as we know it is concerned, the present Zanzibar version is much better than that written by our friends in Kenya . . . In a word, it seems to us that Messrs. Butcher and Pittway and Miss Deed are not Swahili scholars of the same caliber as those responsible for the present Zanzibar version."[55] The Rev G. Capon of CMS Limuru, in defense of his Mombasa friends, wrote to the Rev H. D. Hooper of CMS London on 17 January 1941, "a fairly close study of Hellier's work makes me very doubtful whether he should be an assessor over Butcher, or indeed over anybody else at all."[56]

Clearly, as with today's translators, personal, academic, denominational, and doctrinal sensitivities bedeviled the translation teams of yesterday. Canon Hellier's subsequent tragic mental breakdown in England was probably due to the many strains and stresses he suffered in the course of his work as the chief translator to the Swahili Union Version. Canon Hellier never forgot his native collaborators. On 15 September 1952, he wrote to BFBS asking them to send a copy of the first editions of the SUV from the press to the Rev Paulo Kihampa because "he made some original and really helpful remarks in the discussion and I felt that for a native he was quite outstanding."[57]

It is a reminder of the miracle of God's grace that such a great translation could emerge from individuals subject to so wide a range of human frailties. Clearly BFBS was right in claiming in a letter written to the widow of Canon Hubert J. Butcher (1879–1956) at his death that: "The Union Swahili Version

---

52. BFBS East African language files, ESC Minutes of 6.11.35, p. 38; see also 16.6.37, pp. 20–21 (BSA/E3/3/545/5).

53. BFBS East African language files, ESC Minutes of 6.11.35, p. 38; see also 16.6.37, pp. 20–21 (BSA/E3/3/545/5).

54. BFBS East African language files, ESC Minutes of 6.11.35, p. 38; see also 16.6.37, pp. 20–21 (BSA/E3/3/545/5).

55. BSA/E3/3/545/5 – see letter dated January 20, 1938.

56. BSA/E3/3/545/5 – see letter dated January 20, 1938.

57. BSA/E3/3/545/5 – see letter dated January 20, 1938.

has already taken its place as one of the monumental achievements of the Bible Society."[58] The launching was front page news in the local media. The *East African Standard* of 12 September 1952, carried a story and picture of the arrival of initial copies of this Bible at the local airport. The first copy was in a protective case of blue leather, bearing the initials and symbol of the airline BOAC and the inscription: "The First copy of the Union Version Swahili Bible, flown especially from London by Comet jet liner and presented to St Stephen's Church, Nairobi, by the British and Foreign Bible Society."[59] The following members of the committee were presented with complimentary copies at the dedication and launching: the Rev Dr Rickard Reusch, Archdeacon R. G. P. Lamburn, Archdeacon Lionel J. Bakewell, Miss E. B. M. Lloyd, Canon Hellier, Canon Hubert J. Butcher, Mr Harry Banks, and Bishop L. J. Beecher.[60] It is significant that the Rev Paulo Kihampa of Muheza who was cited by Canon Hellier as having lent him much help was left out, as were the other African contributors to this whole project.[61]

It is not surprising that a proposed reprint of the Roehl Bible in 1960 was strongly resisted. The Rev Frank Frederick Bedford of the Bible Society in East Africa wrote to BFBS on 7 October 1960, saying "I think it is now accepted as a general principle that the Union Swahili Bible has superseded all other Swahili versions and it certainly would be a retrograde step if a German Bible Society of its own initiative resurrected the Roehl Version."[62] His successor at Bible House, Nairobi, Rev L. V. D. Ashley, echoed the same sentiments in his letter to Stuttgart: "I think it would be a great pity if another Bible in the Swahili language were to be given wide circulation, and at another price . . . [and] it certainly would be disastrous to have this Roehl Bible circulating alongside our Union Swahili Bible."[63] Meanwhile the BFBS held that printing the Roehl Bible "does seem to be retrograde as it certainly tends to be a divisive step."[64] The Swahili Union Version was seen by the churches there as "a God-given means of furthering the sense of unity among Christians in East Africa."[65]

---

58. Newspaper cuttings in BSA/E3/3/545/8.

59. Newspaper cuttings in BSA/E3/3/545/8.

60. See Frank Bedford's letter to W. J. Bradnock, dated May 6, 1952 (BFBS – BSA/E3/3/545/8)

61. We will discuss more fully in the concluding chapter how little recognition was given by the missionaries and agencies to the Africans involved in translation work.

62. Newspaper cuttings in BSA/E3/3/545/8.

63. Newspaper cuttings in BSA/E3/3/545/8.

64. Newspaper cuttings in BSA/E3/3/545/8.

65. Newspaper cuttings in BSA/E3/3/545/8.

The view from Stuttgart was different. The General Secretary of the Bible Society in Stuttgart, Dr Theodor Schlatter, had written on 19 January 1961, to Dr Oliver Beguin, the UBS General Secretary, in defense of the proposed reprint: "It is not a matter of rivalry but of the richness of the translation of God's Word. Africans are continually asking for the Roehl Bible."[66] Dr Beguin in turn observed: "I am aware, of course, that the Stuttgart Society never quite swallowed the introduction of the Union Version . . . I am simply aware that behind this project there is the sense of grudge which Stuttgart feels against the BFBS in this matter."[67] A second edition of the Roehl Bible was produced by the Württemberg Bible Society in 1961 and was reprinted again by the Bible Society of Tanzania in 1995, perhaps with faint echoes of Dr Schlatter's position.

The Deuterocanonical books of the Bible, also referred to as the Apocrypha, were translated into Union Swahili by D. V. Perrott, an Anglican missionary and linguist,[68] assisted by a committee of reviewers. These books were published by the Tabora Mission Press (TMP), in 1967. This text was used for a Roman Catholic edition of the Bible with the Deuterocanonical books containing notes based on *The Jerusalem Bible*. Martha Lagerstrom and a native speaker named Mtipura prepared Arabic transliterations (i.e. in Arabic script) of the Union Version text of the Gospels published in 1969, and Acts in 1970.

The Swahili Union Version has been the major Bible of most Swahili speakers and readers in East Africa since its publication. As already indicated, the SUV was based on the grammatical and morphological forms of Kiunguja, but freely used lexical items from Kimvita. It reflects a formal correspondence approach to translation. Its vocabulary is outdated in places and some of its expressions are meaningless or unnatural. Nevertheless, it remained an excellent translation even though many recognized its need of both linguistic and textual revision.

The work of revising the SUV text was eventually undertaken by the Bible Societies of Kenya and Tanzania in 1999 and the finished product, the Revised Swahili Union Version (RSUV), was published in early 2007 by the two Societies. It was released in two editions, a Catholic edition, with the Deuterocanonical books, and a Protestant edition, without the Deuterocanonical books. Mr Timothy Kamau, a Kenyan Anglican churchman trained as a linguist, and the Rev Wilson Rugakingira, a Tanzanian Lutheran pastor and theologian,

---

66. Newspaper cuttings in BSA/E3/3/545/8.

67. Newspaper cuttings in BSA/E3/3/545/8.

68. Perrot is well known for developing the popular *Teach Yourself Swahili* grammar and dictionary (1951).

were given the responsibility of leading the work. A committee of reviewers from Kenya and Tanzania collaborated in the task to help ensure quality and acceptability. In an interview and report on the work, Kamau had this to say:

> The revisers began the task by revising the Old Testament as at [i.e. starting from] Genesis onwards. Each reviser read an alternate book noting areas that needed to be revised according to a set of criteria originally suggested in Eugene Nida and Jan de Waard's book, *Functional Equivalence*:[69]
>
> i. Where literal rendering would give an entirely wrong meaning.
>
> ii. When a borrowed term gives "zero" meaning or if it is entirely meaningless.
>
> iii. When a literal rendering leads to obscurity in meaning.
>
> iv. When a literal rendering leads to bad grammar style in the receptor language.
>
> v. When a literal rendering leads to ambiguity not in the source text.
>
> vi. When the style and syntax of the source language is too complex and difficult.
>
> The procedure was that each of the revisers would read a given book noting areas that require to be revised and take the lead in discussing it during the subsequent team meetings. The first such team meeting that served as the launch of the project was held between 8th and 9th [of] April 1999 at the United Bible Societies Offices off Ngong Road in Nairobi. It was attended by all the three General Secretaries of Kenya, Uganda, and Tanzania, Dr. Mojola, as well as the two SUV revisers.[70]

The Bible Societies and churches have not vigorously marketed and promoted this 2007 SUV revision, so few readers are using it yet. It looks like a major switch from the SUV to the RSUV will take some time.

---

69. The full title is *From One Language to Another: Functional Equivalence in Translating* (1986).

70. See appendix D, for full reflections.

Some Catholic Translations into Standard Swahili

Note should be made here of two notable Roman Catholic translations in standard Swahili. Already mention has been made of Father Emile Brutel's work in producing the Gospels and Acts in Kiunguja. Father Alfons Loogman of the Roman Catholic Holy Ghost Fathers was perhaps the first Catholic to attempt a translation in standard Swahili based on a standard orthography. His labors culminated in the publication of the Gospels and Acts in 1947 and the complete New Testament in 1958. The Gospel and Acts were revised and published in 1960. These were all produced at the Holy Ghost Press in Morogoro, Tanzania. Like the Brutel effort, this work was not produced in adequate quantities and made little impact, and has been unavailable and out of print for a long time. The same may be said of the translation of the NT by the Benedictine Fathers that appeared for the first time in 1986. As early as 1972, portions of this translation were published by the Ndanda Mission Press in southern Tanzania. The Psalms portion which had appeared earlier – and which would later appear in a revised edition in 1985 – was published by Father P. Isaya. These German missionary priests were assisted and supported by local Swahili experts including Father Filipo Mrope.

Interconfessional Cooperation and *Biblia Habari Njema*

All the above-mentioned translations were strictly speaking not interconfessional, even though they were often used across confessional and denominational lines. The Swahili Union Version has dominated the field as the leading Swahili Bible for all Christians. Indeed, it has become in a very short time the King James Version equivalent for the Swahili-speaking world, that is, the one Bible that many readers see as the only authoritative translation. Nevertheless, it is the new *Biblia Habari Njema* (Good News Bible) which has from its inception been a truly interconfessional and interdenominational effort. Sponsored by Bible Societies of Kenya and Tanzania at the request of the Protestant and Roman Catholic Churches in both Kenya and Tanzania, the *Biblia Habari Njema* translation sought the participation of all churches at all levels from the two sponsoring countries.

Biblia Habari Njema is the first major Swahili translation for which East Africans themselves have been wholly responsible and in which they have fully participated at all levels. In April 1969, John Ole Tompo Mpaayei, the pioneer Bible Society leader of East Africa and the first African General Secretary of the Bible Society in East Africa (BSEA), reported that a number of church leaders had requested a revision of the Swahili Union Version, although they felt that a new translation would be better than a revision. On 25 June 1969, he observed that "At the moment it would seem that there are no competent nationals to undertake this work and it is doubtful whether the church in East Africa would be willing to accept another Swahili translation made by expatriates."[71] But eventually the need for a new Bible became acute. In the words of the eminent biblical scholar Peter Renju who worked throughout the region for many years as a UBS Translation Consultant:

> The Catholic Church in Tanzania had by this time grown rather very weary of the existing Bible translation of the Union Version, first because it did not cover its interests [the Catholic canon includes, besides all the books of the Protocanon, other books from the Deuterocanon], and secondly, [because] the language used in this particular translation was generally unacceptable, especially with regard to its lexicon.[72]

The need was apparent to many and soon the churches and Bible Societies found "competent nationals" to be translators. The new translation in contemporary Swahili was initiated in the early 1970s. Among those who participated as translators at one stage or another during the translation process were the following: Peter Renju (Catholic), Cosmas Haule (Catholic), Jared Mwanjala (Anglican), Amon Mahava (Lutheran), Amon Oendo (Seventh-Day Adventist), Douglas Waruta (Baptist), David Mhina (Anglican), and Leonidas Kalugila (Lutheran). The first test portion of this translation was the Gospel of Luke which appeared in 1975, published by the Bible Societies of Kenya and Tanzania. The NT appeared in 1977 to an enthusiastic reception. It has since become a best-seller, outselling all other books in the region. An edition of the NT with Psalms was published in 1987 by the two Bible Societies. In 1988 the *Habari Njema* NT appeared with the Jerusalem Bible notes translated especially for this edition. Roman Catholic authorities granted an imprimatur for this edition to encourage wide use by Roman Catholic readers. The completion of the OT encountered some delays, but the complete Bible, which included a revised NT, was eventually sent to the printer in 1994 and was released simultaneously in Kenya and Tanzania on 24 March 1996, in two editions, one with the Deuterocanonical books and the other without them.

While the launching and dedication ceremony in Kenya was held in Nairobi, the capital city, the launching and dedication ceremony in Tanzania

---

71. BFBS East African language files (see TLC June 6, 1969).

72. For a partial transcript of the complete interview, see appendix D.

Figure 2.3. Dr Peter Renju, biblical scholar and former Roman Catholic priest who worked as translator on the Biblia Habari Njema. Photo © Aloo Osotsi Mojola

was held in the little backwater town of Manyoni, situated on the old slave route and on the main central railway line to western Tanganyika. The choice of Manyoni was significant. The idea was to make an intentional symbolic statement delinking modern standard Swahili from the "original" Swahili dialects of the East African littoral and of the traditional Swahili Islamic settlements.

The language of *Biblia Habari Njema* (*BHN*) is predominantly Swahili as currently spoken especially in Tanzania and as taught in institutions throughout the region as the standard form of the language. It is interesting that the translation freely employs the terminology created and popularized by the socialist government of Tanzania at the time the translation was carried out. The translators did not take up the Roehl agenda of de-Arabizing standard Swahili. Thus, where Roehl uses, for example, the Bantu terms *kumtegemea Mungu*, *tambiko* and *matoleo* ("faith," "sacrifice," and "offering," respectively), *BHN* uses the traditional Swahili Arabic terms for these concepts, going back to Taylor and Steere's terms (i.e. *imani*, *dhabihu*, and *sadaka*). Roehl's terms are perfectly good Swahili Bantu words going back to the roots of Swahili Bantu's traditional religious heritage. Their use in *BHN* would certainly have advanced the cause of enculturation or indigenization, at least as far as it relates to the current non-ethnic, non-Muslim Swahili speakers who are now the majority target users.[73]

In general, however, Roehl's agenda of de-Arabizing standard Swahili has been bypassed by the current practice of borrowing, primarily from Bantu languages first and thereafter from foreign languages. In the area of science and technology, for example, modern standard Swahili has borrowed heavily from English. Borrowings from Arabic are at a minimum since Arabic is not much used these days even in the coastal areas, except perhaps in Arabic or Islamic contexts. The translators of *BHN* followed this practice and employed such terminology as is current in the churches, which basically means the

---

73. Renju, "Passover Lamb," 229–234.

terminology already established in church usage and liturgy by the Taylor and Steere translations.

Biblia Habari Njema is a meaning-based translation, a dynamic translation of the functional equivalence variety. Translations of this type, such as the English Good News Bible or Contemporary English Version, as a matter of policy set out to give priority to the meaning of the source text and how this is to be faithfully captured in the receptor text (i.e. the language of translation) as accurately, clearly, and naturally as is possible. These translations place priority on the sense of the original text. In contrast, translations such as the Swahili Union Version are of the formal correspondence variety. They place more emphasis on the words and forms of the original text than on the contextual meaning of the original text. Translations of the formal correspondence variety are sometimes faulted for being unnatural, unclear, inaccurate, and ambiguous. Many of the pioneer missionary translations referred to in this text fall in this category.

The *Biblia ya Uzima* and *Neno* Translations

Another recent contemporary translation of the Bible in modern standard Swahili was attempted by Living Bibles International (East Africa) who used the English Living Bible as a model. The first edition of this translation called *Biblia ya Uzima* ("The Bible of Life") was published by Living Bibles East Africa in Nairobi in 1984. It turned out to have quite a number of serious mistakes and shortcomings, so that it had to be withdrawn from the market. It was thereafter extensively revised. However, the second edition of this translation of the NT, which appeared in 1989, is hardly a mere revision. It is in effect a completely new translation with a new title, *Neno* ("The Word"). *Neno* is certainly more readable and representative of contemporary standard Swahili than its predecessor. Later a Swahili-Arabic diglot based on this *Neno* NT and the Arabic NIV equivalent was published for use in East Africa. The OT translation, which has been in progress for a long time, is under the sponsorship of the International Bible Society (IBS). The IBS later merged with Living Bibles International, eventually taking over its name and functions. The IBS eventually completed and launched its Swahili translation of the Bible at a special ceremony held in Moshi, Tanzania, toward the end of 2009. It was released by the IBS under its current name, Biblica, and the translation appeared under the title *Neno*. Although the new *Neno* translation of the Bible claims to be based on the NIV, it seems to have been heavily reliant on both the Swahili Union Version and the *Biblia Habari Njema*, freely adapting from one to the other. However, its textual base seems to have been heavily influenced by the King James Version.[74]

Bible Translation in Congolese Swahili

In addition to the East African Swahili translations, a number of equally good translations have been flourishing in the vast Swahili-speaking areas of Zaire, renamed the Democratic Republic of Congo (DRC) in 1997 as it had also been previously known from 1960 to 1971. The widespread use of Swahili in the Congo goes back to the eighteenth century and to the eastern African trade in slaves, ivory, gold, and other valuables. This trade, with its main operational center at Zanzibar, was instrumental in the Swahili-ization and to a certain extent the Islamization of certain parts of the continent's interior, especially along the trade routes. Missionaries and explorers contributed to reinforcing the reach and establishment of Swahili. It is no wonder that missionaries saw the need to translate the Bible into Congolese Swahili. The challenge was to determine in which of the varieties of Congo Swahili the translation should be made, the dialect situation in the Congo being rather complex. After early traders and missionaries introduced Swahili into the Congo, local languages gave color and diversity to the language so that three major dialects emerged: the northeastern variety with Bunia as a base, the central variety with Bukavu-Goma as a base and the southern variety with Lubumbashi-Kalemie as a base. Spoken mostly in the eastern part of the country, the dialects form a continuum that stretches from the northeast, probably as far as Kisangani-Mahagi-Bunia-Beni, to Goma-Bukavu-Shabunda-Maniema-Kindu in the center, and to Kalemie-Lubumbashi-Kolwezi-Kamina in the south.

In 1921 the BFBS published a translation of NT portions in Kingwana-Ituri Swahili that a missionary named James Lowder had prepared. The complete NT was eventually published in 1937 after undergoing revision by a team consisting of B. Litchman; J. Bell and his wife; Elizabeth P. Prost; Birdie and A. P. Uhlinger; Anne M. Cowell; William A. Deans; Ella Spees; and G. D. Searle. Proverbs was translated by Cowell and the Psalms by Cowell, Birdie Uhlinger and Ella Spees. The BFBS published the two books in 1951 and 1954, respectively. Psalms was bound with the NT of 1927. Another translation started by missionary C. T. Studd in Kingwana-Ituri resulted in the publication of the Epistles of James, 1 and 2 Peter, 1 John, Jude, and selections from the Psalms in 1925 by Scripture Gift Mission (SGM) in London. The complete NT was printed in 1929 by SGM.

---

74. See, for example, at 1 John 5:6–8.

Studd's translations of the complete book of Psalms as well as Proverbs were also published in 1929 by SGM.

Another form of Kingwana is the so-called Kingwana-Lualaba. As early as 1905 a missionary named W. H. Stapleton had translated parables and miracles from the Gospels that were printed at Yasusu by the Baptist Missionary Society (BMS), and H. Sutton Smith had translated a collection of OT stories that was printed in 1907 also at Yasusu. However, the NT in Kingwana-Lualaba, which would be published by BFBS in London in 1938, was the work of G. J. Wilkerson and C. B. Wilkerson, who had translated the Gospels and Acts which BFBS had published in 1937.

Following the example of East Africa, a number of missionary societies in the Congo took seriously the idea of a "union Swahili" that would bring together all the Kingwana dialects. At a conference at Yakusu in January 1934 the missionaries tried to assemble all the missions and persuade them to accept Kingwana. The first attempt to render Scripture in this new Kingwana Union Version was the Gospel of Matthew translated by a team representing seven missionary societies and published in London by BFBS in 1934. Unfortunately, the effort was premature and the idea of a union or standard Congo Swahili did not meet with success at this time.[75] However, serious work on this union version did continue and resulted in the publication of the Gospel of Luke in 1952 at Ibambi. The work of a team consisting of John F. Carrington, D. Ridely Chesterton, William A. Deans, Ella Spees, C. E. Taylor and Anne M. Cowell, augmented by R. E. Harlow, Gertrude Koppel, J. Grainger, C. White, Moses Penge, Simon Ambaume and Yosiya Butso eventually resulted in a Union Swahili Congo Bible based on the East African Swahili Union Version. The NT was published in 1955 and the complete Bible in 1960, both by BFBS.

Roman Catholic translations in Congo Swahili started with selections from the OT and NT published as early as 1895 and 1903 in Einsiedeln and Freiburg, translated by Father Laurentius Wulfers and others. A number of other Scripture selections translated by Father Léonard Goffiné and Father Léonard Massman followed in 1913. Work by Father Charles Sacleux appeared in 1921, by Father Gabriel Grison in 1923, and by Théophile Avon in 1926; other subsequent lectionaries by Josef Peeters and André Rommelaere appeared between 1971 and 1975.

All of these publications sought a kind of union approach and therefore ignored the language as it was spoken on the ground. One can easily see why this should be so, for example, in the case of Father Emile Brutel and Father Sacleux

---

75. BFBS ESC Minute Cards, vol. 6.

who had begun their work in Tanganyika and thus had already translated and published in Kiunguja Swahili. The first Gospels and Acts published in Algiers by the Maison-Carrée in 1913 were the work of Father Brutel. In 1953 Marie-Jules Celis's four Gospels were published at Beni by the Mission Catholique. In 1961 Thomas Neve's four Gospels were published at Lubumbashi by the Mission Catholique. The first NT by Catholics was published by Editions St. Paul at Lubumbashi in 1975. It was the work of Father Josef Peeters, Father André Rommelaere, Thomas Kitombo, Osimo Okongo wa Njoku, and others. In 1985 the Verbum edition of the NT appeared, followed by the complete Bible in 1986. Both were published in Kinshasa by Verbum Bible, being the work of Father Peeters and Father Denys Cooreman.

Lastly, mention should be made of the common language translation of the Bible in Congo Swahili. This work was mainly sponsored by the Bible Society of DRC-Kinshasa and was based at Bukavu in eastern DRC. The common language NT was published in 1981; it was reprinted in 1990, and a revised edition was released in 1997. The publication of the complete Bible in contemporary Bukavu Swahili with the title, *Biblia – Maandiko Matakatifu Kwa Watu Wote* (Bible – Holy Scriptures for all people), followed in 2000. Those involved in this translation included Waso Lulinda, Chasinga Ntumulo, and Bishikwabo Francois. They were assisted by a dedicated team of the American-sponsored, Africa Christian Mission consisting of Ron Butler as co-coordinator and John Schirle, together with the sponsorship and technical support of the Bible Society of Congo (DRC) through the translation consultants of the United Bible Societies.

The union Swahili Congo Bible based on the East African Swahili Union Version and more recently the common language Swahili Congo Bible closely related to the East African *Biblia Habari Njema* have helped to spread and popularize a type of DRC standard Swahili. Today, however, the trend is for all these dialects to be increasingly influenced by East African Swahili, a trend driven by Tanzanian usage. It is this standard Swahili that dominates the radio air waves – Radio Tanzania, Kenya Broadcasting Corporation, the British Broadcasting Corporation, Voice of America, Radio Deutsche Welle, Radio Japan, Radio India, and Radio China, among others.

Julius Nyerere's Translation of the Gospels and Acts

Julius Kambarage Nyerere (1922–1999), the founding father of the modern Tanzanian nation, is to be credited with the current prominent place of modern standard Swahili, not just in Tanzania, but in the entire East Africa area. He played a pivotal role in making Swahili the primary language of education as well as of political and social discourse in his nation. The heavy use of Swahili in Tanzania led to the development of the Swahili lexicon and technical terminologies by a number of professional committees that were put into place for that purpose. A number of dictionaries and word lists reflecting current developments in the language proliferated, the most prominent being the *Kamusi ya Kiswahili Sanifu* (1981), *Kamusi ya Kiingereza-Kiswahili* (1996) and the *Kamusi ya Kiswahili-Kiingereza* (2001).[76] Nyerere not only played his role in the arena of Swahili language policy planning and implementation, he also contributed through his political writings and speeches, which were all published in Swahili. His translations of two of Shakespeare's plays, namely, the *Merchant of Venice*, which appeared as *Mabepari wa Venisi*[77] and *Julius Caesar*, which appeared as *Juliasi Kaisari*,[78] received wide acclaim in East African literary circles.

Towards the end of his life, Nyerere turned his attention to the field of Bible translation. His approach was quite innovative and new. He set out to translate the New Testament and the Psalms into Swahili using the ancient traditional poetic style of the *utenzi* of the East African coastal belt. A number of famous poems going back several centuries are in this style.[79] His Scripture translation followed the tradition of such poets as Mathias E. Mnyampala of Dodoma who translated the Gospels in this poetic style as *Utenzi wa Enjili Takatifu* (translated 1962, published 1967), and *Utenzi wa Zaburi* (1965, pub. 1967), and Mwalimu Evaristo M. Mahimbi in *Utenzi wa Yusufu* (1975). These differed from Mwalimu Julius K. Nyerere's work in the sense that Mwalimu Nyerere created a verse-by-verse rendering of the Gospels and Acts while Mahimbi and Mnyampala adapted and offered a condensed poetic rendering of the original stories. Nyerere's translations appeared in 1996 as *Utenzi wa Enjili – Kadiri ya Utungo wa Matayo* (Matthew), *Kadiri ya Utungo wa Marko*

---

76. These were all prepared and published in Dar es Salaam, Tanzania, by the Taasisi ya Uchunguzi ya Kiswahili (TUKI), (i.e. the Institute of Kiswahili Research) based at the University of Dar es Salaam with the participation of Baraza la Kiswahili Tanzania (BAKITA), (i.e. Kiswahili Council of Tanzania). The laudable effort of Kirkeby, *English-Swahili Dictionary* (2000), is worthy of mention.

77. Nyerere, *Mabepari wa Venisi*.

78. Nyerere, *Juliasi Kaizari*.

79. See Noss and Renju, "Tenzi of Mwalimu Nyerere," 19–34. See also Noss, "Mwalimu Julius Nyerere's Scripture Translation," 391–409.

(Mark), *Kadiri ya Utungo wa Luka* (Luke), *Kadiri ya Utungo wa Yohana* (John) and *Utenzi wa Matendo ya Mitume* (Acts).[80]

President Nyerere's translations have received widespread acceptance and are read by both Christians and non-Christians alike. The use of Islamic terminology in the translations, especially in the terms used for God's name, makes this translation particularly easy for Muslims to understand.[81] It should be noted, though, that the Muslim name for God, Allah, is not used in this translation. Interestingly, East African Swahili Muslims commonly use the Bantu expression *Mwenyezi Mungu* (Almighty God) to refer to God. The popularity of Nyerere's translation of the Gospels and Acts is probably due to the poetic style adopted, the quality of the work itself, and to the personality of the translator himself – a popular and widely respected president who has left a lasting imprint and influence not only in his nation but throughout the African continent and perhaps even beyond.[82]

The Swahili Bible and Its Contribution to Laying the Foundations for Colonial, Nationalist, Postcolonial and Christian discourses

The Swahili Bible is perhaps the most widely read book in East and Central Africa. This is due to the fact that Swahili is one of the most widely spoken linguae francae in Africa. Estimates of Swahili speakers vary from fifty million to more than a hundred-million people.[83] Obviously, this figure includes people whose command of Swahili varies from mother-tongue competence to functional use in limited areas. Prior to the standardization of Swahili by Christian missionary Bible translators, linguists, and educators, with strong support from the colonial British government, there was no single variety of Swahili. Each coastal Swahili settlement was associated with its own variety or dialect of the cluster of languages that is now commonly referred to as Swahili. The need to standardize Swahili was clear and unavoidable if it was going to serve as a lingua franca in the region and be used for trade in the East African hinterland stretching into the interior of the Congo, for colonial administration

---

80. Published at Peramiho, Tanzania, by the Benedictine Publications, Ndanda, and given an imprimatur by Cardinal Polycarp Pengo of Dar es Salaam, Tanzania.

81. For example, use of such terms as Karima (in Acts 1:2, 3), Latifu (Acts 1:5), Maulana (in Acts 1:6), Jalia (Acts 1:8), Jalali (Acts 1:14).

82. For an assessment of Nyerere's impact, see Legum and Mmari's *Mwalimu*.

83. According to a BBC news report in 2005, Microsoft had launched software in Swahili "targeting more than 110 million speakers of the language" ("Microsoft Swahili Speakers Launch," http://news.bbc.co.uk/1/hi/world/africa/4527876.stm).

and education, as well as for missionary and religious purposes. Despite the inevitability of this fact, it can be argued that the translation of the Bible into Swahili and the widespread use of this Bible in the region played no small role in this process. As has been stated already, the missionary contribution to the spread and use of Swahili in the interior is well documented. So is the missionary contribution to the development of a unified Romanized Swahili orthography, and of Swahili lexicons as well as grammars with which the names of missionary scholars and pioneer Bible translators such as Johann Krapf, Edward Steere, Charles Sacleux, Arthur C. Madan, and W. E. Taylor are inextricably associated.

The Christian missionaries who took the challenge to translate the Bible into Swahili had to contend with the problem of operating with cultural and linguistic systems that were not only different from their own but also different from one another and often conflicting. As the historian Adrian Hastings has put it, "Christians had to decide their faith in terms of words and concepts whose usage and meaning hitherto had other purposes and other senses."[84] In the case of Swahili, the Islamic scholar Farouk Topan points out that initially Islam faced the daunting task of formulating its own theological concepts and terms in Swahili.[85] Later, Christianity had to do the same, having to contend with both the Islamic-Arabic heritage and worldview, as well as with the underlying original Swahili-Bantu heritage and religio-cultural worldview. This dual heritage could not be brushed aside. It is not clear that the early missionary translators who undertook this task realized the magnitude of what was before them. Translators of the Bible in Mombasa Swahili (the men from CMS, Johann Krapf and Johannes Rebmann to W. E. Taylor), and translators of the Bible in Zanzibar Swahili (the men from UMCA, Edward Steere and his colleagues), were clearly scholars steeped in the study of the culture and dialects in which they worked as well as its literature. Steere's NT of 1879 and Bible of 1891 were widely used throughout the region. This was the Bible that the first missionaries in the hinterland and as far away as Buganda – and indeed the whole Great Lakes region – used. As we will see in subsequent chapters, this Bible had a great impact on Bible translations in other languages of this region such as Luganda (Bible 1896), Yao (NT 1907, Bible 1920), Gogo (NT 1899), Runyoro-Rutoro (NT 1905, Bible 1912), Kitaveta (NT 1906), and Giriama (NT 1901, Bible 1908), among others. Taylor's Bible in Mombasa Swahili, which came out in 1914 (NT 1909), was not as widely used in the region as that of

---

84. Quoted in Topan, "Swahili as a Religious Language," 334.
85. Topan, 334.

Steere. Moreover, its impact was drastically reduced by the decision to create a regional Swahili standard from the 1930s onwards that virtually bypassed it. Adrian Hastings had this situation in mind when he wrote:[86]

> In many parts of East Africa, including Buganda, missionary teaching was initially imparted either through the medium of Swahili, or in a local language much affected by Swahili borrowings. Reasons for this were several. Swahili being a coastal language its missionary use preceded that of any other language by decades. Up-country missionaries . . . had Swahili grammars, dictionaries and Bibles to make use of in coping with their own still unwritten but kindred languages.

Working in a Swahili Muslim environment, Krapf and Rebmann, Taylor and Binns, and Steere and his colleagues, all relied heavily on Swahili Muslims for their knowledge of the language and its underlying religious and cultural life. This had an effect on their respective translations even though all four Swahili Bibles, (namely, Steere's Bible of 1891, Taylor's Bible of 1914, Roehl's Bible of 1937, and Hellier and Butcher's Swahili Union Version of 1952), were not produced with a primarily ethnic Swahili target audience in mind. Of course, first-language speakers were envisaged, but they were not the primary audience. These missionary translators were to all intents and purposes resident at the coast among Swahili-speaking heavily Islamized people. It is therefore safe to conclude that these translations were influenced by the Islamic culture of the ethnic Swahili people to whom we owe the Swahili language. Islamic terminology and concepts were adopted and used extensively in the translations.

This influence is evident in the generous use of Islamic religious terms in these translations, even in cases where suitable Swahili terms of Bantu origin do exist. For example, words for "priest," "prophet," "spirit," "holy," "sacrifice," "altar," "offering," "life," "blood," "impure," "sin," "cleanse," "condemn," "believe," "faith," "hope," "human being," "good news," "book," "psalm," "glory," "blessed," and "earth" – and numerous others in these translations are all derived from Arabic. Even in cases where a particular term was not in use in Swahili Islamic discourse, these translators invented a term derived from the Arabic. In this connection P. J. L. Frankl and Yahya Ali Omar write:

> The available evidence, which dated from the mid-nineteenth century, suggests that the Swahili people had no need of a word

---

86. Quoted in Frankl and Omar, "Idea of 'the Holy' in Swahili," 112.

for "holy" to express their sense of "The Holy." In order to translate the word "holy" for speakers of *kiMisheni* (the Kiswahili spoken by European-Christian missionaries and their followers) a Swahili word *takatifu* was derived to translate "holy" – this probably occurred in the late 1850s or in the 1860s. But the Kiswahili language has a genius for absorbing new words, and so since the Second World War, the *maShekhe* (Muslim Sheikhs) have used the "Christian" *takatifu* in their qur'anic interpretations for the qur'anic words derived from the Arabic consonantal root q d s. Whatever the origin of *takatifu* as a printed word, it is true to say that in their conversations of Swahili folk *takatifu* has been until recently a word unknown and therefore a word unheard.[87]

Through the influence of these translations, the word *takatifu* was widely adopted in numerous translations of the Bible in the East African Bantu languages. Professor Adrian Hastings draws attention to this in the case of Luganda. He writes:

In Luganda *takatifu* was at first only one of many Swahili words employed . . . Between 1908 and 1912, however, there was a systematic removal of unnecessary Swahilisms from Christian Luganda undertaken by both Protestants and Catholics. Swahili had come to be regarded as an alien and – perhaps also – a threateningly Muslim language . . . *Takatifu* was at this point changed to the indigenous *tukirivu* or *tukuvu* (i.e. holy).[88]

Farouk Topan notes that "almost all major terms for an Islamic discourse in Swahili are derived from Arabic,"[89] a claim that is echoed by Patricia Romero, who writes, "All of the words referring to Islam and religion, of course, are Arabic."[90] No wonder a number of writers, among them Ali Mazrui and Pio Zirimu, speak of Swahili as an Islamic language or an Afro-Islamic language.[91] It seems that when the original Swahili Bantu culture was Islamized, the Bantu religious component was transformed and given a new linguistic component. This process never completely eliminated the original Bantu factor. In spite of the power of Islamic transformation, the Swahili Bantu name for God, *Mungu*,

---

87. Frankl and Omar, 113.

88. Quoted in Frankl and Omar, 113.

89. Topan, "Swahili as a Religious Language," 335.

90. Romero, *Lamu*, 3.

91. Mazrui and Zirimu, "Secularization of an Afro-Islamic Language," 25–53.

which Swahili shares with a number of other Bantu languages in the region, still dominates in Swahili Islamic discourse.[92] Topan thinks that the process of Islamizing Swahili Bantu religious discourse and terminology could have proceeded as follows:

    i. the original Arabic term was Swahili-ized, e.g. Ruah (Arabic) → Roho (Swahili) [i.e. Spirit]

    ii. the original Arabic term was Swahili-ized and, additionally, given a Bantu synonym, e.g., Rasul (Arabic) → rasuli/ mtume (Swahili) [i.e. apostle]

    iii. the original Arabic term was generally not adopted but the concept was given a Swahili term, e.g., Mungu was preferred to Allah [i.e. God].[93]

It should be noted that even when a term from the Bantu was retained, if it related to the religious sphere, it was given Islamic meaning. Thus *Mungu* (Allah) in Swahili Islamic discourse is always qualified as *Mwenyezi Mungu*. Farouk Topan correctly notes that *Mwenyezi* is a "compound of Kiswahili and Arabic elements respectively: *mwenye* denoting 'possessor' and *ezi* (from 'izza), 'power' and 'might'. The full phrase is taken to express the omnipotence, sovereignty, and regality of the Almighty."[94] Mazrui and Mazrui exemplify this process by offering a few more examples as follows:

> The word for God in Kiswahili (*M'ngu* or *Mungu*) comes from Bantu, whereas the word for angels (*malaika*) comes from Arabic. The word for the heavens (*mbingu*) comes from Bantu whereas the word for earth, especially when used religiously (*ardhi*), comes from Arabic. The word for a holy prophet (*mtume*) comes from Bantu, whereas the word for a devil in a religious sense (*shetani*) comes from Arabic. Curiously enough, the words for paradise and hell (*pepo* and *moto*) come from Bantu, whereas the word for the hereafter as a whole (*akhera* or *ahera*) comes from Arabic.[95]

In general, however, it can be argued that Swahili seems to have synonyms or alternative ways of expressing many of the ideas for which the Arabic

---

92. See article on this topic by Frankl and Omar, "Word of 'God' in Swahili," 202–211.

93. Topan, "Swahili as a Religious Language," 335.

94. Topan, 336.

95. Mazrui and Mazrui, *Swahili State and Society*, 22.

expression is now dominant, unless, of course, the term in question is about entities or realities that were absent from the original Bantu world.

Krapf, Taylor, and Steere, and their collaborators, and even Butcher and Hellier later, apparently had no problem with the Arabic-Islamic component of the Swahili lexicon or its suitability as a medium for expressing Christian ideas. On the contrary, this component made their task lighter. They did not have to struggle to look for, or to invent, suitable Bantu words for expressing Christian concepts and ideas. Krapf spoke for the rest when he pointed to the fact that this Arabic-Islamic component of Swahili "affords to the translator the resource of being able to adopt at will an Arabic word when in difficulty for a proper expression in Kisuaheli [*sic*]."[96]

This Arabization of Swahili Bantu in the translation of the Christian Scriptures extended to quite a number of the languages of the East African hinterland. Naturally, many Christians felt that using Islamic words in Christian Scriptures posed a problem, and it was the German Lutheran missionary translator, Dr Karl Roehl, who undertook to address the problem. He wondered to what extent the Christian missionaries should facilitate an Arabization program while promoting a parallel program of Christianizing the local cultures and languages. Topan has put it well: "If Swahili, as a lingua franca had to be used, then it had to be de-Arabized," or freed from its Arabic character.[97] In fact, as noted earlier, Roehl refused to collaborate with the British team of Butcher and Hellier on the translation of the Swahili Union Bible precisely on the issue of what he felt was its excessive use of Arabic words.

Although Swahili has borrowed heavily from Arabic, a situation that has given the false impression that it is close to Arabic and related Semitic languages, it is actually in every respect a Bantu language in terms of its syntax, its morphology and phonology, its core lexicon, which is closely related to Proto-Bantu (i.e. Ur-Bantu), and its links to the present-day neighboring Bantu languages. It is, for example, much easier for a speaker of a related Bantu language to learn Swahili than it is for a speaker of Arabic or related Semitic languages. In fact, Swahili has not borrowed words exclusively from Arabic but from all the languages that it has come into contact with. Freeman-Greenville estimated "20 to 30 percent of the (language) is composed of loan words that come from such disparate areas as Persia, Hindustan, Gujarat, Turkey,

---

96. Krapf quoted in Topan, "Swahili as a Religious Language," 338.

97. Topan, "Swahili as a Religious Language," 339.

Malaysia, Portugal, Germany, and of course, England . . . Some words, too, are from 'special Arabian dialects.'"[98]

Swahili in Résumé

By looking at the various translations of the Bible in Swahili over time, one can trace the changes in the development of the language and of theological expressions. As an example, one could compare how the Lord's Prayer has been rendered in five of the key translations in East African Swahili, namely the Swahili Zanzibar Bible 1883, the Swahili Mombasa Bible 1914, the Roehl Bible 1930, the Swahili Union Version 1952 and *Biblia Habari Njema* 1996.

Close comparison of these texts will make clear to Swahili readers and speakers that there are some minor shifts in the development and formation of the Swahili Bible, but they will note in particular how close to each other the Kimvita and Kiunguja dialects are, a factor which no doubt facilitated the successful creation of a standard Swahili and a Union Bible.

In summary, the translations of the Bible in Swahili have played a key role in the process of standardizing the language and in the development of a strong literacy and educational program. Scholars recognize the Swahili Bible's role in contributing to the development of a national language and culture in both Kenya and Tanzania, as well as an international language for use across national boundaries. For Christians, the Swahili Bible has become the major tool of inter-ethnic or cross-cultural Christian ministry and communication in the entire East African region as well as in the eastern parts of the Democratic Republic of Congo. Virtually all the earlier Protestant versions as well as the 1996 interconfessional version, *Biblia Habari Njema,* have been and continue to be widely used by all the churches across confessional groupings.

---

98. See Romero, *Lamu,* 3, quoting from Freeman-Grenville, *East African Coast.*

3

The People of Pwani: From Lamu to Mtwara

Pokomo, Boni, Mijikenda, Digo, Zaramo, Makua, and Makonde

Introducing the People of the Coastal Areas

The East African coast, *Pwani* in Swahili, or *Mwambao*,[1] as it is popularly called, stretches from the Somali border right down to the Mozambique border. It spans about 3,000 kilometers of coastline, consisting of beautiful sandy beaches, warm waters of the Indian Ocean, deep and secure harbors, and numerous offshore islands such as Zanzibar, Pemba, the Mafia Island, and Kilwa Kisiwani. Some islands such as Lamu and Mombasa are separated from the mainland only by narrow channels.

The people of Pwani are by no means homogeneous. They form a multiplicity of ethnic groups and speak a diversity of languages. From their strategic location along the coast, they have acted as intermediaries, traders, and cultural brokers between the peoples of the interior and newcomers to their shores. Indeed, since time immemorial these coastal communities have grown accustomed to incursions, invasions, occupation, as well as friendly visits from people of diverse nationalities. Even before the rise of Islam, they maintained contact with people from the Arabian Peninsula, the Indian subcontinent, China, and southeast Asia. In recent times the contacts with the Europeans have been the most defining and influential. These contacts have naturally left their imprint on the local languages and cultures, both material and spiritual.

Archaeological evidence – for example, the excavations at Shanga in the Lamu archipelago and at Manda and Pate[2] – has shown that there were

---

1. *Pwani* refers to where there is a tide; *mwambao* means the region where the dry land meets the sea or ocean, (i.e. coastline).

2. Insoll, *Archaeology of Islam*, 152–205.

numerous settlements along the coast of pre-Islamic indigenous peoples. The present-day peoples are predominantly of Bantu stock. The outsiders are mainly of Asiatic origin, particularly from the Arabian Peninsula, the Indian subcontinent, and southeast Asia. Those of European origin form a tiny minority and are of more recent origin, even though an account by a Greek writer about trade in the Indian Ocean entitled the *Periplus of the Erythrean Sea* (that being the contemporary name for the Indian Ocean), written around 130–140 CE refers to the activities of the Greeks and Romans and their trade with the Arabs and the peoples of the eastern African shores. The Greek writer Ptolemy in a book entitled *Geographia* written in the second century CE, with a later extant edition dated in the late fourth century, refers to trading posts along the Somali and Kenyan coast. However, by the seventh century the position previously held by the Greco-Romans had been taken over by the Arabs. The influence of the Arabian Peninsula and the Persian Gulf was on the increase, especially after the rise of Islam. By 1000 CE many peoples from those areas had settled along the East African coast.

The influx of newcomers from the Arabian Peninsula and the Persian Gulf area led to the slow beginnings and development of an Afro-Arab culture centered on the spread and expansion of Islam. These Muslims learned the languages of the local populations and created new Afro-Arabic urban settlements along the eastern African coast stretching from present-day Somalia to Mozambique. The greatest expansion is said to have begun in the twelfth century. Newcomers came into contact with the Swahili-speaking communities around this period. They intermarried with many of the other coastal peoples, but adopted Swahili as their lingua franca for use along the expanding island and coastal settlements.[3]

As stated in the previous chapter, Swahili is a member of the Bantu group of languages, a fact that is evidenced by its basic structure, grammar, morphology, lexicon, and phonology. It is very closely related to the northeastern coastal Bantu languages such as Elwana, Pokomo, and the Mijikenda dialects.[4] The Bantu origin of Swahili was obviously a factor in its use as a lingua franca. Some people have assumed that Swahili is an Arabic-based creole or that it is of Arabic origin. This is not the case. Swahili is an African language.[5] The

---

3. For more on this period of transition, see Abungu, "City-states of the East African Coast," 204–218. See also J. Middleton, *World of the Swahili.*

4. For more, see Nurse and Spear, *Swahili.*

5. Sutton, in his *Thousand Years of East Africa*, 60, writes:

> It is often pointed out that Swahili vocabulary contains a large number of words of Arabic derivation. That is correct; and it is easy to pick out many such words of non-Bantu origin (adapted though they have been by sound shifts and

coastal settlements that developed were referred to as Swahili settlements, or Swahili town-states,[6] despite their Afro-Arabic and Islamic culture. These settlements became the new power centers and sites for the spread of Islam and Arab culture in East Africa. Among the most famous of these centers were Lamu, Shanga, Malindi, Mombasa, Pemba, Zanzibar, and Kilwa.[7]

Swahili communities in their ancient town-states were, of course, not the only people at the coast. There are several dozen languages and communities along the eastern coast of Africa from north to south (see maps 3.1 and 3.2 below), including the following:

- the Boni, Pokomo, and various members of the Mijikenda group (the Kauma, Giriama, Chonyi, Jibana, Kambe, Ribe, Rabai, Duruma, and Digo);[8]
- the various people who speak some dialect or variety of Swahili, including the Bajuni or Tikuu, Pate (on Pate Island), the Siu (also on Pate Island), Amu (on Lamu Island), Mvita (on Mombasa Island), Cifundi (spoken north of Vanga), Vumba, Mtangata, Pemba, Tumbatu, Hadimu, Makunduchi, Unguja, Mafia, Mgao, Mwani, Ngazija (spoken on Grand Comoro Island), and Nzwani (spoken on Anjouan Island in the Comoros);[9]
- the people of Tanga, namely, the Bondei, Zigua, Shambala, Doe, and Kwere;
- the peoples of Dar es Salaam, specifically the Zaramo;
- the peoples south of Dar es Salaam, the Ndengereko, Rufiji, Matumbi, Mwera, Machinga, Makonde and Maraba.[10]

Swahili prefixes). What is less well understood however is that the bulk of these borrowings are not ancient in Kiswahili, but belong to the last two hundred years or so (the period of the "new" Arabs and the Zanzibari state).

6. As in Nurse and Spear, *Swahili*, 80–98.

7. See Moon's *Kilwa Kisiwani: Ancient Port City on the East African Coast*, for a recent study of one of these influential ancient coastal city states; or see Ghaidan's *Lamu: A Study of the Swahili Town*. Romero's *Lamu: History, Society and Family in an East African Port City* (1997) is a fascinating account that brings the story to the present.

8. [130] Spear, *Kaya Complex*, 1–15.

9. Polome, *Swahili Language Handbook*, 19–29; and Nurse and Spear, *Swahili*, 52–67. The Swahili dialects are usually included in Guthrie's Group G40.

10. The Zigua, Kwere, Zaramo, Ngulu, Lugulu, Kami, Kutu, Vidunda, Sagala, and Doe belong to Guthrie's Group G30, while the Ndengereko, Rufiji, Matumbi, Ngindo, and Mbunga belong to Guthrie's P10. The Yao, Mwera, Makonde, Ndonde, and Mabiha are part of Guthrie's P20. The Makhuwa is part of P30, together with such Mozambican languages as Lomwe, Ngulu, and Chwabo. See Maho, "Classification of the Bantu Languages," 649; Odden, "Rufiji-Ruvuma (N10, P10-20)," 529–545; and Nurse and Philippson, *Bantu Languages*, 529–545.

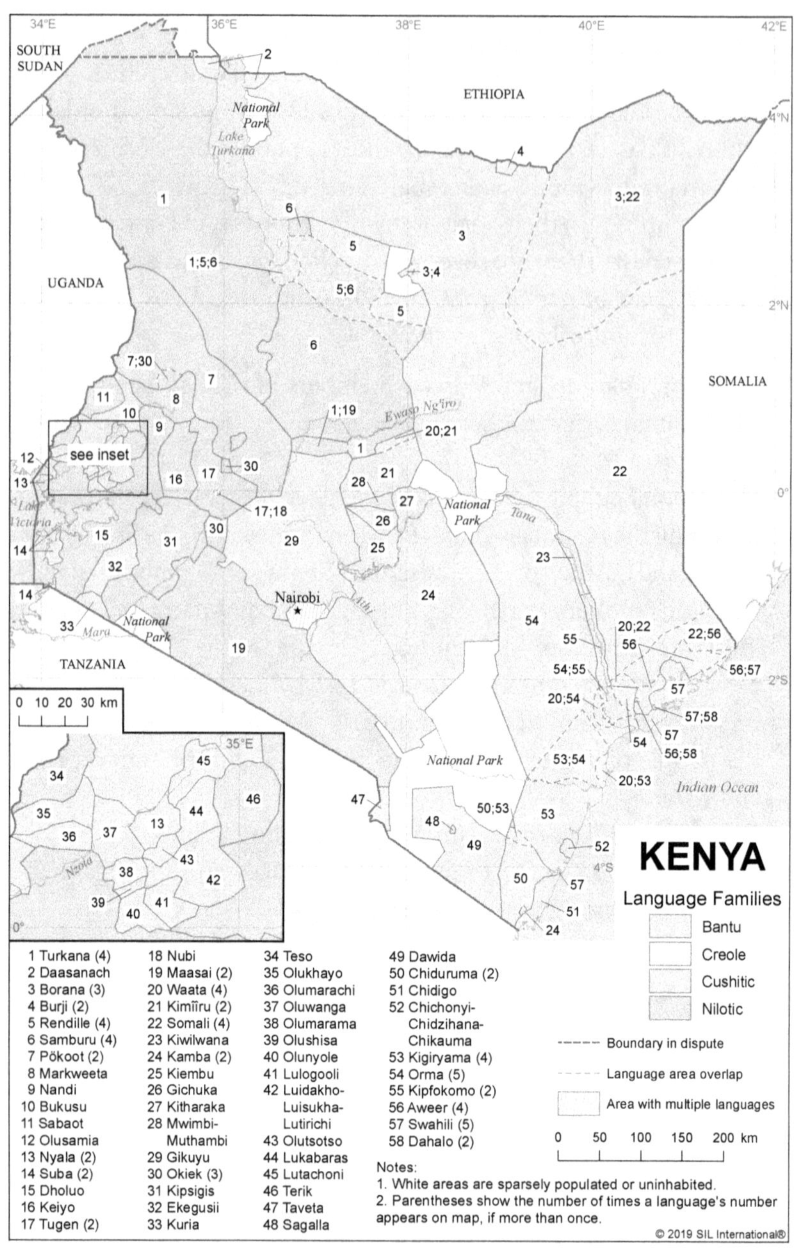

Map 3.1. Language Map of Kenya[11]

---

11. Used by permission, © 2005 SIL International, Ethnologue: Langauges of the World. 18th edition. M. Paul Lewis, Gary F. Simons, and Charles D. Fennig (eds.), further redistribution prohibited without permission.

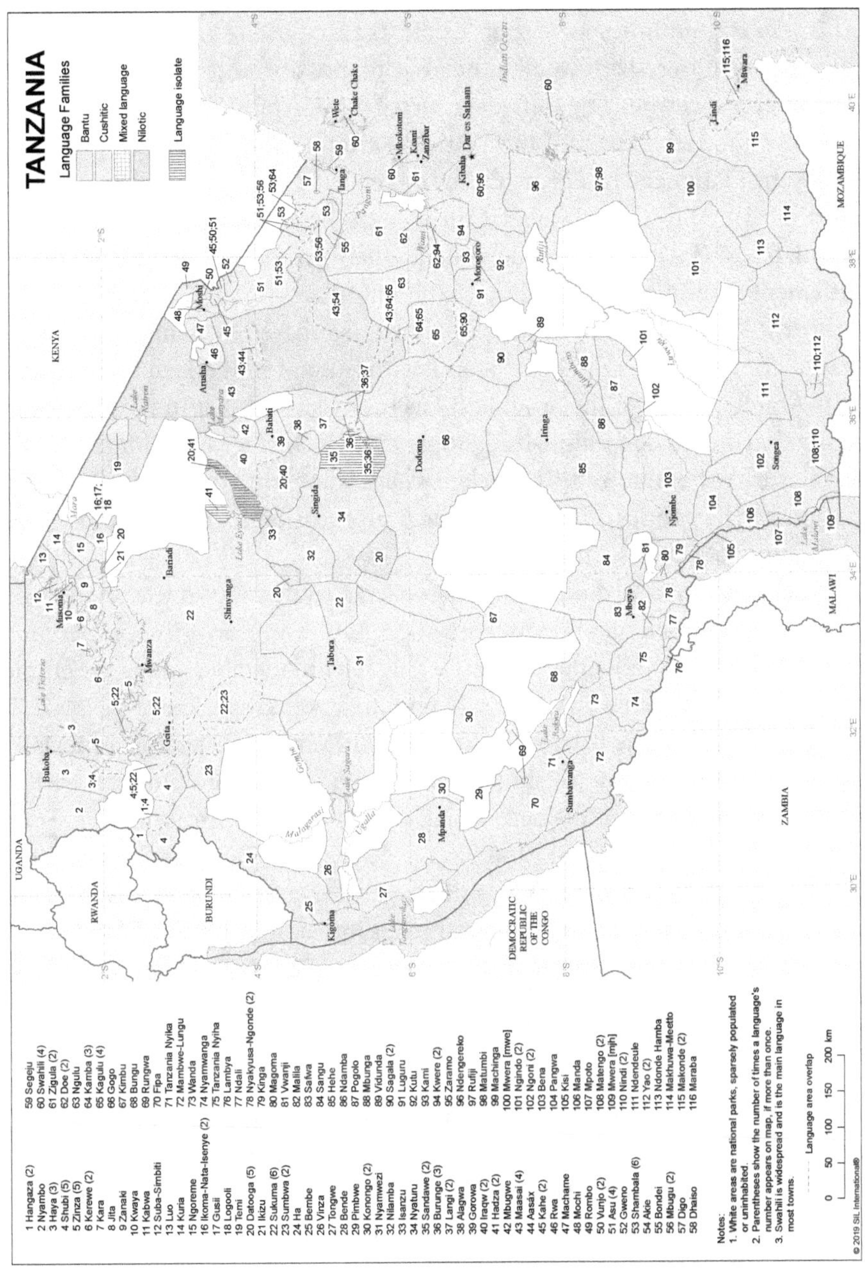

Map 3.2. Language Map of Tanzania[12]

<hr>

12. Used by permission, © 2005 SIL International, Ethnologue: Langauges of the World. 18th edition. M. Paul Lewis, Gary F. Simons, and Charles D. Fennig (eds.), further redistribution prohibited without permission.

These communities have roots as old as those of the Swahili. They have, however, been overshadowed by the Swahili, possibly due to the substantial Swahili empowerment by outsiders, first by the Arabs and in more recent times, by the Germans and the British. Paradoxically, while the power of the Swahili language has grown, the influence of the Swahili communities has diminished to the extent that the Swahili have been marginalized. The Swahili have been further fragmented into their various dialect groupings and settlement communities. What unites them is their common Islamic religion and Afro-Arab culture. But this is a feature also shared by many of the other coastal communities who have been Islamized and influenced by the same Afro-Arabic culture of the Swahili. It has been claimed that in East Africa to be Islamized is to be Swahili-ized. Some even go further to claim that to be Islamized is to be Arabized. These claims have some truth but need to be taken cautiously. The politics of African versus Arab occasionally crop up and makes such claims complex to untangle.

The question of Swahili identity has been a contentious one as evidenced in recent publications and discussions.[13] At the present time, a person's identification as Swahili does not necessarily refer to membership in the ethnic coastal Swahili communities. It could refer to any first speaker of the Swahili language in any of the urban areas of coastal Kenya or Tanzania, especially if such a person is also a Muslim. In fact, some coastal communities are fast losing their languages or dialects, which are threatened with extinction. Such communities as the Digo of Mombasa in Kenya and Tanga in Tanzania are increasingly being identified as Swahili, largely because of the linguistic factor, but also because they are predominantly Muslim. Swahili-ization, Islamization and Arabization are three key factors that dominate the realities of the East African coastal areas and threaten, to a certain extent, some parts of the hinterland. The earliest Christian missionaries to the East African coast and the immediate hinterland had to contend with these factors that are still critical in all current discussions of Christian mission and evangelization, especially in the current climate of religious and political fundamentalisms.[14]

During the nineteenth century a considerable part of the coastal belt was under the influence and political control of the Arabs and their Swahili

---

13. See, for example, Allen, *Swahili Origins*; Mazrui and Shariff, *Swahili*; Mazrui and Mazrui, *Swahili State and Society*; Mojola, "Post-colonial Translation Theory," 77–104; and Askew, *Performing the Nation*.

14. For historical context, see Sim's *Fundamentalist World*, and Ali's *Clash of Fundamentalisms*.

collaborators. Zanzibar emerged as the leading center of power during this period. Authority was exercised by a dynasty of Omani sultans who had relocated and moved their power base to Zanzibar. The most famous of them were Seyyid Said (ruled 1806–1856), Seyyid Majid (ruled 1856–1870), and Seyyid Barghash (ruled 1870–1888). The influence of Zanzibar extended as far as the Great Lakes area of East Africa and the Congo. As the proverb puts it, "When one pipes in Zanzibar, they dance on the lakes"; but as Abdul Sheriff comments, "The tune that was being played was not one of political control, for the Sultan's sway did not extend beyond the narrow coastal belt even at the height of his power. Zanzibar did control the external trade of a large part of the region."[15]

Zanzibari power during this period derived from control of the inhuman trade in ivory and slaves, as noted by Abdul Sheriff, "Zanzibar in the nineteenth century was the seat of a vast commercial empire. Its economy was based partly on the production of cloves and coconuts on the islands themselves, using slave labor and partly on the eastern African transit trade for which Zanzibar was almost the sole entrepot."[16] To ensure success in this trade, the Zanzibaris needed intermediaries in the interior. For this they collaborated with some inland ethnic communities, such as the Yao, the Nyamwezi, and even the Kamba. The trade in slaves, ivory, and animal skins led the Zanzibaris and their collaborators to venture further into the interior, as far as Tabora in central Tanganyika, to Ujiji of Livingstone and Stanley fame on the shores of Lake Tanganyika, and right into the Congo. The role of Swahili as a lingua franca of the region was enhanced in the course of these activities. Some of the early European explorers and missionaries such as David Livingstone contributed much to the eradication of the horrors and brutalities connected with this inhuman trade, and in the process opened these territories for European "colonization, civilization and Christianization."[17]

Bible translation was one of the beneficial outcomes of this process. It led to the development of the local languages and the creation of writing systems for these languages, and gave rise to readers in the vernacular. Christianization could not proceed without the Bible, and the Bible that made sense was the Bible in the languages of the people, a Bible that spoke to the hearts of the people

---

15. Sheriff and Ferguson, *Zanzibar under Colonial Rule*, 1. Sheriff's, *Slaves, Spices and Ivory*, covers the case of Zanzibar during the period under discussion here in greater detail. See also Gilbert, *Dhows and the Colonial Economy*.

16. Sheriff and Ferguson, *Zanzibar under Colonial Rule*, 4.

17. It is David Livingstone who in an 1857 lecture tour in Great Britain saw these three Cs as providing the key to the future of Africa.

in their own idioms and cadences. The Bible in the vernacular empowered speakers of these languages to read the Bible for themselves, to interpret it for themselves, and even to challenge missionary interpretations. In the process, it opened up the doors for the appropriation, ownership, and enculturation of the new faith in a gradual and complex process.[18]

We have noted that during the Portuguese period in East Africa nothing significant happened to advance either the cause of the gospel or the translation of the Bible into the local languages. Apart from their impressive monuments and other ruins such as Fort Jesus in Mombasa and the Vasco da Gama pillar in Malindi, Kenya, traces of the Portuguese legacy in East Africa can only be gleaned from a few words bequeathed to the Swahili language that are still in use, for example, *meza* for "table," *sapatu* for "slipper," and *mvinyo* for "wine," among others.[19] For wine the German derived *divai* is also used. These borrowed words appear in the various Bible translations.

Mission Work and Bible Translation at the Coast

The church historian and missiologist Kenneth Latourette correctly described the nineteenth century as "the Great Century of Missions."[20] A number of religious societies and missionary organizations that were founded in Europe established work in East Africa and were responsible for the spread of Christianity to these shores. Johann Ludwig Krapf, the first missionary to East Africa after the Portuguese exploration, began his work at the coast. Krapf and his wife landed at Zanzibar on 7 January 1844. They were welcomed by the British consul, but later stayed at the American consulate. The population of Zanzibar at that time included only twenty Europeans, most of whom were involved in the ivory trade as well as the trade in such items as rubber, cloves, and animal skins in exchange for cotton, guns, knives, and swords.

Sultan Seyyid Said welcomed Krapf, treated him well, and even offered him help in his mission. Given the hegemony of Zanzibar and of the sultan

---

18. For thoughtful discussions of this process, see the following texts: Welbourn and Ogot, *Place to Feel at Home*; Barrett, *African Initiatives in Religion*; Barrett, "Spread of the Bible"; Barrett, *Schism and Renewal in Africa*; Mbiti, *Bible and Theology*; Walls, *Missionary Movement*; Walls, *Cross-Cultural Process*; Sanneh, *Translating the Message*; and Bediako, *Christianity in Africa*.

19. For more on the influence of Portuguese on Swahili, see Strandes, *Portuguese Period in East Africa*.

20. Professor Latourette devoted volumes 4, 5, and 6 of his 7-volume *A History of the Expansion of Christianity*, (1941, 1943, 1944) to the ninteeth century. No wonder he called it the great century!

throughout the length and breadth of the East African coast, his help counted for much. The sultan sent a letter recommending Krapf to the coastal rulers asking them to treat the missionary well and serve his needs any way they could. This letter accomplished what the sultan intended and facilitated the task of Krapf and his colleagues in mission. It symbolized the perception that their activities were not inimical to the interests of the ruling authority.

The pioneering work begun by Krapf was carried forward by his colleagues, Johannes Rebmann and Johann Erhardt. However, it was the Methodists rather than the Anglicans who were the real heirs of Krapf's work at the coast. For example, on 23 March 1862, Krapf returned briefly to Kenya to help establish a center at Ribe for the United Methodist Free Churches. In that year two Methodist missionaries, Thomas Wakefield and James Woolner, were brought to Ribe by Krapf, who was intent on pursuing the vision of his Galla mission. Another missionary, Charles New, arrived later in 1863. Thomas Wakefield turned his attention to learning and mastering the language spoken at Ribe. From this base he translated into Ribe the book of Jonah, which was published by the Methodist Press at Ribe in 1878, and the Gospel of Matthew, published by BFBS in 1882.

Translation work among the Pokomo was pioneered by the Neukirchen Mission. F. Würtz translated the Gospel of Mark into Pokomo, assisted by a certain Abdullah, and it was published by BFBS in 1894. A. Kraft of the same mission, together with the assistance of unnamed mother-tongue speakers, saw to the finalization of the NT translation with the publication by BFBS of Matthew–Acts in 1901 and Romans–Revelation in 1902.

In 1984, a group from the Bible Society of Kenya visited the area to study and discuss the Pokomo churches' request to the Bible Society for a new translation of the Bible into Pokomo. It became clear that these pioneer translations had not really been well received or extensively used. They never became King James translation equivalents for their respective languages. Illiteracy may have been a factor, as was an inadequate orthography. But most important, perhaps, was the fact that these translations never captured the genius of the local receptor language, or the richness, the natural rhythms, and the native flavor expected in a good translation that becomes authoritative for the users.

This was equally true of Giriama, the biggest of the native languages spoken along the Kenya coast, notwithstanding the involvement of a native speaker in the translation team. Scripture translation in Giriama was led by the Church Missionary Society. W. E. Taylor, D. A. Hooper, and a local Giriama, Johana Gona, constituted the translation team. In 1892 Luke was published and in 1901 the entire NT was printed. The OT appeared in print in 1908, thus making the complete Bible available in the Giriama tongue in that year.

Like the Pokomo and the Duruma,[21] none of these missionary translations met the test of acceptability and widespread use. The first portion ever translated into Duruma was the Gospel of Luke, translated by Johann Krapf in 1848, and printed in Bombay, India, by the American Missionary Press, after which Scripture translation into Duruma ceased.

Although the lack of widespread literacy among the coastal communities may have been a reason for the limited effective use of the other vernaculars, the dominant use of Swahili by early missionaries and outsiders who preferred to use this lingua franca may also have been an important factor. Nevertheless, it seems that the poor quality of these translations and issues of naturalness and intelligibility were also major factors. It should not be surprising then that the current ongoing translation of the Giriama Bible by BTL/SIL makes no reference whatsoever to the 1908 Giriama Bible. This is unfortunate as there is always something to learn from past mistakes or endeavors.

The Scriptures into the Kenyan Coastal Languages

Of the nine Bantu languages or dialects of the Mijikenda cluster along the Kenyan coast, only three, Giriama, Duruma and Ribe, had at least parts of the Bible or the entire Bible itself by the beginning of the twentieth century.[22]

The nine Mijikenda communities are distinct, yet very closely related both linguistically and culturally, and in terms of historical origins. They refer to themselves as *kaya*, that is, "villages," "homesteads," or "communal settlements." These communities were at one time referred to as *Nyika* by the neighboring Swahili communities and by the early foreigners arriving in Kenya. The term *nyika* means "bush, wilderness" and tended to have a derogatory connotation. Therefore, the communities chose the term *Mijikenda* in the 1940s to describe themselves and to strengthen their unity and solidarity. *Mijikenda* literally means "the nine villages" in all the related dialects and in Swahili: *miji* "villages or towns" and *kenda* "nine."[23]

---

21. It should be noted that Duruma is the same language that Krapf translated the Gospel of Luke into in 1848. He referred to it as the Kinyika Rabai.

22. The nine languages are Giriama, Kauma, Chonyi, Jibana, Kambe, Ribe, Rabai, Duruma, Digo, and Chwaka.

23. For a brief survey of these communities, see Mwangudza, *Mijikenda*, or Spear, *Kaya Complex*.

To the north of the Mijikenda and of the Pokomo are speakers of the little-known language Malakote. This is a Bantu language-speaking community that is also called Ilwana. Very little has been written about this group; consequently, it has not attracted much outside attention and almost nothing by way of Scripture translation was attempted. Currently, however, BTL, the local Kenyan arm of SIL, is carrying on translation and literacy work in a number of Bantu languages on the Kenyan coast, including Malakote as well as Pokomo, Giriama, Duruma, and Digo.[24]

These new translations are all expected to be of the common-language or dynamic equivalence translation variety. Various Scripture portions have already been printed in these languages. For example, a new Duruma translation effort was launched in 1987 under the leadership of John F. Newman of SIL. The Gospel of Mark and the book of Acts appeared in 1989 as test portions, published by BTL and the International Bible Society (IBS). The Gospel of John was published in 1991 and 1 Peter in 1999. The first entire NT in Duruma was published in 2000, the work of a team under the leadership and guidance of John and Heidi Macaulay of SIL, together with two mother-tongue speakers, Raphael Mkala Ndurya and Stephen Mwatela Mwendwa of BTL. Work on the OT is still ongoing under the leadership of Gideon M'Mbetsa who also serves as a member of the translation team.

The Duruma had received their first Gospel (Luke) in 1848 translated by Johann Krapf, but unfortunately, this Gospel was not followed by any other Scripture in the early period. Perhaps the fact that Krapf did not plant a church among the Duruma meant that there was no community to own this text or use it as a basis for their worship and life. This explains why many current SIL translation missions have a church-planting component. The present-day translation effort faces some of the same challenges as in the early days – for example, the challenge of Islam and traditional religions as well as that of poor literacy. The focus and emphasis on literacy by BTL may lead to success where earlier efforts ended in failure.

The first efforts to produce the Scriptures for the Digo community were by the German missionaries. As early as 1911, H. H. Günther of the Evangelische Missionsgesellschaft für D. O. A. had worked on selections of the Bible which he titled "A Bible history, containing two Psalms." These were soon forgotten, as there was no established church community among the Digo to make full use of them or to request a continuation of the work begun that might culminate

---

24. These Kenyan coastal languages are usually listed under Guthrie's Group E70. See Maho, "Classification of the BantuLanguages," 639–651.

in the publication of the entire Bible. More recently, in 1980, Scripture Gift Mission (SGM) also attempted to produce selections from the Gospels called "The Four Things." This work was intended for use among the few Digo Christians and other interested Digo readers. Again, this translation had no impact. New work on the translation of Digo Scriptures was started in 1987 by BTL in collaboration with SIL missionaries Martien and Arisa de Groot working together with mother-tongue speakers including Rogers Maneno. This team produced Genesis, the first-ever portion of Scripture in Digo. This was dedicated and released for use in 1993. Andrew P. Clark of SIL/WBT has continued assisting a team of mother tongue speakers. A number of other books were published, and then the NT,[25] which was launched and dedicated at Kwale on 8 December 2007. Work on the OT has been completed and publication is expected sometime in 2020. The past and present team has included Gideon M'Mbetsa, Joseph Mwalonya, Sayuni Kaole, Edward Chome, and an SIL couple, Steve and Alison Nicole, in the early stages who worked as translation consultants. The BTL/SIL efforts have been mostly concentrated on the Digo of Kwale district in Kenya. Some interested parties expressed the view that it was important to involve the Digo of the Tanga area in Tanzania who were not involved in this translation.

The Pokomo who live along the Tana River have had a significant Christian presence in their area going back to the nineteenth century. As stated above, the first Scripture in Pokomo, namely, the Gospel of Mark, appeared in 1894, with the NT following in 1901–1902, and Psalms in 1911. A reprint of the NT was done in 1930. Subsequently, no one did any further translation into Pokomo and these Scriptures are no longer in use. This is strange in a community with a dynamic and living church. A UBS consultant and colleagues from the Bible Society of Kenya visited the area sometime before work on the current Bible sponsored by BTL commenced. The local Christians informed the team that they were unable to use the first NT in their language, which they found unintelligible and unclear due to archaic speech and unnatural expressions. Another reason for failing to use the NT in their own language was the presence of the Scriptures in Swahili. There is therefore a need for a contemporary and meaningful translation in the Pokomo tongue for use by today's Christians.

Local churches invited the BSK to partner with them in an effort to prepare such a translation, but the Bible Society was unable to do so. The churches made

---

25. The publications by this team were: Acts of the Apostles (1997); Exodus 1–20 and selections from 24–40 (1999); Galatians, Philippians, Colossians, James, 2 Peter (all 2000); Gospel of John (2003).

the request of BTL/SIL, who agreed to undertake the task. A team consisting of mother-tongue speakers, including John Galole, Vincent Hiribae, and Edward Jillo, commenced the work in 1985. The Gospel of Mark was the first fruit of their labors in 1993; Luke followed in 1995, and in 1998 First Timothy–Titus as well as 1 Peter–3 John. In 2002 the entire NT as well as Genesis and Exodus were published. The current team includes Shedrack Falama as team leader and translator. Other members of the translation team have included Vincent Hiribae, John Galole, Ruth Gwiyo, Henry Koroso, and Julie Buya. BTL is very active in promoting literacy work that is intended to support this project. The complete Bible in Kipokomo is expected in 2020.

The Giriama situation is not dissimilar to that of the Pokomo. The Giriama are the largest of the Mijikenda communities. They have a large Christian presence in their midst and they still actively use their language. A natural question is why the large Giriama Christian community did not express a need or interest in the Giriama Bible that was prepared for them at the beginning of the twentieth century by the pioneer Christian missionaries. An answer is that the presence of the Swahili Bible and its use in their churches led to the neglect of their own Giriama Bible. A sociolinguistic study by a BTL/SIL team in the mid-1980s concluded that there is a real need for Giriama Scriptures. A reprint of the earlier Scriptures could have solved this problem, but the BTL/SIL team determined on the basis of their survey that a new translation was needed. The archaic language and unnatural structures of the earlier pioneer translation made it unusable by modern-day Giriama-speakers. It is not surprising that this should be so. The first Giriama Bible had been in existence for over eighty years at the time of the survey, and for most of those eighty years it was not used. The answer was to do a new contemporary translation. BTL/SIL set up the Giriama project in 1989 with a team of mother-tongue Giriama speakers, composed of Stephen Sirya, Stephen Nzomo, Alfred Mthawali, and James Mramba, to carry out the task. Three of these have since left the project. Samson Iha was the project leader, with Alfred Mthawali and Edward Chome serving as translators. Simon Thoya and Clemence Yongo have been active in literacy work to promote and support the translation effort. The New Testament was dedicated and released for circulation on 18 December 2004 and the Old Testament on 6 April 2019.

It is noteworthy that there was no SIL expatriate expert on this team. This follows a model that was also used by other BTL/SIL translation teams, such as the ones for the Pokomo and Tharaka projects. These examples are illustrative of changes that have been going on in the SIL and their new National

Bible Translation Organizations (NBTOs) such as BTL to pass on the baton to mother-tongue speakers. It reflects the realization that translation needs to be indigenized, and that a good translation is best done by competent native speakers of the target language. A foreign speaker of a language can hardly master all its aspects like a native. A non-native speaker's command of the language with its rhythms and idioms, as well as folklore, and the underlying culture and traditions is always limited. Although many years are needed to master a new language, a missionary translator typically begins translation work after only a year or two of learning the target language. It is doubtful that a thorough understanding of the genius and complex figures of the language is possible in such a limited period, not to mention the time needed to immerse oneself in the diverse and complex cultural life of the people.

Scriptures in the Coastal Languages of Tanzania

The Digo of Tanzania, who mostly live in the neighborhood of Tanga, are predominently an Islamized community and, like other coastal communities who are Muslim, are to a large extent Swahili-ized. They share in the Afro-Arabic cultural characteristic of these communities. It must be said, though, that in nearly all these coastal communities, there is a strong presence of key elements of the traditional African religious world. These are intricately intermixed with those from the Islamic and Arabic worlds. One may speak here of dynamic syncretistic practice.

The Digo of Kenya and the Digo of Tanzania are basically the same people only separated by an international border that can be explained by their colonial past. Attempts by Christian groups to evangelize the Digo on either side of the border have been slow in bearing visible fruit. There is nonetheless a small but vibrant group of Digo Christian believers. The Digo Scriptures translated under the auspices of the BTL and SIL are due to be published sometime in 2020. They were mainly done with the participation of the Kenyan Digo, but are also expected to be used by the Tanzania Digo. The key challenges both in Tanzania and in Kenya are the "Swahili challenge" and the "Islamic challenge," that is, the linguistic and the religious challenges. This does not mean that the Digo language is in danger of extinction, at least not in the short term. The language's fate will depend on trends in language use in Tanzania in general and in the Tanga area in particular. What is needed to prevent the disappearance of the language are community and government programs to support its use by speakers, for example, literacy programs and the publication of Digo stories, proverbs, traditional songs, and folklore.

Among the missionaries who landed on the East African shores were those sent by the UMCA. Their first port of call was naturally Zanzibar. Bishop George Tozer relocated from Central Africa to Zanzibar in 1864, accompanied by Dr Edward Steere, whose work in Swahili we have already described. Consolidating their work in Zanzibar fully occupied these missionaries of the UMCA, but their eyes were also turned to the mainland. By 1875 they had set up a station in the Usambara Mountains to the west of Tanga. This followed initial exploratory visits by Rev Charles Argentine Alington in 1867 and by Bishop Tozer himself in 1868. Magila, not far from Tanga, was the first mission center in this area. It was intended to serve the four or so major communities in the area, namely the Digo, Zigua, Bondei, and Shambaa.[26]

The interest of the UMCA missionaries in Bible translation was logical given their experience in Zanzibar with Bishop Steere's Swahili endeavors. Responsibility for translating the Scriptures into Bondei, the language spoken around Magila, fell to the UMCA missionary team of John P. Farler, Herbert W. Woodward, Henry C. Goodyear, and Godfrey Dale, but only three of the Gospels were translated into Bondei, namely, Matthew (1887) and Luke (1888), both printed at the UMCA Press, Zanzibar, and the Gospel of John (1895) printed at the UMCA Press at Holy Cross, Magila. A revised edition of Matthew was produced in 1890 by BFBS, London. Nothing else appeared in Bondei after this. It is not clear why these missionaries never finished the task of translating the NT. One reason could have been their preference for using Swahili in their mission work after they realized that Swahili was well understood in that part of the world by many people.

Towards the end of the nineteenth century, UMCA missionary Walter H. Kisbey undertook to do translation work in the related neighboring language Zigula, or Zigua. He was assisted by Arthur Mbezi, a mother-tongue speaker. As in the Bondei case, all Kisbey accomplished was a translation of the Gospel of Matthew, which was published in 1906 by BFBS, London.

The UMCA missionaries also turned their attention to the southern coast of Tanganyika and its hinterland. Starting in 1876, they established mission centers at Masasi among the Yao and Makhuwa and at Newala among the Makonde in present-day Mtwara Region. These bases soon became centers for the Christianization of indigenous communities and for improving their general well-being.

---

26. Note that the Bondei and Shambaa together with the Taveta and Asu belong to Guthrie's Bantu classification group G20, while Zigua belongs to G30 together with the Zalamo and the other languages along this coastal belt between Dar es Salaam and Tanga.

In general, both the UMCA and the Roman Catholic Holy Ghost Fathers favored use of Swahili throughout Tanganyika, especially in education and liturgical worship. They did not pay much attention to the development of literacy or Scriptures in the vernaculars. The dominance of Swahili and its widespread use throughout most of present-day Tanzania probably discouraged these two groups of missionaries from engaging in other language learning and study. This may be the reason for their subsequent minimal overall contribution to translation in their other mission areas.

In contrast, the German Protestant missions and the Roman Catholic White Fathers believed in the value of the vernaculars in touching the African soul, as evidenced in their efforts into translate in the various languages. Cardinal Charles Lavigerie, the founder of the White Fathers, encouraged missionaries of his order to master the local vernaculars and the underlying cultures as a prelude to successful mission work. They set up a number of mission presses in various places to support this work. Adrian Hastings notes:

> More than anything else it was the instruction of Lavigerie and the practice of the early White Fathers from the 1870s which put a considerable segment of the Catholic missionary force in the forefront of the struggle to understand both language and custom . . . [W]hen Pilkington, best of the early CMS linguists in Uganda, arrived in 1890 and began studying the language, he found the French, White Father, Luganda grammar far better than the English.[27]

The German Lutheran Bethel Mission in the Usambara Mountains

Carl Peters landed at Zanzibar in September 1884. He began his activities on the mainland of Tanganyika starting from Eastern Ukaguru, called Usagara, just before the Berlin Conference for the Partition of Africa, which took place from November 1884 to March 1885. Peters was viewed as a harbinger of things to come and helped to lay the ground for the colonization of Tanganyika by the Germans. In 1887 German East Africa, *Deutsche Ostafrika*, became a reality, bringing Tanganyika under the hegemony of the Germans. Other missionaries were not far behind Peters.

The Lutheran mission to German East Africa, Evangelische Missionsgesellschaft für Deutsche Ostafrika, was represented by Johann Jacob

----

27. Hastings, *Church in Africa*, 267.

Greiner, who landed at Dar es Salaam on 2 July 1887. In 1892 Greiner moved his center to Kisarawe. He retired to his estate at Minaki in 1897, died in 1905, and was buried at Kisarawe. The landmark Azania Front Lutheran Church in Dar es Salaam was built during this period in 1902.

In 1889 August Krämer joined Greiner. Krämer later moved up north to Tanga where he settled. It was at Tanga that fifteen-year-old Michael Koba became the first Tanganyikan to become a Lutheran Christian in German East Africa. He was baptized on 24 April 1892. In 1894 Krämer's Swahili hymnal was published at the UMCA Press at Magila. This was essentially a translation of German Lutheran hymns. Krämer died soon thereafter in 1896.

From Tanga the work proceeded to the Usambara Mountains among the Shambaa.[28] The Shambaa peoples live in the beautiful mountainous area of Usambara among *shambaai*, "the area where banana trees thrive." This is a fertile area blessed with good rainfall. The area is associated with Kimweri ye Nyumbai, considered "one of the greatest rulers in Tanzania's history."[29] He ruled from the early nineteenth century until the 1860s. He is remembered together with such leaders as Mkwawa of Uhehe (1855–1898) in the Southern Highlands of Tanzania,[30] Nyungu ya Mawe (died 1884) and Mirambo of Unyamwezi (c.1840–1884) in Central Tanzania from Tabora to Ujiji,[31] and the Chagga chiefs or *mangi* of Kilimanjaro. Kimweri was a powerful benevolent ruler who ruled for many years as a priest-king. He had control and influence over neighboring local rulers. Economic and political contacts increased during Kimweri's reign. Among the foreigners he met were Krapf (1848 and 1852), Richard Burton and John Speke (1857), and Dr Otto Kersten and Baron Karl Klaus von der Decken (1861).[32] The breakup of Kimweri's kingdom in the 1860s led to the weakening of traditional values and practices and the influx of foreigners into the territory: Arabs, Swahilis, and later the Germans. It was the Lutheran German missionaries who opened up Christian mission centers in the Usambara Mountains. They set up mission work at Mlalo in 1891, Mtae in 1893, Vuga in 1895, Lutindi in 1896, Bubuli in 1899, and Bungu in 1903. The missionaries responsible for this early Usambara mission were Ernst Johanssen

---

28. As noted above, the Shambaa, together with the Bondei, Taveta, and Asu, belong to Guthrie's Bantu classification group G20, while their closely related neighbors, the Zigua, are included in G30. For historical and cultural information on the Shambaa, see Feierman, "The Shambaa," 1–15, and more fully in Feierman, *Shambaa Kingdom*.

29. Kimambo and Temu, eds., *History of Tanzania*, 60.

30. For more on this period, see Redmayne, "The Hehe," 37–58.

31. For more, see Roberts, *Tanzania before 1900*, 117–150.

32. Feierman, "The Shambaa," 9.

and Paul Wohlrab. Ernst Johanssen moved to Rwanda in 1907, but in 1910 he moved to Bukoba from where he established the Lutheran work in Buhaya and North-West Tanganyika.

These Lutheran missionaries – particularly Ernst Johanssen, Paul Wohlrab, and Karl Roehl of Swahili Roehl Bible fame – immediately recognized the need for translating the Holy Scriptures into Shambala. In 1896 the German publisher Bertelsmann printed the Gospel of Mark. The Württemberg Bible Society published the Gospel of John in 1901 and Matthew in 1902. The Gospel of Luke, however, was published by BFBS in 1903. The complete NT in Shambala was published in 1908 by BFBS and was reprinted in 1930 with some slight revisions.

Later on, Dr H. Waltenberg of Mlalo assisted by Elisa Chaghuza, O. Shauri, and B. Mnkama started a revision of the NT, and also translated the Psalms. The Gospel of Luke in this new revised edition and new orthography was published by BFBS at Nairobi in 1960. However, Waltenberg's remaining revision and translation work was never published despite his report of "a steady demand for this NT" and that "there were no signs that Swahili would take its place."[33] Later developments ran counter to this argument.

At the time of writing little interest has been shown in revising the 1908 Shambala NT or of working on a contemporary translation. The consensus of the churches is that the Swahili Bible is good enough. As for the future of Shambala or Bondei or Zigua languages, although some linguists wonder if they face extinction, it is not evident that the speakers are concerned about the danger of losing their languages. They seem to be quite happy using the national language Swahili which the government has been vigorously promoting since the days of the president Mwalimu Nyerere.

It took a long time for anything significant to happen with respect to Scripture translation in the coastal languages spoken in the area between Tanga, Bagamoyo, and Dar es Salaam. The Roman Catholics were the first Christians to establish work in this area. The first Catholic missionaries to arrive in Tanganyika came from St Denis on the Indian Ocean island of Reunion, landing at Zanzibar in 1860. A member of this team, Father Fava, moved on to the mainland and set up camp in Bagamoyo in 1862. Moved by the plight of the slaves, the sick, and orphans, he saw an opportunity for Christian witness here. However, he died after a short time. His place was taken by the Holy Ghost Fathers who arrived in Zanzibar on 16 June 1863. The group

---

33. BFBS correspondence.

consisted of Father Antoine Horner, Father Edward Baur,[34] Celestine Consol, and Felician Grüneisen. They moved to Bagamoyo in Zaramo country in 1868 and set up a Christian "freedom village" or settlement there with the aim of ransoming slaves, caring for the sick and the orphans, and offering a new start to those under their care.

Bagamoyo was at that time the main entry and departure point for traffic to and from Zanzibar and the outside world, as well as the chief export and import town on the Tanganyika coast. Dar es Salaam was not yet on the map. The main trade route passed through Bagamoyo and on to Tabora, Ujiji, and the Congo. Many of the early explorers and missionaries passed through the doors of Bagamoyo as did the slaves on their way to the Zanzibar slave market and to their horrible fate. The work of the Holy Ghost Fathers with freed slaves at Bagamoyo served as a model and inspiration to other missions. Further, their contribution to Swahili research has been memorialized in the outstanding and monumental work of Father Charles Sacleux and his colleagues, as we described in the previous chapter.

From Bagamoyo, the Holy Ghost Fathers later expanded into most of the Morogoro area, to Mhonda in 1877, Mandera in 1881, Morogoro in 1882, Tununguo in 1884, and to Kilosa (Ilonga) in 1885. They moved to the fertile mission field of Kilimanjaro in 1890 starting off at Kilema, and from there to Kibosho in 1893, and to Kilomeni in 1909. From the Moshi area work expanded to Kondoa among the Warangi in 1902 and in 1908 to Gallopo. Nevertheless, these dedicated and indefatigable missionaries have left us little or nothing in terms of published translations of the Holy Scriptures in the languages of the people among whom they worked. The Holy Ghost Fathers did not generally take a keen interest in learning the local vernaculars or developing any Scriptures in these languages. Swahili was their chosen tongue and most of their work was carried on in this language.

It was not until sometime in the middle of the twentieth century that anyone showed interest in the Zaramo language, the most widely spoken vernacular in this area between the coastal town of Tanga and the Tanzanian capital city Dar es Salaam, including such the major Zaramo towns as Bagamoyo, Minaki, Kisarawe, Pugu, Maneromango, and Kibaha. The Zaramo are to be found mainly in the environs of Dar es Salaam and as far north as Bagamoyo. They are said to be matrilineal, and traditionally a segmented society that

---

34. Historical records give both names, Etienne and Edward, apparently for the same person, as well as a German spelling, Eduard Bauer. For Etienne Baur the translator, see ch. 2, n.35.

lacks a political head or hierarchy. They share this feature with many other communities in their neighborhood such as the Kutu, Lugulu, and Kagulu, but also especially with peoples in southern Tanzania. They are well-known for their lively and moving traditional *ngoma* or music. Although generally associated more with Islam and greatly influenced by their Swahili neighbors and their Afro-Arabic culture, the majority of Zaramo are still deeply steeped in their traditional religious practices.[35]

When Johann Greiner arrived in Dar es Salaam in 1887, he was the first missionary to the Zaramo people. August Krämer, who joined him in the Zaramo area two years later, produced the first Lutheran Swahili hymnal which he translated from German in 1894. However, it was Rev W. Gottmann of Kisarawe and Rev Artur Worms of Maneromango who pursued a linguistic interest in the Zaramo language, eventually translating some OT selections and NT selections. These translations, however, did not lead to any serious work in completing the Gospels, the NT, or the OT. These early pioneers eventually settled on using Bishop Steere's Bible in Swahili which had already appeared in 1890. It was left to E. Dammann of the Bethel Mission and E. F. Tscheuschner of the Berlin Mission, collaborating with a team of Zaramo mother-tongue speakers, Samsoni Samatta, Tuheri Abraham, and Paul Lawi Sozigwa, to give the written Scriptures to the Zaramo people in a project undertaken in the 1960s. In reference to Professor Tscheuschner, who had been appointed by the Cannstein Bible Society in Berlin to translate the Zaramo Bible, H. A. W. Pilkington, a Bible Society consultant (not to be confused with George L. Pilkington of the Luganda Bible), on a visit to the project, noted in his translation report that Professor Tscheuschner, besides having a good command of Zaramo, also had a good knowledge of the Greek and used the Good News Bible, Swahili, and other versions. He moreover had lived in Africa for forty years. Evangelism and church planting among the Zaramo have remained a perennial challenge.

The challenge of Islam and Swahili, as well as of traditional religious practices, made Zaramo soil particularly hard for the Gospel. The Gospel of Matthew was produced in 1967 and John in 1970. These were published by the Bible Society in East Africa in Nairobi, but copyrighted to the Cannsteinsche

---

35. For some description of this, see Swantz, *Ritual and Symbol*. For a description of some early missionary work in Zaramo country, see von Sicard, *Lutheran Church on the Coast of Tanzania*.

Bibelanstalt.[36] The complete Zaramo NT was published in 1975 by the Bible Society of Tanzania.

It is not surprising that this NT was not enthusiastically received and sales were slow. The use of the Swahili Bible, which was entrenched among the Zaramo Christian congregations, was no doubt a contributing factor.[37] Moreover, in this coastal culture and community, bilingualism with Swahili is commonplace. The prestige of Zaramo is in serious decline and the use of the language itself is also in decline. The Zaramo homeland has been infiltrated by an influx of people from all over Tanzania moving to Dar es Salaam and its environs looking for work. This has had the effect of marginalizing the Zaramo in their own indigenous territory. The national Tanzanian policy of promoting Swahili at the expense of the other more than 120 vernaculars has also had its toll on the Zaramo. The result is that the Bible Society of Tanzania is not at present considering any reprints or revisions of the 1975 Zaramo NT, or even a continuation of this task to the translation of the OT that would lead to eventually having the entire Bible in Zaramo.

The immediate neighbors of the Zaramo such as the Nghwele, Doe, and Kwere are not likely to have any Christian Scripture any time soon. The fate of all the other communities and languages to the south of Dar es Salaam is more or less similar. No translation has taken place so far among the Ndengereko, Rufiji, Matumbi, Mwera, Machinga, or Maraba.[38]

The Makonde live on both sides of the Tanzania/Mozambique border, and like the Zaramo they have largely been influenced by Islam and the majority of them are reckoned to be Muslims. Yet they are deeply steeped in their traditional religious beliefs and practices. Like the Zaramo, they are matrilineal, and traditionally do not have political hierarchies. Their world-famous art and carvings are derived from and influenced by their traditional religious cosmology and values. Groups of Makonde artists can be found in the major tourist centers and urban areas of both Tanzania and Mozambique. Christian work among the Makonde has been slow, partly due to the Islamic influence, but also due to their strongly held traditional beliefs. Some selections from the Bible are said to have been translated into the Makonde language, but evidence for this work cannot be found. It is a pity that the Makonde people,

---

36. See, for example, copies at the Wuertembergische Landesbibliothek, Stuttgart (Ref. No. B Afrika 196709).

37. For more on Christianity and the Zaramo, see Kimambo, "Impact of Christianity," 63–82.

38. These languages are part of Guthrie's P10, P20, and P30.

despite their importance, are a long way from having a New Testament or a complete Bible. There is a ray of hope in the fact that an SIL/WBT team has been involved in a sociolinguistic survey as well as literacy work among the Makonde from their base in Mozambique.

Some Roman Catholic Initiatives

The German Benedictine Fathers and Sisters focused much of their attention on the southern parts of Tanganyika. They first arrived in Dar es Salaam in January 1888. Their first station was at Pugu in Dar es Salaam. It was here that during the Bushiri resistance in 1889 some of their missionaries were killed. Later in the year a station was established at the site where we now find St Joseph's Cathedral in downtown Dar es Salaam overlooking the harbor. In 1895 two mission stations were opened at Lukuledi and Nyangao near Lindi in southeastern Tanganyika. In 1897 the Wahehe were reached by the opening up of the Tosamaganga station.

Father Cassian Spiess opened a station at Peramiho in 1898 after making friends with the Ngoni chief Mputa Gama, son of Zulu, the founder of the Njelu branch of the Ngoni.[39] Peramiho was later to become an important center for theological and biblical study similar to Kipalapala in Tabora. Father Spiess pioneered and laid the foundations for the later translation and linguistic work now characteristic of the Benedictines. He is said to have translated a catechism into Swahili as well as a prayer book containing Scripture selections and readings for liturgical use. He was consecrated bishop in 1902 and moved to the coast. During the Maji Maji rebellion of 1905–1906 he tried to return to his former mission at Peramiho, but he and his party were attacked while en route and he was killed. The Benedictine interest and contribution in literature work has been significant. For example, their Ndanda publishing house in Peramiho has produced and distributed volumes of theological and religious materials for use all over Tanzania. It is noteworthy that this Peramiho-based publishing house publishes almost entirely in Swahili. Their most important publication in recent times has been the Scripture translations of Mwalimu Julius Nyerere, namely, the Gospels and Acts in classical Swahili verse.

The Roman Catholic Mission to Tanganyika and indeed to East Africa, did not demonstrate a strong interest in Scripture translation for most of the early period. The use of Latin in liturgy may have been a factor in underplaying the

---

39. Sundkler and Steed, *History of the Church in Africa*, 534; see also Baur, *2000 Years of Christianity in Africa*, 253–254.

power of the vernacular. The post-Vatican II period marked a sea change in this regard. Before then the exception that demonstrated this general tendency could be seen in the laudable efforts of the White Fathers, starting with the Gospels and Acts in Kiunguja Swahili; the work of Father Emile Brutel and of the Holy Ghost Fathers in the Kiunguja NT of Father Charles Sacleux; and the pioneer Catholic NT in standard Swahili of Father Alfons Loogman of Morogoro. The recent input of the Benedictine Alkuin Bundschuh certainly benefited from the stimulus emanating from Vatican II pronouncements. The failure of the Holy Ghost Fathers, pioneers in mission and linguistic inquiry, to equally pioneer in Scripture translation into local languages was perhaps due to a lack of emphasis or encouragement by the Catholic authorities. Yet their failure in contributing to the development of vernacular Scriptures was compensated for by their contribution to the development and widespread use of Swahili, particularly in the Catholic liturgy and lectionary used throughout Tanzania and in the urban areas of Kenya.

4

A Leap into the Interior

Maftaa, Pilkington, Kitaakule, and the Luganda Bible

Introducing the East African Interior

In 1996 the Bible Society of Uganda organized celebrations to commemorate one hundred years since the publication of the complete Bible in Luganda. The first publication of Scripture in Luganda (Gospel of Matthew), a first in any Ugandan language, appeared in 1887, followed by other publications of individual books of the Bible. The year 1896 saw the culmination of this pioneer process with the publication of the Luganda Bible.

This Bible was destined to become a model to be followed by others; it was a precursor of Bible translation work in other Ugandan languages. Luganda, a Bantu language spoken by the Baganda people of the kingdom of Buganda,[1] is the most widely spoken African language in Uganda. The country itself was named for this, its largest ethnic group. This language is also spoken or understood in parts of northwestern Tanzania and western Kenya. Buganda was at the time of the publication of the first Bible in Luganda the dominant power in the region of the Great Lakes. The great political power exercised by the kingdom of the Kabaka (the king of Buganda) naturally gave the language an advantage over neighboring languages. It is therefore not surprising that the 1896 Luganda Bible was destined to exercise great influence and power over languages not just in the kingdom of Buganda, but in the whole of Uganda, as well as in Buhaya in northwestern Tanganyika (now Tanzania) and Buluyia in western Kenya.

---

1. Luganda is usually listed under Guthrie Bantu classification group E10. The "lu-" prefix signals that the *Ganda* language is being referred to, the "ba-" prefix is the plural form referring to the *Ganda* people, and the "bu-" prefix indicates the place or kingdom of *Ganda*. "Uganda" is the Swahili name that was adopted by the British colonial authorities.

This impact can be observed as far away as in the town of Bukoba in Buhaya, Tanzania, where the inscription on the foundation stone of the old Lutheran church on Kashura Hill reads as follows:

> Ekyokwijukilao EKANISA y'Obulokozi tukagyombeka kusima OMUKAMA KATONDA na YESU KRISTO n'OMWOYO OGULIKWELA. Tukataho eibale eli omu bugenyi bwaitu 1910 28 Juli 1935.

> To commemorate the Church of Salvation, which we built to praise the Lord God and Jesus Christ and the Holy Spirit. This stone is to mark our celebration in 1910 – dated 28 July 1935.[2]

The Luganda words for the "Lord God," *Omukama Katonda* are used in place of the Ruhaya *Omukama Ruhanga*. It is also interesting that the stone recognized 1910 as the date of the beginning of the church in Buhaya rather than the mid-1890s when the Baganda Christians first evangelized this area.

Similarly, the religious terminology and style used in the Anglican translation of the first New Testament in the Luhanga dialect of Buluyia in western Kenya was also influenced by Luganda key terms. A clear example of this can be quickly seen when one compares the Lord's Prayer in Luganda to the Luhanga or even the Union Oluluyia versions. The structure, the style, and the terminology of the latter show close dependence and borrowing from the Luganda text. Even the orthography of the Luhanga translation was much influenced by that of Luganda. For example, the Luganda letter "Kya" which in current Luyia orthography is represented as "Cha" and in Luganda as "Ki" and which is represented in current Luluyia as "Chi," took the Luganda form in the older translation. There is hardly a translation during this early period in the interlacustrine region – or even beyond – that evaded the influence of the Luganda Bible. Luganda became the medium of Christian religious discourse in the region and the Luganda Bible provided the terminology. The widespread use of Luganda throughout this region by missionaries and their Luganda-speaking agents or evangelists no doubt contributed to this phenomenon.

Present-day visitors to the kingdom of Busoga in Uganda will be struck by the continuing use to this very day of Luganda and the Luganda Bible. If they were to visit Padhola country near the town of Tororo in southeastern Uganda, they would be struck to find that the Luganda Bible and language are used in Christian worship and prayer, and this in an area which is the domain of a Nilotic-speaking people. This situation is similar in such places as Sebei on

---

2. Translated by the author with the help of a local Ruhaya mother-tongue speaker.

the slopes of Mount Elgon in Uganda where, instead of Kupsapiny, Luganda is used, and likewise, among the Bamasaba, the Basamia, the Bagwere, and the Banyole in other corners of Uganda. Such is the power of the Luganda Bible.

When the Luganda Bible was published in 1896 it was the first Bible to appear in any of the languages of Uganda. Indeed, it was, after the Kiunguja Swahili Bible of Zanzibar, the second complete Bible to be published in any of the languages of East and Central Africa. It was also the first Bible in East and Central Africa to be bound in one volume.[3] It was popularly called the "Biscuit-tin Bible" because it was the size of the tin boxes used by Baganda to store biscuits and, incidentally, also to store and protect books. This printed Bible was designed to be stored in these biscuit-tin boxes. Though it was pioneered by CMS missionaries Alexander M. Mackay, Robert Pickering Ashe, and Edward Cyril Gordon, it was principally the work of the remarkable translator George L. Pilkington together with William A. Crabtree and local indigenous Luganda translators – Duta Kitaakule, Sembera Mackay, Samwili Mukasa, and Nuwa Nakiwafu.

The year 1896 marks not the beginning of Bible translation in Uganda, but only one stage in a movement whose roots are marked by the first missionaries to Uganda. Perhaps the first visible representative of this movement was the journalist and explorer Henry Morton Stanley. When he arrived at Kabaka Mutesa's court in April 1875 during his second trans-Africa Expedition of 1874–1877 (his first expedition of 1871–1872 had been in search of Dr Livingstone), he was in the company of two African guides and interpreters, Robert Feruzi and Dallington Maftaa.[4] Both these men were freed slaves who had undergone some training and rehabilitation at Bishop Steere's UMCA school in Zanzibar. Feruzi (who like Maftaa was of Nyasa ethnicity) was a noted caravan leader and one of Stanley's most trusted men in the explorer's famous journey from Zanzibar to the source of the great Congo River.

When Stanley left Buganda carrying with him ground-breaking stories for the Western news media, he left Maftaa behind to teach the Kabaka and his people about the "Whiteman's Book."[5] Stanley had apparently been led by force of circumstances to take on the role of missionary to Mutesa, extolling

---

3. The volume was divided into four parts as follows: Genesis–2 Samuel; 1 Kings–Song of Solomon; Isaiah–Malachi; New Testament.

4. Also known as Dallington Scorpion Maftaa.

5. See Reid and Medard's "Merchants, Missions," 98–108, for a picture of what Stanley and his other foreign visitors might have seen. See also Gutkind, *Royal Capital of Buganda*. For information on Ganda traditions, beliefs, and practices, see Wrigley, *Kingship and State*, and Ray, *Myth, Ritual and Kingship*.

to him the message of Christianity. Gwen Anderson of BFBS made this point more dramatically when she noted:

> The first sentence of Scripture ever written in Luganda was dictated not by a missionary, but by a very famous traveler. In order to give the king some idea of the Christian religion, explorer Henry Stanley and the king's scribe – a man named Idi – worked out a translation from the Swahili version of the Ten Commandments into Luganda.[6]

It is very unlikely that Stanley knew Luganda. It is equally unlikely that he had learned or mastered the rudiments of Swahili well enough to attempt a translation from or into it; hence his need of Maftaa as an interpreter.[7]

Stanley's background did not associate him closely with the gospel, yet finding himself alone in a faraway land, he saw himself as an ambassador not only of Western civilization but of Christianity as well. In this instance he took on the role of missionary evangelist. In a joint dispatch to The *New York Herald* and The *Daily Telegraph* in November 1875, Stanley reported that "by one conversation" he had convinced Mutesa of the superiority of Christianity and that "if it were only followed by the arrival of a Christian mission . . . the conversion of Mutesa and his court to Christianity would be complete."[8] Stanley claims to have seen in Mutesa, "[a] man who if aided timely by virtuous philanthropists will yet do more for Central Africa and civilization what fifty years of gospel teaching unaided by such authority cannot do. I see in him the light that shall lighten the darkness of this benighted region . . . In this man I see the possible fruition of Livingstone's hopes."[9] It is interesting that others such as the Rev Charles Thomas Wilson, a member of the first group of Anglican missionaries to arrive in Buganda, saw in Mutesa a "murderous maniac"[10] due perhaps for his penchant for shedding blood at the slightest opportunity either to demonstrate his power or to eliminate any threats to his kingdom and authority.

In his impassioned appeal to "leading philanthropists and the pious people of England," Stanley wrote the following: "Here gentlemen, is your opportunity – embrace it! The people of the shores of the Nyanza call upon you. Obey your

---

6. G. Anderson, "Bringing the Bible to Africa," n.d., 2, mimeographed document at BFBS, Swindon.

7. See for example, Tuma and Mutibwa, *Century of Christianity in Uganda*, 93.

8. Bierman, *Dark Safari*, 176–177.

9. Quoted in Bierman, *Dark Safari*, 175.

10. Faupel, *African Holocaust*, 5.

generous instincts and listen to them, and I assure you that in one year you will have more converts to Christianity than all other missionaries united can number."[11] The reputation of Henry Morton Stanley was in certain respects akin to that of Dallington Maftaa, whom he left behind at Mutesa's court to carry on the gospel light. The UMCA chronicler speaks of Maftaa – who at the UMCA station in Zanzibar "had not been looked on as a credit to the Mission" – as an example of "the bread 'cast upon the waters' (which) is found 'after many days.'"[12] From Buganda, Maftaa wrote to Bishop Steere, his bishop in Zanzibar, as follows:

WANTAGALA, April 23, 1876.

My DEAR BISHOP,

Let thy heart be turned to thy servant, and let me have favour in thy sight; therefore send me Swahili prayers, and send me one big black Bible. I want slates, board, chalk, that I may teach the Waganda the way of God. I been teach them already, but I want you to send me Litala Sudi, that he may help me in the work of God. Oh! My lord, pray for me; oh! ye boys pray for me. And if thou refuse to send me Litala Sudi, send me John Swedi. Your honour to the Queen, and my honour to you.

Dallington Maftaa.

I am translating the Bible to Mtesa, son of Suna, King of Uganda. I was with Henry M. Stanley, together with Robert Feruzi, but Robert is gone with Stanley, but I being stop in Uganda, translating the Bible.[13]

Maftaa eventually attempted a translation of selected portions of the Bible into Luganda as well as a complete Gospel of Luke. He also participated in regular preaching and teaching of the basics of the Christian message, and in regular public reading of the Christian Scriptures. These gave the Baganda an introduction and initial preparatory taste of the Christian religion. Maftaa is reported, however, to have later abandoned the Christian faith, thereby greatly compromising the faith he had once embraced.

Meanwhile, in Europe, Stanley's stories and reports as well as his challenge to the English missionary societies were given wide circulation and coverage

---

11. Quoted in Bierman, *Dark Safari*, 177.

12. Anderson-Morshead, *History of the Universities' Mission*, vol. 1, 78–79.

13. Quoted in Anderson-Morshead, *History of the Universities' Mission*, 79.

by the mass media, notably The *Daily Telegraph* of 15 November 1875. These reports played no small part in preparing the ground for the missionaries to establish work in Uganda. The Church Missionary Society was the first to take up the challenge. The pioneer CMS party, led by Lt Shergold Smith and The Rev Charles Thomas Wilson, arrived in Buganda on 30 June 1877. The other members of this party, which included Alexander M. Mackay, arrived later after a short spell at the coast. They found Maftaa engaged in the preparation of the ground for the gospel.

The French Roman Catholic party of the White Fathers arrived in Buganda on 17 February 1879, led by Father Simeon Lourdel and Brother Amans. Inevitably rivalry, mistrust, hostility, and fights later resulted from this coming together of the British Protestant Anglican CMS group, the French Roman Catholic White Fathers, and the Arab Islamic factor.

The Scriptures into Luganda

The Arabs arrived in Buganda much earlier than any of the new Christian groups. It is generally agreed among historians that it was Islam that initially created a thirst for literacy in Buganda, especially among the young *bagalagala* "pages" at the Kabaka's court. The first Arabs arrived in Buganda in 1844 during Kabaka Suna's reign, bringing with them their Islamic religion and the Arabic language as well as their culture. As part of their effort to Islamize the kingdom, they introduced the idea of a holy book and the concepts of a transcendent God and a holy day. The Christian missionaries were therefore confronted with this Islamic reality as well as with the indigenous cultural and religious beliefs and practices. Some of these ideas were taken up to good advantage by the Christian missionaries, for example, the idea of a holy book. Because of this, Maftaa easily undertook the task of teaching literacy and of teaching and translating the Christian message from the Holy Bible in Swahili.

The pages, known locally as *bagalagala*, formed a ready captive audience for instilling new ideas, teaching new skills, and winning over to the new faith. The missionaries, both Catholic and Anglican, gathered around them groups of enthusiastic *bagalagala* who in no time were ready to die for their new-found faith. It is therefore no wonder that many of the early Christian martyrs in Buganda came from this group. These young enthusiasts, after acquiring new literacy skills, naturally hungered for something to read. The only logical and obvious choice of reading material was the Christian holy book in a language they could understand. And so, the imperative to render the Bible into Luganda was forced upon the missionaries right at the onset of their labors.

Father John Baur speaks of a "Readers' Revolution or the young Baganda movement towards Christianity."[14] He notes:

> The number of people from the court, especially the pages, who came to read and to hear the Good News, increased from day to day. The term "reader" became identical with "Christian" and "man of the new elite". These young Christians were not only convinced but grew also very apostolic in mind . . . There emerged prominent lay leaders who gathered the Christians into prayer groups: Joseph Mukasa Balikuddembe, at the court, Andrea Kagwa around the capital and Matia Mulumba at Mityana. The number of Catholic catechumens more than doubled to well over five hundred.[15]

Anderson speaks of a "Christian revolution" that he says began among the *bagalagala* but eventually spread among even ordinary Baganda and within no time beyond Buganda. He observes, "The most characteristic element in the revolution was *kusoma*, reading. It was literacy. It was education. It was learning the ways of Europe. It was reading God's Word."[16]

The spread and growth of the new movements – Catholicism, Anglicanism, and Islam – no doubt threatened the power and authority of the young Kabaka Mwanga who acceded to the throne in October 1884 while only eighteen years old. He was not as adept at controlling and manipulating these forces for his own ends as his father Kabaka Mutesa had been. His inability to hold the center, coupled with the unceasing rivalry, hostility, and suspicions among all the contending forces led to bloody feuds and scandalous wars of religion. Tragically, this led to a period of social turbulence and political upheavals, and to open clashes and confrontation between the traditionalists and believers of the new faith, between Muslims and Christians, and between Christian and Christian, that is, between Catholic and Anglican.

It should be borne in mind that the Kabaka was not a democrat. John F. Faupel, the author of *African Holocaust: The Story of the Uganda Martyrs*, describes him as follows:

> The Kabaka, or king of Buganda, was an absolute monarch of the type described in Genesis 41:44 – "The King said to Joseph: I am Pharaoh: Without my command no man shall move hand or foot in all the land of Egypt." The Kabaka had uncontested rights

---

14. Baur, *2000 Years of Christianity in Africa*, 236.

15. Baur, 236.

16. Anderson, *Church in East Africa*, 37.

over all his subjects, was a law unto himself, and master of life
and death. The only limitations to his power lay in the sacrosanct
customs established by his ancestors and handed down to him,
but if these acted as a check upon the Kabaka himself, they were
at the same time a motive for loyalty on the part of his subjects,
over whom the Kabaka claimed absolute and complete authority –
not only over their bodies but over their minds and hearts also.[17]

The Kabaka Mwanga II could therefore not tolerate this challenge to his
authority by the foreigners and by these youthful pages of his royal court.[18] The
religious upheavals during his reign from 1884 to 1897 took their first toll on the
young *bagalagala*. The first to fall on 31 January 1885, as martyrs of this chaotic
period, were three from Mackay's group of Christian youth, namely, Yusufu
Lugalama, Marko Kakumba, and Nuwa Serwanga. Dying on 15 November
1885, Joseph Mukasa Balikuddembe was the first Catholic to be martyred. He
was killed apparently for criticizing Kabaka Mwanga for ordering the murder
at Kyando in Busoga on 29 October, of the first Anglican bishop of East Africa,
James Hannington. The day of the bishop's martyrdom coincided with the day
Mackay is reported to have finalized his revised translation of the Gospel of
Matthew in Luganda. These horrific murders increased, culminating in the
terrible slaughter of twenty-six pages, at Namugongo on 3 June 1886, thirteen
of whom were Anglicans and twelve were Catholics. The twenty-sixth martyr,
Charles Lwanga, who was their leader, was killed at a location that would later
be consecrated as the Catholic Martyrs' Shrine at Namugongo-Bulooli.

The blood of these martyrs ensured the spread of the new faith. A modern-
day visitor to Namugongo, located about fifteen kilometers east of Kampala
along Jinja Road and about five kilometers from Kireka trading center along
the Kyaliwajjala-Namugongo Road, will be shown both the Catholic and the
Protestant sites where these tragic events occurred. At the two shrines the visitor
will see the sad and moving pictures of these youthful martyrs. Namugongo
has now become a place of pilgrimage by the faithful. Even Pope John Paul

---

17. Faupel, *African Holocaust*, 1.

18. The kingdom ruled by the Kabakas dates to the late thirteenth or early fourteenth
centuries. The present Kabaka is the thirty-sixth in the ruling line, which from 1857 to the
present is as follows: Muteesa I (1835–1884; ruled 1857–1884); Mwanga II (1867–1903; ruled
1884–1897); Daudi Chwa II (1896–1939; ruled 1897–1939); Muteesa II (1924–1969; ruled
1939–1969, in exile from 1967); Interregnum (1969–1993, traditional kingdoms and rule
abolished by presidential decree); Mutebi II (born 1955; ruling from 1993 to the present). The
burial place of the Baganda kings is the Kasubi tombs in Kampala. The crowning of the present
Kabaka, Ssabasajja Ronald Muwenda Kimera Mutebi II, in 1993, led to a revival of Kiganda
culture and traditions.

II visited these sites in 1993 to honor the youthful Uganda martyrs who gave their lives for the faith. The Catholic martyrs have since been canonized and are now saints of the Roman Catholic Church.

The Luganda Bible was translated during this time. Some historians have interpreted this eventful period as strategic in the Christianization of Buganda. The "Christian revolution" is described as falling into five phases as follows:

> Revolution of the new *dini* "religion" (1888);
> Muslim revolution (1888–9);
> Christian counter-revolution (1889);
> Protestant seizure of power (1892); and
> The consolidation of the revolutionary changes by the British take-over and loss of Buganda's sovereignty (1894–1900).[19]

Thereafter, Christianity in its Protestant and Catholic forms became a dominant factor in the social and political life, not only of Buganda, but eventually of the whole of Uganda.

To encourage and promote literacy as well as to help in the spread and establishment of Christianity, translation of the Holy Scriptures was indispensable. The Anglicans led the way. Alexander M. Mackay pioneered the development of a Romanized orthography for Luganda, an orthography which was later refined and developed into the present standard system. This orthography was quickly adopted to provide the basis of the literacy programs of the *bagalagala* and for the new Scriptures into Luganda.

The first book of the Bible to be translated and published was the Gospel of Matthew. This was translated by Alexander M. Mackay and Robert Pickering Ashe. The first thirteen chapters of this Gospel were printed in 1886 at the CMS Mission Press at Natete. This was the earliest published edition of Scripture in Luganda. The complete text of Matthew was finalized and printed at the CMS Press at Natete in 1887. It was reprinted in 1888 and in 1890 in response to overwhelming demand for copies from the new readers. Mackay died in February 1890. Concerning this first Gospel translated by Mackay, George L. Pilkington wrote:

> [A] tentative translation of St. Matthew's Gospel was made by Mackay and Ashe; this was printed in the country, eagerly read, and criticized, and revised, reprinted, again revised, and again reprinted; and so on, until a version was produced which was

---

19. See, for example, Ward, "History of Christianity in Uganda," 91.

faithful to the original and idiomatic, a splendid piece of work, and a grand basis for future translation.[20]

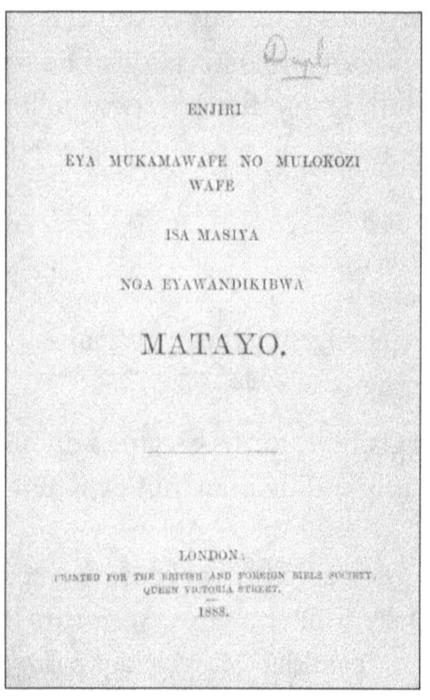

ENJIRI

EYA MUKAMAWAFE NO MULOKOZI
WAFE

ISA MASIYA

NGA EYAWANDIKIBWA

MATAYO.

LONDON:
PRINTED FOR THE BRITISH AND FOREIGN BIBLE SOCIETY,
QUEEN VICTORIA STREET.
1888.

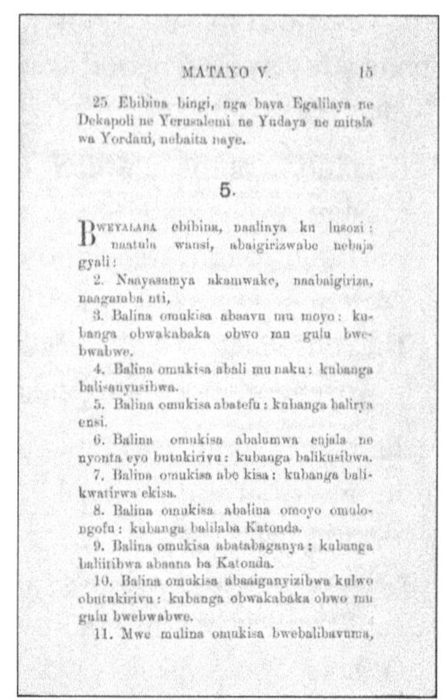

MATAYO V.   15

25 Ebibina bingi, nga bava Egalilaya ne Dekapoli ne Yerusalemi ne Yudaya ne mitala wa Yordani, nebaita naye.

5.

BWEYALABA ebibina, naalinya ku lusozi : naatula wansi, abaigirizwabe nebaja gyali :
2. Naayasamya akamwake, naabaigiriza, naagaraba nti,
3. Balina omukisa abaavu mu moyo : kubanga obwakabaka obwo mu gulu bwebwabwe.
4. Balina omukisa abali mu naku : kubanga balisanyusibwa.
5. Balina omukisa abatefu : kubanga balirya ensi.
6. Balina omukisa abalumwa enjala ne nyonta eyo butukirivu : kubanga balikusibwa.
7. Balina omukisa abo kisa : kubanga balikwatirwa ekisa.
8. Balina omukisa abalina omoyo omulongofu : kubanga balilaba Katonda.
9. Balina omukisa abatabaganya : kubanga baliitibwa abaana ba Katonda.
10. Balina omukisa abaaiganyizibwa kulwo obutukirivu : kubanga obwakabaka obwo mu gulu bwebwabwe.
11. Mwe mulina omukisa bwebalibavuma,

Figure 4.1. The Gospel of Matthew in Luganda, title page and chapter 5. American Bible Society Library and Archives. Used by permission.

The next Scripture portion to appear was the Gospel of John, translated by Robert Pickering Ashe and printed privately in 1891 at Wareham in England at the translator's expense. Another edition of this book with the BFBS imprint followed in the same year. In 1892 the Gospel of Mark, translated by Edward Cyril Gordon, who was assisted by native speakers, was published by BFBS in London. In the same year, BFBS published a new edition of the Gospel of John, revised by Alexander M. Mackay, and after his death in 1890 further revised by Gordon, assisted by Duta Kitaakule and Sembera Mackay. The book of Acts, translated by Pilkington with the assistance of Duta Kitaakule, was published also in 1892 by BFBS London. This was followed the same year by the publication of the Gospels and Acts in one volume. Romans, Galatians–Colossians, the book of Revelation, 1 Thessalonians–Philemon, and Jude, all appeared in 1892 translated by Pilkington together with his Baganda collaborators. Pilkington is known to have been involved with the translation

---

20. Quoted in Omulokoli, "Contribution of George L. Pilkington," 3.

of all the books from Acts to Revelation, with the exception of 1 John which was translated by E. C. Gordon with the assistance of Mika Sematimba.

The 1893 Luganda NT was the first NT in a language of Uganda. The Swahili NT had appeared in 1883, ten years earlier, the first NT in all of East Africa. This Luganda NT was issued in one volume. The Gospels and Acts, Romans–Hebrews, James–3 John and Jude–Revelation were also published separately as portions by the BFBS that same year.

The cooperation between the CMS translators in Buganda and BFBS in London continued with more translation and publication of Old Testament books. Between 1893 and 1896 the BFBS published various books of the OT, as well as a revision of the NT.

- 1893 Exodus and Joshua by Pilkington
- 1894 Genesis, Psalms, Daniel by Pilkington
- 1895 NT new edition, corrections by Pilkington
- 1896 Pentateuch by Pilkington
- 1896 Bible

All this was the work of Pilkington except for some of the books of the Minor Prophets, which were translated by Alexander M. Mackay.

As is already evident, these CMS missionaries could in no way have translated the books of the Bible without the help and assistance of the native speakers of the language. The missionaries' short stay in the country was not adequate to make them masters or experts of Luganda in all its idiomatic complexities and intricacies, much less in its social and cultural ramifications. They depended greatly on native speakers.

Among native Luganda speakers to be noted for their outstanding contribution to the translation of the Luganda Bible are Duta Kitaakule, Sembera Mackay, and Mika Sematimba. Duta had studied at Bishop Steere's UMCA school in Zanzibar and was therefore equipped to contribute to this great task. It is interesting to note that Duta was "sent out of Uganda in 1881 as a punishment for 'reading,' but was allowed to go down to the coast with Pearson, who arranged for him to be taught in the school of the Universities Mission at Zanzibar."[21] It was at Zanzibar that Duta mastered Swahili and thoroughly familiarized himself with the Swahili New Testament. It is not surprising that on his return to Buganda, he was, as Anderson notes, "translating the Swahili

---

21. Tuma and Mutibwa, *Century of Christianity in Uganda*, 96.

Bible into Luganda for preaching and teaching. Pilkington found that the religious terms and phrases had already been worked out by Duta."[22]

In this way Duta and even Maftaa before him brought something of the powerful influence of the Zanzibar Swahili Bible upon the Luganda Bible. Pilkington himself alluded to this fact when he observed:

> For a long time the Swahili New Testament was the text-book of Uganda; day after day the most intelligent of the Christians translated from it into their own language; day after day they discussed among themselves the proper rendering of terms, appealing to the European as to the exact force of the original; for years they were occupied in hammering out a version on a native anvil.[23]

He referred to Swahili as "a temporary bridge, on which to stand to build what from the first was recognized as the only permanent bridge between God's thoughts and the native mind, a version in the Ganda tongue itself."[24]

The fact that Swahili, like Luganda, is a Bantu language obviously had certain advantages and meant that many translation problems of interest to Luganda had already been grappled with and solved in Swahili. However, this did not absolve the translators of the Luganda Bible from working through these problems anew.

George L. Pilkington was born on 4 June 1865 of Irish descent. He had a conversion experience in 1886 while still a student, and graduated with a Cambridge University Classical Tripos BA in 1887. He received a call for missionary service and arrived in Buganda in 1890. Pietistic and charismatic in outlook, he became deeply involved in the Christian revival that swept Buganda starting from the 1893–1894 period. Pilkington has been described by Adrian Hastings as "the ablest of the CMS linguists in Uganda." In a letter home, Hastings commented that "the majority of men whom I've seen in the field closely, wouldn't learn a new language without help in twenty years" and he added, "[I]t was worse than useless to send a man without special training in language into a place where the language was not already mastered, yet that was what many societies had been doing from the start."[25]

---

22. Anderson, *Church in East Africa*, 39.

23. Quoted in Omulokoli, "Contribution of George L. Pilkington," 5.

24. Omulokoli, "Contribution of George L. Pilkington," 5.

25. Hastings, *Church in Africa*, 279.

In contrast, William Anderson writes, "George Pilkington was one of the most sensitive missionaries. He learned Luganda very well. He was close to Africans and understood them far better than most Europeans of his time."[26] Pilkington was thus far better qualified and more suited for the task of translation than many missionaries who later took up this task. His closeness to the people and his sensitivity, as well as his sense of identification with the people he was serving, eventually led him to his death in 1897 while serving as their chaplain during the Nubian rebellion. The 1896 Luganda Bible is therefore his main legacy to the Buganda mission. Duta Kitaakule eulogized him at his death:

> We sorrow very much, beyond our strength; we do not see among the missionaries whom we have anyone who can fill his place and take on his work. I worked very hard at teaching him Luganda; he learnt it well, and was able to speak Luganda like a native, and could translate any book into Luganda without my help, and I was not afraid of him making any mistakes.[27]

Andrea Mwaka, Pilkington's Swahili teacher at the coast, and Nuwa Kikwabanga, his first Luganda teacher as they traveled from the coast to Buganda, would probably have shared Duta Kitaakule's satisfaction in acknowledging Pilkington's extraordinary success in language learning and his monumental contribution to the translation of the Luganda Bible. Given Pilkington's very close and warm relationships with Baganda Christians, it is no wonder that he was instrumental in spearheading the Christian revival of his day that was a precursor of the Tukutendereza revival movement in East Africa some years later.[28]

The use of missionary Arthur Brian Fisher's reading houses and the great interest and enthusiasm for reading among the novice Christians gathered a lot of momentum during this period and their numbers grew, even though it was not clear at that time whether there was a corresponding growth in Christian maturity and understanding. It is reported, for example, that by March 1896, nearly seven thousand people had been baptized as members of the Anglican Church in Buganda while well over fifty thousand were actively seeking baptism. This phenomenon obviously provided great motivation for Bible translation.

---

26. Anderson, *Church in East Africa*, 38.

27. Quoted in Omulokoli, "Contribution of George L. Pilkington," 8.

28. *Tukundereza* is a Luganda word which roughly means "Praises to God."

An indication of the popularity of this Luganda Bible is shown by the fact that between 1888 and 1913, 16,000 Luganda Bibles and 6,400 New Testaments were printed. Altogether 213,290 Luganda Scriptures were printed during this period if Scripture portions and selections are included.[29] Considering the realities of this period in terms of literacy, education, and economic development, this was no mean achievement.

A revised edition of the 1896 Bible appeared in 1899 published by BFBS in London. It was the product of a revision committee consisting mainly of native speakers of Luganda, including Duta Kitaakule, Ham Mukasa, Natanieli Mudeka, Tomaso Senfuma, and Bartolomayo Musoke. This team was assisted by Jane E. Chadwick, a CMS missionary. A corrected edition of the NT appeared in 1914. This was in large type and had *Isa Masiya* (the Arabic-influenced rendering of "Jesus the Messiah") altered to *Yesu Kristo* (Jesus Christ). A half-century later, in 1968, the Bible Society in East Africa, Nairobi, published a new edition of the 1899 text of the complete Bible. Christopher M. S. Kisosonkole prepared this revision.

Pioneer Catholic Efforts at Translation of the Bible into Luganda, as well as Recent Interconfessional and Confessional Efforts

The 1896 Bible and its 1899 and 1968 editions were considered by the Catholics to be essentially a Protestant endeavor. The Catholics had, of course, their own parallel translations, which also go back to the beginning of the missionary effort in Uganda. The founding Catholic missionaries, compelled by the same forces and circumstances that had motivated the Protestants were similarly led to engage in linguistic study and translation. Furthermore, they belonged to the White Fathers' order, whose founder Cardinal Lavigerie emphasized that successful mission work depended on working in local languages. The members of the order believed in the value of the vernaculars in touching the African soul.

Father Leon Livinhac prepared a Luganda grammar, Father Louis Girault translated the catechism, and Father Simeon Lourdel translated the Gospels for liturgical use. Thus, the Catholic translations of the liturgical Gospels and Scripture narratives into Luganda were variously published in 1891, 1892, and 1913. In 1894 the Gospels of Matthew, Mark, and Luke translated by members

---

29. According to Bible Society practice, a portion is a publication that is less than a Testament but has at least one complete book of the Bible. A selection refers to a publication of verses from one or more books in the Bible that are joined by a particular theme.

of the Roman Catholic Uganda Mission were published at the Imprimerie de l'Oeuvre de Don Bosco, Marseilles, France. In 1896 the Gospel of John was published by the Imprimerie Notre-Dame des Prés, Montreuil-sur-Mer, France. In 1905 another Catholic translation of the Gospels and Acts was published by the Imprimerie des Missionaires d'Afrique at the Maison-Carrée in Algiers, Algeria, a reprint of which was published in 1915.[30]

However, the most popular of the Catholic translations is the New Testament done mainly by Father Modeste Raux and his colleagues. The Gospel of Matthew in this translation was published in 1933, the Gospels of Mark, Luke, and John were published in 1934, Acts in 1936, and Romans–Revelation in 1953. All these were printed locally at the White Fathers' press in Kampala. A revision of the Raux version of the NT in Luganda was prepared by William Mpuuga together with J. Muswabuzi and S. Kok. This revised NT was published by the Kampala Archdiocese of the Catholic Church at the Kisubi Marianum Press in 1965 and has been reprinted many times since. The Psalms appeared in 1980. The Catholics are currently involved in a major effort to produce a distinctively and exclusively Catholic translation of the Bible in Luganda. This will be the first Catholic Bible in Luganda when it appears some years from now.

In recent times, the Bible Society of Uganda (BSU) has sponsored and promoted an effort to produce an ecumenical or interconfessional translation of the Bible into Luganda. This effort brings together Catholic, Protestant, and Orthodox Church representation and contributions aimed at producing a new major translation in common everyday modern Luganda. Publications of this common language interconfessional translation started appearing with the publication of Mark in 1974; Matthew, Luke, and John in 1975; Ephesians in 1977; and culminated with the publication of the NT in 1979. This new translation is acknowledged by many to be more readable and understandable than earlier versions and is deemed likely to appeal much more to the younger generation of users who have not been brought up on either the Pilkington-Duta version or the Raux version.

The Committee responsible for the interconfessional New Testament translation included Father Francis Xavier Mbaziira (Roman Catholic); Yafeesi Mwanje, Samuel Ssekadde, and Christopher Ssenyonjo (Anglican); Archbishop T. Nankyama (Orthodox Church); and C. Ssendawula (SDA), among others. Those who worked on the interconfessional Old Testament included Father

---

30. For information on Catholic translations, see Rijks, *Guide to Catholic Bible Translations*, vol. 2.

Mbaziira, Stephen Keewaza Ssenyonjo (Anglican), John Baptist Ssemwanga (Roman Catholic), Fehekansi L. Nyanzi (Anglican), and Edward Kironde (Anglican). The head of the Orthodox Church participated as a member of the management committee. Work on the OT was slowed down by the fluctuations in the availability of full-time as well as part-time staff. The work proceeded at a rather slow pace mainly due to a high turnover of translators. It was, however, Father Mbaziira and The Rev Kironde who saw to the finalization of this common language translation.

Figure 4.2. The Rev Father Dr Francis Xavier Mbaziira, main translator of the common language Luganda Bible. Photo © Aloo Osotsi Mojola

5

The "Mountains of the Moon"

The Bible in Southwestern Uganda, Northwestern Tanzania, Rwanda, and Burundi

Understanding the Rwenzori Mountain Area

The major geographical feature of southwestern Uganda is the Rwenzori Mountains, which have been nicknamed the "mountains of the moon" after the second-century geographer Claudius Ptolemy who wrote that "the Nile sprang from two circular lakes fed by perennial snow: the Lunae Montes, or the Mountains of the Moon."[1] This area covering the borders of both Uganda and the Democratic Republic of Congo, and further south to the Rwanda border, is reckoned to be so beautiful that Winston Churchill famously referred to it as "the pearl of Africa" during his visit to this area in 1907 when he was a thirty-three-year-old member of Parliament for Manchester.[2]

The evangelization of southwestern Uganda, as indeed of most of Uganda, was largely the work of what church historian Father John Baur calls "lay apostles." This was equally the case in the Anglican Church and in the other churches that followed, where Father Baur asserts, "the lay apostles played an unparalleled role."[3] He writes: "Among them, a revival movement, initiated by the missionary George Pilkington, took place in 1893–94 and aroused a storm of evangelism, bringing Baganda evangelists as far south as Rwanda and the Congo to the West. They set out, in their hands the Bible that Pilkington had arranged to have translated for them by an African-European team."[4] Baur is, of course, referring to the 1896 Luganda Bible that George L. Pilkington and

---

1. Pennacini and Wittenberg, eds., *Rwenzori*, xiii.

2. Roberts, *Uganda's Great Rift Valley*, 58–60.

3. Baur, *2000 Years of Christianity in Africa*, 241.

4. Baur, 241.

co-translator Duta Kitaakule had translated. This Bible proved to be a powerful tool in the hands of these lay evangelists, who not only went to the Congo and Rwanda, but also as far as northwestern Tanganyika and western Kenya, armed with the Luganda Bible. In all these places, their converts formed the nucleus of the nascent church in their communities.

The names of Apolo Kivebulaya (ca. 1864–1933) and Yohana Kitagana (ca.1858–1939) stand out as exemplary and indicative of the outstanding work performed by these lay apostles. Unfortunately, African missionary historiography did not always recognize the input, contribution, and independent initiatives of these "black evangelists."[5] It is only in recent times that the balance is beginning to be restored and the "black evangelists" are being given their rightful place in the roll-call of the saints and heroes of faith. Apolo Kivebulaya stands out among those who lit the flame of the gospel in Toro. He later moved on into the Congo to work among the Mbuti pygmies of the Ituri forest, where he became renowned as the "Apostle of the Pygmies." He died in 1933 while a canon at Namirembe Cathedral in Kampala.

The story of Kivebulaya's suffering and endurance in the course of his missionary labors among the pygmies of Aruwimi forest in the eastern Congo, to the west of Uganda, was an inspiration to many Christians in Uganda and throughout East Africa. He was beaten and abandoned in the forest to die at the instruction of a local chief. He was found and secretly nurtured back to health by a female convert. After recovery he continued to proclaim the Gospel fearlessly to his persecutors. They did not believe that he was still alive and thought he had come back from the dead. Afraid to touch him again, they carefully listened to his message and many are reported to have turned to the faith he proclaimed.[6] The Bishop Stephen Neill writing in *A History of Christian Missions*[7] reminds us that "Baganda teachers were the pioneers in the kingdoms of Unyoro, Toro, and Koki," and that the "[m]ost famous of all these pioneers was Apolo Kivebulaya, later canon of the cathedral in Kampala, the story of whose heroic witness and sufferings is a modern epic. From his westerly station in Toro, Apolo pressed on into the primeval forest, and won the confidence of the shy and dangerous pygmy people."[8]

Neill adds that Kivebulaya's "greatest achievement was the translation of St. Mark's Gospel, apparently from the Runyoro version, into the pygmy language;

---

5. For more on this subject, see Pirouet, *Black Evangelists.*

6. See "The Chronicle" of the London Missionary Society of December 1928, 267.

7. Neill, *History of Christian Missions*, 326.

8. Neill, 386.

using his work [Western] linguistic science was at last able to answer the question whether the pygmies had a language of their own."[9] Neill was perhaps writing for effect here, or to correct those who out of ignorance believed that pygmies did not possess a language of their own. Kivebulaya prepared a primer in the language in 1926. In a letter dated 14 September 1932, a representative of BFBS wrote to Canon Apolo as follows:

> As you know I have heard of your work amongst the Pygmy tribe for many years, and have been especially interested in the translation of the Gospel which I understand from Archdeacon Lloyd you are preparing. May I urge you to do all you can to get this very great translation finished, so that we could get copies of the Scriptures printed. Many friends are interested in you and what you are doing, praying for you and giving contributions for the publication of the Gospel which you are preparing.[10]

In a related letter to the Venerable Archdeacon A. B. Lloyd of BFBS dated 20 June 1932, the Editorial Superintendent Dr R. Kilgour wrote encouraging him: "I am perfectly certain that when we see the book we could put it into shape. Canon Apolo is getting to be an old man and I would like to see something out before he passes away. Personally too I would like to see the book out before I leave the Bible House at the end of the year."[11] Regarding doubts that Kivebulaya was up to the task, Dr Kilgour wrote a letter to Archdeacon Lloyd urging him to do everything in his power to let Kivebulaya's version see the light of day. He wrote:

> May I say from my long experience of translation work that even what appears to be a poor translation made by a man like Canon Apolo who evidently has not had very great educational chances, is often of great value as a tentative edition. . . . But I shall be very disappointed if the Bible Society does not at least get the opportunity of issuing such a work. If you could get hold of Canon Apolo's draft and send it to me even though your own knowledge of Mbuti is not much and mine is absolutely nil, I think we could produce something at least that would be a first step towards the version in the Pygmy tongue.[12]

---

9. Neill, 326.

10. BFBS EA languages correspondence files (ESC Min. 9.8.25).

11. BFBS EA languages correspondence files (ESC Min. 9.8.25).

12. BFBS EA languages correspondence files (ESC Min. 8.8.25), 19.

After Apolo Kivebulaya's death in 1933, his work was taken up by two young CMS missionaries, Reginald C. Palin and C. A. Rendle. A biography of Kivebulaya by A. B. Lloyd was published by CMS with the telling title, *Apolo the Pathfinder: Who Follows?*[13]

Yohana Kitagana was the Catholic counterpart of the Anglican Kivebulaya. He was a polygamist who sent away his five wives before baptism as a Christian. He is credited with having pioneered the introduction of Catholicism among the Kiga and Ankole people in the mountainous areas of Kigezi, Bufumbira, and Ankole. He died in 1939.

The Christianization of the southwestern kingdoms of Bunyoro, Toro, and Ankole relied to a great extent on the work of lay evangelists. The Christianization of the rulers of this region facilitated and contributed significantly to this process. Acceptance by the rulers of the new faith tended to speed up the rate of conversions and the spread of the faith in the kingdom. It remained for the Catholic and CMS missions to consolidate and give structure and form to the young, growing church.

The Scriptures into Runyoro

The Bunyoro[14] kingdom traces its origins to the mythological and legendary Chwezi conquerors and rulers sometime in the sixteenth century. The Chwezi are said to have ruled and dominated the entire Great Lakes area including Ankole, Toro, Rwanda, Burundi, Buhaya in Bukoba district in Tanganyika, Buganda, and even the Wanga Kingdom of western Kenya.[15] The Chwezi Empire is usually referred to as Bunyoro-Kitara. The Chwezi were preceded by the Batembuzi, the original rulers who were believed to be demi-gods, *embandwa*. The Chwezi were in turn succeeded by another group of foreign conquerors and rulers known as the Lwoo-Bito, who were Nilotic speakers from

---

13. Published by CMS in London, n.d. Out of print.

14. The Bantu languages in the Great Lakes area mostly use the prefix "mu-" as in *Muganda, Mutooro, Munyarwanda,* and *Muhaya* to refer to an individual human being. The prefix "ba-" is its plural god and refers to more than one person. Thus, *Muganda* is an individual of *Ganda* identity or ethnicity, and the plural is *Baganda*; *Mutooro* is a person of *Tooro* ethnicity, and the plural is *Batooro*; *Munyarwanda*, a person of *Rwanda* ethnicity with the plural *Banyarwanda*. The prefixes "lu-," "ru-," and "ki-" are used to refer to a language. Thus *Luganda, Runyoro, Rutooro,* and *Kiswahili* refer to the *Ganda* language, the *Nyoro* language, the *Tooro* language, and the *Swahili* language, respectively. The prefix "bu-" refers to a place, a kingdom, or a nation, as in *Bunyoro, Buganda,* and *Buhaya*.

15. For a detailed study, see Archie Mafeje, *Kingdoms of the Great Lakes*, or Steinhart, *Conflict and Collaboration*.

the north and who arrived in Bunyoro about the beginning of the sixteenth century. The Bito dynastic rule and control lasted until 1967.[16]

According to the traditions of the Banyoro, the founder of the Lwoo Bito dynasty of Bunyoro was Isingoma Mpuga Rukidi, a brother to Kimera, who is claimed to have founded the ruling dynasty of Buganda. Other traditions maintain that Kintu was the founder or first ruler of Buganda. Whatever the case may be, there is a link between the Nyoro and Ganda ruling dynasties either through the Chwezi or through the Bito. Professor Byaruhanga Akiiki, a Munyoro himself, notes that, "Isingoma Mpuga Rukidi, twin son of Kyomya and grandson of *muchwezi* Isimbwa, was the first legally established *biito* king in Bunyoro. From that time, the Babiito ruled for 18 generations until 1967, with King Kabalega Winyi as the 26th king in that line."[17]

Thus, the people of Bunyoro could lay claim to one the oldest kingdoms in the entire Great Lakes area. Bunyoro was ruled by a king or *Mukama* with his center in the Mubende area. The Mukama of Bunyoro held the kingdom together. As the judicial, religious, and ritual leader, he was the head of government.

It was clear that a people with such an illustrious history as the Banyoro needed the Scriptures in their own language.[18] As the young Christian church grew and spread in southwestern Uganda among the peoples of this region, so did the demand for the Holy Scriptures in languages the people could understand. Initially, as already noted, the Luganda Scriptures were widely used, forcing many people to learn Luganda. However, the Banyoro could not meaningfully use the Luganda Bible. Even though both languages belonged to the Bantu family, Runyoro was a wholly different language from Luganda.

CMS missionary Harry E. Maddox felt called to respond to this need some time in the late 1890s. He set out to reduce Runyoro to writing and thereafter prepared a grammar and lexicon for the language. These were only secondary to his major task of translating the Scriptures into Runyoro. With the help of mother-tongue speakers, he eventually translated the complete Bible. The earliest publications of the Maddox Runyoro translation appeared steadily, the first publication being the Gospel of Matthew which was printed in 1900. This was followed by the Gospels of Mark, Luke, and John in 1901, the Psalms, Acts, and a revised Gospel of Matthew in 1902, a revised volume

---

16. Byaruhanga-Akiiki, *Religion in Bunyoro*, 32. See also Were and Wilson, *East Africa through a Thousand Years*, 29.

17. Byaruhanga-Akiiki, *Religion in Bunyoro*, 29. Italics in original.

18. For a fascinating picture of this period, see Doyle, *Crisis and Decline*.

of Matthew–Acts and a volume of Romans–Revelation in 1905. The complete New Testament became available for the first time in 1905, followed in 1912 by the first complete Bible published by BFBS.

It is interesting to note that some CMS missionaries resisted the Runyoro Bible. In the minutes of a translation report sent to BFBS dated 7 January 1914, W. J. W. Roome, a CMS representative of BFBS in Uganda, reported:

> There is a growing feeling among CMS missionaries that it was a mistake originally to produce a version in Nyoro besides that in Ganda, for the two languages closely resemble each other. The time has not yet come, however, for a fusion of the two versions, and the increasing use of Ganda in Bunyoro may eventually lead to the Ganda version being adopted in place of the other. In any case, no new editions in Nyoro are likely to be wanted for some years.[19]

This feeling was not shared by many and its prediction about a fusion of the two versions, namely the Luganda and Runyoro, was based on the lack of a proper linguistic understanding and appreciation of the two languages.

The Roman Catholics attempted various translations of selections from the Bible into Runyoro for their own liturgical use. The earliest was a harmony of the Gospels which was published at the Maison-Carée in Algiers, Algeria, in 1905, and reprinted in 1924. Various OT and NT selections and Bible stories were translated and published at the same press and at White Fathers Mission Press at Bukalasa in 1923, followed much later by a number of lectionaries at the Kisubi Marianum Press in 1972, 1977, 1980, and 1984.[20] Unfortunately, none of these Catholic translations is extant. It is possible that they were for use mainly by the clergy.

The Scriptures into Runyoro-Rutooro

The Batooro are near neighbors of the Banyoro to the south. Their language is so close to that of the Banyoro that the two languages are generally accepted as being mutually intelligible. The current Runyooro-Rutooro interconfessional Bible translation effort is an acknowledgement of this fact. The Tooro and Bunyoro kingdoms have a common root, but at some point, the people of the kingdom of Tooro claim they broke off from their kinspeople of the Bunyoro kingdom. The pioneer *mukama* or king Kaboyo laid the foundations and

---

19. See the Archival Records in the Bibliography, BFBS Files.
20. Rijks, *Guide to Catholic Bible Translations*, vol. 2, 477.

consolidated the new Tooro kingdom from Kabarole, the seat of the Tooro court, now better known as Fort Portal at the foot of the Rwenzori. A traveler moving from Bunyoro going down south would pass through Tooro and thereafter pass through the country of the Banyankole and Bakiga. This is beautiful territory, renowned for the Rwenzori Mountains which border the Congo, and which is famous as well for its magnificent national parks with their great diversity of wild animals. Travelers could leave Uganda and cross the border into Rwanda to the country of the Banyarwanda.[21] They would cross the border again further south into Burundi among the Barundi. Starting from Bunyoro they would encounter the Runyoro language. They would pass from Runyoro to Rutooro, to Runyankole and Rukiga, and then to Kinyarwanda and Kirundi.[22] If they were to then cross south into Tanzania along Lake Tanganyika, they would find themselves among the Kiha-speakers. These languages form a continuum or chain of very closely related dialects and languages. This fact explains why many observers have seen the need to create common Scriptures, often called "union versions," for neighboring dialects. The current Runyoro-Rutooro translation has been a result of this logic. The Rukiga-Runyankole forms a similar pair. Kinyarwanda-Kirundi could have formed another viable pair except for the politics of language, Kinyarwanda being the language of one country, Rwanda, and Kirundi being the language of another country, Burundi. Each of these countries has its own sovereignty as represented by its army and flag. This is akin to the Nordic languages – Norwegian and Swedish. Other languages, such as Kiha to the south of Kirundi, or Kishubi to the west, could easily have been accommodated as well by a single translation, if the sole criterion were mutual intelligibility.

The question of union or common Scriptures however, is a sensitive one, as it may call into question the identity and integrity of a community and their traditions and their pride in these. From a purely linguistic perspective, it would simply be a matter of mutual intelligibility between any two or

---

21. This territory is now famously associated with the protected mountain gorillas of the Virunga, Bwindi, and Mgahinga national parks and popularized by the writings of anthropologist Diane Fossey and such films as *Gorillas in the Mist*, based on her work in these mountain terrains. See, for example, Roberts, *Uganda's Great Rift Valley*, 117–130.

22. These languages are part of Guthrie's E10 (including – Nyoro, Tooro, Nyankole, Chiga, Ganda, Soga, Gwere, Gungu, Talinga-Bwisi); E20 (including – Nyambo-Karagwe, Haya, Zinza, Kerebe, Jita, Kara, and Ruri), as well as D60 (including – Ruanda, Rundi, Fuliiro, Vira, Shubi, Hangaza, Ha, and Vinza). These are of course part of the interlacustrine Bantu languages of the Great Lakes area, grouped under Guthrie classification – zones D and E or in Meeussen's zone J, (i.e. JD and JE). See Maho, "Classification of Bantu languages," 645, and Bastin, "Interlacustrine Zone (Zone J)," 501–528.

more neighboring dialects or language varieties. Measures for testing mutual intelligibility have been prepared by qualified agencies, such as the SIL.[23]

The Runyoro-Rutooro translation was one of the first viable pairs in the effort of creating union versions in this area. The existence of the Maddox Runyoro translation provided a foundation and basis for this effort. The intention was to link, not just two neighboring dialects, but also two theological traditions, namely, the Roman Catholic and the Protestant. An attempt to prepare an interconfessional translation of the Bible acceptable to both Catholics and Protestants was sponsored by the Bible Society of Uganda (BSU) beginning in the early 1970s for use in Bunyoro and Toro. A translation committee for this proposed Runyoro-Rutooro Bible included George McInnes (Anglican), Joseph Balinda (Roman Catholic), Nkoje (Anglican), Fenehasi Isoke (Anglican), Benedicto Bitamazire (Roman Catholic), and James Rabwoni (Anglican). Some publications resulting from this effort include the Gospel of Luke which appeared in 1972, the Gospels of Matthew and Mark in 1974, and the Gospel of John in 1975. The NT was published in 1977. All these publications were by BSU. Work on the OT took place at a rather slow pace. After the drafting of the OT books including the Deuterocanonical texts, it took many years to move to the editing and final preparation stages. It took over thirty years for this Bible to see light of day. As part of the editorial team working on this project, the following contributed: Fathers P. Isingoma and J. C. Tibakunirwa (both Roman Catholic) and the Revs S. Mwesigwa and George Williams (Anglicans), representatives of the two main sponsoring churches. A new interconfessional Bible serving the needs of both Banyoro and Batooro was launched by the BSU in 2012.

The Scriptures into Runyankole

Ankole is the home of the Banyankole and also the home area of the Ugandan president Yoweri Museveni. It was also the home of the late Anglican Bishop Festo Kivengere. It is a beautiful area of rolling hills and the great Rwenzori Mountains. Since its rise even up to the coming of the British hegemony, the Kingdom of Ankole was weaker than the kingdoms of Buganda and Bunyoro. The king was called the *Mugabe*. Oberg explains:

> The position of the Mugabe was exalted, his authority supreme,
> his leadership all-embracing. As high status was sanctioned, in

---

23. See, for example, Casad, *Dialect Intelligibility Testing*.

the first place, by his descent from Ruhinda, the originator of the Abahinda dynasty, and in the second place, by his possession of the symbols of kingship – the royal drum, *Bagyendanwa*, and the beaded veil, *Rutare*. Both descent and the symbols of kingship are said to date from the times of the semi-mythical Abachwezi kings.[24]

The word *mugabe* is a common Bantu word that means "the one who freely distributes or gives" and is derived from the verb *okugaba*, "to distribute, to give." The Ankole society consisted of two distinct communities, namely, the Bahima or Bahuma pastoralists and the Bairu, or Bahera, agriculturalists. The pastoralists constituted a kind of ruling class while the agriculturalists were something of a working class. The Bahima were at one time united and in charge of a great empire called Kitara that later broke up into the kingdoms of the Great Lakes area, including those of Bunyoro, Toro, Ankole, Rwanda, and Burundi, as well that of Buganda. Historian Edward Stinehart notes:

> In most of the lacustrine kingdoms they (the pastoralists) probably numbered no more than 5 to 10 percent of the population. The agricultural class or Bairu worked their own small land holdings, growing millet, sorghum, maize, matoke (cooking bananas), beans, and vegetables. They were by and large excluded from both political power and from accumulating wealth in cattle and the associated social standing.[25]

Stinehart goes on to relate the following about the domination of the Hima:

> [It] was based on the possession of cattle and the superiority of the Hima military organization, the greater social cohesion of the Hima group, and the acceptance of the Hima superiority by the Bairu class. This acceptance was in turn based on a combination of fear and reciprocity in social and economic matters tempered by the geographical and social separation of two classes, which limited the degree of penetration of Hima government and economic presentations into Bairu life. Dominance was further tempered by a very slight upward mobility of (especially) talented Bairu. This mobility allowed Bairu to assume positions

---

24. Oberg, "Kingdom of Ankole in Uganda," 136.
25. Stinehart, *Conflict and Collaboration*, 6.

of authority and eventually to assume the role, if not the "race" of Hima pastoralists.[26]

Stinehart is perhaps right in concluding:

> Structurally, the dominance of the Bahima rested on a set of three hierarchical institutions: the royal administration, the clientage structure, and the military system. These institutions gave substance to the cultural domination, which revolved around the complex ideology of racial superiority, the superiority of cattle and cattle keeping, the Hinda monarchy as a "national" institution and the religious beliefs of the drum and the Bacwezi cults.[27]

The divide between the pastoralist class and the agricultural class, between the Bahima and Bairu, has persisted in Ankole to this day and is the cause of much hostility, discrimination, and prejudice.[28] However, the Hima and Iru have never erupted into a spate of mass killings as has characterized their southern neighbors the Tutsi and the Hutu.

Among the pastoral people of this region, the Banyankole are said to be the most "cattle conscious."[29] They are a deeply religious people. In fact, the Tukutendereza revival movement, now referred to as the East African revival, had its roots in Ankole, Kigezi, and in the neighboring area of Rwanda sometime in the 1920s among a group of the Rwanda Mission Anglican missionaries led by a Dr Church. From there, its center moved to Buganda and spread like wildfire throughout East Africa. The Luganda song *Tukutendereza Yesu!* ("We praise you Jesus!") became its anthem and signature song. The song is still sung today in evangelical revival meetings in East Africa, even by those who do not understand what it means. Christianity is now very deeply entrenched in Ankole, perhaps the lingering result of this revival movement.[30]

Pilkington and Duta Kitaakule's Bible was the first Bible to be used in Ankole. It was obviously not well understood, hence the need for a Bible in

---

26. Stinehart, 9.

27. Stinehart, 10–11. See also the excellent article by Oberg, "Kingdom of Ankole in Uganda," 121–162.

28. See, for example, Keane, *Season of Blood*; Berry and Berry, *Genocide in Rwanda*; Guillebaud, *Rwanda*; and Pottier, *Reimagining Rwanda*, among others.

29. Stinehart, *Conflict and Collaboration*, 5.

30. For an overview of the history of the East African revival, see Church, *Autobiographical Account of the East African Revival*; Kinoti, "Christology in the East African Revival." See also Osborn, *Fire in the Hills*; Ward, "'Tukutendereza Yesu,'" 113–144; and Gusman, "Being a Mulokole," 318–340.

a language the people could understand. The complete Bible in Runyankole took many years to complete. This meant that the Banyankole revivalists depended on the Luganda Bible for their devotional study of the Bible and for their preaching and fellowship meetings. Furthermore, the shift of the revival movement's epicenter to Buganda strengthened the place of the Luganda Bible. However, pressure and the need to use the local vernacular won the day. Translation work into Runyankole started in the early 1900s. Miss Mabel T. Baker played a leading role in the work of translating the first Gospels into Runyankole. Herbert Clayton and Walter Edwin Owen, as well as a number of mother-tongue speakers who served as resource people, made significant contributions. The four Gospels in Runyankole were published by BFBS as follows: Matthew in 1907, translated by Clayton; John in 1910, translated by Owen and revised by Herbert Clayton and Mabel T. Baker; and Mark and Luke in 1915, translated by Mabel T. Baker.

In 1927 a volume of Scripture narratives in Runyankole translated by the White Fathers was published by the White Fathers Mission Press at Entebbe. Sometime later with only the Gospels in print, the Rev W. J. Mowll's 1936 report to the BFBS noted that "No more translation will be done in this language. The Banyankole speak Ganda now."[31] Mr W. J. Wiseman's report of April 1939 to the BFBS modified Mowll's report somewhat when he noted as follows: "The Rev Arthur E. Clarke of the CMS, Mbarara, also a Native deputation, requested that we begin a revision of four gospels published in 1918, but the difficulty is to find a suitable translator. *It is not now correct, as last reported, that the people are using Ganda. They are talking Nyoro almost wholly.*"[32] A more definitive view was reflected in the report by C. G. Gasyonga of an interview with the King (Omugabe) of Ankole. He reported:

> The Omugabe made a plea for the translation of the Bible into his language – Nkole – on the grounds that neither the Nyoro nor the Ganda Scriptures meet the needs of his people. The Society published three Gospels prior to 1918. Nothing has been done since as we had been informed that the people were able to use the Nyoro Bible. The Omugabe says that this version is quite unsatisfactory for his people.[33]

---

31. See the Archival Records in the Bibliography, BFBS Files.

32. See the Archival Records in the Bibliography, BFBS Files. Italics added.

33. See the Archival Records in the Bibliography, BFBS Files.

The Rev Reginald C. Palin of CMS, Kampala, in agreement with the Omugabe's position, wrote to the BFBS in 1953 explaining as follows:

> Up to five years ago the Banyankole were happily using the Runyoro Bible, but the position is different today with the rapid growth of national self-consciousness. The younger generation are jealous for their own language and resent having to use Runyoro in Church services. Because of this pressure Nkole has been recognized by the Education Department as one of the literature languages of Uganda, though, of course, there is very little literature in it.[34]

The Scriptures into Runyankole-Rukiga

Subsequently the BFBS took up the matter of Bible translation. The evident need and pressure from the people of Ankole eventually led to the launch of a Runyankole Bible translation project, which was in due course expanded to cater to the needs of Rukiga speakers in Kigezi. The man who pioneered this effort was Dr A. C. Stanley Smith of CMS, Mbarara. He was set aside for this task by the Rwanda Mission initially for two years starting from 1956, but this assignment was successively renewed until the completion of the task nearly eight years later. He was assisted by a team consisting of Lazaro Tabaro, P. Kalebya, E. Katate, and Eliezer Mugimba. Some input on orthographic matters was received from the missionary linguist Charles Taylor. The team also had to take into account dialectal differences between the Ankole and Kigezi idioms. This translation was constituted to allow not just for Ankole usage, but Kiga usage as well, hence its being referred to as the Runyankole-Rukiga translation or the Ankole-Kigezi translation. The Gospel of Mark which appeared in 1957 was the first fruit of this effort. This was followed in 1962 by the publication of the complete NT and in 1964 by the complete Bible. These publications were all by the BFBS London.

The Roman Catholics started producing translations of OT and NT selections and stories as early as 1923. However, it was only in 1956 that the Gospel of Matthew was translated by White Father Michel Biewer and published at Mbarara at the White Fathers Mission Press. This was followed by Biewer's translation of the Gospel of Mark and the Acts in 1962, and of the

---

34. See the Archival Records in the Bibliography, BFBS Files.

Gospels of Luke and John in 1963. Unfortunately, Biewer's work on the NT was not completed.

Later on, BSU noted the need for an interconfessional translation in current common-language Rukiga-Runyankole. With the collaboration and involvement of the Catholic and Protestant churches, a representative translation team of native speakers was set up in the early 1970s consisting of W. R. Bamutungire (Roman Catholic), Aloysius Katate (Roman Catholic), V. Kanyonza (Anglican), Phinehas Gantunu (Anglican), and Eliezer Mugimba (Anglican). The first publication of this ecumenical translation was the book of Psalms which appeared in 1972. It was followed by Acts in 1973, the Gospels in 1974, and the complete NT in 1977. The complete Bible appeared in two editions in 1989, a Catholic edition with the Deuterocanonical books and a Protestant edition without them. This was the first interconfessional version of the Bible in Uganda, and the second in East Africa after the Luo version in Kenya and Tanzania in 1977. It was very enthusiastically accepted, with copies being requested from as far as away as Bukoba, where the related Ruhaya language is closely intelligible. Minor but extensive corrections to the 1989 Runyankore-Rukiga Bible have been affected and a reprint of the corrected edition was released sometime at the beginning of 2009.

Scriptures into Olhukonzo

Konzo (Olhukonzo),[35] a Bantu language, is spoken north of Lake Albert along the slopes of Mount Rwenzori, mostly in Kasese and Bundibugyo districts of Uganda. The neighbors of the Konzo on the DRC side are the Banande. Their language, Kinande, is considered mutually intelligible with Olhukonzo to a very high degree.[36] Cecilia Pannacini notes that the "Bakonzo and Banande speak the same language, which is well identified among the other languages of the area, but the social and political organization that characterized the two groups during the nineteenth century is quite different. While the Bakonzo

---

35. Konzo belongs to Guthrie's Bantu classification group D40, which also includes the Nande and Nyanga of DRC in the Great Lakes Area.

36. See Mutaka, "Kinande Bilingual Dictionary," 153–199. Tom Stacey has written that "What essentially distinguishes the approximately 900,000 Bakonzo from the four million or more of their fellows of blood and language in the lowlands of Congo-side, the Banande, is the Bakonzo's presence on Rwenzori or in the mountain's immediate vicinity." See Stacey, "Snows of Rwenzururu and the Kingdom," 9.

remain an a-cephalos [*sic*] society, the Banande developed central political structures."[37] She adds,

> Despite a small number of differences in the lexical repertory of the two variants (Lukonzo and Kinande) produced after the establishment of the colonial frontier, Bakonzo and Banande speak basically the same language and can understand each other very well. On the other hand, Lukonzo-Kinande is quite distinct from other languages spoken on the Ugandan side of the Rwenzori massif, and especially from the languages of the "Runyakitara" group."[38]

The Bakonzo are mostly farmers along the slopes of the mountain. The Olhukonzo word for their homeland is Rwenzururu, (i.e. "place of snow"). The name of the mountain is, in fact, a mispronunciation of "Rwenzururu" ("snow" is *nzururu*). The famous Uganda railway has its terminus at Kasese, the main urban center in their territory. The presence of copper and other precious minerals in this area and the mining activity at the Kilembe mines played a role in attracting the railway to this part of the world. Christianity came to this area as part of the westward expansion and evangelization movement that originated in Buganda. The Bakonzo, however, were dominated for a long time by their more powerful neighbors, the Banyoro-Batooro and the Banyankole. No wonder in the 1960s, at the time of transition from British rule to independence, the Bakonzo and their neighbors the Bamba violently challenged the hegemony of the Tooro kingdom. They formed a rebel movement referred to as the Rwenzururu which sought to create a Rwenzururu kingdom. They sought to assert the use of Lhukonzo and Kwamba languages which had not been given much importance or priority in official spheres or even in Christian church worship or preaching. It had been assumed by Christians and others that the language of their more powerful Batooro-Banyoro neighbors would be adequate for official use and even for Christian worship and Scripture reading among the Bakonzo.

Although the first portion of Scripture into Olhukonzo, namely, the Gospel of Mark translated by the CMS missionary Walter Edwin Owen, was published

---

37. Pennacini, "Rwenzori Ethnic 'Puzzle,'" 73.

38. Pennacini, 78. The Runyakitara group of languages includes Rusongora, Rutuku, Runyabindi and Rubwisi (Lubwisi) dialects, as well as Rutooro with which they are often confused. Oswold K. Ndoleriire notes that "mutual intelligibility is very high, generally above 80%. Rubwisi (Lubwisi), however, shares with Rutoro 73% of words, which is still quite high compared to Lukonzo's 57%." See his "Language Use and Attitudes," 145.

by BFBS as early as 1914, the churches in the area have not deemed the need for a follow-up as urgent. Little else has been done by way of translating the Bible into this language to this day, despite attempts by BSU to do something to this end. The BSU attempted to create Bible selections for new readers and for literacy work. This effort has borne some fruit, but a Konzo Bible or even NT is yet to see the light of day.

Rugungu and Rubwisi

The Rugungu language is spoken by the Bagungu who live at the upper northeast corner of Lake Albert and in the extreme northwest corner of Bunyoro in Hoima and Masindi districts. The Babwisi who speak Rubwisi (also know as Lubwisi or Talinga-Bwisi),[39] on the other hand, live high up in the Rwenzori Mountains to the southwest of Fort Portal and to the north of the Konzo in Bundibugyo district, next to the DRC border. These minority languages have never had their own Scriptures. They have been evangelized largely by means of Scriptures in the language of their more powerful neighbors, the Banyoro-Batooro, which the missionaries expected them to speak and understand. Lately, however, SIL and their local collaborators have shown interest in these languages and are making attempts to do something about the situation. A few Scripture selections and portions have appeared.

The Scriptures into Ruhaya of the Bukoba district in Tanzania

Buhaya is geographically, linguistically, culturally, and religiously contiguous with southwestern Uganda. The links that Buhaya shares with the lacustrine kingdoms of southwestern Uganda go back hundreds of years. The people of Buhaya trace their ancestry to Bunyoro. They are closely related to the Banyambo of Karagwe with whom they share the Bukoba District of northwestern Tanzania. The observation by the late Bishop Josiah Kibira of the Lutheran Diocese that the "Bahaya and Karagwe are almost two different countries in one region,"[40] is certainly an overstatement intended to accentuate the differences between the two. In reality, the Bahaya and the Karagwe are very close, and there is close mutual intelligibility between their two languages. Bishop Kibira did acknowledge that both belonged to the larger group referred to as the

---

39. Both Rugungu and Rubwisi (Lubwisi) belong to Guthrie's E10, (i.e. the Nyoro-Ganda Group).

40. Kibira, *Church, Clan and World*, 11.

"Western Lacustrine Bantu" that includes the Banyoro, Toro, Nyankore, Kiga, Jita, Kerewe, and Zinza.[41] He depicted this larger group as follows:

> Almost all were segmentary societies of a feudal type. All included two distinct ethnic groups of Bairu and Bahima. In all the cases the Bahima, believed to have migrated southward from the north, ruled the others. They have a common history of the immediate period prior to the colonial era where the Nilotic Lwoo-speaking group Babito ruled most of the kingdom of Bunyoro, Toro, Koki and Kiziba. History has it that these tribes of strong and dominating men came down from Ethiopia (Bahima and Babito) and founded a great kingdom that embraced the area of these tribes, called "Kitara". Almost all of them had a "magic-religious system", but with belief in a vague, distant moral creator. They almost all had locally dispersed lineage and clans spread over the area they occupy. The clans were totemic and exogamous. Bahaya has over 130 clans, and Bunyoro and Toro might have 150. They settled in agricultural villages and kept cattle. . . . Their marriage and kinship systems are generally similar. They are almost all patrilineal in inheritance.[42]

Bishop Kibira adds, "This relationship must have had meaning in the effect and spread of the revival movement which started in Ruanda and spread to Uganda and Tanganyika, having its very centre precisely in the areas mentioned above."[43]

The beginnings of Christianity in Buhaya go back to the work of Baganda evangelists rather than to European missionaries. In 1985 the church in Buhaya wanted to celebrate its seventy-fifth anniversary as it had celebrated its twenty-fifth anniversary in 1935 and its fiftieth in 1960. However, in January 1981 the synodal council of the Lutheran Church, North Western Diocese, disputed the matter and could not come to an agreement. Wilson B. Niwagila, who highlights this disagreement, writes:

> During the debate two positions were held; those in favour of the celebration argued that the church of Buhaya began in 1910 when the first German missionaries built their mission station

---

41. Linguistically Ruhaya is classified in Guthrie's E20, (i.e. the Haya-Jita group that also includes the Kerebe, Jita, Kwaua, Kara, Zinza, and Ruri).

42. Kibira, *Church, Clan and World*, 11–12.

43. Kibira, 11–12.

on Kashura hill in Bukoba. Those opposed to the celebration argued that the church of Buhaya was not started by the German missionaries, who came in 1910, but was started earlier in the 1890s by different groups of Africans who had contact with the Ganda Christians in the neighbouring country of Buganda. When the vote was cast the former group lost the motion and all the preparations were cancelled.[44]

In recent times the celebrations focus not so much on the arrival of Christianity in this region but on the setting up of the current missionary-instituted church in the area.

Buhaya had already received the gospel from Buganda by 1890. The first Muhaya person to be baptized was Zakari Ikati in 1901 by CMS. Aburahamu Mpandakyaro, Isaya Kibira, and Andereya Kajerero also belonged to this first group. Kajerero was baptized in 1906 and confirmed by Bishop Tucker in 1908. Mzee Isaya Kibira was the leader of these pioneers and his house at Kashenye on the Tanzania and Uganda border became their meeting place. Later on, Mzee Isaya Kibira's son Josiah Kibira became the first African bishop of the Lutheran Church in Bukoba and later a president of the worldwide Lutheran World Federation. Another son, Emmanuel Kibira, after a distinguished career of service in the government of Tanzania, made a tremendous and enviable contribution to the work of the Bible Society of Tanzania (BST) as its General Secretary until his retirement in 1990. He guided the Bible Society to new levels as well as to expanded responsibilities in its task of the translation, production, and distribution of God's word in the vernacular languages of Tanzania.

The first Western missionaries to Buhaya were Ernst Johanssen, Ernst Doehring, and Wilhelm Rascher of the Lutheran mission to German East Africa. Johanssen, who had already served in the Usambaras in Tanganyika and in Rwanda, was called together with Doehring and Rascher to start Lutheran missionary work among the Bahaya. They arrived there in 1910. The partnership between the new German Lutheran missionaries and the infant local church in Buhaya combined to speed the growth of the church. This partnership was evident in the translation of the Gospels into Ruhaya. In the task of translation Doehring was assisted by Andereya Kajerero and Yokana Nsodo. In the course of the World War I, Bukoba fell to the British in 1916 and the German missionaries had to leave. Andereya Kajerero became the virtual leader of the young church in Bukoba, filling the leadership vacuum

---

44. Niwagila, *From the Catacombs*, 13.

that had been created. He later received assistance from CMS in Uganda, who had been invited by Paul Doehring.

In 1917 Canon Harry Leakey, a CMS missionary, came to Bukoba in response to the felt need there. It was he who prepared the Doehring translation for publication, adapting the proper names to Luganda usage. This is an example of the powerful influence of the Luganda Bible and Kiganda Christianity not only in Buhaya but throughout Uganda and her neighboring territories. The Gospels were published in 1920 and Acts in 1921 by BFBS London. In 1930 the Doehring version of Acts and Revelation adapted by Leakey and revised by Ernst Johanssen of the Bielefeld Mission was published by BFBS in Bielefeld. Anna Rascher and Otto Hagena of the Bethel Mission embarked on a new translation of the Scriptures into Ruhaya. They were assisted by Heinrich Scholten, Ernest Kalembo, Samuel Ishebaki, and Jonathan Karoma. In 1936 their translation of the Gospels was printed at the Lutheran Mission Press at Bukoba and in 1952 the NT was published by BFBS in London. It is interesting to note what Canon Leakey had reported to the BFBS on 5 February 1919. "A committee," he wrote, "consisting of CMS missionaries and natives, has met to discuss the question of providing one version for Lu-nyoro, Lu-toro, Lu-nyankole, Lu-kiga and Lu-haya. It was thought that it was possible to prepare a Union Version to cover these languages."[45] This idea had contributed to the delay in the printing of the NT in Ruhaya. Further, the CMS Haya Mission decided to hand over their work to the Methodist Mission of the South African Conference under charge of the Rev J. Martin White.

The Roman Catholic Church in Buhaya was also active in the task of Scripture translation. In 1959 the Gospels and Acts were published in Bukoba at the Marianum Press. Selections of Bible stories from the OT and NT were also published variously in Trier, Germany, in 1913 and 1926, and also in Bukoba in 1926. These were, however, not widely used or circulated. Pressure therefore arose within the Catholic Church for Scriptures in contemporary language. The recognition of this need contributed to the strong support the Catholic Church would give to the Bible Society-initiated translation project in common Ruhaya.

A third Lutheran translation of the NT into Ruhaya was undertaken by Else Orstadius of the Swedish Lutheran Mission and Gerhard Jasper of the German Lutheran Mission, assisted by Philip Tibaijuka and Joel Kibira, (a brother of

---

45. BFBS–ESC Minute Cards, vol. 3.

Emmanuel and Josiah Kibira[46]), who also worked as Secretary of the Buhaya Native Authority. The Gospel of Matthew was published on its own in 1967. The complete NT appeared in 1968 and Psalms in 1972, all published by the Bible Society in East Africa.

The First Ruhaya Bible – a Tool for Interconfessional Dialogue and Cooperation

In 1982 a new translation project was started with the aim of providing the complete Bible in Ruhaya. This was a joint effort of both the Catholic and Protestant churches in Buhaya. Both the late Bishop Josiah Kibira of the Lutheran Church and Bishop Nestorius Timanywa of the Roman Catholic Church were instrumental in initiating and promoting this union interconfessional effort. Bishop Mushemba, who succeeded Josiah Kibira, was equally supportive of collaboration among the Ruhaya-speaking churches in this translation venture. Among the participating churches were the Baptist, Pentecostal, and Anglican Churches of Buhaya on the Protestant side and the Catholic Church under Bishop Timanywa. Bishop Timanywa had a keen personal interest in this project and offered exemplary support. It is not surprising that Emmanuel Kibira, then General Secretary of BST, following his brother's lead, had a special interest in this project and lent it much support. Among the translators who worked on this interconfessional project were Father Damian Kyaruzi, now Catholic bishop of Sumbawanga; Father Philibert Rwehumbiza, formerly a Rector of Kipalapala Senior Theological Seminary in Tabora; and Father Odillon Kajwahura on the Catholic side. On the Protestant side the following were actively involved: the Rev Bernard Kyamanywa; the Rev Elisa Buberwa, now a retired bishop of the North Western Lutheran Diocese; and Philip Tibaijuka. This work started with the translation of the OT, which was immediately followed by the translation of the NT. The last stages of the entire Bible, including the translation of the Deuterocanonical books as well as overall editorial work, were undertaken by Father Odillon Kajwahura, the Rev Bernard Kyamanywa, and the Rev Elisa Buberwa. Amos

----

46. The Kibira family were very influential in the growth of Christianity in Tanzania. Josiah Kibira was the first Lutheran bishop of the Buhaya area and also the first African president of the Lutheran World Federation. Bishop Josiah's elder brother Emmanuel Kibira was Julius Nyerere's classmate in Tabora Secondary School and he played a major role in the Tanzania adult education program under Ujamaa. This helped to greatly raise the literacy rate of Tanzania above the rates of all neighboring countries. After a stint in the Tanzania parliament, Emmanuel became the General Secretary of the Bible Society in Tanzania. Their father, Mzee Kibira, belonged to the first generation of Christians who were converted by the Baganda evangelists in the 1890s.

and Hosea were published as portions in 1986 by BST. In November 2001 BST released the complete Ruhaya Bible including the Deuterocanonical books. It was launched and dedicated at an interconfessional celebration attended by Christians from all the participating churches, as well as by all interested speakers of the language and civil and government officials.

For the Bahaya community of northwestern Tanzania, 18 November 2001 was a unique and memorable day. On that day, for the first time since the Christian church arrived there in the 1890s, Christians were receiving the complete text of the Holy Scriptures in their own language. The Christian community in northwest Tanzania is a strong and thriving community of believers, self-supporting, self-propagating, and self-governing. It has produced some of the leading Christian leaders in Africa, among them such well-known names as Cardinal Laurean Rugambwa, the first Roman Catholic Cardinal to be appointed from Africa; Bishop Josiah Kibira, the first African President of the Lutheran World Federation and successor to Bishop Sundkler of Sweden, who was a Lutheran Bishop in the area for many years; and former head of the Evangelical Lutheran Church in Tanzania, Bishop Samson Mushemba. The story of the church in these parts has been well narrated, for example by Wilson B. Niwagila who focused on the Protestant beginnings and the Lutheran growth,[47] and by Method Kilaini who described the Catholic beginnings and early developments.[48]

The creation of the Bible in the Ruhaya tongue did not happen overnight. It was the result of a long process. There had been earlier attempts at translating Scriptures in Ruhaya both by the Lutheran and Catholic Christian communities in northwest Tanzania, but none of these had resulted in a complete Bible. It was evident to all at the launching celebration that this new and first complete Bible in Ruhaya was special. The procession leading to the Lutheran Cathedral in Bukoba, where the official service of dedication and thanksgiving took place, was led by the Catholic bishop of Bukoba, the Rt Rev Nestorius Timanywa, and the Lutheran bishop of Bukoba, the Rev Elisa Buberwa, together with the heads and representatives of the Anglican, Pentecostal, and Baptist churches. In the procession were priests, pastors, Catholic sisters, brothers, and Christian workers, as well as ordinary Christians from all the Christian denominations active among the Ruhaya-speaking communities of northwest Tanzania. The procession was accompanied by choirs dressed in colorful garments, dancing

---

47. See Niwagila, *From the Catacombs.*

48. See Kilaini, *Catholic Evangelization.*

to the sound of harmonious singing, accompanied by lively rhythmic drums and instruments and the crowds cheering and enjoying the whole spectacle.

This Bible was a clear and visible demonstration of the common purpose and unity of all the Ruhaya-speaking Christian communities, the culmination of nearly twenty years of interconfessional cooperation among the five Christian confessions – Catholic, Lutheran, Anglican, Baptist, and Pentecostal. Since its inception in 1981 the project had enjoyed the participation of both laity and clergy at all levels represented by various committees. For example, the Consultative Committee brought together the heads of all the participating churches and only dealt with policy issues, while the fully representative Administrative Committee dealt with administrative and financial issues affecting the project. The Translation Committee consisted of three to four translators from both the Catholic and Protestant communities and focused mainly on the actual translation process and on making editorial changes to the text of the translation. The fully representative Theological Committee dealt with questions of theology and special terminology, of exegetical and doctrinal sensitivity, and of diverging confessional traditions, among others. The Review Committee consisted of groups of Ruhaya-speaking readers with interests in questions of orthography, language and linguistic matters, theological and doctrinal matters, together with textual and original-language matters. They also represented the concerns of the young, the old, the female readers, and other groups, as well as the various dialectal variations of the Ruhaya speech community. The aim was to be as inclusive as possible to ensure the widest possible reception and acceptability of this first Ruhaya Bible.

This Bible was therefore received as an instrument of interconfessionality and unity among the Haya-speaking communities of northwest Tanzania. It represented a long struggle to bring closer together differing confessions and traditions. In this endeavor, a number of compromises had to be made at the terminological level (see table 5.1).

Table 5.1. Theologically sensitive language and the Ruhaya interconfessional Bible

Term	Catholic	Protestant	Compromise
God	*Mungu*	*Rubaho*	*Ruhanga*
Church	*Ekelezia*	*Kanisa*	*Nteeko*
Wine	*Vini*	*Mvinyo*	*Divai*
Priest	*Omusaserdoti*	*Omweza*	*Omukuhani*
Worship	*Okuhabudu*	*Okwegashaniza*	*Okufukamira*

The different terms indicated above are variants or synonyms derived from differing traditions and even languages. *Mungu*, *Rubaho*, and *Ruhanga* all mean "God." Similarly, *Ekelezia*, *Kanisa,* and *Nteeko* all have the same meaning as the English word "church." *Vini*, *Mvinyo*, and *Divai* all mean "wine." *Omusaserdoti*, *Omweza*, and *Omukuhani* all mean "priest." Some terms are based on Latin, Italian, German, Arabic, or Hebrew via Swahili or even the Greek, as in the case of *Ekelezia*. The compromise terms mostly settled on a vernacular term except for *divai* ("wine") and *omukuhani* ("priest"), where it was felt that the traditional vernacular term had negative connotations.

The new Bible represents a united tradition resulting from the cooperative effort and the desire to create a common Bible for all the Ruhaya-speaking community. Two editions of this Bible were simultaneously produced, a Protestant edition without the Deuterocanonical (DC) books and a Catholic edition containing the DC books along with the imprimatur granted by Bishop Nestorius Timanywa, the Catholic bishop of Bukoba.

Kishubi, Kihangaza, Giha, Kinyarwanda, and Kirundi

Both Kishubi and Kihangaza are spoken in the area southwest of Buhaya and south of Karagwe in the Ngara area close to the Burundi border. These are part of the Kinyarwanda-Kirundi-Kishubi-Kihangaza-Giha continuum.[49] They are part of the old Bunyoro-Kitara empire and its cultural traditions. No portion of the Holy Scriptures has as yet been translated into Kishubi. But Kihangaza has at least something – the Gospel of Mark. This was the work of F. E. Shaw of the Church Army, an evangelistic arm of CMS. It was published in 1938 by BFBS London. Captain Shaw relied heavily on his students and was discouraged from continuing by objections to his work from the Harold E. Guillebaud, a former translator of the Rwanda and Kirundi version who argued that Kihangaza was a dialect of Kirundi. As already indicated, CMS work in the western part of the Lake region owes its origins to the Uganda CMS Mission and the Baganda evangelists. This work received a push during the period when Canon Leakey was most influential, from 1917 onwards, and was further consolidated from 1929 onwards.

---

49. These are part of Guthrie's D60.

Translation into Giha

A number of Catholic missionaries throughout the Lake Region saw the need to communicate the gospel in the local languages to help facilitate the communal celebration of the sacraments. Many embarked on the difficult and demanding task of translating the Holy Bible into the local languages. Among these was Father Jan Martin van Sambeek of the Holy Ghost Fathers. He worked on Giha, a language spoken by well over a million people in Kigoma province along Lake Tanganyika.[50] Giha is spoken in Kasulu, Kibondo, and Kigoma districts along the eastern shores of Lake Tanganyika and even as far north as Biharamulo. Ujiji, the town where Henry Morton Stanley met Livingstone, is also in Giha-speaking territory. The people were evangelized by the Catholics and the Anglicans, and both groups attempted translations of the Bible. Unfortunately, to this day this important ethnic group has no complete Bible in their own language. Perhaps the belief that they could well use the Kirundi Bible played a part. In any case, the pressure to have a complete Bible in Giha has in recent times gathered momentum, but it is still hampered by the twin obstacles of Swahili dominance from the Tanzanian side and the influence and impact of Kirundi, the neighboring language on the Burundi side. It is interesting, though, that by 1960 Father van Sambeek had translated the New Testament into Giha. This was published by the Tabora Mission Press, who also published the text as portions: the Gospels in 1960, Acts in 1961, and Romans–Jude in 1962. In 1962 the Gospel of Mark was also published in Giha by the Bible Society in East Africa. This was, however, an effort of the Anglican mission led by the venerable Lionel J. Bakewell, Gideoni Mudala, Rubeni Gikanake, and Rubeni Mbiha.

When Archdeacon Bakewell left Africa for service in Australia in 1962, Matthew, Mark, Romans, 1 and 2 Corinthians, Hebrews, and Revelation were in final draft form. He noted in correspondence, "The Africans have translated Luke, John, Acts 1–21, Galatians and Ephesians 1–4."[51] These were, however, never finalized and have never been published.

The Giha Christians and church are eager to bring this task to an end, by providing for a completely new translation. A new project is being constituted to take on this assignment. A team of translators consisting of Silas Anderson Nkwakuzi, Joram Ntakije, and Cleophas Nyaruchali were appointed by both the Anglican and Catholic churches. Work is ongoing for a New Testament

---

50. As noted above, Giha belongs together with Kinyarwanda, Kirundi, Fuliiro, Shubi, Hangaza, and Vinza to Guthrie's D60.

51. See the Archival Records in the Bibliography, BFBS files.

and a complete Bible is expected under the sponsorship of the Bible Society of Tanzania.

Kinyarwanda and Kirundi

Kinyarwanda and Kirundi are spoken in the countries of Rwanda and Burundi respectively. The two countries and languages are like twins who share much in common. The two languages are mutually intelligible. Kinyarwanda is spoken by nearly eight million people in Rwanda, Uganda, DRC, Tanzania, and Burundi, while Kirundi is spoken by nearly seven million people in Burundi, Rwanda, DRC, and Tanzania. The three ethnic groups found in both countries, namely Hutu (comprising over 80% of the population in both countries), Tutsi (over 15% in both countries), and Twa (less than 5%) all speak the same language in each country and all, by and large, share the same culture, customs, and traditions. The hostility and history of genocide in recent years is not linked to language or cultural practice, but rather to irrational prejudices and beliefs, some of which have been attributed to colonial practices of the recent period.[52]

The first Europeans to arrive in this area, on 4 May 1894, were Germans led by Gustav Adolf von Goetzen, exactly one hundred years before the 1994 genocide. After the Berlin Conference of 1884–1885 and the ensuing scramble for Africa in 1899, Rwanda and Burundi were incorporated into German East Africa, which included Tanganyika. German rule in these territories lasted only until World War I when these territories were taken over by the victors. Thus, mainland Tanganyika was taken over by the British while Rwanda and Burundi were handed over to the Belgians by the League of Nations in 1926. The German missionary presence in these territories suffered the same fate as that of the German colonial administrators: they were all expelled. Both countries were therefore Christianized by Belgian Catholic missionaries as well as by British Anglican missionaries working from their base in Uganda. This led to the dominance of these two groups of Christians. They were later joined by groups of Presbyterian, Baptist, Seventh-Day Adventist, and Pentecostal missionaries, leading to the emergence of local Christian communities that were representative of these various missionary groups. The two countries

---

52. A number of recent books offer vivid pictures of this story, among them Prunier, *Rwanda Crisis*; Keane, *Season of Blood*; Berry and Berry, *Genocide in Rwanda*; Melvern, *A People Betrayed*; Gatwa, *Rwanda—Églises*; Guillebaud, *Rwanda*; Pottier, *Re-imagining Rwanda*. For an appreciation of the related issues in Burundi, see Ndarubagiye, *Burundi*; Lemarchand, *Burundi – Ethnic Conflict and Genocide*; and Watt, *Burundi – Biography of a Small African Country*.

were therefore considered predominantly Christian, even at the time of the 1994 genocide.

The official language used in both Rwanda and Burundi is French due to the Belgian colonial experience. They have been therefore a part of *Francophonie*. Historian John Conteh-Morgan reminds us that this term "has been strongly contested" in recent times. He argues:

> With its emphasis on French and its place in Africa, and the new French derived culture to which this language has given rise, the word it is claimed, marginalized the numerous African languages and non-Francophone, that is non-French-derived, cultures in these countries. At the very least, it gives a misleading, exaggerated picture of the place of French in them; exaggerated because it is only one of two official languages in a number of "Francophone" African countries . . . the idea of a French-speaking sub-Saharan Africa community is a myth, . . . it corresponds more to a will to impose French and thus entrench France's influence, than to an accurate description of its place in the community.[53]

Although Rwanda and Burundi traditionally have been proud members of *Francophonie*, in recent times they have tended to move away from it. This is partly due to poor relations with their former colonial master, Belgium, and also partly due to France's alleged role in the 1994 Rwanda genocide.[54]

Rwanda and Burundi are both recognizing the realities of globalization and of their own linguistic diversity and geopolitical interests. A major factor in this trend has been the close geographical, cultural, linguistic, and economic links between the peoples of Burundi and Rwanda and the neighboring countries of Uganda, Tanzania, and Kenya. Rwanda and Burundi are landlocked countries and depend on their three neighbors to the east for an outlet to the sea, as well as for trade and business links. It is interesting to note that many of the leading elite in the government of Rwanda after the genocide were former refugees and leading lights in Uganda and to a lesser extent also in Tanzania and Kenya. Similarly, thousands of Rwandese and Burundi refugees fleeing trouble at home found their way into Uganda and Tanzania. These and other related factors have led to close economic and regional links between these two countries and the countries of Kenya, Uganda, and Tanzania. Rwanda and Burundi were

---

53. Conteh-Morgan, "Francophone Africa," 85–137.

54. See, for example, Wallis, *Silent Accomplice*, which points a finger more directly to France's complicity in the genocide than Melvern does in, *A People Betrayed*.

admitted to full membership of the East African Economic Community, where the dominant languages are Swahili and English, in 2009. Moreover, in 2009 Rwanda was also admitted into membership of the Commonwealth of Nations (formerly the British Commonwealth), where English rather than French is the official language.

This linguistic and political change has influenced Bible Society relations and structures. The Bible Societies of Rwanda and Burundi previously belonged to the UBS Francophone Africa Region, but then shifted to the Anglophone Africa Region. They have also applied to be members of the UBS Africa Swahili Publishing Committee[55] on the grounds that they use Swahili Scriptures widely. At home, however, Kirundi and Kinyarwanda continue to be the languages of choice.[56]

Translation into Kinyarwanda

During the German period, during the late nineteenth and early twentieth centuries, the German Lutheran missionaries understood well the importance of the vernacular. Among these missionaries was a young German by the name of Karl Roehl, who, together with Ernst Johanssen and Paul Wohlrab of the Evangelical Missionary Society for German East Africa, would later distinguish himself as a translator of the Kishambala New Testament of 1908. As recounted above in chapter two, Roehl also later single-handedly translated the influential Swahili Bible now fondly referred to as the Roehl Bible. This same Roehl immediately after his labors in the mountains of Usambara found himself in the hills of Rwanda where he is remembered as the translator of the first Scriptures in Kinyarwanda, the Gospels published in 1914 by BFBS. This splendid effort to translate the full NT was never completed, no doubt due to complications arising out of the war years. But his Gospels would serve as a fine foundation and example to those who followed him.[57]

---

55. The Swahili Publishing Committee is a committee of UBS that promotes the joint publication of Swahili Scriptures with a view to serving Swahili speakers in the entire East and Central African region, as well as elsewhere, in an effective and efficient manner. The committee has members from Bible Societies from countries with significant numbers of Swahili speakers and users of Swahili Scriptures, including Tanzania, Kenya, Uganda, Congo, Rwanda, and Burundi.

56. They are important members of the Interlacustrine Bantu language family which includes many of the languages classified in Guthrie's Zones D and E, combined as Meeussen's Zone J. See Yvonne Bastin, "Interlacustrine Zone (Zone J)," 501–528, and map 25.1 at page 503.

57. Guillebaud, *Rwanda*, 27–28.

The task of translating the complete Bible into Kinyarwanda is credited to a team that included of Harold E. Guillebaud and A. C. Stanley Smith, both of CMS; J. Honore of the Belgian Missionary Society; and H. Monier and A. L. Hands of SDA. However, Samsoni Inyarubuga, a mother-tongue speaker, was really the pillar of this team, as it was he who taught Guillebaud the language and later helped to create the first drafts.[58] This team was assisted by Gideoni Kabano and Paulo Gatunzi. The team produced the Gospel of Mark in 1927, the four Gospels in 1929, the NT in 1931, Psalms in 1933, and the Pentateuch and Ruth in 1939. Daniel followed in 1942; Isaiah, Jonah, Zechariah, Malachi in 1943; and the complete OT in 1954, the year of the first complete Bible in Kinyarwanda. The Bible was published with a revised NT in 1957. All these were published by BFBS in London.

In the 1980s the Bible Society of Rwanda (BSR), working together with the Protestant and Catholic churches, embarked on a project to produce a contemporary interconfessional translation of the Bible in Kinyarwanda. This was to be a fresh translation and not a revision of the 1954/1957 Bible. This common-language interconfessional modern translation in Kinyarwanda was the work of Peter Guillebaud (a CMS missionary and son of Harold E. Guillebaud), and of Giles Williams, a CMS missionary who took over from Peter Guillebaud after his retirement; together with Pierre Gakwandi (Presbyterian); Esdras Kayonga and Eliezer Wunyekarama (SDA); and Innocent Samsoni and Juvenal Kassasira (Roman Catholics). Other Catholic collaborators included Jean Baptiste Rugengamanza, Privat Nkarama, and Emmanuel Rwangombwa. This team published the Gospel of Mark in 1981, John in 1985, Matthew and revised Mark in 1986, Luke and Acts in 1988, Ruth and Jonah in 1989, and the NT in 1991. The New Testament with Psalms came out in 1996 with a slightly revised NT. The entire Bible with a revised NT and Psalms came out in 2004, published by BSR in Kigali.

Work on the contemporary interconfessional translation coincided with the time of tribulation and the genocide of 1994. This was a most difficult time for the team of translators. The Bible manuscripts and drafts on which they were working were miraculously preserved in the translation office situated in downtown Kigali at Bible House during the takeover of Kigali by the Rwandan Patriotic Army that drove the former government from power. The manuscripts on which the translation team were working on had been left in the BSR office the night the presidential plane was shot down. This was the event that sparked the subsequent massacres. In the ensuing days of violence,

---

58. Guillebaud, 24–30.

looting, mayhem, and mass murders, the Bible House miraculously was not looted or destroyed. The manuscripts were recovered several days after relative calm had returned and it was possible to go to the office. The coordinator of the translation team, the Rev Giles Williams, managed to take copies with him to his home in the UK from where, through communication and consultation with the surviving members of the translation team, the task was completed. It is sad to note that one member of the translation team lost his life during the genocide, as did some family members, close relatives, and supporters of the project. Hopefully, the 2004 interconfessional common-language Kinyarwanda Bible will contribute to healing the land and to bringing reconciliation and lasting peace and hope.

The Catholic involvement in Scripture translation in Kinyarwanda was slow. The early focus led by, among others, missionaries Paul Barthélémy in 1902 and Paul Cogniaux in 1911, both of them White Fathers, was on translating lectionaries and Bible story books.[59] The Epistles were published much later in 1950 under the supervision of Father Leopold Vermeersch, also of the White Fathers, followed by the Gospels and Acts by the same team in 1960. These were published at the Imprimerie de Kabgayi, at Kabgayi. The first attempt at a complete NT was by the Catholic priest and well-known scholar Alexis Kagame. Kagame's translation of the NT into Kinyarwanda was published in 1971 by the Imprimerie de Kabgayi in Kabgayi, reprinted in 1975 by the Presses Lavigerie in Bujumbura, revised in 1979, and reprinted again in 1986, this time by BSR. Alexis Kagame, it should be noted, is renowned for his writings on Bantu philosophy from a Rwandese perspective[60] and for his support of the ideas of Belgian Catholic philosopher and priest Father Placide Tempels, whose book *Bantu philosophy* (published in 1959 in Paris by Présence Africaine), was quite controversial and was widely discussed by African and Africanist academics. Edward Gakwandi, another Catholic priest, produced translations of Genesis and Exodus that were published by the Catholic Mission at Nyundo. Alois Bigirumwami followed this example with his translations of the four Gospels: Matthew in 1978, Luke in 1980, Mark in 1982, and John in 1984. These were also published by the Catholic Mission in Nyundo.

Credit for the publication of the first Catholic translation of the Bible into Kinyarwanda goes to the Verbum Bible publishing house in Kinshasa, DRC.

---

59. Rijks, *Guide to Catholic Bible Translations*, vol. 2, 333–336.

60. Among Kagame's books are the following: *Les organizations socio-familiales de l'ancien Rwanda* (1954), *La philosophie bantu rwandaise de l'être* (1956), *Un abrege de l'histoire du Rwanda de 1853–1972* (1975), *La Philosophie bantu comparée* (1976).

Verbum Bibles are translations of the Bible by Catholic priests and biblical scholars fully supported by the Roman Catholic Church.[61] The Kinyarwanda Verbum Bible came out in 1990. It was commissioned in November 1983 by the Rwanda Episcopal Conference. The translation project proceeded initially under the leadership of Francois Xavier Niyibizi and later, from March 1985 after the death of Bishop Niyibizi in a motor accident, by Father Jean Van der Meersch, a Belgian biblical scholar from the Society of the Missionaries of Africa. All the Belgian priests and members of the translation team belonged to this order. This translation – now referred to as the *Bibiliya Ntagatifu (BN)* – was the work of a large team of Rwandan priests and biblical scholars composed of Father Leonidas Gombaniro, Simon Habyarimana, Father Callixte Kalisa, Father Ignace Kanyagana, Venuste Linguyeneza, Augustin Misago, Francois Xavier Niyibizi, Father Denis Sekamana, Father Real Tardiff, Father Guy Theunis, Father Jean Van der Meersch, and Father Leopold Vermeersch, as well as others.[62] Considering that the *Bibiliya Ntagatifu* project appeared to be in competition with the Bible Society's interconfessional *Bibiliya Ijambo Ry'Imana* project, the common-language project that was started around 1979, Father Jean Van der Meersch in his report to the Verbum Bible publishers in Kinshasa entitled, *Une expérience de traduction de la Bible en Afrique (Rwanda)* wrote as follows:

> D'abord, se posa la question fort débattue d'une éventuelle collaboration avec les autres Églises chrétiennes au Rwanda, en vue de la production d'une TRADUCTION OECUMENIQUE. Le problem fut examiné très sérieusement, même avec l'aide de la FEBICAM (Fédération Biblique Catholique Mondiale), et finalement on arriva à la conclusion suivante dans un premier temps, l'Église catholique a le besoin pressant de parvenir rapidement à une traduction complète de la Bible qui ne soit pas trop différente de notre vocabulaire réligieux habituel, et qui puisse se prêter à l'usage liturgique (lecture à la messe par ex.) et à different usages dans la vie chrétienne. Une édition catholique pourrait d'ailleurs être munie d'introductions et de notes infra-

---

61. Verbum Bibles has published a number of translations of the Bible in African languages, among them, Congo Swahili, Lingala, and Kinyarwanda.

62. Rijks, *Guide to Catholic Bible Translations*, vol. 2, 335.

paginales relativement abondantes, suivant les directives du Concile Vatican II (Dei Verbum, n, 25).[63]

Translated as:

At first a hotly debated question arose regarding an eventual collaboration with the other Christian Churches in Rwanda with the objective of publishing an ecumenical translation of the Bible. The problem was very seriously examined, together with the help of the WCBF (World Catholic Biblical Federation). It was finally concluded that the Catholic Church had a pressing need to quickly develop a complete translation of the Bible that closely mirrors the current church terminology or vocabulary, and that is suitable for liturgical use,(public reading in worship services, for example) as well as for a variety of uses in the Christian life. A Catholic version of the Bible could also include introductions as well as relatively generous notes in the page margins, following the guidelines of the Second Vatican Council (Dei Verbum, no. 25).[64]

The Pentateuch was completed and published in December 1986, the NT in 1988, and the entire *Bibiliya Ntagatifu* was published in Kinshasa by the Verbum Bible publishers in 1990.[65]

We thus have now three translations of the complete Bible in Kinyarwanda, the *Bibiliya Yera* (BY) of 1957, the *Bibiliya Ntagatifu* (BN) of 1990, and the *Bibiliya Ijambo Ry'Imana* (BIR) of 2004.

Translation into Kirundi

The first translations of Holy Scripture into Kirundi were by the Catholic White Fathers. Scripture narratives translated by the White Fathers Mission were published as early as 1906 in Trier in Germany. In 1909 the liturgical Gospels were printed in France. These were followed by the translation of the Gospel

---

63. Quoted in Himbaza, *Transmettre la Bible: Une Critique exégètique de la traduction de l'AT, le cas du Rwanda* (2001), 65–66. This work was originally produced as the author's PhD thesis in theology at the University of Fribourg, defended on 12 May 1998, under the supervision of Professors Adrian Schenker, Christopher Uehlinger, and Leo Karrer.

64. Translated by the author.

65. For a detailed overview of the history of the *Bibiliya Ntagatifu* as well as the *Bibiliya Yera*, see Himbaza's book *Transmettre la Bible*, ch. 2, pp. 31–71. The rest of the book presents a detailed book-by-book exegetical critique of the *Bibiliya Yera* and *Bibiliya Ntagatifu* translations. This work is invaluable to specialists and will prove very helpful in future revisions of these two translations.

of Luke by Father Bonneau and its publication in 1920, with a reprint in 1928, in Algiers at the Maison Carrée.

A team of Danish Baptist missionaries composed of N. P. Andersen and Hans P. Jensen took up the challenge to move beyond the Catholic effort. Wondering whether the Barundi could use the Scriptures already prepared for the Wanyarwanda, Andersen wrote:

> We do not say that our Barundi do not understand the language used in the Ruanda translations, but quite a lot of words and expressions are different and sometimes the same word has a different meaning. The grammar differs too, tenses as well as other things in the accidence. The [Roman Catholic] translations have translation for each of the two colonies, Ruanda and Urundi, and they have been working in the field for 35 years.[66]

Dr A. C. Stanley Smith of the Church Missionary Society Ruanda Mission based in Kabale, Kigezi-Uganda, and a translator on the then ongoing Kinyarwanda translation of the Bible, supported Andersen's case by writing to BFBS as follows in a letter dated 6 December 1933:

> I am not personally an authority on the Urundi language but I have stayed with the Andersen's & have spoken to a certain number of the Barundi. I feel quite sure that though Ruanda is intelligible to them, they need the New Testament in their own tongue. There are quite a number of key words which have different meanings, and I believe the tenses do not correspond closely in some cases. The two languages are close enough to have enabled the Danish Baptists to use Mr. Guillebaud's work in the initial stages; but as soon as they can get a version of their own, they ought to have it.[67]

Andersen and Jensen's efforts resulted in the translation and publication of the Gospels of Matthew and John in 1935. They were assisted by Emmanuel T. Sibomana and Ruka Moukiye. These translations were poorly received and were considered to be in urgent need of revision. Under the leadership of Rosemary Guillebaud and Harold E. Guillebaud of the CMS, the translation of the Bible into Kirundi took big strides forward. The Guillebauds were assisted by Hans P. Jensen, Hans P. Emming (Danish Baptist Mission), Stefano Ndimubandi, Danieli Mudende, Emmanuel T. Sibomana, and Yosefu Sinkema. They oversaw

---

66. BFBS EA language correspondence files (see ESC Mins. 3rd January 1934), 48.

67. BFBS EA languages correspondence files (ESC Mins. 11.12.1934), 52.

the following publications: the four Gospels, Galatians–1 Thessalonians, 1 Peter, and 1 John in 1938; the complete NT in 1951; and the OT books of Ruth, Psalms, and Isaiah in 1951, and Genesis in 1960. The complete Bible appeared in 1967. This has now been revised.

The authorities in the Catholic Church in Burundi have never felt quite at home with the Protestant Bible, the *Bibliya Yera*, even though it is the only Bible that is available for anyone who needs a Kirundi Bible. Their desire to create their own distinctive translation was, however, a priority. A group of Catholic missionaries translated a NT which was published by the Presses Lavigerie in Bujumbura in 1967 with reprints in 1973, 1975, and a revision and correction in 1984. Parts of this translation had appeared earlier, Mark and Luke in 1956, Matthew in 1957, and the Gospels and Acts in 1960. The Deuterocanonical books were issued in 1977 in mimeographed form by the Center for the Study of African Languages. These were all published by the Presses Lavigerie at Bujumbura.

A project that was started in the early 1980s by an interconfessional team of Zachary Kiganahe (Roman Catholic), Stanislas Mahinja (Methodist), and Martin Nyaboho (Anglican) was expected to produce an interconfessional Bible in Kirundi. Due to disagreements and misunderstandings between the Catholic Church and the Bible Society of Burundi, this project was eventually suspended. It appears that the Catholics were not keen on participating in an interconfessional translation project with the Protestants who already had their own Bible (the Kirundi *Bibiliya Yera*) before they could have a Catholic Bible of their own – as was the case in Rwanda.

It appears that the Catholics were not eager to participate in an interconfessional translation project with the Protestants since, unlike the Protestants, they did not have a translation of their own to draw upon. The only evidence of the team's efforts is the publication of a portion, the Gospel of Luke in 1986 by the Bible Society of Burundi in Bujumbura. In place of following through with this interconfessional translation, the Catholics embarked on another project to produce a Catholic translation of the entire Bible. This project, which started in the mid-1980s, has encountered many challenges related to the political turbulence and instability in the country. However through the persistence of the translation teams and the General Secretary of the society (Marjorie Niyungeki), steady progress was made and the complete Bible was finalized and published toward the end of 2018.

6

The Eastern Bantu Neighbors of the Baganda

Basoga, Bagwere, Banyuli, Bamasaaba, and Abaluyia

Translation of the Bible into the Bantu languages of Eastern Uganda

The spread of Christianity into Eastern Uganda was facilitated by Semei Kakungulu's subjugation of the local communities by force of arms, especially in the regions of Teso and Lango. Semei Kakangulu was born in 1868 in Koki, a sub-kingdom of Buganda. He was recruited by the British colonial agents to help extend British rule in Eastern Uganda. Kakungulu established himself in these parts through the use of "guns, gun caps and bullets."[1] He set up an administrative structure consisting of *saza* ("county") and *gombolola* ("sub-county") administrative units based on the Kiganda system. These administrative units were manned mainly by Baganda. Kakungulu was himself based at Budaka in Bukedi, thus earning himself the title of "Kabaka of Bukedi." His actions, however, merely prepared the ground for the British.

Michael Twaddle in his book *Kakungulu and the Creation of Uganda*[2] describes a plaque he was shown at Budaka in 1963 by a local government official who told him, "That man (Kakungulu) created the Uganda we Ugandans are fighting for today," and yet as Twaddle notes, "the local people had had the plaque removed to a bicycle shed." The plaque read:

> At this spot in the year 1901 the British flag was first hoisted
> by Semei Kakungulu, emissary and loyal servant of His Majesty
> the King. He built here a *boma* which was for a short time the

---

1. Twaddle, *Kakungulu*, 20.
2. Twaddle, 20.

headquarters of the district. From this beginning came the establishment of peace and the development of orderly progress in this part of Uganda.[3]

When the British took over Bukedi in 1902, Kakungulu himself moved on to Mbale from where he subjugated the Bamasaba and set in place the same structures as in Teso and Lango. When the British took over Bumasaba in 1903, Kakungulu moved on to Busoga from whence he took control of the local *Lukiko* (i.e. local parliament) as its president in 1906 and put in place a Kiganda-type system of administration. Kakungulu is reputed to have been without an equal in Uganda in the zeal with which he served the interests of British colonialism.[4]

Kakungulu was the epitome and classic exemplar of the British use of Baganda agents to colonize and rule, and control indirectly the acephalous societies of eastern and northern Uganda. These communities did not have institutions of centralized rule and power as were typical in Buganda, Bunyoro, Toro, and Ankole. Kakungulu's conquest of Teso, Lango, Bukedi, Bumasaba, and Busoga brought in its train many Baganda settlers, some of whom used the opportunity to spread the Christian faith. Here, as in the southwest, it was the "lay apostles" or "black evangelists" who took the initiative. Thus, Baganda evangelists and catechists could be found all over eastern Uganda preaching the good news of Jesus Christ.

It is of interest that Kakungulu himself became terribly disillusioned with his own collaboration with the British. He became very bitter towards them for their lack of appreciation of his labors on their behalf and for the way they callously exploited him. It is not surprising that he became staunchly involved in one of the earliest separatist and independent churches in Uganda, indeed in all of East Africa, namely the Society of the One Almighty God. This sect, described as anti-European by some, was formed around 1913–1914 and nicknamed the *Bamalaki* after its founder Malaki Musajjakawa. It gained thousands of adherents. A member of this sect is reported to have explained that the reason for the emergence of the *Bamalaki* sect "was that we saw the Europeans who brought us the Bible were not doing what it said, though they told us to do what it said." For example, "The Europeans disregarded the real

---

3. Twaddle, viii.

4. This is in essence one of the main arguments of Twaddle's book.

Sabbath on which God rested: they chose to observe another day which is not commanded in the Bible."[5]

Kakungulu left the *Bamalaki* sect to found another sect, the *Bayudaya* ("the Jews"), which is a kind of Jewish sect that sought to study and live in accordance with the Hebrew Scriptures.[6] The *Bayudaya* has made persistent contacts to gain acceptance and assistance from the World Jewry, but with very limited and disappointing success.[7] The *Bayudaya* members use the Luganda Bible for their worship and Bible reading and are still unable to access the Hebrew Scriptures in the original language since they have not had the opportunity to learn Hebrew.

Translation into Lusoga

The Basoga are the neighbors of the Baganda. They number over one million people and live mainly to the east of Buganda, east of the Nile River starting from the Ugandan city of Jinja to the south of Lake Kyoga. They share many customs and practices with the Baganda. Their language, Lusoga,[8] is a Bantu language. It is not, however, uniformly spoken. It breaks down into certain dialectal groupings with varying degrees of mutual intelligibility, a factor which has a negative bearing on the solidarity of the Basoga or any strong sense of unity or identity. Historian Tarsis Kabwegere argues that "there was no one organized authority structure [in] the whole district" or area referred to as Busoga. "Instead there were kingdoms, entities in their own right linked by relations of marriage and formal inter-unit relations."[9] Citing the Busoga Draft Constitution, he lists these groups as follows: Bugabula, Kigulu, Bulamogi, Luuka, Bugweli, Bukedi, Bunyuli, Busiki, Butembe-bubya.[10] Both linguistic and political fragmentation prevented the area known as Busoga from being united.

Consequently, the *Kyabazinga*, the king[11] of Busoga, did not wield much power. It has been claimed that he was in fact a creation of Kakungulu who

---

5. Twaddle, *Kakungulu*, 267.

6. See a detailed examination of this in Oded's book, *Religion and Politics in Uganda*, especially pp. 75–114.

7. Oded, *Religion and Politics in Uganda*, 75–114.

8. Lusoga shares many linguistic features with Luganda. It is classified with Luganda in Guthrie's Group E10, together with many of the languages listed here, such as Lugwere.

9. Kabwagyere, *Politics of State Formation*, 30.

10. Kabwagyere, 30.

11. *Kyabazinga* is the title for the King of Busoga and is roughly equivalent to that of *Kabaka* of Buganda or titles for local ethnic heads.

wanted to create a centralized authority in this area following the Buganda model, but one which was answerable to the British colonial government. Kabwegyere writes:

> When the British came into Busoga, they found these units too small for administrative purposes. They went ahead to amalgamate them where necessary, and Kakungulu was called upon to construct the Kiganda administrative system in Busoga, a duty he undertook from about 1909. He was made President of Busoga and clan areas were used as sazas (counties). He was succeeded by Wako, a Musoga, as President in 1919, but later in 1938 the title was changed to that of Kyabazinga, simply substituting a local title for an English one. The actual post is one of our creation purely and simply.[12]

Kabwegyere's point is that the administrative unit called Busoga was a colonial creation, as was the post of the *Kyabazinga*, the Muganda Kakungulu having been used and supported to bring it about.

This fact and the linguistic fragmentation of Busoga were no doubt factors in its weakness. Similarly, the Basoga's long period of survival and defensiveness under the shadow of Buganda have greatly contributed to their lack of development or progress in a number of areas. One of these is certainly the area of language use. It is of interest that the Baganda referred to the whole area inhabited by their eastern neighbors, the Bantu communities – that is, Basoga, Bagwere, Banyole, and Bamasaba, as well as the Nilotic communities, Jopadhola, Iteso and Ngakarimojong – as *Bukedi*, meaning "the territory of naked people" or "the territory of people who do not know how to rule themselves."[13] It is a fact that most of these societies were not as centralized as those of Buganda or southwestern Uganda. Nearly all the societies to the east of Buganda were acephalous, that is, without centralized authority.

Even though the Basoga were Christianized at the very beginning of the missionary era in Uganda, they were late in getting the Holy Scriptures in their own language or dialects. In the mid-1890s two CMS missionaries, William A. Crabtree and Frank Rowling, attempted a translation of the Scriptures into Lusoga, but eventually gave up, acquiescing to the argument for the use of Luganda Scriptures. It is possible, though, that they came to terms with the complex dialect situation and the lack of significant support for the dialect

---

12. Kabwagyere, *Politics of State Formation*, 31.

13. Ward, "History of Christianity in Uganda," 94.

Crabtree had chosen to execute his task. They therefore only succeeded in producing the Gospel of Mark in 1896, translated by Crabtree with some assistance from Rowling, and the Gospel of Matthew in 1897, translated by Crabtree. Both were published by the CMS Press, Busoga. The Gospel of John was then translated by Rowling with the assistance of Baganda teachers, and was published by the BFBS, London, in 1899. In addition to these, Crabtree also translated a catechism in 1895, a reader and hymnbook in 1896, and portions of the Book of Common Prayer in 1897. These were all published at the CMS Press, Busoga.

Over a century later, it was clear that the need for the Holy Scriptures in Lusoga was still as urgent as ever. A consultant for the Bible Societies made a visit to Busoga in the mid-1990s to help the Bible Society of Uganda evaluate a request by the Lusoga-speaking churches for a translation of the Bible in their own language. The consultant was surprised to find how extensive the use of Luganda in Busoga was. Luganda and Lusoga in Busoga constitute a situation which linguists refer to as *diglossia*. An indigenous Lusoga-speaking family could at one moment be carrying on a mundane conversation in Lusoga, their own mother tongue, and yet immediately switch to Luganda if a prayer or a religious homily was called for. A traditional ceremony could be held using Lusoga, but a Christian worship or prayer service in a church or some other formal place would require use of Luganda.

This situation is not unique to Busoga. The consultant was surprised even more during visits to the territory of Padhola in eastern Uganda where the Nilotic-speaking Jopadhola live. This is somewhere in the environs of the Ugandan town of Tororo, not far away from Mount Elgon on the border with Kenya. Here again the Jopadhola used their own language, Dhopadhola, freely and extensively in all forms of communication. However, whenever they switched to Christian worship or prayer, Bible reading or liturgy, they immediately turned to Luganda. In the case of Lusoga and Luganda it could be argued that these two languages are closely related. They both belong to the large Bantu language family, and moreover the two languages are mutually intelligible to a very high degree. Thus, it is relatively easy for a speaker of Lusoga to learn to speak Luganda or even understand large chunks of conversation in Luganda without much effort. Such is not the case with Dhopadhola and Luganda. Dhopadhola is a Nilotic language, belonging to a different language family, and the degree of mutual intelligibility between Luganda and Dhopadhola is virtually zero.

Nonetheless, for the Basoga as for the Jopadhola, the decision to have a translation of the Bible in their own language was an affirmation of the intrinsic worth of their own language, an affirmation of their ethnic and linguistic being, a recognition of their identity as a people, and an affirmation of their traditions, values, and history. In the 1989–1990 period, interconfessional efforts were made by the Roman Catholic and Anglican churches under the sponsorship of the Bible Society of Uganda to start an ecumenical Lusoga Bible translation project. This was officially launched in December 1990. A translation committee consisting of Father John Kajolya (Roman Catholic), Richard Isabirye (Anglican), and Daudi Waidhuuba (Anglican) has been busy working to make the Bible available in the language of Basoga. The first publication of this translation, the Gospel of Mark, came out in 1996 as a trial edition. The entire New Testament appeared in 1999. It was received with great rejoicing and much celebration and was reprinted in 2004. Another reprint of the NT with Psalms was reissued in 2011.

For many Basoga, the availability of the NT, even though only a part of the complete Bible, was an affirmation that God speaks Lusoga and understands Lusoga. God could now be addressed directly by means of Lusoga. The people understood that Lusoga was as good as Luganda and was just as holy and acceptable for Christian religious use. This fact, though simple, is revolutionary and has liberating consequences. It makes room for thought and reflection in the language of Scripture, and naturally leads to dialogue with indigenous thought forms, world views, concepts, and values. In short, it opens the door for inculturation and indigenization and a full and true incarnation of the word. Demand for this NT proved to be high. Work was then started on the Old Testament. The translators included Rev Father Frederick Kyuka (Roman Catholic) and Daudi Waidhuuba (Anglican) who worked from their base at the Iganga Catholic Center in eastern Uganda. The complete Lusoga Bible was published in 2014 in two editions, a Protestant and a Catholic edition. These had been keenly awaited and were very warmly received.

Lugwere and Lunyuli

Despite the success with the Lusoga translation work, the complex dialect situation in Busoga still remains an issue and may prove an obstacle to the full use and comprehension of the new Scriptures. Linguistic surveys have shown that some of these groupings of people speak dialects that are sufficiently different from one another to justify their own Scriptures. Examples are Lugwere and Lunyuli. At times these have been seen to be part of the Lusoga dialect cluster. Yet speakers of these dialects are recognized as linguistically distinct and are cited in official records as such.[14] They are therefore not represented or included in the ongoing Lusoga Bible translation project. Further, the Lusoga Scriptures already produced are not used in these communities that instead continue to use the Luganda Scriptures. SIL workers are currently busy working with churches in Bugwere and Bunyuli with a view to producing Scriptures in these languages. Many with an earnest desire to serve this population hope the SIL project will meet with success.

Translation into Lumasaaba

Lumasaaba is currently spoken by over half a million people in eastern Uganda. It is part of a continuum of over nineteen Bantu dialects spoken mainly in Kenya with varying degrees of mutual intelligibility under the cover term of "Luyia." Lumasaaba, however, is very closely related to the neighboring Lubukusu in Kenya, a member of the Luyia group. Lumasaaba itself has inter-dialectal problems and intelligibility problems among its northern, central, and southern speakers. This problem has inevitably spilled over into translation and orthography. Churches and linguists are still seeking an adequate solution. It is clear that whatever common orthography is established for the Bible will influence future use as well as establish a popular standard.

The first Scriptures into Lumasaaba were pioneered by the gifted linguist William A. Crabtree of CMS, who is credited with the development of the first Lumasaaba orthography. It should be recalled that this same Crabtree participated with Pilkington in the translation of the Luganda OT. He also did some work on the first Lusoga Scriptures. The first Lumasaaba Gospels were translated by Crabtree with the help of local helpers and published by BFBS in 1904. Later, Walter Holden revised Crabtree's Gospels and also translated the book of Acts. These were published in 1910 by BFBS, London. Use of the Luganda Bible hindered the progress of translation toward a complete NT or Bible. It was only in the 1970s that momentum was gathered for another effort at translating the complete NT. A translation committee headed, until his passing in 1973, by Bishop Akisoferi M. Wesonga (Anglican) and thereafter by Charles Shillimi, was assisted by a local review committee, and eventually saw to the completion of this task. The Gospel of Luke was published in 1972,

---

14. See, for example, Karibwije, *Uganda Districts Information Handbook: Expanded Edition, 2011-12*, pp. 107 and 122. Lugwere, as noted above, is part of Guthrie E10, while Lunyuli falls into the Masaba-Luyia Group, (i.e. Guthrie E30).

followed by the Gospel of Matthew in 1974, while the Gospels of Mark and John appeared in 1975. The complete Lumasaaba NT appeared in 1977. These were all published by the Bible Society of Uganda, Kampala. This translation had problems of orthography due to dialectal problems among the three major dialects, northern, central, and southern. A standard orthography based on the central and southern dialects was agreed upon and serves as the basis for the recent translation work. The 1977 NT has been revised and was reissued in 2011.

Work on the OT began in 2007. The translation team was composed of the Rev Milton Eridadi Shissa (Anglican) and the Rev Father Deogratias Syambi (Catholic). Progress was hampered by the dialectal and orthographical difficulties mentioned above. A committee of language experts and linguists who speak the language was charged with helping to iron out some of the challenges and weaknesses of the orthography and dialect chosen for the 1977 NT. The committee's work and advice proved to be helpful and fruitful. Their suggestions were incorporated in the revised 1977 NT issued in 2011, and in a complete Bible launched in December 2016.

The Luyia Dialects

Translation work among the Abaluyia of western Kenya was rather disjointed, as were the Abaluyia themselves. In fact, the term "Abaluyia" is a cover term for a cluster of several contiguous dialects found in western Kenya and parts of eastern Uganda. Linguist P. A. N. Itebete suggests that the term and its cognates first came into existence in June 1935 as a cover term for all the groups in western Kenya now commonly called by that name.[15] It was brought into popular vogue in the 1930s and 1940s in order to galvanize these groups into political solidarity, forging a new and singular ethnic identity, as was happening elsewhere in Kenya. Similar cases around the same period include the creation of the Kalenjin group in the Rift Valley region, the Meru group in central Kenya, and the Mijikenda group at the coast. A parallel in the 1970s and even in the 1990s was the unsuccessful attempt to forge the Gikuyu, Embu, Meru Association (GEMA) bringing together the Agikuyu, Embu, and Meru communities.

In those pioneer missionary days, the cover term "Abaluyia" did not as yet exist as the name of an ethnic group. What existed was a chain or continuum of mutually intelligible dialects, starting with Lubukusu and Tachoni in the

---

15. Itebete, "Language Standardization," 103.

extreme north, continuing to Lunyole and Lulogooli in the extreme south, and ending with Lusamia in the extreme west. Table 6.1 below represents the groupings of Luyia as Itebete understands them.

Table 6.1. Luyia dialect clusters according to Itebete

Region of Kenya	Dialects Spoken
Northern	i. Babukusu ii. Batachoni (those speaking Lubukusu)
Central	i. Bawanga, Bamarama, Batsotso, Bashisa, Bamarachi ii. Basamia, Bakhayo, Banyala (Lake) iii. Banyala (North), Bakabras, Batachoni (those speaking Lukabras) iv. Banyole
Eastern	Bisukha, Bidakho, Batiriki
Southern	Balogoli

Historian John Osogo in *A History of the Baluyia* includes the Abasonga in the Kenyan Luyia cluster as neighbors of Abanyala and Abasamia of Busia.[16]

In her 1980 PhD dissertation for the University of Texas, focusing on the Luyia dialects, Rachel Angogo Kanyoro divides the Luyia into six groups, what she calls "a possible practical grouping for literary purposes,"[17] demonstrated in table 6.2 below.

Table 6.2 Luyia dialect groupings according to Kanyoro

Region of Kenya	Dialect groupings
Northern	1. Bukusu
	2. Saamia, Nyala (Kakamega), Nyala (Busia), Khayo and Marachi
Central	3. Wanga, Marama, Tsotso, Kisa and Kabras
	4. Nyole and Tachoni
Southern	5. Idakho, Isukha and Tiriki
	6. Logooli

16. Osogo, *History of the Baluyia*, 14. See also Were, *History of the Abaluyia*.

17. Angogo, *Unity in Diversity*, 80.

Kanyoro's classification and Itebete's classification were carefully considered but are not being followed in the current translation work of the Bible Society of Kenya. It should be noted, for example, the Tachoni and Nyole are not as close in terms of mutual intelligibility as Kanyoro suggests. These two dialects are at two extremes of the Luyia continuum with the Tachoni at the extreme north and the Nyole at the extreme south. Moreover, while the Lunyole Bible has already been translated and published (2001), there is no evidence of its use or demand by the Tachoni. Likewise, it is unlikely that the Nyala-Kakamega would accept a Lusamia Bible. The Nyala-Busia are however more likely to be more at home with a Lusamia Bible. There is now, however, ongoing work by the BTL to produce a Tachoni Bible. A first Gospel in this language is already in print. There is also ongoing work to produce a Lunyala-Kakamega Bible under the auspices of BSK. There is also an ongoing translation of the Kabras Bible under the auspices of the BTL, however they have not followed the expectations of the Itebete or Kanyoro classifications.

The Lulogooli Bible

The nineteen or so Luyia dialects cannot be served by the same shared literature written in any one of the dialects or by an artificial union language created to maximize communication among them. The history of Bible translation among the Abaluyia attests to this observation. Kanyoro's study cited above was essentially intended to prove this point. Although some of her conclusions may be debated, her general thesis is convincing.

The Friends Mission to Kenya was the first Christian mission among the Abalogoli, that is, the speakers of Lulogooli. The Friends immediately concluded that without learning the local language and having the Scriptures translated into this language, progress would be slow and uncertain. The Gospel of Mark in Lulogooli was the first Scripture portion in any of the Luyia dialects. It was the work of one of the first missionaries in the Luyia world, Emory J. Rees, who was assisted by Joel Litu, a mother-tongue speaker. It was published privately in 1911 in Marion, Indiana, USA. A revised edition of this was later published by the American Bible Society in 1914. This was followed by the Gospels and Acts printed privately by the Friends African Industrial Mission Press, Maragoli, Kenya, in 1917 and reprinted in revised form by the ABS in 1921. The rest of the NT appeared between 1921 and 1928,[18] printed locally

---

18. First John also appeared in 1921; 1 and 2 Corinthians in 1922; Galatians–2 Thessalonians in 1923; Romans in 1925; 1 Timothy–2 Peter and 2 John–Revelation in 1928.

in five parts by the FAIM Press, Maragoli, due to the limited capacity of the press. But in 1929 this NT was issued in a single volume by the ABS although it was dated 1928.

Soon after the translation of the NT, Jefferson W. Ford of the Friends Mission to Kenya took over responsibility for the translation of the OT. He was assisted by Joel Litu, Helen K. Ford, and James Songore. Ford based his translation on the English Revised Version (1885), but he also consulted the Authorized (King James) Version (1611) and the two Swahili versions of the time, namely, the Zanzibar and Mombasa versions. The book of Daniel appeared in 1927 together with the NT book of Revelation, a rather interesting combination reflecting a strong interest in apocalypticism. Genesis appeared in 1930; Exodus, Ruth, Esther, Joel, and Jonah in 1932; Psalms in 1934; Leviticus in 1935; Numbers in 1937; and Proverbs in 1939. All these were initially published locally at the FAIM Press, Maragoli. The ABS report on this translation is as follows, "In 1938 the manuscript of most of the Old Testament in Luragoli was received in New York. Fortunately, the translator of the Lulogooli New Testament was now living in Illinois. The manuscript of the Old Testament was entrusted to him for final correction before publication." That there were some problems is clear from the following:

> As Mr. Rees is now retired and running a truck farm, he has not had much time to devote to this work without hurting his business, which is his livelihood. The American Friends Board of Mission has sent him $100 but would like the Society to make him a grant of $150 to enable Mr. Rees to hire help to free him to work on the text[19].

The ABS committee responsible consequently voted for Mr Rees to be granted this amount "if it can be found in the budget."[20]

There were, however, still some delays in finalizing the complete OT in Lulogooli. Among the causes was an attempt to develop both a union Luyia orthography and a union translation. The ABS report notes:

> It was feared that an early publication of the Luragoli Old Testament could prejudice the development of a union orthography . . . Then again, there were problems which were not linguistic. It seemed impossible to secure cooperation between missions in the area. Mr. Ludwig of the Church of God distrusted the Ragoli, and

---

19. American Bible Society, Unpublished Historical Essays, No. 16, VI-E, 112.
20. American Bible Society, Unpublished Historical Essays, No. 16, VI-E, 112.

> desired an independent Old Testament in Nyore . . . and Mr. Rees
> found the translation by Mr. Ford unsatisfactory in many places,
> requiring considerable revision.[21]

The ABS Versions Committee, on 3 June 1941, agreed "to defer publication of the Ragoli OT pending further information on the linguistic situation."[22] In the end, the orthographical changes recommended to clear the way for a union Luyia orthography and translation were rejected by the Executive Committee of the American Friends Board of Missions, who requested the ABS to publish the OT without the changes requested. "The Friends missionaries on the field reportedly felt that the only way a union language can develop in the field is slowly through the experience of the Africans themselves through intermarriage and travel."[23] Because of these delays, the OT together with a slightly revised edition of the NT published in 1929 were completed and published by ABS in 1951. Mr Ford had died on 16 December 1949, before completing the proofreading of the NT. This task was completed by Mrs Ford and other FAIM missionaries on furlough from Kenya.

A new common-language Lulogooli translation was started in 1987. The old existing translation was felt to be too literal, inaccurate in a number of places, unnatural in style, and written in an unsatisfactory orthography. The new translation has made minor orthographical changes and is mostly a meaning-based translation of the common-language variety. The entire team of translators are mother-tongue speakers of Lulogooli, and has included Peter Asava (Church of the Holy Spirit), Ernest Mugunda (Friends), and Wycliff Ganira (Pentecostal Assemblies of God). The common-language NT was published by BSK and launched at the Kidundu Friends Church in Vihiga in April 1997. Christians in the area received the text very positively, and all copies of this new NT were sold out. A reprint was put on hold to allow for the entire Bible, which was eventually released at a dedication and launching service held at the Mbale Stadium in Maragoli on 4 July 2009. It was well received with a number of key church leaders in attendance.

---

21. American Bible Society, Unpublished Historical Essays, No. 16, VI-E, 112.

22. American Bible Society, Unpublished Historical Essays, No. 16, VI-E, 112.

23. American Bible Society, Unpublished Historical Essays, No. 16, VI-E, 113.

The Lunyole Scriptures

Translation work in the neighboring Luyia dialect of Lunyole was carried out by the Church of God Mission based at the Kima mission station that was established in 1905 as the South Africa Compound and Interior Mission. This translation was mainly the responsibility of Gertrude B. Kramer assisted by Daniel Asiachi and other mother-tongue speakers. According to the ABS report:[24]

> In 1912 in agreement between the CMS, the American Friends, the Interior Branch of the South Africa Compound Mission (Kramer's Mission), the Friends began translating in the Ragoli, the CMS in Oluhanga and the Interior Mission in the Nyore. From a study of Mr. Rees's Ragoli Mark and Archdeacon Chadwick's Matthew, it seemed evident that the languages though related were not mutually intelligible.

At a conference held in February 1922 attended by the Venerable Archdeacon Walter Edwin Owen (CMS), W. J. W. Roome (BFBS), Emory J. Rees (FAIM), Jefferson W. Ford (FAIM), H. C. Kramer and Gertrude Kramer (Church of God African Mission), and A. J. Leech (CMS) "the conference agreed that the adoption of one selected dialect from the area would be a more hopeful proposition than to attempt to construct a union dialect, and decided to meet again in a month's time."[25] Interestingly, in his letter to Dr R. Kilgour of BFBS, W. J. W. Roome reported that "the Bunyore language conference that seemed hopeful at one stage has at last proved fruitless." He quoted Archdeacon Owen, who had written:

> Ref the Bunyole language conference. It was a hopeless stalemate. Rees would not budge an inch, and to our chagrin Mrs. Kramer has received a consignment of St. John's Gospel in Lunyole from America, and announced her decision to go on and complete the New Testament in Lunyole, so interested were the Banyole she said, in having books in their own dialect. We talked to a standstill. Dr. Jesse Jones urged the view that we ought to drop the project of unity on language for the sake of larger unity on educational and other mission matters . . . Can we make Swahili effective?[26]

---

24. See American Bible Society, *Unpublished Historical Essays*, Part V, Section E, 17.

25. BFBS EA languages files (ESC minute 9.4.24), 4.

26. BFBS EA languages files (letter dated April 9, 1922).

Later, Mrs Kramer wrote to the ABS reporting about a language conference held in Kima in 1924 under the auspices of the Phelps-Stokes Commission at which the renowned Ghanaian Dr Kwegyir Aggrey was present and had pleaded "that since so many people spoke these different dialects they should each be given the New Testament in their own dialect, which pleased most of the missionaries."[27] Mrs Kramer embarked on her translation in Lunyole. The first portions to be completed were Philippians, James, and 1 John, all printed in 1915 by Gospel Trumpet Company in Anderson, Indiana, USA. These were followed by the Gospel of John in 1923; 1 Corinthians–Colossians in 1926; and Mark, Acts, and 1 Thessalonians–Jude in 1927. By the time of Mrs Kramer's retirement in 1929, she had completed her translation of the NT in Lunyole even though much of it remained to be published. For example, Matthew, Luke, Acts, Romans, Hebrews, and Revelation were still in draft form needing some polishing. She was, however, able to correct and revise her translation of the whole NT using the various check-lists supplied by ABS. This was completed in 1934 and the galleys were sent to Kima mission for correction, being returned by Mr J. S. Ludwig of the African Mission of the Church of God to ABS a year later for printing. The ABS Translation Committee noted, "Mr. Ludwig and his assistants have given consideration to the many questions raised, and have sought to bring as much uniformity as possible into the text. Their corrections have been so carefully made that it will probably not be necessary to send further proofs to Africa."[28]

The NT was published in July 1936 in an edition of 3,000 copies. A reprint in 1941 of 4,000 copies incorporated some sixty corrections contributed by Miss Mabel A. Baker of the Church of God Mission. By September 1948, Miss Baker had completed her translation of the Psalms into Lunyole. This translation of the Psalms together with a corrected edition of the Kramer NT text was published by ABS in 1953. No other OT book was attempted in Lunyole during this period.

The efforts to translate the Lunyole Scriptures were mostly the work of the Church of God Mission for use by all the Luyia communities among whom they worked. The Anglicans did not support or use the Church of God Scriptures even in Bunyore itself among their Lunyole speakers. This is surprising considering that there were as many Anglicans in Bunyore as there were Church of God members.

---

27. ABS files. See the Unpublished Historical Essays, Part V, Section E, 115.

28. In minute V of their meeting of November 15, 1935. See the Unpublished Historical Essays, Part V, Section E, 115.

A project to produce a new translation of the complete Bible in Lunyole was started in 1985. This was intended to be of the common-language, dynamic equivalence translation variety. In contrast to the first translation, which was entirely a Church of God endeavor, this time nearly all the churches active in Bunyore partnered in the effort. There was still a marked dominance by the Church of God, as was to be expected. The team appointed to do this work was composed entirely of mother-tongue speakers: Jairo Asila, Obed Ochwanyi, Joseph Osotsi, and Raba Okola (all of the Church of God), and Ezekiel Jako (Pentecostal). Ezekiel Jako and Raba Okola carried the bulk of the work after the untimely deaths of Jairo Asila and Joseph Osotsi and the resignation of Obed Ochwanyi. The common-language NT was published and launched at the Church of God Cathedral in Kima, Bunyole, in February 1997. The entire Bible in Lunyole was completed a few years later and launched at the same Church of God Cathedral in Kima, in 2001. With the discontinued publication of Appleby's Union Oluluyia Bible, this is now the only Bible available to the Banyole for use in worship and private reading.

The Luhanga New Testament

The Luhanga translation was the first CMS translation in any of the Luyia dialects. Archdeacon W. Chadwick, who had arrived in Butere in 1912, had his first translation of the Gospel of Matthew published by BFBS, London, in 1914. Chadwick had mainly targeted the Lumarama- and Luwanga-speaking communities. His colleague, Canon A. J. Leech, who took over responsibility for this translation after the death of Chadwick in Kilwa Tanzania on 2 October 1917, decided to create a union translation for the Lumarama, Luwanga, Lukisa, and Lutsotso dialects, but with some lexical items taken from Lusamia, Lukhayo, and Lumarachi. This union translation was given the name *Luhanga* which is different from Luwanga, a real language. The Gospel of Luke in this union translation was published in 1916 while revised versions of Matthew and Luke as well as the Gospel of John appeared in 1922. The entire NT in Luhanga appeared in 1939.

This is the version that was used in all Luyia-speaking CMS churches. For example, CMS churches in Lunyole-speaking areas continued to use the Luhanga version of the NT, even some years after the availability of a Lunyole version of the NT.[29] The problem may have been that the Lunyole translation

---

29. Author's note: I can remember using the Luhanga version of the New Testament in our CMS village churches in Bunyole in the 1950s and 1960s despite the availability of the Kramer and Baker Lunyole NT and Psalms.

had been done by the Church of God Mission rather than by CMS. The Luhanga version was used as far north as the Bukusu, indeed by all Anglicans in Luyialand. Similarly, the Logooli translation was used in all areas of the Friends Missions as far north as among the Babukusu. The difficulty with which the Luhanga version was understood in many areas, and the new solidarity and ethnic consciousness being developed by the new Luyia identity that began in the late 1930s, contributed to the demand for a new union Luyia which all Luyia speakers could understand.

The Oluluyia Union Version

Already in 1920 the following had been noted in a BFBS report prepared for that year:

> It seems a waste of time and money to produce independent versions in three such closely related dialects (Hanga, Ragoli and Nyole), and several missionaries agree with Mr. Roome in thinking that an effort should now be made to prepare a Union Version for the Bantu Kavirondo, or to select one dialect which may serve the whole area. To promote this object Mr. Roome is trying to arrange a Conference, to meet in Maseno in Jan. 1921.[30]

Table 6.3. Dialect groups served by the Union Luluyia Translation

Region of Kenya	Dialects spoken
North	Lubukusu and Lutachoni
South	Lulogooli
East	Lwisukha, Lwidakho, Lutiriki, Lukabras, Lunyala (Kakamega)
West	Lusamia, Lukhayo, Lunyala (Busia), Lumarachi, Lusonga
Central	Luwanga, Lumarama, Lukisa, Lutsotso
South-Central	Lunyole

With the availability of the NT in Luhanga in 1939, it was decided in 1942 by a committee chaired by Archdeacon Walter Edwin Owen of CMS to prepare a translation of the OT in a union Luluyia designed to serve almost all the Luyia groups (See table 6.3 above). Lugishu and Lunyoli of eastern Uganda were not included. Linguistically, they qualify as members of this cluster of

---

30. BFBS ESC Minute Cards, vol. 5 (see 5.1.21), 28.

closely related dialects. Their exclusion from the newly created ethnic entity called Abaluyia was simply the result of political factors; they were located in Uganda as a result of historical colonial accident while all those groups that were included happened to be in Kenya. The committee met some obstacles in getting support for this project, but after relentless efforts by all concerned, and after some years, it was finally agreed to prepare a Luluyia Union Version. Eventually all the missions – including Anglican, Roman Catholic, and Church of God – gave their support. The main exception was the Friends Mission, who felt that Lulogooli speakers could not be served by this proposed version, but they also had in view their own translation of the whole Bible, which was quickly moving toward completion.

The task of translating the Union Luluyia Bible fell to Deaconess Leonora Lee Appleby of the Australian CMS who had her translation office at Butere in western Kenya. She set out to create a new standard orthography of Luluyia, and to use the grammar of the central dialects – Luwanga, Lumarama, Lukisa, and Lutsotso – but to be free to use vocabulary from all dialect areas. Her linguistic work resulted in a prescriptive grammar of the Union Luluyia that was published in 1947. This also spelled out the rules of the new orthography to be used. Appleby headed the translation team for the new Union Luluyia Bible. She was assisted by Mr Jared Isalu and by a committee consisting of representatives from the various Luyia dialect communities.

The committee meeting held in Kisumu on 25–25 July 1951, included Mrs Donohew, Miss Baker, Messrs Jairo Asila and Daniel Wako (Church of God); Miss Hendrickson and Mr D. Undusu, (PAEA); the Rev E. Kellum and Mr J. Adede (FAIM); Messrs F. Ainsworth and Y. Awori (AAC); with Jared Isalu and Leonora Appleby serving as translators.[31] The translation sought to be inclusive of all Luluyia dialects and the translation team made various visits to different dialect areas. For example, on 7 July 1952, Miss Appleby reported that

> [S]he and Mr. Isalu the assistant translator had visited various language centers: Bujumba (Marachi), Nambobota (Samia), Nambale (Bukhayo) and Butonge (Bukusu). The aim of the journey was to investigate the distribution of various words that had arisen in the course of the translation. Special mention should be made of the Bugishu Language Committee appointed by Jonathan Barasa and their Secretary Mr. John Musundi.[32]

---

31. BFBS ESC Minute Cards, vol. 5 (see 1951), 10.

32. BFBS ESC Minute Cards, vol. 5 (see 1952), 9.

Bishop Festo Olang was also a member of this committee. Others who later joined the committee included the Rev D. Udali, Hudson Andembe, and Y. Namanda, all from the Anglican Church.

The first portion of this translation to be published was the book of Genesis in 1954. It was followed by Proverbs in 1956; Isaiah in 1957; and 1 and 2 Samuel, as well as the Gospel of Luke, in 1960. The Gospel of John appeared in 1962. The NT with Psalms was published in 1968 by the Bible Society in East Africa. The complete Bible was published in 1975 by the Bible Society of Kenya. This new Bible was officially received and dedicated by the Luyia churches and people at a ceremony held at the Kima Church of God station near Maseno, on 18 January 1976.

Ever since its publication this Bible has been poorly received except in the area of the central dialects, Marama, Wanga, Kisa, and Tsotso. In other areas, intelligibility has been generally low. It is said that the translator of this Bible, Miss Leonora Appleby, was the foremost expert and best speaker of union Luluyia, since she is known to have corrected even elderly people universally accepted as competent speakers and masters of their own languages. To better serve the neglected Luyia dialect groups – Lubukusu, Lulogooli, Lunyole, and "central Luluyia," comprising Lumarama, Lukisa, Luwanga, and Lutsotso – four new common-language versions have been translated and published.

The Lubukusu Bible

Lubukusu is mainly spoken in the Bungoma district of Western Kenya on the southern slopes of Mount Elgon. The Babukusu Christians have for a long time not had access to a good translation of the Scriptures. The Lulogooli and the Luluyia Bibles were widely used in the Friends and Anglican churches respectively. It is the need for their own Scriptures which led to the request for their own translation of the Scriptures. Dr Kees de Blois, a missionary to the Reformed Church of East Africa who later became a UBS translation consultant, played a very active part in assisting the churches in Bukusu area to get started. De Blois was very knowledgeable in this language, having written his PhD dissertation on its phonology. He worked very closely with local church leaders, including the Rev Joshua Biboko of the Reformed Church and Jonathan Barasa, a retired colonial chief of the Friends church. The project was formally launched on 20 April 1976, at a meeting held at the Friends Church in Bungoma.

The first translation team for this project included three mother-tongue speakers, Jonathan Barasa (Friends), William Welime (Reformed), and John

Masete (Baptist). Their labors resulted in the first NT in Lubukusu which was published by the Bible Society of Kenya and launched at the Reformed Church in Bungoma in March 1993. Copies of this NT are no longer in print. It was, however, revised in readiness for inclusion in the new complete Bible in Lubukusu. Work on the OT started as soon as the NT was completed. A new team of translators consisting of Robert S. Wafula and the Rev Elivered Nasambu Masika (both Anglican) were involved in the OT work, but both left to pursue biblical and theological studies overseas. Among those who took over from the above and saw the OT to completion were Father Daniel Wekesa (Roman Catholic), Father Christopher Wekesa (Roman Catholic), Bernard Musima (Roman Catholic), John Machuka (Pentecostal), and Francis Walusaka (Pentecostal). The Catholic Church made a significant contribution to the work, making it fully interconfessional. This is to be appreciated, given that Bungoma is one of the strongholds of the Catholic Church in Kenya. The first Catholic Cardinal in Kenya, Cardinal Otunga, was a member of this community and spoke Lubukusu. Similarly, the Archbishop of the Anglican Church of Kenya at the time of dedicating the project, the Most Rev Eliud Wabukhala, also hails from this area, where he previously served as the bishop of the Bungoma Diocese of the Anglican Church of Kenya. Work on the entire Bible was completed in early 2007. An imprimatur for the complete Bible with Deuterocanonical books was granted by the Bishop Okombo, who is also responsible for the Catholic Biblical Apostolate in Kenya. The dedication and launch of this first Bible in the Lubukusu tongue took place at the Masinde Muliro Stadium in Bungoma, Kenya on 22 May 2010. The Anglican Archbishop was the guest speaker at this crowded event, characterized by excitement, joy, song, and dance.

New Translation in the Central Luyia Dialects of Luwanga, Lumarama, Lushisa and Lutsotso

The failure of Appleby's Oluluyia Union Bible experiment led to the fragmentation of the Luyia communities in terms of Bible use. One of the people who were most unhappy about this development was the late Anglican Archbishop Festo Olang, who had been one of the staunchest supporters of this experiment. One of the reasons for his support had certainly been rooted in his desire for the elusive Luyia unity. After numerous studies, the Bible Society of Kenya decided to support translation in the Lubukusu, Lulogooli, Lunyole, Lwisukha-Lwitakho-Lutirichi, and the Luwanga-Lumarama-Lushisa-Lutsotso dialects. Meanwhile, the Bible Society of Uganda took up support for the Lusamia translation. Participation of Kenyan Basamia Christians has been enlisted. This makes the Lusamia translation a joint project of the Bible Societies of Kenya and Uganda and serves the needs of speakers on both sides of the border.

Work on the Luwanga-Lumarama-Lushisa-Lutsotso translation was fully representative of these four Luyia dialects. It was further, interconfessional in nature with all the churches working in this area, including the Roman Catholic Church. The location of the translation office was in the compound of the Anglican cathedral at Mumias in Wanga. Mumias is a historically important center in western Kenya. It was the seat of the only Luyia centralized kingdom, that of Nabongo Mumia. This Luyia kingdom was certainly influenced by that of Buganda to the west.

The first European to arrive at Mumia's court, then called Kwa-Shiundu after Mumia's father, was the intrepid Joseph Thomson, who came there on 2 December 1883. The second European to arrive at Mumia's court was the man appointed in England to head and pioneer expansion of the Anglican Church in Eastern Africa, Bishop James Hannington. He arrived in 1885. On the orders of the young Kabaka Mwanga, the king of Buganda, the bishop was subsequently murdered at Lubwa in Busoga on his way to Buganda. Local Baganda prophets had prophesied that from the east of the country would come foreign and strange invaders who would conquer this illustrious kingdom. Arab traders at Kabaka's court had supported these prophecies and pointed out that the incoming Europeans had evil plans against his kingdom. They encouraged the Kabaka to do everything to prevent this from happening. Thus when news of Bishop Hannington's arrival from the east was received at Kabaka's court, he took necessary precautions. One of the Bishop's companions who escaped was Otsyalo, a young Wanga boy from Kwa-Shiundu, that is, from Mumia's court. Otsyalo is said to have lived in the area of the murder for the next four years "until one day in March 1890, he was ordered to leave Busoga and take the remains of Bishop Hannington back to Kwa-Shiundu."[33] The remains of Bishop Hannington were laid to rest not far from the present translation office of the Luwanga-Lumarama-Lushisa-Lutsotso project, and the grave site is maintained to this day by the Anglican Church.

The new translation is expected to serve the four Luyia dialects that share a very high level of mutual intelligibility. The main idea of this translation is to use the grammar and syntax of Lumarama and Lushisa as a base since these two are so close that it is not easy for speakers from the other neighboring

---

33. Osogo, *Nabongo Mumia*, 11–12.

dialects to distinguish between them. The vocabulary of this new central Luluyia translation, although essentially derived from these two core dialects, was expected to also be drawn freely from the other two dialects, Luwanga and Lutsotso. The intention here was to avoid another artificial translation, such as A. J. Leech's Luhanga translation which had also targeted these same four dialects. This project was started in 1993 with Naftali Tsuma (Kisa – Church of God) and Matthias Khalumi (Tsotso – Roman Catholic) as the main translators. Among those who have been members of the translation team have been the following: John Masinde (Wanga – Anglican), Peter Muniafu Osore (Marama – Anglican), Angeline Were (Marama – Anglican), Gladys Hopilo (Marama – Anglican) and Peter Afubwa (Tsotso – Roman Catholic). The NT was completed and launched at a ceremony held at Ebutsinga School in Butsotso, Kakamega, on 7 May 2005. The full Bible was completed in 2016. It is hoped that the complete Bible in this new "union dialect" will be a workable successor to Appleby's Oluluyia Union Bible experiment, which everyone agrees was unable to serve all the dialects usually referred to as Luyia.

Lusamia/Lugwe Translation

Lusamia/Lugwe is spoken in both sides of the Kenya and Uganda border. For many years Basamia speakers have been using the Union Oluluyia Bible. On the Uganda side, however, the tendency has been to use the Luganda Bible. This dual usage has led to divergence in the use of certain religious and liturgical terms and expressions with Luganda-influenced Lusamia in Uganda, and Swahili-influenced (as well as Union Oluluyia-influenced Lusamia usage) in Kenya. Translation work started officially in 2001 and is supported by both Roman Catholic and Protestant churches. The translators for this project were the Rev Father Augustine Odaro (Roman Catholic) and the Rev George Okambo (Anglican); they worked from the Catholic Center in Lumina on the shores of Lake Victoria. Their Kenyan counterparts included Julius Ojanji and Philip Egesa. The reviewers were selected from all the churches active in the area. The work was supported by the Bible Society of Uganda, the Bible Society of Kenya, and the Uganda and Kenya based Lusamia-speaking churches. The aim was to create a translation that would be accepted on both sides of the national border and would reflect Lusamia usage as common to all speakers. The translators completed work on the NT and the OT translation. The complete NT was dedicated and launched in Busia, Uganda, in 2011. Justice Ogolla, a renowned Musamia and a Principal Judge of the Uganda High Court, was the guest of honor at the launching ceremony. The complete

Lusamia-Lugwe Bible was completed and launched in 2019 by the Bible Societies of Kenya and Uganda. Interestingly some Bagwere in Uganda have not been happy with this Union Lusamia-Lugwe version and continue to agitate for their own Bible in Lugwere, which they claim is different from Lusamia.

The Lukakamega-Lutiriki Translation

In response to widespread interest and persistent requests from the churches in the Luyia dialect areas of Isukha, Idakho, and Tiriki,[34] the Bible Society of Kenya finally agreed to support a new project to translate the Bible into these dialects. These dialects are closely related and have a very high degree of mutual intelligibility. The two dialects, Lwisukha and Lwitakho, commonly called Lukakamega, are almost indistinguishable by speakers of other Luyia dialects. Lutiriki (also called Lutirichi) is closer to these two and shares an acceptable level of mutual intelligibility. Isukha and Idakho are all in the neighborhood of the local town of Kakamega, which is also the county headquarters. Their common name, Lukakamega, derives from the county. Lutirichi, on the other hand, has Kaimosi as its main urban center. Kaimosi has been a major educational and religious center, not just for the Tiriki, but for the entire western region and the entire country. The Friends Africa Mission made Kaimosi their center from the onset of their mission activities in 1902 and set up numerous institutions in this Tiriki town. Among these are the East African Yearly Meeting of Friends, the Friends Bible College, the Friends Teachers College, and the Friends Girls Secondary School. Yet the Tiriki are not exclusively Friends. The Salvation Church has a strong foothold here, as does the Pentecostal Church. The Catholic Church, the Reformed Church of East Africa, as also the African Independent Churches, have been in this area from the beginning of the Christian enterprise.

What is true of Tiriki is equally true of the whole area of Idakho and Isukha. The early Christian missions did not distinguish among these areas. It is interesting to note that although the Protestant denomination popularly known as the Quakers or the Religious Society Friends, which originated in England sometime in the seventeenth century and, due to persecution, spread to America and later to East Africa, now has the majority of its adherents in this corner of western Kenya. The Quakers who first arrived in western Kenya

---

34. It is interesting that of the Luyia dialects only these three, together with Logooli, belong to E40, which includes languages spoken to the south of the Kenyan Nyanza Gulf, such as Gusii, Kuria, Suba, and Zanaki.

were said to be "quaking" and "manifesting the gifts of the Spirit." Later some of there number were accused by others to have abandoned the true way of the Spirit.

Some adherents broke off to form a splinter church. The African Church of the Holy Spirit (ACHS) formed in 1927 was the result of this split and is thus one of the first so-called African Independent churches in East Africa, so well documented by David Barrett in his classic book, *Schism and Renewal*. The church has its Kenyan headquarters at Lugala, not far away from the translation office of the Lukakamega-Lutiriki translation project. One of the translators in the Lukakamega-Lutiriki project, John Akhura Muhambi, was installed in 2008 as the High Priest of the ACHS. He continued his work as translator of the Bible in this project. He was committed to work until the Bible in this language saw light of day, even though, as he asserted, "From the time I have been alive on this earth, I have never come across a job which is very challenging like Bible translation." He considers the new first Bible as being very critical to the mission of his church among his people – the Betakho, Besukha, and Batiriki. In a recent interview he stated, "This Bible is very essential to our people for them to understand clearly and naturally the Word of God in their own language."[35]

Figure 6.1. Bishop John Akhura Muhambi and parents. Bishop Muhambi was a translator on the Lwisukha-Lwitakho-Lutirichi project. Photo © Aloo Osotsi Mojola

The various Bibles from the neighboring dialects are used with varying degrees of comprehension, for example, the Lulogooli Bible, the old Oluluyia Bible, and to a certain extent, the Lunyole Bible. On the whole, however,

---

35. For an edited version of this interview, see appendix A.

African independent churches are weak in their use of the Bible and where the Bible is used, the interpretation is heavily influenced by traditional practices, rituals, and beliefs. It is hoped that the participation of people like High Priest John Muhambi Akhura in Bible translation will have a positive impact on the growth and re-alignment of his church with sound biblical doctrine and practice. The fact that High Priest Akhura is one of the first in his church to benefit from theological and biblical training should encourage members of his church and others to follow his example. Akhura was trained at the Limuru St Paul's Theological College famous for training leading Anglican, Methodist, and Presbyterian Church ministers and pastors. In his own words, "People from this area are eagerly waiting for the whole complete Bible and I hope and believe this will be a starting point for scholars from this region to start developing this beautiful language linguistically."[36]

Figure 6.2. The Rev Philip Muhambi, reading the Lukakamega-Lutirichi New Testament in 2005. Photo © Aloo Osotsi Mojola

The Lwisukha-Lwitakho-Lutiriki translation project started off as an interconfessional project bringing together not just the Protestant and Catholic churches but also the African instituted or African independent churches in the area. It was launched in June 1997 and included a translation team consisting of Evans Lijoodi (Lutirichi – Reformed Church), Protas Luganu (Lwisukha –

---

36. See appendix A.

Roman Catholic), and John Muhambi Akhura (Lwitakho – African Church of the Holy Spirit). Protas Lugano left the project and was replaced by Father Benedict Muchenditsi (Lwisukha – Roman Catholic). The Lwitakho and Lwisukha dialects provide the grammatical basis of the translation. The vocabulary and all lexical issues are equally drawn from all three dialect areas to ensure widespread acceptability and intelligibility. The idea is to use vocabulary that is the most widely understood and used throughout the area. The project had its offices initially at the Lirhanda Friends Centre, but was later relocated to an office in the compound of the main Catholic Church in Mukumu. The NT has been completed and was launched at Kaimosi Teachers College in Kaimosi, Tiriki, on 2 April 2005. Work on the OT was completed sometime in 2009. Thus the translation of this Bible took exactly twelve years from the beginning of the NT work to the completion of OT work. The published Bible reached the language area for dedication and launching sometime in April 2014.

7

The People of the White Mountain

Chagga and their neighbors, Meru, Pare, Dabida, Sagalla, and Taveta

The Chagga – the People of the White Mountain

The Chagga people of Tanzania live "in the shadow of one of Earth's most magnificent structures."[1] The structure being none other than the great Kilimanjaro, the highest mountain in Africa.[2] When Johannes Rebmann, the pioneer European missionary and explorer, sent reports back to his home that he had witnessed, on 10 November 1848, a snow-capped mountain in East Africa almost on the equator, his report was dismissed by William Desborough Cooley in an 1852 issue of the *Athenaeum*, a European scientific publication, as a "most delightful mental recognition, only not supported by the evidence of his senses."[3] Cooley had concluded, "I deny altogether the existence of snow on Mount Kilimanjaro. It rests entirely on the testimony of Mr. Rebmann . . . And he ascertained it, not with his eyes, but by inference and the visions of his imagination."[4] So easily was the testimony of Rebmann dismissed in the name of science!

The Chagga have a special affection and attraction to Kibo, the higher of the two peaks of Mount Kilimanjaro. Charles Dundas, an anthropologist and senior colonial official in the former Tanganyika Territory noted that to the Chagga people Kibo is,

---

1. Dundas, *Kilimanjaro*, 5.
2. Mount Kilimanjaro is 19,342 feet (5,895 meters) high.
3. Dundas, *Kilimanjaro*, 11.
4. Reader, *Kilimanjaro*, 9.

> The embodiment of all that is beautiful, eternal and strengthening . . . the Chagga man has a great love of his country and is more possessed of a sense of nationality than any other Africans known to me. In truth one cannot but expect this, for not only is the magnificence of the mountain such as must compel attachment, but as soon as the mountain dwellers leave it, life becomes intolerable for them. Kibo is the great landmark and focus of the Chagga people.[5]

Moreover,

> [t]he dead are buried with face towards Kibo; the side of the village facing Kibo is the honourable side, where the house master is buried . . . He who comes from above – by which is meant from the direction of Kibo – must give greeting first because he comes from the fortune bringing side. Filial affection requires that a son should face Kibo whilst washing, lest it be said that he thrusts his father into the plain. When meeting a superior on the road it is customary to pass on the lower side of the road, giving him the more honourable side towards Kibo.[6]

Due to the shortage of land and the very high population density in Chaggaland, many Chagga have migrated as businessmen of all kinds, artisans and technicians, professionals, and migrant labor to all parts of Tanzania. Indeed, the Chagga are to be found in almost all the major cities of East Africa engaged in all manner of business and economic activities. It is sometimes said that the Chagga in diaspora have more or less taken over the role of the Indian *dukawallah*, that is "shopkeepers," in Tanzania and in most of the major towns of East Africa. Nonetheless, throughout Tanzania there is a common saying that a Chagga never forgets his origin in Kilimanjaro. Every year during Christmas, and other major feast days, long processions of crowded buses and other means of travel bring the sons and daughters of Kilimanjaro back to their native land in large numbers, carrying back to the land of their ancestors whatever gifts and riches fortune has granted them in their sojourning. Some jokingly refer

---

5. Dundas, *Kilimanjaro*, 39.

6. Dundas, 39.

to it as a Chagga's annual hajj. The Jew's "next year in Jerusalem" is somewhat like the Chagga's "this year in Kilimanjaro."[7]

The peoples who now form the Chagga ethnic group are of diverse origins and speak a cluster of closely related dialects forming a linguistic continuum. As Dundas wrote:

> There is no common name for the inhabitants of this mountain for they originate from various tribes, and even from different races. And having settled in communities whose limits were in the main naturally demarcated by the deep river valleys of the mountain, they know themselves only as the people of this and that ridge, as for instance Wamashame, Wamoshi and so forth.[8]

Writing some years earlier, Johannes Raum, the German Lutheran missionary and Bible translator, had observed:

> The name Wachagga is of Swahili origin. Kilimanjaro people are called Wakirima by their neighbors, which means people from the mountain (kirima – mountain). Chaggaland is called Waha by the Kae and Pare people. But these names are not to be found among the Chagga themselves. When referring to themselves the Chagga people call themselves – *Wandu wa mnden* – which means "the people who live in the [banana] plantations."[9]

He adds, "In a strict sense, one cannot speak of a Chagga people."[10]

The people to whom this term Chagga is now given are said to have migrated to the mountain from the neighboring territories and communities. The roots of the Chagga are to be traced back to the Kamba, Dabida, Taveta, Maasai, Pare, Shambaa, Kahe, Meru, Dorobo, Pokomo, Gikuyu, among other ethnic groups. Raum puts it as follows:

> There is a tradition concerning the settlement of the land which has resulted in the present division of the area: some of the migrants came from the plains while others came from the forest areas. So when the last group of settlers arrived, they found people who were already living there on the mountain. The first people

---

7. The late Anza A. Lema, a former leader of the Lutheran World Federation in Geneva, himself a Chagga, has written a stimulating study on the Chagga, "Chagga Religion and Missionary Christianity on Kilimanjaro: The Initial Phase, 1893–1916," (1999), 39–62.

8. Dundas, *Kilimanjaro*, 32. See also Dundas, *Asili na Habari za Wachagga*.

9. Raum, *Versuch einer Grammatik*, 1. Translations given here are the author's.

10. Raum, 1.

who lived on the mountain were probably of pure Bantu stock, close relatives of the Wateita, Wakamba, Washambaa and Wapare people. Together with these groups they belong to the more recent Bantu people who moved in from the North. For example, the inhabitants of the Mbokomu area, west of Moshi, migrated from the Tana river. The original migrants of Bantu background have intermarried with people of Hamitic as well as Semitic origin. We can thus conclude as follows: The Chagga people do not constitute ethnic homogeneity (unity). The ethnic foundation of this people is Bantu, although there is a strong element of Hamitic (Maasai) as well as Semitic (Wakilindi) origin. The pure Bantu man has a short and heavy stature (strong prognathism and protruding lips) and is of dark color.[11]

Raum's claim of a Semitic element among the Chagga is far-fetched. It derives most likely from prevailing classifications of African peoples and languages at the time. The Maasai are now classified as Nilotic and not Hamitic. What Raum calls Wakilindi refers to the Mbugu or Maa of Lushoto in the Usambara Mountains whose language is currently classified as Cushitic, and about whom he writes, "The ruling clans, i.e., the Wakilindi from the Usambara mountains, are originally of Semitic origin, and are a result of the Arab invasion. Hence the tall, light skinned human type of these clans."[12]

Their language is not Semitic, however, and has never been classified as such. It is clearly Cushitic. Cushitic is the name for what scholars previously called Hamitic, a discredited term because of its association with the racist Hamitic myth.[13] Raum was operating under the influence of the myth whereby all evidence of "civilization" or "development" in sub-Saharan Africa was associated with lighter-skinned intruders from the "civilized" north.

The diversity of the Chagga is easily noticeable both in their distinct physical features and in their differing dialects. An example of this diversity can be seen in the word for "water" in the various Chagga localities – *muha* in Shira (or Kibongoto), *murra* in Machame, *mudha* in Kibosho, *mringa* in

---

11. Raum, 2–3.

12. Raum, 3.

13. In the context of African history, the "Hamitic myth" was the idea or belief that any developments of a higher order or that seemed complex were products of light skinned peoples who migrated and settled in those parts of Africa. This belief has been discredited and is no longer accepted by African and Africanist historians.

Moshi and Marangu, and *mota* in Ngasseni.[14] See table 7.1 for an overview of the key dialect groups of Chaggaland.[15]

Table 7.1. Chagga dialects by locality

Where Spoken	Dialects
Hai or western Chaggaland	Siha, Masama, Machame, Kibosho
Central Chaggaland	Uru, Old Moshi, Vunjo, Kilema Vunjo, Marangu, Mwika, Kahe
Rombo or eastern Chaggaland	Kimashati, Usseri

Yet in this diversity, a unity can be discerned, for example, in the mutual intelligibility of many close dialects in the Chagga cluster. It is also seen in their shared cultural and religious practices. Both Raum and Dundas presuppose this common cultural and religious unity of the Chagga. Thus, for example, Dundas writes, "That there are marked variations of custom and dialect is not surprising, seeing that the tribe has no common origin; rather one may be astonished that, in general, common principles of custom and a more or less common language have been evolved."[16]

Hence an outsider can hardly tell the difference between a Chagga from Machame, Kibosho, Moshi, Kirua, Kilema, Marangu, Mamba, Mkuu, or Usseri. Even the Chagga themselves have this problem, unless they use the dialects they speak as a basis for making distinctions. This is compounded by the fact that Swahili is very widely used by the Chagga, even when speaking among themselves. Some younger-generation urban Chagga no longer speak any of the Chagga dialects.

It is not surprising then that some Chagga openly question the usefulness of having a translation of the Bible in any of their dialects. They fear that their language is threatened with extinction in the not-too-distant future, and that it is progressively and rapidly being replaced by Swahili, the main lingua franca in the area. This fear does not, however, have firm linguistic justification. The main ground for the involvement of the local Chagga churches and the Bible Society of Tanzania in the three Bible translation projects, to translate the

---

14. Dundas, *Kilimanjaro*, 48. It is of interest that the Chagga words for water differ significantly from the Proto-Bantu word for water, which is closer to the Swahili *maji*, Lunyole-luyia *amatsi*, Nyakyusa *amiisi*, Gikuyu *mai*, Chichewa *madzi*, Luganda *mazzi*, Kinyarwanda *amazi*, Ruhaya *amaizi*, and Lingala *mai*.

15. Polome and Hill, eds., *Language in Tanzania*, 15. See also Philippson and Montlahuc, "Kilimanjaro Bantu (E60 and E74)," 475–500.

16. Dundas, *Kilimanjaro*, 48.

entire Bible into the Machame, Mochi, and Vunjo dialects, was to encourage the use of the vernacular language in Christian worship and Bible reading. It is expected that the three Bibles will lead to a deeper understanding and practice of the Christian faith.

The British and the Germans Arrive in the Kilimanjaro Region

CMS missionaries were the first missionaries to come to the Kilimanjaro area. Johannes Rebmann visited this area from 27 April to 11 June 1848, and again in April 1849, thus gaining the honor of being the first white person to see this great mountain. Rebmann, however, found local Chief Mankinga of Machame too demanding and uncooperative, and his second visit apparently ended up being his last visit to Kilimanjaro. He is commemorated today by a monument that has been erected at a place called Kalali where he is said to have pitched his tent during his Machame visit of April 1849.

Some years later, in 1871, Charles New, a Methodist missionary from Ribe near Mombasa, followed Rebmann's footsteps to Kilimanjaro and gained the honor of being the first European to climb Mount Kilimanjaro. New held long conversations with Chief Mandara of Moshi. Later, in 1878, Chief Mandara wrote to New as follows, "Now I want to ask you a question. If you want children to teach, we shall give them to you. And I shall follow you to learn with all my people, if you really want. Meanwhile, send me a Book . . . mind you don't forget it."[17]

The next white man to visit Chief Mandara after Charles New's visit was the naturalist Sir Harry Johnston early in 1884. Johnston attempted to negotiate a treaty with Chief Mandara, which apparently created certain misunderstandings and difficulties when Bishop Hannington visited. James Hannington had been consecrated the first Anglican bishop of Eastern Equatorial Africa on 24 June 1884, and six months later he arrived at Freretown near Mombasa. Later in 1885 he passed through Old Moshi and held lengthy negotiations with Chief Mandara. This led to the purchase of some land on which the first CMS mission house in Old Moshi was erected. A. R. Steggall, one of the first missionaries here, mastered both Kimochi-Chagga and Kitaveta. He reduced them to writing and translated the Gospel of Matthew into Kimochi-Chagga, the first Scripture in any of the Chagga dialects. It was published in 1892 by BFBS.

The same year saw the publication of the Gospel of Mark into Kitaveta, spoken on both sides of the Kenya and Tanganyika border, southeast of Mount

---

17. Church Missionary Society, *CMS Missions in East Africa*, 15.

Kilimanjaro, a neighboring language to the Chagga dialects. John's Gospel in Kitaveta was also published the same year. These had been translated by Yohana Nene Mdighirri a local mother tongue speaker of Kitaveta and revised by missionary A. R. Steggall.

Difficulties with the Germans, whose flag had been hoisted in German East Africa in February 1890, led to the withdrawal of the CMS missionaries to Taveta in Kenya in the autumn of 1892. Before closing his mission, Steggall wrote on 21 May 1892, as follows, "Sorrowfully I express my conviction that our Mission cannot be carried on in German territory. I feel that the attack about to be made, is made really because Moshi is the seat of an English mission."[18]

Exactly a month later, on 22 June 1892, a German invasion led by Lt. Von Bulow and Lt. Wulfram and consisting of a team of sixty Nubians and five Swahili was badly defeated by seven hundred Chagga warriors. The two Germans were killed in the fighting. Steggall had no alternative but to run to the British sphere of influence or territory where they exercised control. Here in the security of Pax Britannica, he was able to proceed with his translation of the Kitaveta New Testament. The table below (table 7.2) shows the different books that were published by various publishers beginning in 1892, when the Gospels of Mark and John came out, until the entire NT was published in 1906 by BFBS.

Table 7.2. Timeline of the Kitaveta New Testament

Year	Scripture Publication	Published By
1892	Mark, John	Church MS, Mochi
1894	1,2 & 3 John	CMS, Taveta
1896	Matthew, Luke	BFBS, London
1897	Exodus	CMS, Taveta
1900	Acts	BFBS, London
1900	James, 1 & 2 Peter, Jude	CMS, Taveta
1903	Mark revision	BFBS, London
1905	Psalms	SPCK, London
1906	Romans – Revelation = New Testament completion	BFBS, London

---

18. See the Archival Records in the Bibliography, BFBS files.

At their departure to British Kenya in 1892, CMS handed over its Kilimanjaro work to a German Lutheran missionary group, the Leipzig Mission. The first five missionaries of the Leipzig Missionary Society arrived in Chaggaland in August 1893. These were Emil Müller, Gerhard Althaus, Robert Fassmann, Albin Boehme, and Theodore Passler. They came through Mombasa as had Krapf, Rebmann, New, Hannington, and Steggall. These German missionaries tended to be academically oriented with an emphasis on a culturally and socially relevant gospel which focused on education and nurture. They disdained the evangelistic and individualistic approach thought to have been characteristic of the Moravians, the CMS, and the London Missionary Society (LMS).

The Leipzig Mission started work at the former CMS station in Old Moshi, but soon moved to Nkwarungo in Machame where Chief Shangali warmly received them. It is said that the Old Moshi people burned down the station to protest the transfer to Nkwarungo. The Leipzig Mission expanded rather quickly. In 1894 Passler and Althaus established work in Mamba, while Fassnab settled in Old Moshi. Jessen and Bleicken began work in Shira in 1901, Stamberg in Mwika in 1906, Gutmann in Masama in 1906, Raum in Uswaa in 1907, and Arno Everth in Marangu in 1912.

It was missionary linguist and anthropologist Bruno Gutmann who pioneered the translation of the Scriptures into the local language. Gutmann arrived on 9 August 1902, together with his missionary colleagues of the Leipzig Mission, Hermann Fokken and Dr Plötze, the first medical missionary in this area. Initially assigned to work at Mamba, Gutmann later moved to Machame, Masama, and finally settled at the Old Moshi station with which his life is very closely identified. The people of Old Moshi revere him and hold him in the highest regard. It is said that Gutmann prepared his own burial tomb at the church he built at Kidia, Old Moshi, but was never buried there as the problems of post-World War II Germany made it difficult for him to return to Kidia. He was finally laid to rest in his native country on 17 December 1966. As an ethnologist and cultural anthropologist, he delved deeply into the life, values, and traditions of the Chagga people and mastered the local language as well as its idioms, proverbs, folktales, riddles, and thought patterns. Through his numerous writings and publications he introduced the Chagga, and their society, to the scholarly world. Out of respect, he was given the nickname *Wasahuye o Wachaka*, "Grandfather of the Wachagga," because early on he espoused a contextualized and culturally relevant gospel. It is indeed this perspective that dominated and informed his mission theology.

However, Gutmann will be best remembered for his translation of the New Testament into Kimochi-Chagga, an accomplishment to which his fellow missionary colleague of the Leipzig Mission, Robert Fassmann, also contributed. Although their names are not usually mentioned in the missionary annals, a number of local native Kimochi speakers participated in this achievement, among them the Rev Ndesaryo Kitange, the father of Seth Kitange, former General Secretary of the Evangelical Lutheran Church in Tanzania, Northern Diocese; Filipo Njau, father of artist Elimo Njau of today's well-known Paa ya Paa Gallery of African Art in Nairobi; and the Rev Imanuel Mkony. This was not, of course, the first attempt to translate the Holy Scriptures into the local language. A. R. Steggall of CMS had already translated and published the Gospel of Matthew in Kimochi by 1892. This German team had the Gospel of John translated into Kimochi and published in 1905 by the Saxon Bible Society at Leipzig. The Epistle to the Romans was published in 1908 at the Lutheran Mission Press, Moshi, and the Gospel of Mark in 1911 by the Saxon Bible Society, Leipzig. The entire NT was published in 1939 by the Württemberg Bible Society at Stuttgart as *Mkundana Mhya fu mbike ni Mndumi odu Yesu Kristo Mokira wandu wose kui mdedye fo kidi kya Uchaga* (The New Agreement established by our Lord Jesus Christ Savior of all people in the language of the Chagga seat).[19]

More than fifty years later, the church in the Kimochi-speaking area of the mountain took up the challenge to revise Gutmann's NT. Chosen for this task were Pastor Sebastian Mrema of Sango Parish and Pastor Boanerge Moshi of Mbokomu Parish, assisted by a team of reviewers. The work of revising the NT started in 1993; it was completed and finalized in 1996, and printed in 1997. The dedication and celebration of this revision was held in Old Moshi in June 1999. Work on the translation of the OT into Kimochi followed in earnest, but was slowed down and eventually halted after the passing on of Pastor Mrema and the transfer of Pastor Moshi to Kae. The project was, however, revived in 2008 after consultations between the Bible Society General Secretary and the leadership of the Lutheran church in the area. Three translators were seconded to the project and commenced work in 2008; the three are all pastors from the Lutheran church northern diocese. Rev Gilbert Mekameka Olotu and the Rev Elishonguo Ndisanjo Macha, who were new to the project, and the Rev Boarnege Moshi was reappointed to the project.

---

19. The word "seat" in the translation is literal. It expresses the idea of homeland, ancestral land, dwelling space, etc.

Work on the Kimachame-Chagga dialect began much later than the Kimochi project. Pastor Johannes Raum of the Leipzig Mission only succeeded in having the four Gospels translated and published by BFBS in 1932. An edition with a revised orthography was published in 1950 by BFBS. Among native Kimachame speakers who worked on the Gospels were the Rev Solomon K. Nkya, the Rev Timoteo B. Mushi, the Rev Alfayo Salema, and the Rev Alelio N. Mushi. It took some time, however, before efforts could be directed toward producing a complete Bible, which had been the original desire. In 1991, a team of three Machame pastors – Kalebi Shoo, Barnabas Munuo, and Stefano Ntindi – assisted by a team of reviewers, began translating the New Testament. They thoroughly revised Raum's four Gospels and completed translating the entire NT. This was dedicated and launched at a ceremony held at the Hosiana Lutheran Parish, Machame, in September 2000. Work on the Kimachame OT is now complete. The office base remained at the Nkwarungo Lutheran Parish where the first Leipzig missionaries set up their station on 5 October 1893. The complete Bible is projected for dedication and launching sometime in 2020.

Figure 7.1. The Revs Kalebi Shoo and Barnabas Munuo who, along with Stefano Ntindi, translated the Bible into Kimachame Chagga. Photo © Aloo Osotsi Mojola

The third Chagga dialect to have a translation of the Holy Scriptures is the Kivunjo-Chagga dialect. This translation is currently in progress, having started only in 1991. The principal translators were Pastor John Mlay and Pastor Godson Maanga, assisted by a team of reviewers. The complete NT was published by the Bible Society of Tanzania and was dedicated and launched at a joyful celebration held in Marangu on 6 November 1999. Work on the OT resulted in good progress and was completed at the end of 2012. It is expected to be dedicated and launched sometime in 2020.

Figure 7.2. The Revs Godson Maanga and John Mlay, principal translators of the Kivunjo-Chagga Bible. Photo © Aloo Osotsi Mojola

A Tragic and Sad Beginning in Meru and the Kirwa New Testament

Kirwa, a language which is popularly known as Kimeru, belongs to the same continuum as the Chagga dialects. In fact, the level of mutual intelligibility between Kirwa and Kimachame is much higher than that between Kimachame and Kirombo on the extreme east of the geographic continuum. The degree of cultural and linguistic closeness between the Wachagga and Wameru is quite high.[20]

The first missionaries to Meruland were Ewald Ovir and Karl Segebrock sent by the Leipzig Mission. They arrived in 1895 in Chaggaland, but on 20 October 1896, on a tour of Meruland, they were murdered at Akeri, where they had been permitted to pitch their tents by the local Meru Chief Matunda. They were suspected of harboring evil intentions and of being a danger to the community. This act probably dampened the interest of the Leipzig Mission in immediately sending in a replacement team to evangelize and Christianize the Meru people. Nearly a hundred years later, echoes of these deaths were

---

20. It is to be noted that the Meru of Tanzania are quite distinct from those of Kenya.

replayed as the new Meru Lutheran Diocese was being formed from the mother Northern Diocese which they had shared with the Chagga Christians. The creation of this diocese in the 1990s under very difficult circumstances led to intra-communal and intra-ethnic violence, deaths, and other deplorable acts.[21]

Edward Ittameier, another missionary of the Leipzig Mission, the man who translated the Kirwa New Testament, arrived at Nkoaranga in 1909. Although he did not spend his whole time among the Meru, his interest in their language never waned. His translation of the whole NT into Kimeru was completed by 1939, but due to the wartime difficulties of that period, it did not get printed at that time. The whole text was eventually finalized by reviewers and published in 1964 by the Leipzig Mission at Erlangen Germany. Among local mother tongue speakers of Kirwa, the names of the Rev Zakaria Urio and the Rev Ndelilio Kaaya are very closely associated with this translation. There is no doubt that without such local collaborators, missionary translators such as Ittameier would have been less than successful. There has been an evident lack of interest from the church leaders in the area in further work, and so attempts to revise the Kimeru NT and to complete the whole Bible have not yet borne fruit. The claim here, as elsewhere, has been that the Swahili Scriptures are sufficient for the needs of the church.

The Leipzig Mission and the Seventh-Day Adventist Mission in Upare and the Chasu Translation

As a result of the difficulties in Meru, the Leipzig Mission turned its attention toward expansion among the Pare. The term "Pare" actually refers to two communities: the people of South Pare, who are also called Vasu and who speak a language called Chasu, and the people of North Pare, who are also called Wagweno and who speak Kigweno. Both these communities occupy hills of North Pare and of South Pare as well as their respective slopes and the plains

---

21. The story of this tragic event is well narrated by the late Professor Omari in his article, "The Making of an Independent Church: The Case of the African Missionary Evangelical Church among the Meru of Tanzania," 196–212. The Meru Lutheran church had been under the hegemony of Chagga bishops for many years. The Meru wanted their own diocese under their own Meru bishop. This was not easily granted. The violent political intrigues leading to a forced breakup of the old diocese into two dioceses, one for the Chagga and another for the Meru, led to much bloodshed and loss of life. It is tragic that the first Lutheran missionaries in Meru were victims of violence. The new Lutheran Meru diocese also tragically started under circumstances of bloodshed.

below.[22] The missionaries of the Lutheran Leipzig Mission established a number of mission centers in Upare. For example, Hans Fuchs moved to Shigatini in 1904, Paul Rother started work at Gonja in 1904, Albertini at Mbaga in 1908, while Fochen and Stamberg opened a mission center at Vudee in 1909. From these centers the teachings and practices of the Christian faith penetrated the surrounding villages. Lutheranism expanded in this area and was consolidated to its present form as the predominant Protestant denomination in the area.

German Seventh-Day Adventist (SDAM) missionaries also started work among the Wapare around this same period. The first to arrive were W. Ehlers and A. C. Enns, who landed at Dar es Salaam in December 1903 and thereafter moved to Upare. Their first mission station was at Suji which they christened Friedenstal. From Friedenstal they expanded to Kihurio and Vunta. Realizing the importance of using the vernacular language, they set themselves to learning and mastering it. This naturally led to the translation of the Holy Scriptures into Chasu. The responsibility for this work fell to Ernst Kotz and A. C. Enns who immediately set themselves to this task with the help of mother-tongue speakers of Chasu. The Gospel of Matthew was translated and published in 1910.

Around the same time, a Mr Dannholz of the Leipzig Mission also translated the Gospel of John into Chasu. Dannholz and his colleagues apparently sought the co-operation of the SDAM team in preparing a common translation, but this proved futile, because, as he noted, "they found it impossible owing to the [Adventists'] ignorance of Hebrew and Greek and their refusal to consider even a knowledge of Greek necessary for translation work."[23] The SDAM translation was therefore carried out with the help of mother tongue interpreters who also knew either Swahili or Shambala, the Swahili and Shambala versions being the source text for the Chasu translation. The Leipzig Mission could not accept this approach and so went their separate way. The Gospel of John translated by Herr Dannholz was published by the Saxony Bible Society in Leipzig in 1912.

The SDAM team completed the NT in Chasu and assured BFBS that "it contained nothing of a sectarian nature. It can be used by any Christian Mission."[24] This was published in 1922 by BFBS. The SDAM team later translated and issued OT Bible stories in Chasu.

---

22. Kimambo, "The Pare," 16–36. It is interesting that Gweno (North Pare) belongs together with Meru, Kahe, and the Chagga dialects to Guthrie's E60. Asu (South Pare) belongs with Taveta, Shambala, and Bondei to Guthrie's G20.

23. See the Archival Records in the Bibliography, BFBS files.

24. See the Archival Records in the Bibliography, BFBS files.

The Leipzig Mission team's approach proved to be too slow. Consequently, they did not realize their dream of translating the complete NT into Chasu for use by the Lutherans. However, the decision to revise the SDAM NT using some kind of "union" Chasu gave the opportunity for producing a NT acceptable to all the churches in the area. It was, moreover, claimed that "this first NT was not very acceptable as it appears to be in a very local dialect."[25] The revision team was chaired by a Lutheran, Pastor Andreas Msechu of Kifula, whom the Rev Bedford of the Bible Society in Nairobi described as "a tremendous character," "one of the best kind of dictators," "the man who has kept the Christian Church together in the Pare mountains through all the vicissitudes of war."[26] On Pastor Msechu's revision team were Nathanaeli Mgaya (Usangi), Martin Shafuri (also Usangi), Danieli Kimbwereza (Mbaga), and Abraham Itunda (Bombo). They were supervised by the Rev Paul Edstrom of the Lutheran Mission. As there were no SDA representatives on the team, the Lutherans approached the SDAM, who not only agreed to a revision of the NT, but also appointed evangelist Yohana Kilonzo to represent them on the Revision Committee.

The plan for this union Chasu NT was to employ all dialects spoken by the Chasu people, with the Mbaga dialect of South Pare providing the point of departure. The Gospel of Mark was published in 1960 by BFBS. Pastor Schomerus, a retired German missionary from the area, returned to assist in the final checking of the NT manuscript. He was supported financially by the United Evangelical Lutheran Church of Germany. The final NT in Chasu was published in 1967 by the Bible Society in East Africa.

This NT is now out of print and no longer being used. For a long time the church leaders in the language area did not express any interest in its reprint or revision. Some church leaders have expressed interest in a revision of the NT and translation of the OT, but this has not gained wide support and the Bible Society is not yet convinced enough of the viability of the project to commit any funds to the idea. The feeling at the moment is that the Swahili Scriptures are adequate to meet the need.

The Scriptures into Kisagalla

Just across the international border on the Kenyan side are to be found the Kenyan neighbors of the Pare and Chagga in the hilly Taita-Taveta area. This

---

25. BFBS files and reports at the Cambridge University Library, UK
26. BFBS files and reports at the Cambridge University Library, UK

area is inhabited by the Dabida on the Taita Hills, the Sagalla on the Sagalla Hills, and the Taveta in the plains, who speak Kidabida, Kisagalla, and Kitaveta respectively.[27] Since Kenya was under British control, the first missionaries to work in this area were those of the CMS. Whereas the Tanganyika side of the border was German territory, the Kenyan side was clearly British territory. J. Alfred Wray of the CMS successfully established in the Sagalla hills in 1883 the first inland station in Kenya among the Sagalla people. Nearly ten years later he had succeeded in having the Gospel of Mark translated into Kisagalla. This was published in 1892 by BFBS; the four Gospels followed in 1912, also published by BFBS. This was the extent of his translation work. The Rev W. J. Mowll of BFBS reported that there was not need for more translation as the people understood both Dabida and Swahili.[28]

It is of interest that the complete Bible in Mombasa Swahili appeared a short while after the publication of the Kisagalla Gospels. It is possible that CMS missionaries in this part of East Africa felt that the Mombasa Swahili Bible could adequately meet the Scripture needs of the people here. It took more than a hundred years after the first book had been published in Kisagalla for the entire New Testament to appear in this language. This NT was translated by a retired Sagalla school teacher, Matthew Gae of the Anglican Church, in collaboration with participants from his local church in partnership with the Bible Society of Kenya and the UBS fellowship. It was published in 1994 and was launched at a very joyful ceremony held in the Sagalla area in January 1995.

Kidawida (Taita) Scriptures

Although translation work in Kitaveta[29] began in 1892, translation in the bigger and more dominant Kidawida (or Dawida) language did not see the light of day until the turn of the last century. The work was spearheaded by CMS missionary R. A. Maynard. With the help of mother-tongue speakers he embarked on a translation of Mark's Gospel which was published in 1904. It took quite a number of years to complete the entire New Testament that eventually appeared in 1922. Soon after its publication it was felt that the NT needed to be revised, a project that took ten years to complete. Maynard and

---

27. Dabida and Sagalla are part of Guthrie's E70, which also includes the Kenyan coastal Bantu languages, i.e., the Mijikenda and the Pokomo. Taveta is part of Guthrie's G20 and is more closely related to Chasu (South Pare), Shambaa, and Bondei.

28. BFBS EA language correspondence files (see ESC Mins. Feb. 9, 1921), 31.

29. The name of the language to its own speakers is "Kidawida"; outsiders refer to it as "Kitaita."

his team of mother-tongue speakers – Stephen Kilelu, Jonathan Kituri, and Jeremia Kibinda – were responsible for this work. The revised Kidawida NT was published by BFBS in 1932. Not much additional translation work took place at the coast after this, perhaps again because of the widespread availability of the complete Mombasa Swahili Bible at the time.

There were renewed efforts at completing the work started by the pioneer missionary translators in the early 1980s when the local church in cooperation with the Bible Society of Kenya launched a new common-language translation project. Work on a new Kidawida New Testament began in earnest in 1982. The NT appeared eight years later in 1990 to a warm reception. The translators of the NT, Evan Mwavua and Daniel Kana Senge, both of them Anglican, were encouraged to continue with work on the Old Testament. With work on the OT virtually complete, the two translators finally rested from their labors, Daniel Kana Senge in 1993 and Evan Mwavua in 1995. This tragedy was compounded in 1996 when the keyboarder to the project, Deborah Mwawuda, also passed away later. Others who had been active on this project who also passed away before the publication of the translation, were the first chairman of the translation committee, Canon Allan Madoka, and reviewers Eliud Mwambi, Alexander Kubo, and Ekiakim Warungu. Their labor in the Lord was not in vain! On 24 October 1998, the first Kidawida Bible was launched with great celebration and joy on the hills of Taita. The ceremonies were held at Wundanyi. It was a day many Kidawida-speaking Christians had been waiting for. The Bible is now in full use on the hills of Taita. It is used, however, side-by-side with the Swahili Bible, from which it is facing stiff competition.

8

The Move to Central Tanganyika

Gogo, Kagulu, Nyaturu, Nilamba, Langi, and Sandawe

Beginnings of Church Missionary Society Work among the Wakaguru and the Wagogo

The CMS was slow in starting serious work in Tanganyika (as Tanzania was once known), considering that already in the 1840s Johann Krapf and Johannes Rebmann had explored its northern territories, visiting both Chief Kimweri of the Usambara Mountains and Chief Mankinga of the Chagga of Mount Kilimanjaro. While in Usambara, Krapf reported that he often retired to the hills, behind a large tree away from the village, "to pray that the Redeemer's Kingdom might soon be established in these heights, and that His songs might be heard on these lofty hills, and in full reliance on the promises of God I took possession of the pagan land for the militant Church of Christ."[1] Within a few years Krapf's prayers were to be answered literally.

Mpwapwa, known locally as Mhamvwa, is situated in central Tanganyika among the Wagogo people and holds the credit of being the starting point of CMS work in this part of Africa. It is a beautiful and peaceful place surrounded by picturesque hills and beautiful baobab trees. The town originated as a place for resting on the ancient caravan route to Uganda and to the Congo through Ujiji.

If Zanzibar was the cosmopolis or the commercial and political center of East Africa during the last half of the nineteenth century, the town of Bagamoyo was the main gateway into the interior, as well as the main exit point for the thousands of slaves savagely uprooted from their motherland. The route from Zanzibar into the interior of Africa passed through Bagamoyo, Mpwapwa or

---

1. Christian Missionary Society, *CMS Missions*, 27.

175

Dodoma, Tabora, Ujiji on the shores of Lake Tanganyika, and thereafter into the Congo, or north to Buganda. This route constituted the main slave trade highway as well as the main route for the export of ivory, various animal products, and minerals. The present central railway line from Dar es Salaam roughly follows this old caravan route. The building of the railway by the Germans started in 1905 at Dar es Salaam, reaching Morogoro in 1907, Tabora in 1912, and Kigoma in Rwanda in 1914.

This well-trodden route saw many of the early European travelers and missionaries, including Captain John Speke; Richard Burton and James Grant; Henry Morton Stanley; Roger Price; and Alexander M. Mackay; and it was along this route that the body of David Livingstone was transported by his trusted companions Chuma and Susi. Alexander M. Mackay and his retinue on their way to open up Uganda for Christ are reported to have set up camp at Mpwapwa along this famous highway. The recommendation to CMS of the suitability of Mpwapwa as a base for their missionary work in the interior was made by Captain Cameron. It was left to a George James Clark, an engineer and architect from northwest England, to pioneer the opening up of the Mpwapwa mission station in 1876. His life, however, was short, as he died in this same year. A more permanent occupation of Mpwapwa by CMS was in due time secured by the arrival in 1878 of Dr Edward John Baxter and Mr Joseph Thomas Last. The latter moved to Mamboya in January 1880 to establish a station there among the Wakaguru. Last's wife, Annie Jackson, who arrived at Mamboya in November of that year, is said to have been "the first English woman to penetrate the interior of Eastern Equatorial Africa."[2] She died there on 10 March 1883. Mrs Last's courage and example were an inspiration to many female missionaries who were to follow. Indeed, the first unmarried women missionaries to move into an up-country station first settled at Mamboya the very next year, in 1894.[3]

After Mpwapwa and Mamboya, CMS set up another mission center at Kisokwe in 1883. Berega, Nyangala, and Itumba in Ukaguru were occupied in 1900, as was Mvumi in Ugogo. Buigiri (Ibwijili) received a resident missionary in 1901, while Kongwa became the chief mission center in the district in 1904. These CMS stations around Mpwapwa that originated as stepping stones on the old caravan route to Uganda were set up by Bishop William George Peel as a remote extension of the Mombasa Anglican diocese. On 1 January 1898, CMS divided the Diocese of Eastern Equatorial Africa into the Dioceses of

---

2. Church Missionary Society, *CMS Missions*, 27.

3. Church Missionary Society, 29.

Uganda and of Mombasa. Bishop Tucker stayed on as the bishop of the Uganda Diocese, which stretched to Western Kenya and the Mwanza area then under the Germans. Bishop Peel was consecrated bishop of Mombasa on 29 June 1899, while Bishop G. A. Chambers of Australia was consecrated bishop of the new Diocese of Central Tanganyika in 1927 at the time of the new subdivision from the mother Mombasa diocese. The move to Dodoma took place in 1927, the year the Australian branch of CMS took over responsibility for the Tanganyika mission from the Diocese of Mombasa.

This remote outpost of the Mombasa diocese turned out to be the cradle of CMS work, and of Anglicanism of the "low church" variety, in Tanganyika. The "high church" variety of Anglicanism, on the other hand, was the preferred official form of worship in Zanzibar, the coastal areas of Tanganyika, and most of southern Tanganyika. The original mother Diocese of Central Tanganyika over time has given birth to all the other low church Anglican dioceses of Tanganyika, including those of Morogoro, Tabora, Victoria Nyanza, Kilimanjaro, and western Tanganyika. Dodoma, the main urban center of central Tanganyika, has become the political capital of Tanzania.[4] The Gogo,[5] in whose territory the city of Dodoma is situated, constitute the majority of the population in Dodoma, and in the Mpwapwa and Manyoni districts of central Tanzania. They speak the Gogo[6] language and are predominantly an agro-pastoralist community. They keep cattle and grow millet, sorghum, and maize, and pumpkin among other food crops. While the Gogo are patrilineal, their Kagulu neighbors are matrilineal. The Gogo are well-known for their polyphonic and rhythmic music. Hukwe Ubi Zawose, a Tanzanian musician who died in 2003, and his family did much to make this music widely known throughout the world.[7]

Translation Work in Kaguru

It is interesting that the pioneer missionary translators did not make their first translation of the Scriptures into the Gogo language. Instead they started with

---

4. For an overview of the Catholic initiatives among the Gogo, see Maddox, "Church and Cigogo," 150–166.

5. For more detailed information on the Wagogo, see Mnyampala, *The Gogo*, and Rigby, *Cattle and Kinship*.

6. Gogo together with Chikagulu (North Sagara) belong to Guthrie's G10.

7. See Arnaud and Lecomte, *Musiques de toutes les Afriques*, 416–419.

Chikaguru,[8] the language spoken by the Kaguru, the Gogo people's eastern neighbors. It was Joseph Thomas Last and his colleague in Mamboya, Arthur North Wood, who were convinced of the importance of Kaguru, or the Kimegi language, for the communication of the Christian gospel. They soon mastered this language and started translating the Holy Scriptures.[9] This effort led to the first Scripture portion in any of the languages of Tanzania, excluding Swahili. The Gospel of Luke was published in 1885 and the Gospels of Matthew and John in 1894, all by BFBS. A shortened Prayer Book published in 1895 also included Scripture selections and readings for liturgical use. Historian Elizabeth Knox writes of Wood's work as follows:

> His translations into Kimegi (the Kaguru language) were now sufficient to cover worship, with Morning and Evening prayer, Baptism and Marriage services, and one hundred hymns. He had also three reading primers . . . The people were now able to participate in the services in their own language. The increased use of the vernacular made the services more meaningful. Previously, Wood had preached in Kikaguru, but the people's participation in worship had been largely confined to Swahili. With the primers in the vernacular, a great obstacle had been removed in learning to read, as pupils would not be confronted with two unknown items together.[10]

Arthur Wood was assisted by Asani Mugimbwa in his translation work. Knox notes:

> Asani Mugimbwa, who had accompanied Wood to Kisokwa during the Bushiri crisis, assisted with these translations and thereby gained some training for the work ahead. He would learn more quickly from translation than from lessons of a more general kind, as translation requires precise examination of the documents being translated. So his stay at Kisokwe was for Mugimbwa a short but intense Bible study course.[11]

It is unfortunate that these pioneering efforts to translate the Holy Scriptures into the Kaguru language did not culminate in a full Bible or even

---

8. Chikagulu/North Sagara, together with Gogo, is included in Guthrie's Bantu referential classification system, Group G10.

9. For information on Kaguru culture and customs, see Beidelman, *Moral Imagination*.

10. Knox, *Signal on the Mountain*, 129.

11. Knox, 130.

a complete New Testament. The Kaguru have had to use the Swahili Scriptures ever since those early days. It is only in recent times, a hundred years after these pioneer Gospels were produced, that the local Kaguru church leaders have expressed a renewed interest in making the complete Bible available in Kaguru. The Anglican and Roman Catholic Churches have taken the lead in this endeavor, with the support of the Bible Society of Tanzania and the Pioneer Bible Translators (PBT).[12] A Kaguru translation team composed of Frederick Chingwaba, Gresford Chitemo, Benjamin Mkuchu, and Michael Peter Nhonya has completed work on the NT. It was dedicated and launched on 8 May 2010, at Gairo, a key town in Ukaguru midway between Morogoro and Dodoma. The excited and joyful participants at the launch marched jubilantly around the town in celebration of this historic event, the first NT in Kikaguru. Unfortunately, Bishop Gresford Chitemo, one of NT's translators and key promoters, passed away in 2009 before he could see the early fruits of his labors. He was much missed by all who attended this memorable celebration. Work on the OT is currently underway and the complete Bible is expected in 2020.

Translation Work in Gogo

Henry Cole, together with John Edward Beverley and John Charles Price, felt called upon to work among the Gogo and to give them the Scriptures in their own language. This was a wise move, given the strategic location of the Gogo in the new emerging Anglican diocese during those pioneer years. Frank Frederick Bedford of the Bible Society in East Africa later observed that, "The Gogo are a very important tribe and the first ground-nut experiment[13] at Kongwa is in their area,"[14] although Archdeacon Oliver Timothy Cordell referred to them as "a non-progressive people engaged in cattle-rearing, wandering from place to place."[15] It is not surprising that translation work in

---

12. PBT, based in Dallas, Texas, has been involved in East Africa since the late 1990s. The organization was formed in 1976 with the purpose of translating Scripture for so-called "Bibleless" people. They also work in literacy and church planting. In 2007 they had up to 206 missionaries working in 43 languages around the world, mainly in East and West Africa, and also in Asia.

13. The British introduced commercial and big scale groundnut/peanut farms in the Gogo area. It was on an experimental basis. The experiment was not however very successful.

14. That is in Gogo territory or land. See Bedford, *Bible in East Africa*, 35, and also BFBS correspondence files: letter dated 19.12.1951.

15. See BFBS ESC Minute Cards – vol. 3.

Gogo[16] eventually overshadowed that in Kaguru. The Gogo are more numerous and their culture more dynamic. Moreover, their love of their language is widely known and evidenced through their popular and much-loved music. Cole, Beverley, Price, and their Gogo assistants completed the Gospel of Matthew and had it printed at the UMCA Mission Press in Zanzibar in 1886. Other books continued to be printed until the entire NT in Gogo appeared in 1899, published by BFBS.[17]

Henry Cole continued with the translation of the Old Testament but he was unable to complete it. His work was revised and continued by John Henry Briggs, Ernest William Doulton, and Thomas B. R. Westgate. This resulted in BFBS publishing Genesis in 1905, followed by Exodus and Numbers in 1910, and a revised edition of the NT in 1911. Doulton and his colleagues were badly affected by the deterioration of relations with the Germans in the period prior to World War I. They were imprisoned for a while at their respective mission stations, but they continued translating the OT during that time. However, this work was all in vain as all their draft manuscripts were destroyed when the Germans looted and burned their stations.

Consequently, the work of translating the Gogo Bible stalled for some years. It was later picked up by Oliver Timothy Cordell, assisted by Samweli Makanyaga, Mika Muloli, Pawulo Musoloka, and Filemoni Chidosa. Archdeacon Cordell's translation was "made with the help of a capable African who prepared the first drafts. These were worked over and typed out by Archdeacon Cordell himself and re-examined by two Africans."[18] This team saw the publication of 1 and 2 Samuel by BFBS in Sydney in 1952, and the complete Bible in 1962 by BFBS in London. This Bible included a revised NT of which the Gospels of Mark and Luke had appeared in 1960 as test editions.

The first Gogo translation of the Bible which was carried out over an eighty-year-period between 1878 and 1962 was of questionable quality. Since it was a more-or-less word-for-word translation, as well as one that was translated

---

16. A summary of the history of Bible translation in Gogo is given in the booklet prepared by the Bible Society of Tanzania at Dodoma in 2002 on the occasion of the launching of the new translation, "Historia Fupi ya Tafsiri ya Biblia kwa Lugha ya Gogo."

17. The Gospel of Luke was published in 1887 by the BFBS, London; John's Gospel was printed in 1889 by the CMS Press at Freretown in Kenya; a revised edition of the Gospel of Matthew appeared in 1891, Ruth and Jonah in 1893, while the Gospels and Acts appeared in 1897.

18. BFBS – ESC Minute Cards, vol. 3.

mostly by foreign speakers of the language, and done over such a long time span, there were naturally numerous shortcomings in the text. It is partly due to a general dissatisfaction with the translation – as well as to the fact that the Bible Societies encouraged the development of meaningful, natural, accurate, and common-language translation of the Bible in current idiom – that the late Bishop Yohana Madinda sought the Bible Society of Tanzania's help in initiating a new translation of the Bible in today's Gogo, to be translated by the Gogo themselves. His successor, Bishop Godfrey Mudimi Mhogolo, proved to be a strong supporter and promoter of this program of translating the Scriptures into the local vernacular.

The first local translator appointed to this task in 1983 was the late Canon Lungwa, who was at the time based in Mvumi. He passed away before much had been achieved and in 1984 the baton was passed to Canon Naphtali Petro Lusinde.

Canon Lusinde was fully convinced of the need for this translation and worked hard to involve all the churches and all the various areas of Ugogo in the effort. He was more than qualified to do this. He was a respected Gogo churchman and elder coming from a highly distinguished family. His grandfather was an influential traditional ruler and his own father had been one of the pioneer African lay evangelists in Ugogo. His younger brother Job Lusinde had distinguished himself in the government of President Julius Nyerere, in which he had served in various ministerial and ambassadorial positions, including service in the People's Republic of China. His cousin John Malecela had served as a vice-president to Julius Nyerere. The family was thus well-connected and through these relationships the translation had support in high places. His co-translator in the translation of the New Testament was John Lesangwa, a representative from the Roman Catholic Church. The Gospels of Luke and John were published together as a single portion in 1989 by the Bible Society of Tanzania. The NT was published in 1991, also by BST.

Canon Lusinde continued to labor on the translation, assisted at various stages by his colleagues on the translation team, the Rev Richard Mazengo, the Rev Yohana Chogolo, and the Rev Yohana Chisoma, as well as a very active committee of reviewers led by Canon Filemoni Chidosa, already mentioned in connection with the 1962 Bible. A number of OT portions were published by BST including Genesis in 1992, Exodus in 1994, and Psalms in 1995. The complete Bible in this new translation was completed and launched at a joyful ceremony held in Dodoma on 2 November 2002, at which the President of the Republic of Tanzania, His Excellency Ali Hassan Mwinyi, was in attendance, as well as other dignitaries, including government ministers and the Archbishop of the Anglican Church of Tanzania, John Ramadhan.

Figure 8.1. The Rev Canon Naphtali Petro Lusinde, member of Cigogo Bible translation team (1986–2002). Photo © Aloo Osotsi Mojola

When asked in 2007 by the author to reflect on his experiences, Canon Lusinde was asked why a new Gogo translation was needed at this time when Swahili is widely spoken and is used even in Gogo churches. His response was as follows:

> No, Kiswahili is not sufficient. There are many Gogo people, especially in the rural areas, who do not understand Kiswahili well or who cannot speak it well. In any case, it is important that a people use their own language given to them by God and that they enjoy and benefit from its use. Thirdly, language changes, and it was necessary to translate a new Bible in contemporary Cigogo to replace the old and outdated Cigogo translation. Although it was printed in 1960 it was actually in very old Cigogo. The New Testament of this Bible came out in 1899. That was why I was keen to be involved in this new translation.[19]

Asked further how the new Bible was received and how the Gogo are responding to it, he replied:

---

19. See appendix B, for a full transcript of author's interview with Canon Lusinde.

> Yes, I am happy that it is out and available now. It was very well accepted. People are very happy to hear it read in churches or in their homes. Unfortunately, the sales of this Bible have not been very encouraging. There are a number of factors for this. First, our people are not used to buying books or reading books . . . Secondly, we have a new younger generation who are more used to Swahili and are not keen to buy and use their Cigogo Bible. They need to be encouraged to love and to use their own tongue. The older generation do not have this problem. They love the language. They love to hear it. Some can read it but some cannot afford to buy it.

A number of church leaders including Bishop Mdimi Mhogolo, the Anglican bishop of the Dodoma Anglican Diocese, confirm that the new translation has been well received and accepted in Ugogo. This translation was, however, based on the central Gogo dialect spoken in the Dodoma area. It has suffered from the problem of poor acceptability in the Mpwapwa and Manyoni areas where other Gogo speakers are to be found. This is a challenge that will eventually need to be confronted by the church and the Bible Society.

The Augustana Lutheran Mission in Singida and Translating the Scriptures into Kinyiramba and Kinyaturu

One of the inevitable results of the World War I was that the Germans were ordered to leave Tanganyika. The missionaries of the Leipzig Mission in northern Tanganyika had to leave in 1920. Consequently, they invited the American Augustana Lutheran Missionary Society to take responsibility for their work, which the Augustana Mission did until the return of the Germans in 1925. In 1926 an agreement was reached whereby the Leipzig Mission took responsibility for northern Tanganyika while the Augustana Mission was given responsibility over the Singida area among the Wanilamba and Wanyaturu (Waremi). The Leipzig Mission had pioneered work in the Ilamba area starting at Ruruma as early as 1911. The first Augustana missionaries to arrive at Ruruma in 1926 were George N. Anderson, F. H. S. Magney, and N. L. Melander. They extended the work to Iambi in 1927, to Ushora in 1929, to Isanzu in 1931, to Kiomboi also in 1931, to Wembere in 1936, and to Kinampanda in 1937, among other places.

This team immediately started learning Kinilamba,[20] a dialect closely related to Kisanzu, for use in their ministry. They inevitably took up the challenge of translating the Scriptures into Kinilamba as part of their strategy to communicate the good news of Jesus Christ to the Wanilamba people effectively. The Gospel of Mark was translated and published in 1940 by BFBS, and the Gospel of John in 1945 by ABS for BFBS. This translation was prepared by F. H. S. Magney, E. R. Danielson, and George N. Anderson, all members of the Augustana Mission. They were assisted by a number of mother-tongue speakers, the most active being Yakobo Ntundu. Anderson, a graduate of the University of Minnesota and Columbia University, reported that in preparing their translations they referred to Nestlé's Greek New Testament prepared by BFBS and that "the native assistants [referred] to the 2 Swahili versions, the so-called Steere version and the Roehl version."[21]

In 1951, Franics J. Bedford of BFBS wrote regarding Iramba as follows:

> This language is known to us as "Ilamba". It is a BFBS language. The original work being Mark's Gospel printed by us in 1940. The arrangement with the ABS was only ad interim and was due to the difficulties caused by the war. They shared with us the imprint on John's Gospel done in 1945. There is no reason why future publications should not revert normally to the BFBS. Dr. Nida reported on this language in 1948 (he was there with Canon Coleman) and pointed out that these people were really literate in Swahili and that only a few hundred could read Ilamba.[22]

The missionary team of Magney, Danielson, and Anderson completed the New Testament, assisted by Manase Yona, Teofilo Makala, Yakobo Nkurlu, and other mother-tongue speakers. The Gospel of Mark, a revision of the earlier one of 1945, was published in 1963 by BFBS, while the NT was published in 1967 by the BSEA.

Translation work in the neighboring Kinyaturu or Kiremi language was carried out by the Rev Howard S. Olson, also of the Augustana Lutheran Mission. Olson had been a missionary among the Remi since 1946. He collaborated with his fellow American Lutheran missionaries, the Rev Leslie Peterson and the Rev David Henry, together with three Remi teachers, Yohana

---

20. Kinilamba, together with Kinyaturu (Rimi), Kilangi, and Kimbugwe, is included in Guthrie's Bantu referential classification system, Group F30.

21. BFBS correspondence files: letter dated 15.2.1939.

22. BFBS correspondence files: letter dated 19.12.1951.

Seme, Benjamin Jingu, and Mikaeli Hape, on the translation of the Gospel of Mark, which was published in 1956 by BFBS. The Gospel of John was translated by Olson, assisted by the Rev Benjamin Jingu, Mr Petro Ibrahimu, and Mr Imanueli Mungwa, representing the three dialects of Remi. This was published in 1964 by the BSEA in Nairobi. Later, Olson moved on to teach at the Makumira Lutheran Seminary in Usa River, Arusha. His textbook on Greek Grammar written in Swahili as *Jifunze Kiyunanicha Agano Jipya*[23] proved most popular among his students and even beyond. Olson, like a large number of missionary translators of his era, was well-trained in both biblical studies and biblical languages. This factor no doubt contributed to the quality of the translations produced by these scholar-missionaries and to their durability of their translations in their areas of use.

In recent years the churches in the Singida area have expressed a renewed interest in completing the task commenced by these Augustana missionary pioneers. They have therefore embarked on a revision of the 1967 Kinilamba NT to be followed by a first translation of the OT. Similarly, the churches also embarked on a first contemporary translation of the NT into both Kinyaturu and Kinilamba. The members of the Kinyaturu translation team consisted of Elia Mande, Simeon Kusina, and Naftali Nghunghu, all Lutheran pastors, while the members of the Kiniramba translation team were Gideon Kahola, Sheila Immanuel, and Zephania Gunda, also all pastors in the Lutheran Church. Work on both the Kinilamba NT revision and the Kinyaturu (Kirimi) NT is complete. Both were dedicated and launched together on 19 December 2010, in Singida, Central Tanzania, at the Lutheran Cathedral grounds before a packed and expectant audience. Work on the OT immediately followed and the translators have made encouraging reports of their progress. The declared aim of completing the entire Bible in both languages is the main motivation of both translation teams.

The Langi of Kondoa and the Sandawe of Kwamtoro

SIL International, organizing projects from their center in Dodoma, have started work in a number of languages in central Tanzania, among them the Kilangi, Burunge,[24] and Sandawe. The preliminary stages of the work have taken much longer than usual. This is due to the fact that the SIL translators

---

23. Olson, *Jifunze Kiyunani cha Agano Jipya* [Teach yourself New Testament Greek].

24. Kirangi, as noted above, is part of Guthrie's F30; Burunge, on the other hand, belongs to the Southern Cushitic language family.

involved have had to learn the respective languages, develop orthographies, and work on trial publications for use in developing basic literacy in the languages. The fact that they are also involved in actual translation as second language translators, albeit with the help of mother-tongue speakers, means that the time spent in grammatical study and analysis, and collecting and understanding lexical material, has tended to slow them down. Oliver and Dorothea Stegen have commenced work on Kilangi, a Bantu language of some 270,000 speakers. The Walangi, whose main urban center is Kondoa, are neighbors of the Gogo living toward the north of Gogo territory on the way to Arusha from Dodoma. A significant number of Walangi are Muslims. Roman Catholics, however, form the majority of the Christian community among the Walangi, followed by Anglicans and Lutherans. Traditional beliefs are also strongly held by some Walangi. Despite nearly a century or so of Christian presence among these people, there is to date no Bible, or portions of it, in this important language. Instead, Swahili is widely used, perhaps because of the presence of the strong Islamic element and its concomitant Swahili-ization. The SIL team has made slow progress. A number of portions and selections of the Bible have been produced. Hopefully, the complete New Testament and a complete Bible will be available in this language in the near future.

The Sandawe and the Hadza are the only communities that speak a click language in Tanzania. These languages are related to the other click languages spoken in Namibia, Botswana, and South Africa by the San and Khoikhoi peoples, previously called Bushmen and Hottentots, with whom these Tanzanian languages share many linguistic, historical, and cultural similarities.[25] The Sandawe and the Hadza are among the oldest inhabitants in this part of Tanzania, and indeed of Africa, judging by the antiquity of their lifestyle as well as the history of African migrations, which indicates that Bantu peoples are later migrants to their areas.[26] They are characterized by a hunter-gatherer lifestyle which is slowly becoming economically untenable and unsustainable. They have been compared to such other groups as "the Shoshoni of the Great Basin, the Australian Aborigines, the Arctic Inuit, the Aka of the Philippines, the Mbuti . . . and Ju/!Hoansi of [Southern] Africa, and the Ache of Paraguay."[27] Their cultures share these features as common patterns:

---

25. Barnard, *Hunters and Herders*; Smith, et al., *Bushmen of Southern Africa*.

26. See Newman, *Peopling of Africa*, 184–187; Olson, *Mapping Human History*, 50–53.

27. Panter-Brick, Layton, and Rowley-Conway, eds., *Hunter Gatherers*, 13.

1. "apparent under-production, and a general lack of material accumulation;

2. routine food gathering;

3. egalitarianism; and

4. despite [the general egalitarianism cited above], a routine division of labor between foraging activities of males and females; men more commonly hunt while women more commonly gather."[28]

Historically, in East Africa most missionary agencies have tended to ignore the Sandawe and the Hadza. Invariably, they approached these people through the languages and cultures of the neighboring peoples with whom these groups tended to assimilate. This trend has posed a threat to the survival of the cultures and languages of these older peoples of eastern Africa. They are, moreover, increasingly being marginalized economically, leading to massive poverty and a state of helplessness, not only in Tanzania, but in southern Africa as well.[29]

Translation work among the Sandawe is being undertaken by a Swiss translator couple, Daniel and Elisabeth Hunziker of SIL. As observed above, the time needed to learn the language, establish a viable orthography, and work on literacy materials is such that the progress has been slow. Some selections and trial portions have been produced, but at the time of writing the New Testament is yet to come out, despite more than a decade or so of work on the language of the Sandawe.

---

28. Panter-Brick, Layton, and Rowley-Conway, 13
29. See, for example Gall, *Bushmen of Southern Africa.*

9

The Spread to the Lake

Sukuma and Their Neighbors, Nyamwezi, Jita,
Kerewe, Zinza, Kuria, Suba, and Gusii

Translation Work of Mennonites, CMS, SDAM, and AIC in the Lake Region

Sukuma[1] is the most widely spoken language in the Lake Region. It is concentrated mainly between Lake Victoria and Lake Rukwa to the west of the southern tip of Lake Tanganyika, between the diamond mining town of Shinyanga to the south of Mwanza and the world-famous Serengeti Plains. With over five million speakers, the Sukuma are the largest ethnic group in Tanzania, inhabiting mainly the districts of Kwimba, Maswa, Shinyanga, Mwanza, and Geita. Their main urban center is the lake shore city of Mwanza. Other important urban areas include Shinyanga and the gold mining town of Geita. A Bantu language, Sukuma is closely related to Nyamwezi (84% lexical similarity), Sumbwa and Nyaturu (59% lexical similarity), Kimbu (57% lexical similarity), Nilamba (55% lexical similarity), and Langi (49% lexical similarity).[2]

The Sukuma are a very religious people, steeped in both the African traditional religions and the Christian faith. The Africa Inland Church (AIC)[3] is well established in this area, as are the Roman Catholics and the Anglicans. The Pentecostals are, however, making huge inroads among the Sukuma as well. This area early became the center of African Inland Mission (AIM) work,

---

1. Sukuma, together with Nyamwezi, Sumbwa, Kimbu, and Bungu, is included in Guthrie's Bantu referential classification system, Group F20.

2. See Grimes, *Ethnologue*, 238. See also Polome, "Languages of Tanzania," 17.

3. The Africa Inland Church grew out of the work of the Africa Inland Mission established in 1895 by Peter Cameron Scott, a Scottish-American missionary. Beginning from Ukambani, Kenya, the work spread to other locations in Central Kenya and in the Rift Valley region of Kenya.

which eventually spread throughout the whole of Tanzania. The Anglicans pioneered the work among the Sukuma, but they were overtaken by AIM.

Similarly, Scripture translation work in the language was initiated by the Anglicans, but AIM soon took over responsibility. The pioneer translation work among the Sukuma was the work of Anglican CMS missionaries, Edward Cyril Gordon, E. H. Hubbard, J. W. Purser, and F. H. Wright. They were assisted by Natanieri Mudeka and Henry Mukasa, among others, to translate and prepare for publication the four Gospels and Acts. Both Mudeka and Mukasa were Baganda catechists who had voluntarily gone to spread the gospel among the Sukuma.[4] The Gospel of Matthew was published in 1895; Mark, John, and Acts in 1896; and Luke in 1897. The letter of James was published in 1903, Romans and Galatians in 1907. The New Testament was completed and published in 1911 by the BFBS in London.

A BFBS report of 1895 noted:

> At the request of the Church Missionary Society the Committee has undertaken the publication of Gospels of St. Matthew and St. Luke. The version is in the language of Nassa, a Church Missionary Society station at Speke Gulf, South Victoria Nyanza. The version was made by the Rev. E. H. Hubbard, of the Church Missionary Society, by the help of Natanieri, a Muganda native catechist who went voluntarily to teach the Basukuma.[5]

During most of this period, CMS work among the Sukuma had been an extension of the Uganda work. In 1909 a decision was made to hand over the CMS Nassa station to AIM. Thereafter, AIM took a leading role in the Protestant mission among the Sukuma. A new translation of the NT was undertaken by an AIM missionary team under the leadership of T. G. Marsh. This was mostly a revision of the 1911 NT. It was published in 1925 by BFBS.

Work on the Old Testament was mainly carried out by Zakaria Balele under the supervision of a team of AIM missionaries. Genesis was published in 1929; Exodus in 1931; Daniel, Joel, Obadiah, Jonah, Haggai, and Malachi in 1932; and Leviticus in 1934. They were printed at the AIM Evangel Press at Lohumbo. Balele was an outstanding Sukuma Christian who earned great respect as a result of his involvement in the translation of the Sukuma Bible. He was recruited to this task because of his life and faith, but also because of

---

4. This is yet another example of the impact of the Luganda work and its role in the Christianization, not just of Buganda, but the entire Great Lakes area.

5. BFBS—Record of Translation Work 1895, 396.

his linguistic gifts, his intelligence, and his humility. He was active in preaching the gospel, and his simple life and faith made an impact on many people. The Africa Inland Church holds him in very high regard to this day.

The revision and re-translation of the T. G. Marsh New Testament as well as the Balele Old Testament was undertaken by an AIM team including Balele, Emile Sywulka, Charles E. Hess, and W. J. Maynard, as well as a team of local reviewers. The NT was published in 1944 and the OT in 1960.

At this writing, a new effort, sponsored by the AIC, Anglican, Lutheran, and Roman Catholic churches, is underway to produce a modern translation of the Bible into current common-language Sukuma. It arises out of dissatisfaction with existing Scriptures, which are not only difficult to comprehend for many Sukuma, people but are also in dire need of revision and correction. It has also arisen out of the desire to have an interconfessional translation to serve the needs of all the churches. Prior to this effort, the Catholics did not have any major Scriptures in Sukuma, although the White Fathers are reported to have translated numerous liturgical selections and Scripture narratives for lectionary and liturgical use from as early as 1899. Between 1921 and 1952 Father Léon Bourget translated a number of Scripture selections for church use.[6] Nearly all of them were published at the White Fathers Mission Press in Mwanza. As Scripture translations, these works were understandably incomplete because these missionaries did not set out to translate the complete Bible or even the complete New Testament. Their main aim was to prepare liturgical texts for use in their Sunday readings and for the catechism. It was only after the Second Vatican Council (1962–1965) and developments in the area of the Biblical Apostolate that Catholics became very actively involved in Bible translation in Africa and elsewhere. This perhaps explains the current eagerness of the Catholics to be part of an interconfessional text that is acceptable to Sukuma-speaking Christians.

Translation work to produce a contemporary Sukuma text of the Bible commenced officially in 1992 under a translation team consisting of Stephini Nikodemo Nzuuli, Masanja Ngweso, Daniel Kipili, and David Magoke. Father Karl Zimmerman, a Roman Catholic biblical scholar worked with the team for a while but was unable to continue due to old age and ill health. The work on the New Testament has mainly involved reworking and restructuring an earlier draft prepared by Masanja Ngweso, as well as having a team of reviewers work through the drafts. The first publication in the new translation, the Gospel of Mark, was launched for distribution in 1995 and was enthusiastically received.

---

6. Rijks, *Guide to Catholic Bible Translations*, vol. 2, 415.

The text of this common-language Sukuma NT was completed in February 2001. Work on the Old Testament, including the Deuterocanonical books, has been completed. It has, however, been subject to delays. The complete Bible is now with the printer and is eagerly awaiting dedication and launching at the lakeside city of Mwanza in Tanzania, hopefully in 2020.

The Scriptures into Nyamwezi

The Nyamwezi are not only immediate neighbors of the Sukuma, but their two languages are very close. As noted above, the lexical similarity between Sukuma and Nyamwezi is as high as 84 percent. The Nyamwezi are to be found in the territory around Tabora. Given their strategic location on the main trade route from Zanzibar and Bagamoyo through central Tanganyika, to Tabora and up to the Congo, the Nyamwezi were significantly involved in trade. Their leader, chief Mirambo (d. 1884), was a great associate of the notorious slave trader Tippu Tip (1837–1905).

Writing about the Nyamwezi, Andrew Roberts begins by noting that, "The Nyamwezi have long been famous as traders and travelers," and "well over a hundred years ago there were Nyamwezi living as far as Zanzibar, Katanga, and what is now Zambia."[7] Their name, which means "people of the moon," is no doubt connected to their love of travel and trade. Roberts observes, "The most important single theme in the history of the Nyamwezi in the 19th century is their involvement in the international ivory trade."[8] Through these activities Tabora became a major urban and cosmopolitan center in the interior of mainland Tanganyika. It is no wonder that it also became a center of Islam, and has remained so to this day.

The London Missionary Society (LMS) was the missionary organization with which David Livingstone was associated. Formed in Leeds, England, in 1875, it became the first Christian missionary group to start work along the shores of Lake Tanganyika. Among the first missionaries to reach Ujiji on the shores of this lake were Roger Price, E. C. Hore, and A. J. Swann in 1877. This mission was, as Roland Oliver points out, "both impractical and unlucky."[9] It burnt itself out after a few years. Another LMS missionary, Dr Ebenezer Southon, started off at the court of the Nyamwezi Chief Mirambo but did not meet much success either.

---

7. Roberts, "The Nyamwezi," 116.

8. Roberts, 122.

9. Oliver, *Missionary Factor*, 42.

It was the LMS missionary T. F. Shaw, assisted by his fellow LMS colleagues Jacob Wainwright, W. Draper and others, who first translated the word of God into Nyamwezi. The Gospel of Mark was published by BFBS in 1897. However, the translation endeavor was subsequently passed on to the Moravians who completed work on the Gospel of Matthew, which was published in 1907 by G. Winter at the historical Moravian center of Herrnhut, Germany. The complete New Testament in Nyamwezi translated by L. R. Stern and his colleagues of the Moravian Mission, appeared two years later, published by the BFBS in London in 1909. The 1909 NT was revised rather extensively some years later by another team of Moravian missionaries: Søren H. Ibsen, N. H. Thygesen, and A. J. Keevill, assisted by reviewers. It was claimed that the 1909 edition of the NT had many serious mistakes and was in a dialect spoken primarily in the northwest corner of the Nyamwezi-speaking area. Some revision work had been started earlier by N. H. Gaarde together with Mose Mhozya and Isai Magaga, assisted by a team of reviewers. It was, however, the Ibsen-Thygesen-Keevill team who completed the task. By 1942, the manuscript of the revised NT was ready for printing, but it was not actually published until 1951 by BFBS. There has been no attempt to translate the OT into Nyamwezi.

The White Fathers, too, have been working among the Nyamwezi since the early period. They set up stations at Tabora and Kipalapala, the latter eventually becoming a major Catholic theological and biblical center. They made attempts at working in the vernacular language despite the pressure to use Swahili. Among their first attempts at translation was a prayer book together with selections from the Gospels for the liturgy. These were published in 1920 at the Tabora White Fathers Mission Press and were reprinted along with a new translation of the liturgical Gospels by Father Ambrose Kaseka. Another White Father, Father Paul Schönenberger, translated Gospel selections for Lent, which were published in 1962. This was followed by his translation of the Gospels, which was published in 1966 at the Tabora White Fathers Mission Press, and the NT in 1975, published at Turnhout, Proost, in Germany. Unfortunately, the use of Nyamwezi for worship has encountered the fate of many Tanzanian languages – succumbing to the overwhelming predominance Swahili.

Several factors may account for this situation. The depth of early Islamization, Arabization, and Swahili-ization among the Nyamwezi, and their early trade links with the eastern Swahili coast may have weakened their allegiance both to their own language and to the newly acquired Christian faith. This is clearly a case where history, commerce, religious ecology, and culture all converge to influence language use. Hence the Nyamwezi church leaders have not been keen to support a revision of the 1942 Moravian NT, or a reprint of the 1975 White Fathers' NT, or a new contemporary translation in modern speech. Among the Nyamwezi, as among the Wairangi of Kondoa, another heavily Islamized and Swahili-ized community, interest in the use of vernacular Scriptures is low. As a result, the churches in the area have not expressed a desire to have a complete Bible in their language.

Translation into Ecijita

Ecijita, also known as Kikara or Kiruri after some dialects in this cluster, is spoken on the islands of Ukara and Ukerewe in southern parts of Lake Victoria. It is closely related to Ruhaya as well as to the other interlacustrine Bantu languages of this zone. The translation of the New Testament into Ecijita was the work of two missions, namely SDAM and AIM. The first SDAM team to land on Tanganyikan soil was led by W. Ehlers and A. C. Enns, who arrived in 1903 and began working in the Pare region. Another team went westwards to the Lake Region, where they founded stations at Busegwe, Majita, and Ikizu in Musoma District in 1908 and at Utimbaru in Tarime District in 1911, moving to Bupambogila near Bariadi in the Shinyanga region in 1912. AIM, on the other hand, started their work in Tanganyika with the arrival in June 1909 of the Australian-American Emile Sywulka and his wife. This was at the invitation of the veteran Uganda CMS missionary Alexander M. Mackay, an invitation extended through the AIM head in Kenya, C. E. Hurlburt. AIM had already been in Kenya since 1895. From the Nassa station in the Sukuma area, AIM expanded to Kijima in 1910, to Makongoro and Mwanza in 1912, and to Kolandoto in 1913.

It was Emile Sywulka together with Ezekiel Kaneza who translated the Gospel of Luke into Ecijita in 1934. This was published with some hymns appended at the AIM Evangel Press at Luhumbo. Around the same time, R. Reider of SDAM, with the help of local Bajita including Abrahamu Maraduzu, started translating the New Testament, eventually completing it. This early draft, however, was never published. Some years later, Sywulka and his AIM team, including Miss T. Fay Toney, Frank E. Manning, and Zakayo Mutema, took this draft and revised it extensively. The Gospel of Matthew was published in 1941 and the complete NT in 1943 by the American Bible Society on behalf of BFBS as a "war emergency service." One of the translators, Frank E. Manning, wrote the following:

> As usual, the Bible Society has published this Testament without
> a question regarding cost. The natives will pay a nominal price

for the Testaments, nominal to us but not to them. The difference between the cost of producing them and the sale price to the natives will be met through gifts received by the Bible Society from interested individuals. Thus the Bible Society is in reality a mission agency and worthy of the prayers and gifts of the Lord's children; for how could the missionary work effectively without the word of God in the native tongue?[10]

Some years later, a further revision of the Ecijita New Testament was undertaken by Donald H. Ebeling of AIM at the encouragement of Dr Eugene Nida of the ABS on a visit to the island.[11] The Ebeling revision of the New Testament was published in 1960 by BFBS London.

Translation into Kerewe

The Kerewe language is closely related to Nyambo-Karagwe, Haya, Zinza, Kerebe, Jita, Kwaya, Kara, and Rori.[12] This group is further related to Nyoro, Tooro, Nyankole, Ciga, Ganda, Soga, Gwere, Gungu, and Talinga-Bwisi.[13] These are all part of the great lacustrine group of languages referred to as the Western Lacustrine Bantu that includes the Banyoro, Toro, Nyankore, and Kiga, as well as Jita, Kerewe, and Zinza. The Kerewe people are found in the northwestern part of Ukerewe Island in the southern part of Lake Victoria to the north of the Sukuma. They share a 76 percent lexical similarity with Zinza, 75 percent with Haya, 69 percent with Nyambo, 68 percent with Nyankore and Chiga, 63 percent with Toro, and 62 percent with Nyoro.[14]

The White Fathers reached the Ukerewe Island about 1880 as part of their evangelization of the southern parts of the Lake Victoria area. These missionaries, through the imposing leadership of the founder of the White Fathers' order, Cardinal Charles Lavigerie, are credited with the penetration of large parts of this area. Arriving in Zanzibar in April 1878, one team led by Father Lourdel moved westwards towards Buganda, reaching Kabaka Mutesa's court on 17 February 1879. From Buganda they set up stations all around the Lake Victoria area as well as on the islands. They went further to Unyanyembe in 1881 and Bukombi in 1883. Another team moved towards Lake Tanganyika

---

10. American Bible Society, *Unpublished Historical Essays*, No. 16, VI-E, 112
11. American Bible Society, *Unpublished Historical Essays*, No. 16, VI-E, 112
12. These are all included in Guthrie Bantu referential classification system Group E20.
13. These in turn are part of Guthrie's E10.
14. Grimes, *Ethnologue*, 233.

and arrived at Ujiji on 24 January 1879. Here they met the LMS missionary E. C. Hore. At Karema on the shores of Lake Tanganyika, the White Fathers established their first permanent station in 1885, and in 1887 they saw J. B. Charbonnier installed as the first bishop on the mainland.

The renowned Catholic medical missionary and catechist, Dr Adrian Attiman, served at Karema on the shores of Lake Tanganyika for nearly seventy years from 1889 until his death in April 1956. He achieved more than most catechists ever dream of achieving and is perhaps better remembered than any other Catholic catechist of his generation. A Songhai from Mali, he was kidnapped as a child by the Tuareg and sold to a slave trader who took him across the desert to Algiers. He was bought and given his freedom by the White Fathers in Algiers, who trained him there and later as a medical doctor in Malta. He was commissioned to do missionary work in East Africa and is reputed to have walked seven hundred miles from Bagamoyo to his station on the shores of Lake Tanganyika. He married a local Bemba woman and worked in Karema until his death at ninety-two years of age. He is remembered for his legendary and exemplary labors as a medical doctor and missionary catechist among the Wafipa. Historian Elizabeth Isichei notes that "He always wore the costume of Algiers," and that "When he died, two thousand people walked in his funeral procession."[15] One writer wrote of him, "He is above all praise. Day and night, good weather and bad, he is at the disposal of the sick." Another wrote:

> His own life was deeply spiritual. It is impossible to estimate the number of people who became Christians through his influence. He never accepted his whole salary and on the death of his wife and the ordination of his son he refused any further payment. He taught himself surgery from medical journals and, because medical supplies were often so slow in coming from Europe, he made a study of local plants and was thus able to prepare his own medicines. He conquered a number of epidemics that broke out among the people. Time and time again he refused important appointments. During his lifetime he received eleven decorations – the French legion of Honour, three from Belgium, three from the Vatican and four from Britain, including the Wellcome Medal of

---

15. Isichei, *History of Christianity*, 222.

the Royal African Society, the only other medical missionary to receive it being Albert Schweitzer.[16]

The White Fathers spread the gospel widely and consolidated their work throughout the whole western half of present-day Tanzania from Bukoba, Mwanza, Musoma, Kigoma, Tabora, and Sumbawanga to as far south as Mbeya and Tukuyu. The Kerewe New Testament published in 1946 at the White Fathers' Mission Press in Bukerewe was a fruit of the White Fathers' labors. The main translator of this NT was Father Almas Simard, who had the help of several mother-tongue speakers. This was, however, not the first attempt at making God's word available in this language. Other publications in Kerewe had appeared earlier, for example, Bible stories in 1899 and 1941, liturgical Gospels in 1921 and 1937, and a gospel harmony in 1930. Unfortunately, these efforts have not been continued.

Translation into Zinza

The Zinza, whose history is intimately tied to that of the Bachwezi and Bito, are part of the Western Lacustrine Bantu. They live along the southern shores of Lake Victoria. The White Fathers were among the earliest missionaries among the Zinza. It was Father Marie Joseph Vekemans who took it upon himself to have the New Testament translated into Zinza. Only Matthew and Acts were published: Acts at the White Fathers' Press at Bukalasa in 1930 and Matthew in 1934 at the Maison-Carrée in Algiers. Later, Richard Dilworth of the Africa Inland Church translated the Gospel of John and the First Epistle of John, which were published in 1945 at the AIC Press in Lohumbo. In recent years interest in doing translation in this language has been revived thanks to the Tanzania branch of SIL. This Bible agency has been actively working on a translation of the NT into Zinza since the early 1990s. Initially headed by Tom Mathews, the work has since passed to other workers. Some portions and selections have been published while work on the NT is progressing slowly.

Translation into Zanaki

Zanaki is a small language spoken in the Musoma-Mara area of the Lake Victoria Region. It falls in the same dialect continuum as Ikoma, Ngurimi,

---

16. Quoted in Sahlberg, *From Kapf to Rugambwa*, 93.

Ikizu, Igikuria, and Ekegusii[17] in neighboring Kenya. Zanaki is best known as the mother tongue of Mwalimu Julius Kambarage Nyerere, the renowned and well-respected first president of Tanzania. The only Scripture portion published in this language is the Gospel of Matthew. This was translated by a Mennonite missionary couple, J. Clyde and Alta Shenk, and was published in 1948 by both ABS in New York and BFBS in London under a joint imprint.[18] Margaret T. Hills, the ABS librarian, wrote in her April 1948 report regarding the Zanaki as follows:

> Inland from the southeastern shores of Lake Victoria in Tanganyika, East Africa, live 20,000 Bazanaki, long considered by their neighbors as fierce and treacherous. Perhaps that reputation is why their language is so different from that of their neighbors . . . Dr. Eugene A. Nida, the Society's Secretary for Versions, visited the mission station, near Musoma, in March in the course of a journey studying African language problems. He was greatly impressed with the sincerity of purpose, the wonderful spirit of harmony and the fine church development in the mission and with its unusual spiritual atmosphere. And this in center of a tribe reputed to be "fierce." An exceptionally able native was of great help in the making of the translation.[19]

The first pioneers of the Mennonite Church in Tanganyika, Elam and Elizabeth Stauffer, together with John and Ruth Mosemann, launched their work at Katuru Hill, Shirati, in the Mara region in 1934, and by 1946 they had established five mission stations at Shirati, Bukiroba, Mugango, Bumangi, and Nyabasi. The first Mennonite missionaries among the Zanaki people were Clinton and Maybell Ferster, together with J. Clyde and Alta Shenk. They started their work at the Bumangi station in May 1937. It fell to the Shenks to initiate the translation and literacy work. They were assisted in this task by Jonathan Nyamhagata, "an interpreter who taught them Zanaki culture and customs,"[20] and Jonah Itine Mirari, a carpenter and evangelist. Reporting on Mirari's contribution, the Shenks noted in their report to the American Bible

---

17. These groups of languages are grouped under Guthrie's E40.

18. ABS report of April 1948 on new languages by ABS librarian M. T. Hills, in BFBS EA languages files.

19. ABS report of April 1948 on new languages by M. T. Hills, the librarian in BFBS EA languages files.

20. This and the other quotes below are from the American Bible Society, Unpublished Historical Essays, No. 16, VI-E, 112

Society that: "an exceptionally able native was of great help in the making of the translation." The unidentified "exceptionally able native" to whom Dr Nida made reference, as recorded in the ABS librarian's 1948 report, was none other than Jonah Itine Mirari. It is a pity that they were not able to proceed beyond the Gospel of Matthew. The only other Scripture publication in Zanaki was a small, thirty-four-page pamphlet of Scripture selections called *Way of Salvation*, published by SGM in 1953.

Mwalimu Julius Nyerere is known to have espoused a great love for his mother tongue Zanaki, as well as for his national language Swahili, and for English as the language of international communication. However, when he turned his interest to translating the Scriptures, he was apparently attracted more to experimenting with the ancient forms of classical Swahili poetry and how to render the age-old biblical message in this medium than to translating into his mother tongue.

Mzee Emmanuel Kibira was a former classmate of Mwalimu Nyerere at the Tabora Boys' Secondary School, as well as a colleague in implementing the Ujamaa program during Nyerere's presidency. Shortly before the end of his tenure as General Secretary of the Bible Society of Tanzania, he paid a private visit to President Nyerere at State House in Dodoma accompanied by the team of Ruhaya Bible translators.[21] The president expressed much interest in Bible translation and shared with this group the work he was engaged in at the time, namely, working on a translation of the Bible into Swahili. He also expressed a desire to do something similar in his own Zanaki tongue. His Swahili Gospels and Acts were eventually published, but he died before completing this project. It is not clear whether he managed to produce any work in Zanaki in accordance with his desire. Perhaps Zanaki would have benefited from his prolific pen had he been granted more years of life.

Translation into Igikuria

Igikuria is spoken in both Kenya and Tanzania and so the Kuria community is to be found on both sides of the border. Four Kuria clans, Abairegi, Abagumbe (Abarenchoka), Abanyabasi, and Abakira, are located on the Kenya side of the border. On the Tanzania side the following twelve clans are listed: Abairegi, Abanyamongo, Abanyabasi, Abatimbaru, Ababwasi, Abakira, Abamera,

---

21. Mzee Emmanuel Kibira was General Secretary of the Bible Society of Tanzania from 1978–1989. Nyerere resigned from the presidency in 1989.

Abakenye, Abakiini, Abasweta, Abakiroba, and Abatobori.[22] The Kuria of Tanzania and the Kuria of Kenya are essentially one people. Despite some dialectal variation, their languages are by and large mutually intelligible.

The translation of the Bible into Igikuria has had a rather checkered history. One of the main reasons for this is the absence of a well-established church with a strong interest in Bible translation. The Roman Catholics carried out the first translation of the Gospels and Acts into Igikuria in 1960–1962. Copies of these Catholic translations are, however, hard to find, as they were never widely distributed. It was left to non-Catholics to see to the completion of the translation task. The charismatic and independent-minded Mzee Chacha Omahe took up the daunting challenge to translate the New Testament into Igikuria. A hard-working and highly motivated worker, Chacha Omahe was basically a self-taught man who dared to do great things for God. He received some help from Rosemary Guillebaud of CMS in the early stages. He translated Mark, published in 1969 by the Bible Society in East Africa, and Luke, published in 1976 by the Bible Society of Kenya. Chacha Omahe and his collaborators employed a linguistically sound orthography which adequately represented the Igikuria sound system. However, the lack of a good literacy program and the use of unfamiliar vowel symbols created difficulties, which readers familiar with the Swahili orthography naturally resisted.

Chacha Omahe went on to prepare the first complete draft of the New Testament on his own. His drafts were found to be dynamic and clear, but closer to what Daniel Shaw refers to as transculturation.[23] They were a kind of cultural translation that uncritically employed much Igikuria traditional, cultural, and religious terminology. Younger and better-trained translators deemed his work to be unacceptable, and so they reduced much of the traditional cultural material as they revised and reworked his translation. Moreover, some orthography revision and adaptation were also thought necessary.

Revision, or retranslation, began in earnest in 1983 under the guidance of Chacha Omahe himself, with William Maswa, Joseph Magige, and Marwa Kubyo as translators, and Ann-Britt Svensson, a Swedish Maranatha Pentecostal missionary, as the coordinator of the translation project based at their center on the hills at Komotobo. After the death of Chacha Omahe in 1986, the high turnover in the translation team delayed completion of the NT. The Gospel of John was printed by the Bible Society of Kenya in 1987 in the revised translation and orthography. The NT was eventually finalized by

---

22. Abuto, *Traditional History of the Abakuria*, 7–8.

23. See Shaw, *Transculturation*.

Gabriel Nyagetari (Maranatha Pentecostal Church) and Raphael Mwita Akiri (Anglican), and was officially launched after publication in a joyful ceremony held at Taranganya on the Kenya-Tanzania border in November 1996. Both the Bible Societies of Kenya and Tanzania as well as Igikuria speakers from both sides of the border were fully represented in the celebrations that followed.

Figure 9.1. The Revs Ezekiel Mwita and Elkana Birore at work translating the Old Testament into Igikuria. Photo © Aloo Osotsi Mojola

The churches then agreed to embark on the work of translating the Old Testament. A new translation team consisting of Jackson Nyangi, Charles Monto, and Emmanuel Kubyo was formed in 2004, but due to certain difficulties, the work was discontinued. At a meeting held in Musoma in July 2007, church leaders from a number of churches, Anglican, Lutheran, Seventh-Day Adventist, and Mennonite, under the chairmanship of the Mennonite Bishop Nyagwegwe of Shirati, agreed to revive and consolidate their flagging efforts and move forward with determination to bring this work to full completion. The project was restarted in March 2008 with a new team of translators composed of Emmanuel Mwita (Anglican), The Rev Ezekiel Mwita (Mennonite), and Elkana Birore (SDA). Father Samuel Habuba, Rev Peter Rosso and Rev Edward Mocha have since then joined. They have diligently worked on the Old Testament books and have completed the entire OT work. The process of preparing the complete Bible is expected to be done by early 2020, with its publication and a dedication hopefully taking place towards the end of 2020.

Translation into Suba

The Basuba are a complex group. They were originally wholly Bantu, neighbors of both the Nilotic Luo and the Bantu Kuria. Even though the original groups are of diverse origins, the majority came from Uganda, especially after the death of the king of Buganda Kabaka Junju around 1760. They are now mainly found on the islands in the Winam (Nyanza) Gulf of Lake Victoria, such as Mfangano and Rusinga, as well as along the shores of Winam Gulf from Ruri Bay to the southern end of Matara Bay in present-day Rusinga, Mfangano, Gembe, Kaksingiri, and Gwasi locations.[24] Today they have been virtually assimilated by their Nilotic Luo neighbors both culturally and linguistically. Many Basuba identify themselves as Luo and speak no other language but Luo. Moreover, this group of assimilated Suba has taken on Luo names and customs and lives in every way as Luo.[25] But there is still a significant remnant of Suba-speakers – a fact which motivated the BTL to initiate moves towards translating the NT into this language. The 1996 Gospel of Mark was the first publication in this language. Subsequent publications were Acts in 1999; and Romans, Titus, and Timothy in 2003. These portions have received a warm reception. In 1995 the government of Kenya created a new administrative district called Suba District to satisfy perceived Suba political and cultural aspirations. This national government action in itself goes a long way to confirm the need for the Suba translation of the Bible already started by BTL. Though the program to translate the NT took some time to get to completion, the NT was launched on 15 April 2011 at Gethsemane Garden Christian Centre, on Mfangano Island. The translation team consisted of Naphtaly Mattah (team leader), Boniface Msaswa, and Jeremiah Okumu. Wycliff Okoth and Peter Odhiambo were involved in literacy work to promote and support the project. These are all mother-tongue Suba translators. Work on the OT is in progress.

Translation into Ekegusii

The Abagusii are to be found close to the Tanzanian border in southwestern Kenya, to the south of Winam Gulf. Their language, referred to as Ekegusii, is closely related to Igikuria and Suba (also spoken in this area), but extends to the Tanzanian side of the border. Ekegusii is the most widely spoken of the three languages and the only one that has a complete Bible. Bible translation work

---

24. For more on these people, see Ayot, *History of the Luo-Abasuba*.

25. The story of this process of the assimilation of the Abasuba into Luo-Abasuba is fascinating, and has been well narrated by Professor Ayot in his book cited above.

was pioneered among the Abagusii by the Seventh-Day Adventist Mission. Starting in the 1920s, E. A. Beavon and Ruth Rait, both SDAM missionaries, assisted by Paulo Nyamweya, saw the Gospel of Matthew published in 1929 by BFBS. The BFBS minutes of 6 January 1926, report that the translation was prepared "from the English version, using also the Swahili and Luo versions, with the help of native Christians."[26] G. A. Lewis, another SDAM missionary, assisted by Paulo Nyamweya and a local committee, went on to translate the entire New Testament. The Gospel of John was published by BFBS in 1945, and the NT in 1948. This was reprinted in 1971.

The present Ekegusii Bible is the product of the cooperation of many of the churches active in the Gusii area, including the Swedish Lutheran, Pentecostal Assemblies of God, Church of God, and Seventh-Day Adventist Mission. Work on this translation was led by the Swedish Lutheran Mission under the direction of Martin Lundstrom beginning in 1957. This effort resulted in the publication of the Gospel of Mark in 1960, John in 1964, a revision of Mark in 1965, a revision of John in 1966, and Matthew and Luke in 1967. These were published by the Bible Society in East Africa. Anna-Brita Albertson took over the direction of the project in 1970 and led it until its completion and the publication of the entire Bible. She was assisted by Josiah Ogamba of the Pentecostal Assemblies of God and a local committee of reviewers.

This second New Testament was published in 1974 with the imprint of the Bible Society in East Africa. Work on the Old Testament followed without interruption. Genesis and Exodus were published in 1977. The entire Bible was published by the Bible Society of Kenya in 1988, and dedicated and launched at Itierio, near the town of Kisii, the main urban center of the Gusii homeland. It has proved very popular with users and remains in high demand. A project to revise the Ekegusii Bible with the objective of preparing an interconfessional edition has been underway, under the sponsorship of the Bible Society of Kenya. An interconfessional team, consisting of Rev Boaz Nyariki, Rev Gwachi Evans Mokua and Father Lawrence Morumbwa, completed the revision of the 1988 Bible and prepared an interconfessional Kisii Bible in two editions – a Protestant and a Catholic edietion. This is expected sometime in 2020.

---

26. BFBS East African languages correspondence file (E3/3/629).

10

The Hills and the Valleys: From the Southern Highlands to the Shores of Lake Malawi and Lake Tanganyika

Hehe, Bena, Kinga, Vwanji, Ngoni, Yao, Nyakyusa, Fipa, and Safwa

German Missions in Southwestern Tanzania

Southwestern Tanganyika became a stronghold of the Lutherans and the Moravians from the very beginning of the German period. The first missionaries of the Berlin Missionary Society (BMS) to arrive in the Southern Highlands were Carl Nauhaus, Christian Schumann, and Christoph Bunk, who came from South Africa. They crossed Lake Malawi on 25 September 1871, and set up a station at Pipagika near Manow. They christened this place Wangemannshöhe in honor of Dr Theodor Wangemann who directed the work of the Berlin Mission from 1866 to 1894. From 1891 at Pipagika, the work of the Berlin mission expanded to Manow in 1892; Ikombe and Mwakaleli in 1893; Bulongwa in 1897; Tanda in 1897; Kidugala in 1898; Ilembula, Jacobi, and Lupembe in 1899; Magoye in 1900; and Pommern in 1912, among other centers. In the process, the Wanyakyusa, Wakinga, Wasangu, Wapangwa, and Wangoni,[1] and other groups, were reached with the gospel.

The first Moravians to arrive in these parts of southwestern Tanzania were led by a South African, Theodor Meyer. Included in this pioneer Moravian group were Theodor Richard, G. Martin, and J. Haefner. Other

---

1. The Nyakyusa, together with the Ndali, as well as the Konde, Kukwe, and Sokili, are part of Guthrie's M30, while the Hehe, Bena, Pangwa, Kinga, Wanji, and Kisi are part of Guthrie's G60.

early missionaries were Oscar Gemuseus, P. Hollan, J. Kretschmer, H. Bauer, E. Boeh, and E. Bechamann. They arrived at Rungwe on 21 August 1891 and set up a mission station there. They expanded to Ipyano and Rutengano in 1894, to Utengule in 1895, to Mbozi and Isoko in 1900, to Ileja in 1906, to Mwaya in 1907, and to Kyimbila in 1908. Within a short span of time after the first woman, Numwagile Fyabalema, was converted in Rungwe on 7 February 1897, the Moravians spread from Lake Nyasa (now Malawi) to Lake Rukwa.

The territory the Moravians actively evangelized expanded when the London Missionary Society handed over their work among the Nyamwezi to them. Thus, in answer to this call, Edmund Dahl, Konrad Meier, and Rudolf Stern became the first Moravians in Urambo and Unyamwezi in 1898. They expanded in 1901 to Kitanda, in 1902 to Sikonge, in 1903 to Ipole, in 1904 to Kipembawe, in 1906 to Usoki, and in 1912 to Tabora. In the same way that Numwangile Fyabalema was a spark for the work in Rungwe, Yohannes Kipamila gave impetus to the Unyamwezi mission starting from Urambo when in 1903 he was among the first group of local Christians to be baptized. He soon became involved in the work of evangelism and remained active in this role until 1936. His influence and outstanding work as an evangelist throughout Unyamwezi has been widely recognized in the Moravian Church of Tanganyika.[2]

Because of the difficulties the Germans faced during World War I, the Scottish Livingstonia Mission was invited in 1917 to come in from Nyasaland (now Malawi) and take responsibility for the Moravian and BMS missions. Between them, the BSM and Moravian missions saw to the translation of New Testaments into Nyakyusa-Ngonde, Nyamwezi, and Nyiha, while their associated missions the London Missionary Society translated the Mambwe-Lungu New Testament, and the Livingstonia Mission translated the Namwanga Bible and the Ngoni Gospel of Mark.

The Scriptures into Nyakyusa-Ngonde and Nyakyusa

The Nyakyusa-Ngonde NT was translated by Carl Nauhaus of BMS. The first portion in this language, namely, the Gospel of Luke, was translated by D. K. Cross of the Free Church of Scotland Mission and published in 1895 at the Mission Press in Livingstonia. The Gospel of John, which appeared in 1896, was also translated by Cross and printed at the Livingstonia Mission Press. In 1898

---

2. See, for instance, Kisanji, *Historia Fupi ya Kanisa la Kimoravian Tanganyika Magharibi* [A short history of the Moravian Church in Western Tanganyika].

an OT history including some Psalms translated by Nauhaus and Christian Schumann was published by the BMS. In 1899 BFBS published the Gospels of Matthew, Mark, and Luke, translated by Nauhaus assisted by Schumann, while the complete NT translated by Nauhaus was published in 1908 by the Prussian Bible Society, Berlin.

BFBS reprinted the Nyakyusa-Ngonde NT at the request of the Prussian Bible Society in 1928. In 1933 and 1940 selections from the Psalms and the Prophets translated by M. E. Faulds and revised by D. R. Mackenzie, both of the Church of Scotland Mission, were published. A revision of this NT was worked on intermittently by Paul Fueter, E. Knudsen, and H. Staub, all of the Moravian Mission; John Nilsson of the Swedish Lutheran Mission; and the Rev Alexander of the Livingstonia Mission; together with A. Mwakasungula, Y. R. Musopole, A. Sebetai, P. A. P. Seme, and G. P. Mwakalukwa, as well as others. Commenting on Staub's abilities, the Rev L. V. D. Ashley of BFBS wrote, "I was in the Southern Highlands with Pastor Staub and was most impressed by his unusual knowledge of the language and his gifts as a translator. I believe we can look forward to a version of exceptional quality."[3] This Staub revision of the NT was published by the Bible Society in East Africa in 1966.

Already in the mid-1970s efforts were being made by the Moravian, Lutheran, and Baptist churches in the area to start a new translation in present-day Nyakyusa. Initially these efforts were intended to include the churches in the Ngonde-speaking areas of Malawi as the two languages are known to have a high level of mutual intelligibility. Unfortunately, these attempts at cooperation, aimed at producing a union translation of Nyakyusa and Kingonde, were never realized. The Nyakyusa people of Tanzania had to go it alone, as did the Ngonde.

The Nyakyusa Bible translation project officially started in 1977. The main translator, Mwalimu Kaisi Mwamatandala, was assisted by the Rev Mwakatobe and by reviewers from the Moravian, Lutheran, and Baptist churches, including Bishop Stephen Mwakasyuka, the Rev Mwatonoka, the Rev Mwasanjala, and the Rev Kapula. Partly as a result of Mwamatandala's unexpected death, work on this translation was delayed. Bishop Mwakasyuka, assisted by the reviewers, took a very active part in doing the final checking and revisions to the Mwamatandala draft of the Bible. Work on this was finalized in 1995 after the proofs had been read by Bishop Mwakasyuka and the text of the Bible sent to the printers. This long-awaited Bible was eventually received with jubilation

---

3. See the Archival Records in the Bibliography, BFBS Files.

and thanksgiving on 21 July 1996, at a crowded launching ceremony in the Nyakyusa town of Tukuyu.

Other Translations by the Moravian and BMS Missions

By 1914, Christian Schumann of the Berlin Missionary Society had completed the translation of the Bena New Testament. He was helped by a number of mother-tongue speakers, including Mzee Mangula of Lupembe, a village to the east of Njombe. The war years (1914–1918) delayed the book's production, but it was eventually published by BFBS in Berlin in 1920. At that time, the Bena NT was intended to be used by the Sangu, Masagati, Hehe, and, of course, by the Bena themselves.

The choice of Bena in the place of Hehe was a kind of German revenge on their erstwhile adversary. The Hehe people are famous for their role in the anti-colonial struggle and especially in the struggle against the German colonialists.[4] They aggressively resisted the Germans, gaining victory over them briefly in 1891. The Germans did not give up. After much preparation and planning they made another attack,

> a fierce hut-to-hut and hand-to-hand engagement. Mkwawa (the Hehe chief) escaped to engage in a guerrilla war for four years. Many German attempts to capture Chief Mkwawa failed. The German governor von Liebert offered 5,000 rupees for Mkwava's head. Mkwava was left in his last days with only two pages. Finally, sick and alone Mkwava shot himself and one of his pages in June 1898 as a German patrol led by a Sergeant Merckel, approached his hiding. Merckel cut off Mkwawa's head which was dispatched to Germany. After the First World War, it was provided in the Treaty of Versailles that the head be returned to the Wahehe. The head was not returned until 1955.[5]

The German missionaries who evangelized the Hehe area translated the NT into Bena for use by the neighboring communities: the Hehe, the Sangu, the Masagati, the Pangwa, and of course, the Bena themselves. These form a linguistic cluster of dialects with high levels of mutual intelligibility. The Bena NT was translated and completed in 1914 by Schumann of BMS with the help of mother-tongue speakers, such as Mzee Mangula of Lupembe. However, it

---

4. Gwassa, "German Intervention," 85–122.

5. Gwassa, 115.

was only published in 1920. The reception of the Bena NT among the Hehe was poor. The Hehe felt slighted. They saw themselves as a people of renown and valor – the people of Chief Mkwava – who should not have to stoop so low. They had their own language and their own songs. If anything, they felt it was the Bena who should use the Hehe language. The Bena were to the Hehe the junior and younger brother.

More recently, Lutheran Bishop Owdenburg Mdegela and his assistant the Rev Mwachusi were at the forefront of the endeavor to have the Holy Scriptures translated into the language of Mkwava. Anglican Archbishop Donald Mtetemela was also very actively involved in supporting this project. The main translators on the project are the Rev Lambert Eliezer Mtatifikolo of the Lutheran Church (who also serves as the project coordinator), and Canon Yohana Mbeho of the Anglican Church. The project was officially launched towards the end of 1995. At long last, the misjudgment of the German missionaries was being corrected.

In the early days of the project, in order to give the people a taste of the new translation, it was decided to publish the Gospel of Matthew as a portion. The launching of this Gospel was celebrated in the cool highlands of Uhehe in Iringa on 14 May 2000. What joy! What sense of pride! After more than a hundred years since the arrival of the first missionaries in Uhehe, the day had at last arrived for the Hehe people to receive the first Gospel ever written in their own tongue. Bishop Owdenburg Mdegela led the launching celebrations and prayers dedicating the Matthew portion. The Lutheran Cathedral in Iringa was not big enough to contain the crowd of worshipers who overflowed all around the church. Naturally, all the members of the translation team, together with the review committee members, were there as well.

In his impassioned launching speech, Bishop Mdegela told the crowd that he reads the Holy Scriptures in seven languages, Bena, Swahili, Zulu, English, German, Greek, and Hebrew. It is a shame, he said, as tears welled in his eyes, that he cannot as yet read the Scriptures in his own mother tongue. He referred to his own mother tongue as the language of the umbilical cord, the language one starts hearing even before one is born into the world. It is the language of the deep things, the language of the heart, the language of the emotions. And what can be deeper than the things of God, the word of God? The launching of the Gospel of Matthew was a great day. Light had dawned on the Hehe people, on the land of Mkwava. And yet this was only the beginning.

As is often the case with translation projects, the challenge after publishing the New Testament is to complete the translation of the Old Testament so that the entire Bible can be published in the mother tongue of the Hehe people.

With the Hehe NT completed, work on the OT has been moving rather slowly. The first NT in the Hehe tongue was dedicated and launched in Iringa on 23 August 2009, before an excited and eager audience who could not believe that at last this day had come. The complete Bible is eagerly awaited, however this may not be available for some time, hopefully in 2021.

Another effort of BMS was the Kinga New Testament. This NT was translated in the 1930s by A. Tramp of the Berlin Mission, assisted by Tupewilwe Sanga, a mother-tongue Kinga speaker. It was, however, revised after World War II by Tramp's daughter. The proofs were corrected by Olle Thurfjell and L. Yessalina Kiluswa and published by BFBS in London in 1961.

Traugott Bachmann was one of the most renowned of the Moravian missionaries. He was nicknamed "Mwalwisi," a local name for someone who has something to do with water (*lwisi* "water") perhaps associating him with the life-giving/life-sustaining water that Jesus gives. Among the Moravians, he ranks possibly with Theodor Meyer who was nicknamed "Mwalusama," a local name for one who looks so hard that he forgets everything else, that is, "someone steadfast, persistent." Bachmann immersed himself in the Nyiha language and culture,[6] eventually translating the Gospel of Matthew, which was published by BFBS in Berlin in 1904. The complete Nyiha NT that Bachmann translated was published in 1913 by BFBS in London. A revision of the Bachmann version was prepared by another Moravian missionary, H. Beck, assisted by, among others, Miss E. Senft, Wamusamba, A. Simukoko, Osia Mwashivuya, Eliezer Mdolo, and Z. Haonga. The Gospel of Mark was published much later, in 1960, and John in 1963 by BFBS. The complete NT was published in 1965 by the Bible Society in Central Africa at Blantyre, Malawi. The Nyiha language is referred to sometimes as Nyasa Nyika.

The UMCA Translations

In general, the UMCA legacy in Bible translation in Tanzania rests mainly with the Swahili Bible. Both the UMCA and the Holy Ghost Fathers favored the use of Swahili throughout Tanzania, especially in education and liturgical worship. They had a dim view of the vernaculars which they considered to have no viable future in the public sphere. This accounts for their minimal contribution to translation in their other mission areas. The German Protestant missions

---

6. Shinyiha belongs with Namwanga, Safwa, and Lambya, among others, to Guthrie's M20. For an overview of Nyiha history and culture, see Brock, "The Nyiha (of Mbozi)," 59–81.

and the White Fathers, in contrast, believed in the value of the vernaculars in touching the African soul.

UMCA was a pioneer in championing the vogue of enculturation or contextualization of the gospel in East Africa. Their idea of "Christian villages" derived from this focus. One of the model UMCA missionaries in East and Central Africa was W. P. Johnson. Besides being a gifted linguist of the stature of his UMCA colleagues, Steere, Madan, and Pennell, he lived as an African. His life was simple, sacrificial, and exemplary. He spent most of his life at Likoma on the eastern shores of Lake Nyasa/Malawi. In the fifty years he spent in East and Central Africa, he only went to his home in England once, during which time he was awarded an honorary doctorate in divinity from his alma mater, Oxford University, not just for his five decades of exemplary missionary work, but also for his valuable book, *My African Reminiscences: 1875–1895*. This amazing man never gave up even after he lost a hand and eye through sickness. He remained single-minded to the very end. He died on 11 October 1928, and was laid to rest in a little church at Liuli in Tanganyika on the shores of Lake Nyasa (Malawi).

Johnson's major translation work was the rendering of the complete Bible as well as the *Book of Common Prayer* into Nyanja[7] in 1908. He also worked on Chimanda[8] together with T. H. Hicks, also of UMCA. In 1913 they had the Psalms translated and printed by UMCA at Likoma. In 1928 the Gospels were published by the BFBS, and in 1937 the complete NT in Chimanda came out, also published by BFBS.

Johnson also had an interest in Mpoto, into which he translated and had the Psalms printed at the UMCA Press in Likoma in 1913. He followed this with the Gospel of Mark, which was also printed at Likoma in 1914. This Gospel was later revised by G. F. George of UMCA and published by BFBS in 1924. Nothing else has appeared in Mpoto thereafter.

UMCA work in those days covered areas of present-day Mozambique and Malawi as well as Tanzania. The Chiyao[9] New Testament, which was translated by A. Hetherwick and published eventually in one volume in 1907, took about fourteen years to complete. Various portions were published by BFBS, London, between 1889 and 1898 as the books were completed. It is to be noted, however,

---

7. This belongs to the Nyanja Cewa cluster of dialects spoken in Tanzania, Malawi and Mozambique. It is listed under Guthrie's N30.

8. Chimanda, together with Ngoni Tanzania, Ngoni Malawi, Matengo, Mpoto, and Ndendeule are listed under Guthrie's N10.

9. Chiyao belong together with Mwera, Makonde, Ndonde, and Mabiha to Guthrie's P20.

that the first portion in Yao, the Gospel of Matthew, was translated by Chauncey Maples and published by BFBS in 1880. Work on the OT was also undertaken by UMCA missionaries, mainly, C. H. Ker, Norah L. Mann, Mary Cornish, Katharine H. Nixon Smith, Christopher B. Eyre, A. G. H. Sargent, R. A. Russell, Yohanna Abdallah, and G. H. Wilson. This OT, which was finalized in 1920, was printed in parts by BFBS at Likoma.

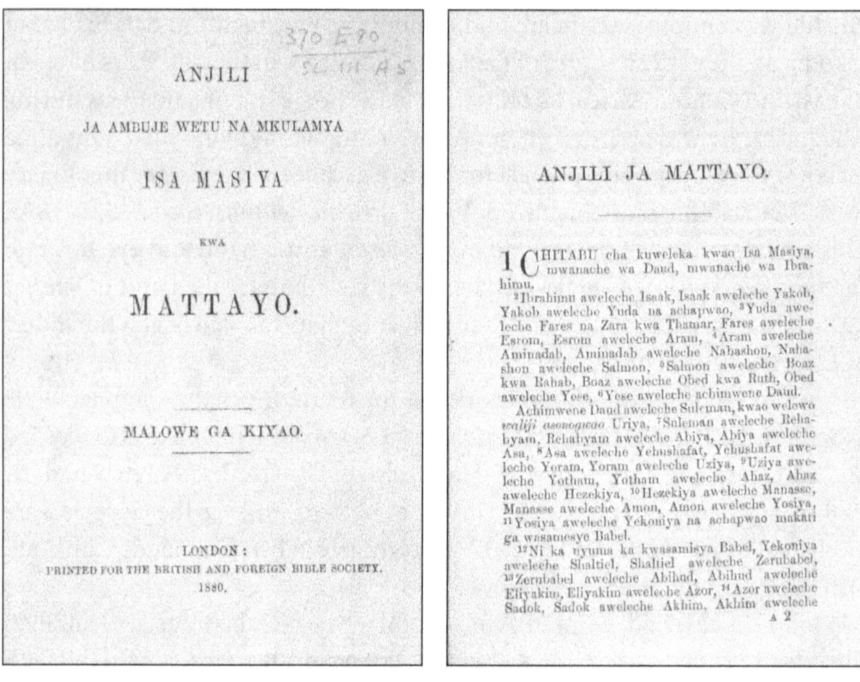

Figure 10.1. The Gospel of Matthew in Yao, the title page and first page. American Bible Society Library and Archives. Used by permission.

The Chiyao NT that was published in 1952 was a new translation begun in 1927.[10] This 1952 version was in a union Chiyao that was intended to accommodate all Chiyao speakers, especially those in Masasi, Tanganyika, and Likwena in Malawi. Work on a common-language translation of the Bible in this language was concentrated and managed wholly in Malawi. Chiyao speakers number about two million people, with about one million to be found in Malawi around the southern tip of Lake Malawi. Half a million are to be

---

10. The publication of Matthew was followed by Mark and Acts in 1932; Genesis and Exodus in 1933; Luke and John in 1934; Matthew (a revised version), Romans, 1 Corinthians, 1–3 John, and Jude in 1935.

found in southern Tanzania, mostly in Tunduru, Mtwara, Masasi, and Ruvuma Districts, and another half a million are to be found in Mozambique, mostly in the Niassa Province to the south and west of Lake Malawi. Historically many Yao were Muslims and in the past many collaborated heavily with the Arab slave and ivory traders. Today, many Yao are Christians. To best serve the Scripture needs of this growing population the Bible Society of Tanzania will likely need to investigate possibilities for joint cooperation with the neighboring countries, especially Malawi. For example, BST could consider adapting the Malawi Chiyao Bible for use by Tanzanian Yao readers.

As noted above, the UMCA contribution to the translation of the Scriptures into the languages of the areas where they worked turned out in the end to be often fragmentary and short-lived. A typical case is the Makua (or Makhuwa) language spoken in southern Tanzania.[11] This is different from a related dialect of Mozambican Makua for which a complete Bible was published in 1982. The Rev Chauncey Maples, who later contributed significantly to the Bible in Kiunguja Swahili, succeeded in translating only the first seven chapters of the Gospel of Matthew. This was published at the UMCA Mission Press in Zanzibar in 1881. In 1927 the Gospel of Mark appeared in Makua, the translation of a committee of UMCA missionaries and nationals including F. Reuben Namalowe, Obed Y. Kasembe, Gerard Sonje, and Isaak Nchiha. The Gospel of John was translated by Dr Lyndon P. Harries of UMCA and published by BFBS in 1946.[12] Nothing else, however, followed in this dialect of Makua spoken in southern Tanzania and in the neighboring parts of Mozambique.

The Scriptures into Mambwe and Mambwe-Lungu

During the 1890s, missionaries of the London Missionary Society worked on the translation of the Scriptures into Mambwe,[13] spoken in both Zambia and the neighboring Fipa area in Tanganyika. D. Picton Jones of LMS translated the Gospels of Mark and John into Mambwe and these were published in 1893 and 1898, respectively, by BFBS. The complete NT in Mambwe, translated by D. Picton Jones, was published in 1901 by BFBS.

---

11. The Makhuwa (Makua) dialect cluster has numerous speakers in Mozambique and southern Tanzania. It is listed under Guthrie's P30.

12. Among other writings, Harries published a grammar of Mwera (1950), and later moved on to academic teaching in the United States where he distinguished himself at the University of Wisconsin-Madison as a leading Swahili scholar.

13. Mambwe and Lungu, together with Fipa, Rungwa and Pimbwe – all spoken in Tanzania and Zambia – belong to Guthrie's M10.

Some years later another team of LMS missionaries, Ernest H. Clark, Harold E. Wareham, and W. Draper, assisted by some reviewers, attempted another translation into Mambwe. They translated the Gospel of Mark and published it in 1909; Acts followed in 1912; and Matthew, Ephesians, and 1–3 John in 1913, as well as a revision of Mark. The Gospel of Luke and Romans appeared in 1914. All were published by BFBS.

In the 1920s there was a proposal to do a translation that would bring together Mambwe and Lungu, two closely related dialects that were considered to be mutually intelligible. This led to a revision of the LMS Mambwe version into a Union Mambwe-Lungu version. This work was prepared by a team consisting of W. Goran Robertson, Ernest H. Clark, Harold E. Wareham, W. Draper, and J. A. Ross, all of the LMS, assisted by mother-tongue speakers. The Gospels and Acts were published in 1921, Romans to Revelation in 1922, the NT in 1923, and the Psalms in 1924, all by BFBS. The Bible Society of Tanzania currently has, however, no knowledge of these Scriptures and has not received any expression of interest in their use from the communities that use this language. It may be that the churches on the Tanzanian side of the border use Swahili Scriptures or obtain their mother-tongue Scriptures from the Bible Society of Zambia where the language is predominantly spoken. Efforts by the Bible Society of Zambia to do something in this language have not been successful.

The Presbyterian Contribution to Translation Work in Southwestern Tanzania

The Livingstonia Mission was founded by the Presbyterian Free Church of Scotland Mission (FCSM). Formerly known as the Glasgow Society, it was named Livingstonia in honor of David Livingstone, their illustrious son. The Livingstonia Mission's area of operation was mainly along the shores of Lake Malawi (Nyasa). A town on the western shores of this lake was also named Livingstonia in honor of David Livingstone. The Livingstonia Mission was the first to reach the lakeshore Tonga people as well as the Ngoni. The first leader of this mission was James Stewart.

The Gospel of Mark in Ngoni[14] was published in 1891, followed by a revised edition of the same Gospel in 1898 and a fifth edition in 1911. These were all published at the Mission Press in Livingstonia. This translation was the work

---

14. Ngoni, as noted above, belongs to the Guthrie's N10, together with Manda Matengo, Mpoto, and Ndendeule.

of Walter A. Elmslie, a missionary of the Free Church of Scotland Mission. Earlier, in 1890, Elmslie also had the Sermon on the Mount and Parables from the Gospels in Ngoni published at the Livingstonia Mission Press. No other Scriptures have been made available in the Ngoni tongue to this day. The Gospel of Mark is now out of print and is no longer remembered by the present generation.

To the northeast of Lake Nyasa (formerly Malawi), southwest of Lake Rukwa, on both sides of the Tanzanian-Zambian border, the Namwanga language is spoken.[15] Though the speakers of this language are to be found in both countries, translation work has been sponsored wholly by the Zambian churches and the Bible Society of Zambia. This provides some explanation for the non-involvement of the Tanzanian churches and the Bible Society of Tanzania in the endeavor to make Scriptures available to the Namwanga-speaking people. A consequence of this fact is that Namwanga Scriptures are not available in Tanzania. Thus, the launching of a new interconfessional version of the Bible in Namwanga, translated by Sinkala and his colleagues and published by the Bible Society of Zambia in 1982, did not generate any interest in Tanzania. Indeed, no copy of this Bible can be found at the Bible Society of Tanzania.

Work on the Namwanga translation of the Scriptures goes back to 1903 when the Gospel of Luke was published by BFBS. It was translated by Alexander Dewar of the Livingstonia Mission. It was, however, James A. Chisholm of the same mission who saw to the translation of the rest of the NT. Various portions were published until the first complete NT was published in 1933 at Edinburgh by NBSS (see table 10.1 below). A corrected edition of this NT was prepared by Ernst W. Burnett of the Livingstonia Mission and published in 1941 at Edinburgh by NBSS. The book of Psalms was translated by Caleb Sikaundi and Fergus Macpherson of the Livingstonia Mission and published in 1953.

Some Individual Initiatives

Nearly a hundred years after the Ngoni Gospel of Mark was published, Mark was translated into Vwanji,[16] a language spoken to the north of the Ngoni in the Njombe section of Southern Highlands near Mbeya. This Vwanji Mark was an

---

15. Namwanga, as noted above, belongs to Guthrie's M20, together with Nyiha and Safwa, among others.

16. As noted above, Wanji (or Vwanji) is part of the Sango-Hehe-Bena-Kinga-Pangwa-Kinga-Kisi group included in Guthrie's G60.

Table 10.1. Timeline of Namwanga Publications

Year	Publication	Published By
1903	Gospel of Luke	BFBS at London
1905	Gospel of John	NBSS at Livingstonia
1910	James to Jude	NBSS at Livingstonia
1913	Gospel of Matthew	NBSS at Livingstonia
1914	Gospel of Mark	NBSS at Livingstonia
1915	Gospel of Luke (Revised)	NBSS at Livingstonia
1923	Acts and Romans	NBSS at Mwenzo
1924	John (revised)	NBSS at Livingstonia
1925	Hebrews	NBSS at Livingstonia
1928	Galatians to Philippians	NBSS at Livingstonia
1930	Acts (revised), 1 and 2 Corinthians, Colossians to Revelation	NBSS at Mwenzo
1933	New Testament	NBSS at Edinburgh
1941	New Testament (corrected)	NBSS at Edinburgh
1953	Psalms	NBSS at Edinburgh
1960	Old Testament Selections	NBSS at Edinburgh and Glasgow
1982	Bible	BS of Zambia at Lusaka

individual effort of one L. S. M. Nsemwa. This work received the endorsement of the Anglican and Lutheran churches with a view to publication by the Bible Society of Tanzania in 1985. The project did not, however, take off, probably because the community did not support or show sufficient interest to sustain the project. The fact that Vwanji is a minority dialect in the Hehe-Bena-Kinga continuum might also be a factor.

In the neighborhood of Lake Rukwa and to the southeast of Lake Tanganyika are to be found speakers of Kifipa.[17] The Fipa people were among the first Tanzanians or Tanganyikans to be converted to Catholicism as a community. Kathleen R. Smythe notes, "Ufipa in southwestern Tanzania, is often seen as a success story for the Catholic Church as it has one of the highest concentrations of Catholics in East Africa."[18] This she attributes to at least three

---

17. Kifipa is part of the Fipa-Mambwe group included in Guthrie's M10. For some historical and cultural information on the Fipa, see Willis, "The Fipa," 82–95.

18. Smythe, "Creation of a Catholic Fipa," 129.

factors, namely, the positive acceptance of the White Fathers' message, their focus on the conversion of children, and the "significant congruence, both cultivated and innate, between the Catholic religion and the roles played by its missionaries in Ufipa on one hand and Fipa religion and culture on the other."[19]

Smythe does not explore the role that the presence or absence of the Bible in Fipa may have played in the present state of Christianity in Ufipa. It suffices to note here that it took a long time before the Fipa had any access to the Holy Scriptures in their language. A hunger for the written word in their own tongue caused some individuals and volunteers to take private initiatives. It was a Fipa school teacher who privately translated the four Gospels. These were later published by Scripture Gift Mission in 1974 as the "Four Things."

A Fipa NT was published by the Bible Society of Tanzania in 1988. This was the work of a volunteer team consisting of Julius Hamisi, Joachiani Malemu, Paulo Mwanauchi, and Jehad Kamansale under the coordination and support of a Dutch missionary, Miss T. Beimers of Muleche Laela, in the Sumbawanga area. Recent attempts by an interconfessional group consisting of all the major churches in the Fipa area to revise the Beimers NT as well as translate the entire OT and the Deuterocanonical books have not yet borne fruit. The Bible Society of Tanzania has made several attempts to support this effort without much success and is eagerly awaiting further initiatives from the Fipa churches.

Work on the neighboring language Safwa, also found in the Mbeya area, was no different. A volunteer team of D. Nkombo and Levi Namunyampa translated the four Gospels using the Swahili Union Version as a base. This was published in a single volume in 1956 by SGM as the "Four Things."

---

19. Smythe, 129.

11

Facing Mount Kenya

Gikuyu, Meru, Tharaka, Embu-Mbeere, and Kikamba

The Languages of Mount Kenya

The languages spoken around Mount Kenya[1] are closely related to each other and are mutually intelligible to varying degrees. This affinity extends to culture and history and, in recent times, has prompted solidarity and collaboration in national politics. Each group, however, has its own distinctive myths of origin and stories of how the different groups came to be where they are and the way they are. This has led one folklorist writing on the Embu-Mbeere, for example, to assert:

> The Embu and the Mbeere have often been erroneously regarded as a splinter group of the Kikuyu ethnic group. Even their language has been dismissed as a "primitive" dialect of the Gikuyu language. However, as oral history testifies, the Embu and the Mbeere are a community with a definite history as well as a culture that qualifies them to be recognized as an ethnic group with a definite cultural identity.[2]

Many years of living in proximity with close Bantu cousins has led to frequent intermarriages and intermingling, regular cultural exchange, and linguistic borrowings among the Mount Kenya ethnic groups. Some historical linguists explain their closeness in terms of the Thagicu hypothesis – that all these closely related Mount Kenya languages go back to an original ethnic

---

1. Mount Kenya, straddling the equator, at 17,021 feet (5,188 meters) is Africa's second-highest mountain, surpassed only by Mount Kilimanjaro.

2. See Chesaina, *Oral Literature of the Embu*, 3.

group "from which they are all derived."[3] These languages and dialects include Gikuyu, Kikamba,[4] Embu-Mbeere, the Meru group (Chuka, Muthambi, Mwimbi, Igoji, Miutine, Imenti, Tigania, Igembe), and Tharaka.[5] The Segeju and Sonjo in Tanzania are also included in this Central Kenya Bantu/Thagicu language group.[6]

Krapf's Travels and Researches and the First Missions into the Interior of Kenya

After Johann Krapf's departure from Kenya in 1853, during most of the rest of the nineteenth century, missionary work was confined to the coastal strip and among coastal communities, save for Krapf's own adventures into the interior and his involvement with the Akamba people and their leader, Chief Kivoi. On one occasion, Krapf and Chief Kivoi, a prominent ivory trader, were on a trip to the Tana River when they were waylaid by bandits. Chief Kivoi lost his life in this incident but Krapf survived. Krapf's involvement with Chief Kivoi led to his attempt to translate Scripture into Kikamba. Krapf succeeded in translating the Gospel of Mark, which was published in 1850. How he accomplished this feat without having ever lived among the Akamba is a puzzling and extraordinary accomplishment. His efforts laid the foundation for later translation work in Kikamba, as well as for the other languages of the Mount Kenya area, and indeed for the rest of East Africa.

Church historian Father John Baur observes that "Kenya had been the first East African country to see missionaries at its coast, but it was the last one to receive some in its interior."[7] Another historian, William Anderson, attributes this to "the difficulty of penetrating the harsh, waterless hinterland before the construction of the railway."[8] The presence of unwelcoming and fierce groups such as the Maasai was also a contributing factor. Nevertheless, after the building of the Uganda Railway which reached its terminus in western Kenya in 1901, Anderson speaks of the "flood of missions" which "began to

---

3. Patrick R. Bennett quoted in Muriuki, *History of the Kikuyu*, 52.

4. *Kamba* is the base form, *Mukamba* is a *Kamba* person, *Akamba* is the plural for *Kamba* people, *Kikamba* is their language, and *Ukambani* refers to the territory they inhabit.

5. These are listed in Guthrie's Bantu referential classification system in group E50. For the members of the Meru cluster, see Nyaga, *Customs and Traditions of the Meru*, and also Mwaniki, *Chuka Historical Texts*, x–xii.

6. Muriuki, *History of the Kikuyu*, 52.

7. Baur, *2000 Years of Christianity in Africa*, 254.

8. Anderson, *Church in East Africa*, 62.

pour into central and western Kenya, at the turn of the century."[9] Consequently, the Anglicans were able to open their stations in Ukambani at Mlango in 1888, in Gikuyuland at Kabete in 1898, on the Luyia-Luo border at Maseno in 1906, and at Kigari in Embu in 1910. The Africa Inland Mission (AIM), later to become the Africa Inland Church (AIC), started its missionary work among the Akamba in 1895 under their founder and director Peter Cameron Scott, later moving to work among the Maasai, Kikuyu, and Kalenjin peoples. The Methodists moved from the coast to their base in the interior among the Meru people in 1910.

The country was now ripe for harvest and missionary workers came in like a flood. The groups who set up operations at this time included the following:

- the Church of Scotland Mission, now the Presbyterian Church of East Africa (PCEA), among the Agikuyu in central Kenya with their centers at Thogoto, Tumutumu, and Chogoria;
- the Friends Africa Mission (also known as the Friends Africa Industrial Mission), now the East African Yearly Meeting of Friends (EAYMF), among the northern and eastern Luyia (Bukusu, Tiriki, Logooli, Isukha, Nyala, and Kabras) with their center at Kaimosi;
- the Church of God Mission among the southern Luyia (Nyole, Kisa, Idakho, and Tsotso) with their center at Kima near Maseno;
- the Seventh-Day Adventists among the Kisii and Luo of South Nyanza with their centers at Kamagambo and Kendu Bay;
- the World Gospel Mission (WGM) among the Kipsigis with their center at Kericho;
- The Pentecostal Assemblies of God among the southeastern Luyia (Logooli) with their center at Nyang'ori.

The Roman Catholics were represented by three of their orders, namely, the Holy Ghost Fathers among the southern Gikuyu in Kiambu and around Nairobi; the Consolata Fathers among the northern Gikuyu in Murang'a and the Nyeri around Mount Kenya; and the Mill Hill Fathers in western Kenya among the Luo, the Luyia, and Kisii.

With no available lingua franca for their use, the missionaries had no alternative but to learn the native tongues of their target audience so as to facilitate communication and the sharing of the gospel with the people to whom they were sent. The need for Bible translation soon became obvious as is evidenced by the profusion of attempts at translation in the local languages

---

9. Anderson, 62.

shortly after the missionaries' arrival and settlement. Catholic participation in Bible translation was negligible or nonexistent during this period. This field of endeavor was dominated by the Protestant missions.

The Bible in Kikamba

Krapf's translation of the Gospel of Mark published in 1850 meant that Kikamba was one of the first languages in the country of Kenya to have a translation of a book of the Bible. It was printed in Tübingen, Germany, by the Ludwig Friedrich Fues Press and its title page reads as follows: "*Evangelio ta Yunaolete Malkosi.* The Gospel according to St. Mark, translated into the Kikamba language by the Rev. Dr. J. L. Krapf, Missionary of the Church Missionary Society in East Africa."

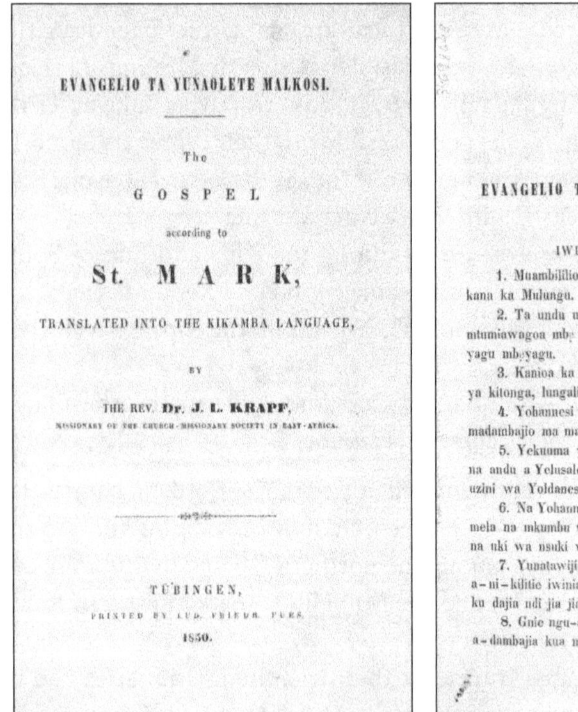

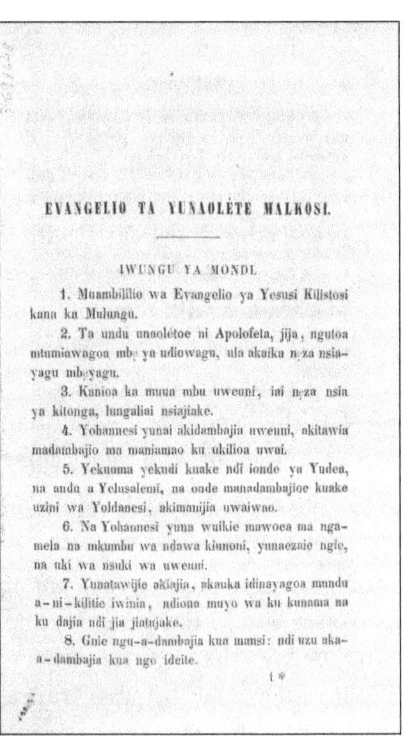

Figure 11.1. The Gospel of Mark in Kikamba, the title page and first page. American Bible Society Library and Archives. Used by permission.

The Kikamba of this Gospel is mostly unintelligible to contemporary speakers of the language. A UBS translation consultant randomly requested a number of Kikamba speakers to give him a back-translation of the first eight verses from Krapf's translation into Swahili or English, only to meet with a negative response. They claimed that the Kikamba in this Gospel no longer made sense.

Krapf's translation may have been for his own academic interest. He never lived in Ukambani, nor did he actively speak the language. No church was planted in Ukambani during his time and this Gospel was never really used there. However, Krapf must be given credit for his vision and for his determination to start something in this language. He clearly planted the seed, even though from a distance. His compatriots, J. Hoffmann, H. Pfitzinger, and Ernest Brutzer of the Leipzig Mission, continued his efforts half a century later by translating and bringing to publication the Gospel according to Luke in 1898, Acts in 1904, and Matthew in 1909 – all by BFBS.[10] Unfortunately, these efforts were not very successful as the texts were not widely used or accepted. This was due to the poor choice of dialect, the fact that the translation was not well received by the Akamba, the difficult German-based orthography, and the decision to leave the field to the Africa Inland Mission.[11] The Africa Inland Mission and the Gospel Furthering Fellowship (GFF) missionaries thus inherited and continued the work of the Leipzig missionaries. It is they who would finally realize Krapf's dream of seeing the entire Bible in Kikamba.

To this end, George W. Rhoad, Nellie Rhoad, Hattie Newman, C. F. Johnston, H. S. Nixon, Rose W. Horton, L. E. Davies, Emma Farnsworth, Clara Guilding, and Frances Johnson all contributed to the task. Aaron Kasyoki and Jeremiah Kyeve were mother-tongue informants or assistants. A new translation of Mark appeared in 1915, John in 1916, while the entire New Testament appeared in 1920. It is interesting that Daniel, released in 1935, was the first OT portion printed in Kikamba, rather than Genesis, which followed in 1936. The entire Bible appeared in print in 1956, more than a century after Krapf laid the foundation. It was published by the BFBS in London. A corrected edition was published by the Bible Society in East Africa in Nairobi in 1974.

This Bible translation was a result of the interest, cooperation, and collaboration on the part of the missionaries. Kikamba speakers welcomed it and it has been widely used throughout Ukambani despite some of its intelligibility problems arising out of regional differences, archaic expressions, and literalisms. It was apparently not sensitive to the sociolinguistic and dialectal situation of Ukambani. For example, some significant differences between

---

10. See BFBS – ESC Minute Cards of 8.4.14, vol. 4.

11. See BFBS – ESC Minute Cards of 11.9.12 and 8.4.14, vol. 4.

Masaku, South Kitui, North Kitui, and Mumoni/North Mwingi speakers seem to have been ignored or assumed to be non-existent; the resulting translation gave preference to Masaku speakers. Problems of unnaturalness, lack of clarity, or even ungrammaticality in this translation were due to the literal approach adopted by the translators. The translation also reflected the limited linguistic competence of the missionaries who learned Kikamba as a second language. The text was in need of revision, a situation common to many translations executed during this period.

Plans to start a new common-language translation of the Bible in modern Kikamba came together in 1995 under the sponsorship of the local Roman Catholic, Anglican, and African Inland Churches. The initial team of translators included Michael Ndonye (Anglican), Urbanus Kioko (Roman Catholic), and Julius Wambua (AIC). They were replaced by a completely new team composed of Father Francis Maundu (Roman Catholic, Masaku), the Rev Jonathan Kilonzo (Anglican, Kitui), and Rev Charles Kimwele (AIC). Later, in 2007, Father Maundu left to pursue biblical studies in Rome. His place was taken over by Father Benedict Mwavu.

This effort to create a new translation in contemporary Kikamba was certainly long overdue, considering that the present pioneer Kikamba Bible is outdated and has become almost unintelligible to most contemporary readers. The translators who worked on the new translation were mandated to take into account many of the factors that have made the existing missionary translation difficult to understand and to create a new reader-friendly version. Their target was an idiomatic translation in modern Kikamba that contemporary readers will be able to read, fully understand, and enjoy. The publication of the NT in June 2003 confirmed the need for a new Bible in contemporary speech. The fact that every copy was bought and the demand for a reprint was high was seen as an endorsement of this goal. Work on translating the OT continued in earnest and was completed and printed in two editions – a Catholic edition containing the deuterocanonical books and a Protestant edition without these books. The dedication and public launch of this second Bible in Kikamba took place at a colorful ceremony on 14 April 2011, at Machakos, a town near Nairobi, Kenya.

Surprisingly, Professor John S. Mbiti, a New Testament scholar and a leading pioneer scholar of African traditional religions, a Kenyan who is a mother-tongue speaker of Kikamba, found this new translation to be unacceptable. In his view it was too paraphrastic and inaccurate in a number of places. Professor Mbiti found it appropriate and desirable to use the ancient Kikamba name for God, *Mulungu*, in place of the one currently in vogue, *Ngai*. *Ngai* is of Nilotic origin, from Maasai, and is widely used by most of the Mount

Kenya groups including the Gikuyu and Embu-Mbeere. It is interesting that Krapf used the old name *Mulungu*. It looks like *Mulungu* was the preferred name in the 1840s when Krapf did his translation into Kikamba. However, reverting to the Bantu *Mulungu* would present problems today, the main one being the current widespread use and acceptability of the Maasai term *Ngai*.

Figure 11.2 Professor John Mbiti (middle) and Professor Jesse N. K. Mugambi (right) with the author. Photo © Aloo Osotsi Mojola

Unhappy and disappointed with the new translation, Mbiti decided to embark on an endeavor to translate the New Testament into Kikamba himself. With a PhD in New Testament from Cambridge University and as a mother-tongue speaker of Kikamba he was ideally suited for this task. With much patience and perseverance Mbiti eventually completed translating the entire NT. He made an offer to the Bible Society of Kenya to consider it for publication. This offer, however, was not accepted. The Bible Society's reason for turning Mbiti's offer down was that the translation was the work of a single author that was not supported by the churches. It was also reasoned that because Mbiti had been resident in Switzerland for many years he was no longer sufficiently in touch with ongoing changes and developments in the language. Further, BSK feared that Mbiti's translation might suffer from literalness and too strong an adherence to the grammatical forms of koine Greek. Some thought that Mbiti's deep understanding of the traditional Kamba religion as a specialist in African traditional religions could have unduly influenced his translation. As noted above, this is evidenced in his use of the old Kikamba name of God, *Mulungu*, rather than the current borrowed term *Ngai*. A close study and a comparison of the two translations is likely to prove interesting and instructive.

Professor Mbiti is to be congratulated, however, for taking this bold step in showing his fellow professionally trained biblical scholars the way. While many are comfortable reading the Bible in foreign tongues, Mbiti has plunged into the deep in an attempt to mediate the language and world of the New Testament with that of his own Kamba traditional religious, cultural, and linguistic milieu. The challenge is for African biblical scholars to cease being strangers to the Bible in their own languages, and to actively embrace the use of the Bible in their own mother tongues. This is a necessary key to the enculturation, indigenization, or the incarnation of the Bible in the African soil; as such it highlights the urgency of developing hermeneutics of the Bible within the framework of African vernaculars.

Also, Mbiti is to be credited also for championing the study of African traditional religions, an interest that goes back to his study and research at Cambridge University, which he published as *New Testament Eschatology in an African Background*. In this study he explored the African view of time. His next two books, *African Religions and Philosophy* and *Concepts of God in Africa*, specifically focused on the traditional religions of Africa but with a view to how they could provide a basis for Christian faith. Sadly, Professor Mbiti passed on on 6 October 2019 in Switzerland where he resided. He was however buried in his home in Ukambani, Kenya.

The Bible into Gikuyu

Gikuyu is the language of the most populous ethnic group in Kenya, numbering well over six million people. The beginning of translation work in Gikuyu was uncoordinated and reflected a certain measure of denominational rivalry and competition.[12] For example, A. W. MacGregor of the Church Missionary

---

12. For information on the traditions of the Gikuyu, see Cagnolo, *Agikuyu*. Also, Kenyatta's *Facing Mount Kenya* (1938), written as a student at the London School of Economics under his mentor Professor Malinowski, is still of great interest. Wanjohi's *The Wisdom and Philosophy*

Society based at Kabete, working with his assistant Enoka Boi, had the Gospel of John published in 1903 by BFBS. A. Ruffell Barlow, representing the Church of Scotland Mission (CSM) based at Thogoto, had the Gospel of Mark published in 1909 by the National Bible Society of Scotland, while F. H. McKenrick of the Africa Inland Mission based at Kijabe had Paul's letter to the Philippians published by their Mission Press at Kijabe in 1912. Thereafter, the missions attempted successfully to follow a unified and coordinated strategy. These efforts resulted in the first Gikuyu New Testament, which appeared in 1926, translated mainly by Cannon Harry Leakey and A. Ruffell Barlow, and was published separately by BFBS at London and by NBSS at Edinburgh. A revised edition with Psalms appeared ten years later published under similar arrangements. Leakey and Barlow were supported by an interdenominational committee consisting of E. W. Crawford (CMS); Dr J. W. Arthur and Miss Stevenson (CSM); L. H. Downing and F. H. McKenrick (AIM); and Dr J. Henderson (GMS). Canon Harry Leakey was the chair of the United Kikuyu Language Committee and A. Ruffell Barlow was its secretary. One of the challenges that this committee had to resolve was that of standardizing the language and its orthography, especially the representation of the vowel sounds.

Canon Leakey worked very closely with Mathayo Njoroge in preparing his translations. In a letter to BFBS Leakey says of Njoroge, "He is simply invaluable to me, and I am deeply conscious of the fact that it is largely due to him that the books I have brought out have met with the favourable reception they have, and have been sold up at such amazing speed."[13] BFBS in response "resolved to recommend that the payment of Mathayo's salary, £72, for the year 1936, to March 31, 1937, be approved."[14] Later in his request for the renewal of that grant, Leakey spoke of Njoroge's "extreme conscientiousness, sense of responsibility and punctuality in regard to his work."[15]

In 1951 the Old Testament was published separately under a comparable arrangement. The chief translators were L. J. Beecher and A. Ruffell Barlow. A revised and corrected edition of this Bible appeared in 1965. R. G. Calderwood together with Ayub Kinyua and Meshullam Wachira were the main workers on the revision. Nonetheless, the whole was a product so to speak of interdenominational cooperation and the work of missionaries in the

---

of the Gikuyu Proverbs (1997), as well as his *Under One Roof* (2001), are fine resources on the life of the Gikuyu people as captured in their proverbs. See also Mugo, *Kikuyu People* (1982).

    13. BFBS – ESC Minutes Cards of 11.9.12 and 8.4.14, vol. 4.

    14. BFBS ESC Minutes, Apr 17, 1936. See 4.3.36, p. 67.

    15. BFBS ESC Minutes. See 7.4.37, p. 3.

area. The 1936 report by the Rev W. J. Mowll of BFBS listed the Committee as consisting of the following members: "The Rev. Canon H. Leakey, Limuru (CMS); Mr. L. J. Beecher, Kahuhia, Forthall (CMS); Mr. R. G. M Calderwood, Kikuyu, (CSM); Mr. A. R. Barlow, Tumutumu (CSM); Mr. F. H. McKenrick, Kijabe (CSM); Mr. C. W. Teasdale, Kijabe (AIM); and Mr. J. W. Dougal, Nairobi (Educational Adviser to Missions in East Africa)." The same report noted: "Canon Leakey has practically finished the Pentateuch and the historical books; he has done also a good deal of Isaiah and Jeremiah. Mr. Barlow is on schedule with the other books. Mr. Beecher has translated Obadiah, Daniel, Haggai, and Malachi, and is doing Zechariah. Mr. Calderwood has done Jonah (published 1928) and is working on Amos."[16]

The input from mother-tongue speakers was considered seriously. Both Leakey and Barlow relied heavily on their mother-tongue assistants. The 1965 revision sought to focus on clarity and naturalness while retaining the formal correspondence character of the translation. The translation has enjoyed overwhelming popularity in all Gikuyu-speaking areas, as well as in areas where Gikuyu is a secondary though related language, as for example in the Embu-Mbeere and Chuka-speaking areas. It is the most sought-after vernacular Bible in Kenya and a regular best seller by the Bible Society of Kenya. Its influence can be discerned from the writings of well-known Kenyan writers, such as Ngũgĩ wa Thiong'o, whose novels, including *A Grain of Wheat* and *Devil on the Cross*, are heavily influenced by this Bible.

A new contemporary translation in Gikuyu was started in 1983. This was intended to be truly interconfessional and sought to enlist the cooperation, not just of Protestant denominations, but of the local Orthodox and Roman Catholic Churches as well. The three translators in the original team included Gabriel Ndichu (Roman Catholic), Samuel Gathage (Greek Orthodox), and Francis Kirika (Presbyterian). Gathage is the only translator from the Greek Orthodox Church to have participated as a translator of the Bible in any of the East African countries.[17] The team of reviewers was likewise representative to ensure that the language of translation was not only intelligible among the dialect areas of Mathira, Nyeri, Murang'a, and Kiambu – as well as Ndia and Gichugu of South Kirinyaga – but also accurate and faithful to the original texts, employing the rich resources, idioms, figures, natural rhythms, and expressions of this important language.

---

16. BFBS ESC Minutes. See 13.5.36, p. 10.

17. In Uganda, the head of the Orthodox Church participated as a member of the management committee on the contemporary Luganda translation project.

Figure 11.3. Mr Maruge (right) and a Reverend read from the newly published Gikuyu Common Language Bible at Bible dedication and launch event held near Mount Kenya, 2008. Photo © Aloo Osotsi Mojola

The new Gikuyu common-language New Testament was published and launched in 1995. Meanwhile, work on the Old Testament continued under a new team of translators composed of Johnson Kamau (Presbyterian), Francis Kinyari (Roman Catholic), and Edward Karani (Anglican). The work was somewhat delayed because of the need to incorporate recent orthographic changes in the writing of the language. There were also delays in typesetting and printing. The complete Gikuyu common-language Bible was dedicated in Nyeri, Kenya, on 12 July 2008. The location on the slopes of Mount Kenya meant that the dedication was done "facing Mount Kenya." The chief guest at this dedication was, then President of Kenya, Emilio Mwai Kibaki, who is also a Gikuyu speaker, born in Nyeri and a Catholic. The enthusiastic crowd sang and danced to the music of the numerous church choirs representing the Gikuyu-speaking Protestant, Catholic, Orthodox, and Africa independent churches from around the Mount Kenya area. The launch was graced by the oldest primary school student recorded in the *Guinness World Records 2009*. Mzee Joseph Stephen Kimani Nganga Maruge enrolled in primary school in his eighties with the aim of learning how to read so as to be able to read the Bible. The old man was one of the readers of this new Gikuyu Bible during the launch. His dream of learning how to read the Bible had been fulfilled after six years of primary school education.[18]

The new Bible includes a revised edition of the NT that was released in 1995. This new translation is not expected to replace the older existing translation but to be used alongside it. The presence of two versions of the Bible among the Gikuyu users of the Bible is considered to be a blessing and will enrich the community of Bible readers in this language. It will allow for choice of versions in a situation where such a choice did not previously exist. Moreover, it will allow readers to benefit from the variety of perspectives and approaches represented by the two translations, one being an older, formal correspondence translation, and the other being a meaning-based or functional equivalence, contemporary translation; one having been translated by missionaries and second-language speakers of Gikuyu, and the new one having been translated by mother-tongue speakers of the language.

Translation into Embu-Mbeere

There has been a long-standing interest in having the Bible translated into Embu-Mbeere. Although they are seen as distinct dialects, Embu and Mbeere are known to share a high level of mutual intelligibility. Speakers of these two dialects communicate and understand each other fully without any need of an interpreter.[19] Thus the decision to share common Scriptures was uncontested, but was widely accepted and supported by all stakeholders. Work was started in 1976 by the Bible Society of Kenya under the sponsorship of the Anglican and Roman Catholic Churches with Canon Bedan Ireri (Anglican) and Father Gabriel Muverethi (Roman Catholic) as translators, but it stalled as a result of misunderstandings about the needs and the purpose of this work. Some leading Embu-Mbeere speakers felt that the Gikuyu Bible was adequate for use by their people. Given the political context of the time and the perceived need by community leaders to strengthen the political and cultural unity of the Mount Kenya Thagicu groups, commonly called GEMA (an acronym for Gikuyu, Embu, Meru, and Kamba communities), it was thought translation into related dialects or languages would weaken the "tribal" unity. However, changed

---

18. Mzee Maruge's death on 14 August 2009, at the age of eighty-nine was reported by the international press around the world.

19. This unity and common traditions and language is assumed, for example, by Chesaina, *Oral Literature of the Embu*, and Mwaniki, *Living History of Embu*.

political circumstances and a new leadership encouraged the beginning of translation in the Embu-Mbeere dialect cluster.

The Embu-Mbeere Bible translation project was relaunched in 1995. The first members of the translation team were Father Wilson Munyi (Roman Catholic) and the Rev John Gichangi (Anglican). Later, the Rev Pithon Njuki, a speaker of the Mbeere dialect, joined this team and helped to give it a balanced dialect representation. Father Munyi was replaced by another Catholic, James Njiru. The local churches have shown a lot of enthusiasm for this project. At present, however, the Gikuyu Bible continues to serve the needs of the Embu-Mbeere communities, though inadequately. A first trial publication, the Gospel of Mark, was launched on 29 March 1998, at the Anglican Cathedral of the Diocese of Embu in an interdenominational ceremony attended by representatives from all around the Embu and Mbeere districts. The NT followed in September 2002. It was very well received. It is not a surprise that copies of the first printing were sold out very quickly. Reprints have since followed. Work on the OT proceeded well and the complete Bible was printed and issued in two editions, a Catholic edition containing the deuterocanonical books and a Protestant edition without these books. The dedication and public launch of this Bible was held at the Embu town stadium in a well attended ceremony on 16 June 2012, at which UBS representatives who were in Nairobi for one of their consultations also participated.

Figure 11.4. The Rt, Rev Henry Kathii, Anglican bishop of the Diocese of Embu and strong supporter of the Embu-Mbeere Bible translation. Photo © Aloo Osotsi Mojola

The former General Secretary of the Bible Society of Kenya, the Rev Henry Kathii, after his consecration and installation as the Anglican bishop of the Diocese of Embu, continued to support and provide sponsorship of this translation in his own mother tongue and this was expected to give it a moral boost throughout the area. In an interview, Bishop Kathii was asked how he saw the place of Bible translation in the Bible Society and in the church. He responded,

> Bible translation forms the basic work for any Bible Society in Africa. The Bible was introduced to us in languages that were not fully understood by the indigenous people. People are only able to commit their lives to Christ because they understand the meaning and the means of salvation in their own language. When the richness of the language is brought out in a translation in the languages of the people, they understand the claims of the gospel message better, and can respond appropriately. Bible translation makes the message of the Church better understood by the hearers.[20]

Bishop Kathii was instrumental in initiating the Embu-Mbeere translation project. In the meantime, the Embu and Mbeere people continued to use the Gikuyu Bible for many years as they eagerly looked forward to the day when they would have the entire Bible in their own language. That day finally arrived as indicated above on 16 June 2012. Bishop Kathii recalls a story of an old schoolmate who teased him about the second-class status ascribed to the Embu-Mbeere, saying that Gikuyu was God's language, the language of heaven, at the time used by all the churches in the area, while Embu Mbeere was the devil's language since it could not at the time be used.

The Bible in Meru (Kimiiru)

The Meru language is spoken around the eastern and north-eastern slopes of Mount Kenya. Translation work in this language was initiated by R. T. Worthington and W. H. Laughton of the United Methodist Mission. They were assisted by Philip Muntu Inoti and Stefano M. Andegwa. Mark was published in 1921, John in 1923, Matthew in 1934 and Luke in 1935. However, the death of R. T. Worthington disrupted the continuity of this translation effort. It fell to W. H. Laughton, A. J. Hopkins and E. Mary Holding, all of the United

---

20. See appendix A.

Methodist Mission, to take over from where the Rev Worthington had left off. They were assisted by Philip Muntu Inoti, as well as Naaman Mwirichia and Silas Mugambi. A committee of reviewers was also appointed to assist them. Sadly, Pastor Inoti lost his life prematurely in a motor accident. However, the drafts he had made of several OT books were revised by subsequent translators. This second attempt at translating the Meru Bible resulted in the publication of Mark in 1941, the Gospels and Acts in 1946, Romans–Revelation in 1955, and the Psalms in 1955. These were all published by BFBS in London. The complete Bible was finalized and published jointly by ABS and BFBS in 1964.

One of the problems of the Bible in Meru has been its handling of the dialect situation in the Meru-speaking area. Although originally intended for use among all so-called Meru people, it was mainly used by the Igembe, Tigania, Imenti, and Miutini dialect groups for whom the Imenti used in the translation was mutually intelligible. The Chuka, Igoji, Mwimbi, and Muthambi of Nithi – as well as the more populous and much different Tharaka – were not well served by this translation. Additionally, this translation did not treat the question of Meru orthography very well. Meru has seven vowels, yet the orthography of the translation used only five vowel characters, a situation which contributed to many ambiguities and inaccuracies in the translation. Unfortunately, this situation was not solved or even taken into account in the new interconfessional common-language translation which was started in 1979 with Francis Mungania (Methodist), P. Kaibung'a (Roman Catholic), Cyprian Kinoti (Roman Catholic), and Joyce Nki (Methodist) as translators. Consequently, the resulting NT was published in 1988 with this deficiency.

An agreement was reached on a new orthography intended to deal with the problems. The new team of translators working on the Old Testament used this new orthography. The team members were Cyprian Kinoti, initially, and later Bartholomew Kaburu (Roman Catholic), John Kobia Ataya and John Nyota (Methodist), and Aaron Mbae Muga (Presbyterian). Ruth was published in 1995 as a trial portion designed to test the translation in its own right but also as a test to popularize the new orthography. This portion was very well received. New Reader portions in Meru, books 1 to 3 (arranged in three levels, elementary, intermediate and advanced), were translated and published by the Bible Society of Kenya and distributed in all lower primary schools.[21] In April

---

21. New Reader books are a series of books developed by the Bible Societies with new literates or readers in mind. The series is intended to teach the new literates how to read their mother tongue using Bible stories that are simplified and graded to allow for a progression

and May 1998, the translators trained teachers on the use of the seven-vowel system of the new orthography that was used in the translation. This effort has proved very popular and successful. Work on the Old Testament, including the Deuterocanonical books, is now complete, with input from a translation team consisting of the Rev Elias Mukindia Kinyua (Methodist), Father Bernard Kaburu (Roman Catholic), and the Rev Wachira Mugo (Presbyterian), as well Mr Richard Baariu (Pentecostal) who resigned in 2005 to pursue PhD studies at the Nairobi Evangelical Graduate School of Theology. The Kimiiru Bible was finally launched at the Kenya Methodist University, in Meru town on the northern slopes of Mount Kenya, on 26 February 2011, at a memorable public ceremony attended by leading Meru church leaders both active and retired from all denominations as well as leading political, civic, cultural, and community leaders. The ceremony was televised live nationally by one of the leading media houses in Kenya. A local Kimiiru radio program also gave a live broadcast of the ceremony. Sales of this Bible, issued in two editions – one Catholic, the other Protestant – could hardly fulfill with the heavy demand.

Tharaka Scriptures

The difficulty for Tharaka speakers to fully understand the Meru Bible pointed to a need for them to have their own Scriptures. The disparity between these dialects had been recognized much earlier, when Muindi wa Ngumbao became the first translator of the Gospel of John into Tharaka, under the direction of H. S. Nixon of the Africa Inland Mission. Elwood L. Davis, the field director of AIM in Kenya, wrote to BFBS in London on 10 March 1933, challenging the need for a Tharaka translation, saying, "Whilst I think the Tharaka boy is to be congratulated on his achievement, I am wondering whether there is not too great a similarity between the Meru language and Tharaka to warrant translations being made in the two languages."[22]

Nixon, however, felt so strongly about the need for the Tharaka to have a translation of their own that he wrote a letter to BFBS, dated 20 June 1933, as follows:

> I do not regard Tharaka and Meru as dialects of the same language, but even should the committee accept this view, the New Testament has been published in Swahili in both Mombasa

---

from easy to difficult. These have proved very popular and effective for readers in a variety of language situations.

22. See the Archival Records in the Bibliography, BFBS EA languages correspondence files.

and Zanzibar. Surely the difference between Meru and Tharaka is greater than Mombasa and Zanzibar Swahili. The Society will not lose anything financially by publishing this edition in Tharaka, for I am prepared to pay cash for the entire edition. So strongly do I feel the necessity for the publication of the Scriptures in Tharaka that if the Society should regard it as being unnecessary, then I should feel obliged to publish it under other auspices. I feel quite confident, however, that the British and Foreign Bible Society will publish St. John's Gospel in Tharaka.[23]

In 1934 BFBS did indeed publish the Gospel of John that Muindi wa Ngumbao had translated and it was reprinted in 1970.

Bible Translation and Literacy, Ltd, identified a current need for Scripture in Tharaka after conducting an initial sociolinguistic survey in the area sometime in the 1980s. The ensuing efforts to translate the New Testament into Tharaka will help to alleviate the problem of Scripture need among the Watharaka by picking up the translation work begun in 1934. BTL/SIL have taken over where Muindi wa Ngumbao and H. S. Nixon left off. Their work was carried forward by mother-tongue speakers, including Zaccheus Kibiubi, Stephen Kindiki, John Nguu, and Albert Kathenya. Kibiubi, the original team leader, and has subsequently been replaced by Kathenya. The Gospel of Mark was published and dedicated in 1993. This was followed by the Acts of the Apostles in 1995, while Galatians, 1 Timothy–Philemon, James, and Jude all appeared in 1996. These portions are reported to have received a very warm reception. The New Testament was published in 2000 and reprinted in 2002. The strong interest in the NT and this whole enterprise encouraged BTL to move forward with the Old Testament work. Those involved in the translation of the OT include John Nguu as translator and team leader, and Onesimus Kamwara and Juliet Ndatho as members of the translation team. Joseph Mbijiwe and Susan Nyaga serve on the literacy team intended to support and promote the translation work. The complete Bible in Kitharaka was dedicated and launched on 13 June 2019 at the Tharaka Boys High School in Marimanti in Tharaka Nithi County, Kenya.

---

23. See the Archival Records in the Bibliography, BFBS EA languages correspondence files.

12

The Nilotes of the Eastern Great Rift Valley

Karimojong, Turkana, Teso, Kalenjin, Datooga, Maasai, and Samburu

The Nilotes of the Eastern Great Rift Valley

The Great Rift Valley is a magnificent geological feature that stretches from as far north as Israel and Palestine down through Ethiopia and Kenya, and as far south as Mozambique. There is a western branch of this valley that goes through Lake Malawi, Lake Tanganyika, and the Great Lakes area of Uganda and the Democratic Republic of Congo. On both sides of the eastern branch of the Kenyan section of the Great Rift Valley are to be found groups of Nilotic pastoralists – the Karimojong, the Turkana, the Teso, the Pokoot, the Kalenjin, the Samburu, and the Maasai, who extend south to the Morogoro region of Tanzania. These pastoralists are described as having a "cattle complex." Their lives revolve around cattle and related cultural activities. They speak closely related languages of the Nilotic family. The Teso, Turkana, Karimojong, Maasai, Samburu, and Ilchamus are referred to as Plains Nilotes and their languages belong to the Eastern Nilotic branch. Kalenjin and related peoples – such as the Sabiny in the Mount Elgon area of Uganda and the Sabaot, immediate neighbors on the Kenyan side of the border, as well as the Pokoot and Datooga in Tanzania – are referred to as the Highland Nilotes and their language forms the Southern Nilotic branch.

The Tunga people

Father Bruno Novelli, author of *Aspects of Karimojong Ethnosociology: A Grammar of the Karimojong Language* and *Karimojong Traditional Religion* has proposed the term *Tunga* as a common name for all the Plains Nilotes.

This proposal was inspired by how the term *Bantu* came to be used, or the term *Jii*, which is a popular way to refer to the River-Lake Nilotes. All three terms mean "human beings." Father Novelli writes with respect to the Plains Nilotes:

> all these peoples . . . in order to ask the basic question: "Who are you?" and to give the answer: "I am a human being", use slightly different words, but all the same root "NGA". The central root to which the Karimojong belong, has an older form, morphologically more complex. Instead of "NGA" they use the root "TUNGA". They say: "NGAe iyong?" (Who are you?) and they answer: "iTUNGAnan ayong" (I am a human being).[1]

Novelli's proposed term *Tunga* ("peoples") refers to all the Nilotes of the plains, which he divides into three groups – the northern group (the Bari and the Lutuho); the central group (the Teso, Itesyo, the Karimojong, Jie, Dodoz, Topoza, Jiye, Nyangatom, and Turkana); and the southern group (the Samburu and Maasai).[2]

Sometime in 1992, the UBS organized a translation workshop in Lodwar in northwest Kenya for three translation teams that belong to the central Tunga group, namely, the Topoza from Sudan, the Karimojong from Uganda, and the Turkana of Kenya in whose territory the workshop was held. It was fascinating to see how easily members of these three teams, Turkana, Topoza, and Karimojong, communicated with one another, each speaking in their own language and yet being able to converse with one another without a break in the communication. The translators in these teams rejoiced at discovering their commonalities and how closely related their languages were. This encounter was fruitful as it facilitated useful exchanges and discussion of common translation problems and possible solutions. The participants said that had members of the Teso or Itesyo groups been present, there would still have been no break in the communication. Both the Turkana and Karimojong teams have since completed the translation of their respective Bibles. At the time of writing, the Toposa translation team is still at work with their SIL coordinator Martin Schroeder.

---

1. Novelli, *Aspects of Karimojong Ethnosociology*, 27.

2. Novelli, 26.

Translation into Karimojong

Ngakarimojong is the name of the language spoken by the Karimojong people.[3] Karimojong, an Eastern Nilotic language, is very closely related to Teso of Kenya and Uganda, the Turkana of Kenya, as well as to the Topoza, Jie, and Nyangatom of Sudan. These form a closely knit cluster of mutually intelligible dialects or languages. Translation of the Bible into Karimojong was pioneered by the Rev Hamilton Paget Wilkes of the Bible Churchmen's Missionary Society (BCMS). Assisted by Lokong Apachopa, Wilkes prepared an orthography for Karimojong as well as a rudimentary grammar and lexicon, and completed a translation of the Gospel of Mark, which was published by BFBS in 1932. The Rev Walter Edwin Owen, also of BCMS, attempted a translation of Genesis in close collaboration with Mr A. Buxton and Arthur Leonard Kitching, the bishop of Upper Nile. Caleb Sogol was one of their close African assistants and informants. Genesis was published by BFBS in 1933. It was followed by the publication of the Gospel of Luke in 1934, also translated by the Rev W. Owen and Caleb Sogol. Some years elapsed before anything else appeared. Mrs Doris Clark's (BCMS) drafts of Matthew, Romans, Galatians, Ephesians, Colossians, 1 and 2 Thessalonians, 1 and 2 Timothy, Hebrews, Titus, Philemon, and James were prepared in the 1930s but were not finalized for publication at that time. However, the Gospel of John and Acts were published in 1951 by BFBS.

The final push for the completion of the New Testament in Karimojong was made by Miss Jessie Bryden (BCMS) and Joshua Akol, who received help from Professor A. N. Tucker of the School of Oriental and African Studies, London, in solving certain orthographical problems. Using the drafts of Mrs Clark as a basis, Bryden and Akol completed the New Testament. They were assisted by a committee consisting of Rufus Lorukede, Joshua Logit, Daniel Apuun, Zakayo Nanero, and Matthew Tuko. The Gospel of Matthew was published in 1967 and Mark in 1970 by the Bible Society in East Africa, Nairobi. The complete NT was published by the Bible Society of Uganda for the first time in 1974.

The Verona Fathers have also played a prominent role in the translation of the Bible into Karimojong. Their translations of OT and NT selections for liturgical use began appearing in 1937. Later, Father Joseph Garavello translated the four Gospels, which were published at the Kisubi Marianum Press in 1969. Father Garavello followed these with his translation of Acts in 1972; Job, Ruth, Tobit, Judith, and Esther published in 1973; and the complete NT in 1976.

---

3. For consistency and simplicity, the language will be referred to herein without the *Nga-* prefix.

An attempt at an interconfessional translation of the Bible fully accepted by both Roman Catholics and Anglicans and sponsored by the Bible Society of Uganda was officially launched in 1987. A translation team consisting of E. Auffray (Roman Catholic), Sabine Burningham (BCMS), Zacharia Locheng (Anglican), and Petero Logiro (Roman Catholic) finalized work on the interconfessional common-language New Testament. This was launched in Moroto, Karamoja, in February 1997.

Work on the OT inevitably followed and was duly completed with its dedication and public launch on 16 April 2011. The inclusion of Fater Simon Lokodo (Roman Catholic) and Martin Odong (Roman Catholic) as new members of the translation team, and the advancement of Zacharia Locheng from a part-time to a full-time basis, helped give an added boost to the team. Further, Locheng and Logiro had the opportunity to study biblical Hebrew in Israel, allowing them to get some idea of the topography and ecology of the Bible lands. This experience and training gave them significant help in tackling some of the problems of translating the Bible into Karimojong. The text was eventually finalized by Father Odong and Locheng. The dedication and launching ceremony for this Bible took place in Moroto in Karamoja, Uganda, on 16 April 2011. This was the first Bible for this community. Both the Uganda Anglican Archbishop and the Catholic bishop of Karamoja were on hand to lead in the launching of this Bible that they claimed would prove mightier than the machine guns, the now common weapon of war and plunder (including the traditional practice of cattle rustling). The Ugandan first lady Mrs Janet Museveni, the special government minister for Karamoja was the guest of honor. She donated some thirty million Uganda shillings (equivalent to twelve thousand US dollars) to help subsidize the sale price of this Bible. The ceremony was a historic day of great rejoicing and thanksgiving among the Karimojong Christians of all churches.

The Turkana Scriptures

To the north of the Kalenjin cluster are the eastern Nilotic Turkana. They are a nomadic pastoralist group who live in the extreme north-western corner of Kenya. Their neighbors to the north are the Toposa, Jie, and Nyangatom of Sudan, and to the west the Karimojong of Uganda. These groups, as well as the Teso of Uganda and Kenya, speak a closely knit cluster of mutually intelligible dialects. The Turkana, like their Tunga neighbors, are nomadic pastoralists who inhabit very hostile terrain with extremely irregular rainfall patterns, hence their nomadism. Livestock are central to their lives. Livestock is their basis of wealth. To have no cattle is to be a truly poor person.[4] No wonder cattle rustling, involving violent confrontations and loss of life, constitutes an ever-present threat in their social structure.

The attempt to translate the Bible into Turkana was started in the early 1970s under the leadership of Joan Anderson and Jenny van der Klis of AIM, with Isaya and Joyce Emanikor as translators. This was the first translation project in East Africa to have a husband and wife translation team of mother-tongue translators. The Gospel of Mark was published in 1972, John in 1973, James and 1–3 John in 1975, Luke and Acts in 1976, and the complete NT in 1986, all by BSK. Genesis was published in 1987, Exodus and Joshua in 1990, and Psalms in 1994. The complete Bible with a revised NT was dedicated and launched in Lodwar, Kenya, in 2000. This was the first Bible in this language. It has provided the Roman Catholic Church, the Africa Inland Church, the Reformed Church, and the Anglican Church, who are active in the area, with a powerful tool for evangelism and church teaching and growth. The main challenge has been in the area of literacy, given the low literacy levels among members of this community. Therefore, there is a great need for audio-Scriptures, and those encouraging the use of portable audio-Scriptures in Turkana face a situation where demand exceeds supply!

Translation into Teso

Teso also belongs to the eastern Nilotic family. There are more than one million speakers in Uganda, living mainly in the eastern Uganda regions of Soroti and Kumi and in the Kwapa area of Tororo. Another group of Teso numbering about 250,000 are to be found in the western province of Kenya. Though the Teso spoken around Ngora is considered standard, there are other Teso with equally valid claims for their language, for example, the Kenyan variety, or the Ugandan varieties, such as Lokathan, Biri, Ketebo, and Orom. Translation work into Teso started at the turn of the twentieth century, led by Bishop Arthur Leonard Kitching of CMS. Bishop Kitching was a gifted linguist who is, however, remembered by some for his notorious and prejudiced book, *On the Backwaters of the Nile: Studies of Some Child Races of Central Africa*.[5] Although he depended on local native speakers, he did not always trust their

---

4. For some understanding of Turkana religion, see Krijn van der Jagt, *Symbolic Structures of Turkana Religion*. Van der Jagt was both a missionary and Bible Society translation consultant in this area for some time. For the Turkana language, see Dimmendaal, *Turkana Language*.

5. Kitching, *On the Backwaters of the Nile*.

competence or their intuition of their own language. The first portion to be published was the Gospel of Mark in 1910, followed by the Gospel of Luke in 1911, a revised edition of the Gospel of Mark in 1913, and a revised edition of Luke as well as the Gospel of John in 1914. The Gospel of Matthew appeared in 1915 and the Acts of the Apostles was published in 1920. A revision of the Gospels and Acts together with 1 Corinthians and the Epistle of James were published in 1924. In 1930 the Teso NT was published for the first time. All these were the work of Bishop Kitching and his translation helpers.

Work on the Teso Old Testament was entrusted to Miss Norah C. Wiggins, who had been a principal of a girls' boarding school and a key member of the government-sponsored Teso Language Committee. Miss Wiggins had already been quite involved informally in Bible translation, having prepared, for example, a complete OT as well as a number of school books. A translation team consisting of mother-tongue speakers Gideoni Orena, Yairo Okiror, and Enosi Odiit, as well as Kenneth W. Prentice, worked very closely with Miss Wiggins in the translation of the OT and in the revision of the 1930 NT. The translators based their work on the Greek text for the NT, but also consulted English, Luganda, and Swahili translations of the Bible. Portions of Luke and John were published by BFBS in 1960, followed by the complete Bible in 1961. It is interesting to note that Prentice's son, Anglican Canon Hugh Prentice, stayed on in East Africa and distinguished himself as a Bible teacher who possessed a fine mastery of Swahili, as well as of Teso, Luganda, and Cigogo. He worked for many years at St Philips Bible College, Kongwa, in central Tanzania, and also served as a reviewer of the Swahili *Biblia Habari Njema* Study Bible.

The Roman Catholic contribution to Teso Scripture translation goes back to Father John Kiggen's translation of the Gospel of John, which was published in 1920, as well as his selections of Old and New Testament stories published in 1922 and 1930. Other translation work includes Jan Hendriksen's Scripture selections of 1938; his Gospel of Mark in 1967; and the selections of Henry Gommans in 1959; those of Hans Smeets in 1967; and those of Andrew Burm, Herman Gutwenger, and John Eneku in the early 1970s.

An attempt at an interconfessional version was made in the 1970s with an interconfessional team consisting of Juventine Ekiring (Anglican), John Ekuru (Roman Catholic), Tomasi Okurut (Baptist), and Benjamin Okiria (Anglican). The Gospels produced by this team were published by the Bible Society of Uganda: Mark in 1978, Luke in 1981, and John in 1986. However, due to certain misunderstandings among the participating churches – as well as problems resulting from the terrible insecurity and civil war of the Idi Amin and post-Amin period – work came to a standstill.

Unfortunately, the Kenyan Teso, being a minority, were not involved in any of the translation decisions or discussions related to all these endeavors. Initial attempts at such cooperation proved to be unsuccessful. A joint cross-border effort involving both the Bible Society of Uganda and the Bible Society of Kenya could have saved the project by simply relocating its operation to whichever side of the border was experiencing greater tranquility and peace. But because of the problems of intelligibility between the two varieties of Teso, cooperation became difficult. The Uganda Teso Bible is presently out of print. Clearly there is the need for a revision. Whether the Teso communities of Kenya and Uganda should be served by one or two Bibles is a decision that will need to be carefully thought through, taking into account the challenges of union translations that are discussed elsewhere in this book. The Kenya Ateso Bible project is ongoing under the auspices of the Bible Society of Kenya. After research that confirmed the need for this project – and a request by church leaders of the Kenya Ateso community – the project was officially launched at a public ceremony held at Amogoro, Teso, Kenya, on 7 July 2011. The project is being hosted at the Anglican Diocesan Center located at Amagoro near Malaba and close to the Ugandan border on the Uganda highway. It is an interconfessional project in partnership with all churches in the Teso speaking area, the Catholic Church represented by translators Father Gregory Ejakait and Father Frederick Odikor, the Pentecostal and Charismatic churches represented by Pastor Fred Etyang the coordinator of the project. The Anglican church was initially represented by the Rev Damaris Anya, who was replaced by Rev Eliud Omonyokit.

The Kalenjin Dialects

The Southern Nilotic[6] neighbors of the Eastern Nilotic Maasai in Kenya's Rift Valley area are the people called *Kalenjin*. This was an invented term which came into political and later linguistic vogue as early as the 1940s, at the same time as similar trends unfolded at the coast among the Mwambao or Mijikenda peoples, and in western Kenya among the Abaluyia, or in central Kenya among the Meru.[7] Benjamin Kipkorir writes:

> Before the late 1950s, hardly anyone spoke of a people called the
> *Kalenjin*. The invention of the word *Kalenjin* to identify a group
> of people was the achievement of a number of educated young

---

6. Rottland, *Die Suednilotischen Sprachen* (1982) is perhaps the best study to date of this group.

7. See, for example, Kipkorir and Welbourn, *Marakwet of Kenya*, 69–88.

men who decided that the peoples then referred to as the *Nandi-speaking tribes* should have a new and more acceptable name. This name was *Kalenjin*. The word *Kalenjin* means "I tell you" or "I say to you." The choice of Kalenjin was guided by the need to find one word common among all the groups.[8]

But as Kipkorir also writes:

Earlier in 1948, a Kalenjin Union had been established at Eldoret. Earlier still, Kalenjin servicemen with the British forces in the Second World War had formed a bond based on the ceremony of *kalek* – a ceremony for those killed in war. The Kalenjin Society then came into being.[9]

Already in 1954 "a monthly magazine called *Kalenjin* appeared. The magazine was published by the Eldoret office of the Government's Department of Information."[10]

According to Taaita Toweett, another term used to describe the Kalenjin peoples is *Mnyoot*,[11] perhaps by the Kipsigis (one of the key members of the Kalenjin community), as Toweett himself claims. The more usual term, however, is *Kalenjin*. This term is now commonly used to include a number of related peoples as though all were indeed one. Toweett's work on Kalenjin linguistics tries to adduce evidence of the unity of the Kalenjin peoples and their language. Those covered under the term *Kalenjin* are as follows:

- the Nandi-Marakweta branch, which includes the Nandi of Nandi district, the Kipsigis (or Kipsikiis) of Kericho district, the Keiyo[12] of the southern half of Elgeyo-Marakwet district, the Tuken (or Tugen) of Baringo district, and the Marakweta (or Markwet) of the northern half of Elgeyo-Marakwet district. Marakwet is a cover term for six sub-dialects: Endo, Borokot, Almo, Kiptani, Sengwer-Cherang'any and the Markweta from whom the whole is named;[13]
- the Elgon branch, which includes the Sapiny of Uganda found around Mount Elgon, and the Sabaot, i.e. the Kony, the Pok, the

---

8. Kipkorir, *People of the Rift Valley* (1978, 1985), 1. See also Rottland, *Die Sudnilotischen Sprachen*, 20 and also the detailed discussion in Gabrielle Lynch's recent text, *I Say to You*, 2–80.

9. Kipkorir, *People of the Rift Valley*, 2.

10. Kipkorir, 2.

11. Toweett, *Study of Kalenjin Linguistics*, xiii.

12. On the Keiyo, see Chebet and Dietz, *Climbing the Cliff*.

13. Kipkorir and Welbourn, *Marakwet of Kenya*, 71.

Bong'om, sometimes called the Elgon Maasai, of Elgon District on the slopes of Mount Elgon, and the Terik (Nyang'ori) of Nyang'ori location in Kakamega district;

- the Okiek branch, which includes the Sogoo (or Kipchorng'onik Okiek) of the southern Mau Forest, the Enderois, and the Kinare Okiek who are thought to have almost been assimilated as Agikuyu, a process believed to have taken place among the Akie Okiek of northern Tanzania who are thought to have been assimilated as Kisongo Maasai; and
- the Pokoot branch which includes the Pokoot of West Pokot and Baringo districts.

Related members of the Kalenjin group include the almost extinct Omotik of Kenya and the nomadic Datooga of Mbulu district in northern Tanzania. The Datooga branch is comprised of the following groups: Bajuta, Gisamjaga, Barabaiga, Isimijega of East Datooga and the Rotigenga, Buradiga, and Bijanjida of West Datooga.[14]

The Bible into Kalenjin

Levels of intelligibility vary across the nine or so languages or dialects of the Kenyan Kalenjin cluster; not all are mutually intelligible. In any case, there is no single distinct language known as Kalenjin. The Bible commonly used now among these communities, referred to as the Kalenjin Bible, is a union translation intended for use among all the Kalenjin groups. Its language is somewhat artificial and hybrid since no one really speaks "Kalenjin." Rather, the language of this translation is based on an attempt to create a union between the already-translated Nandi and Kipsigis Scriptures together with lexical borrowing from the other dialects of the Kalenjin cluster in order to facilitate wider use and comprehension. Although primarily sponsored by AIM, the translation had the participation of the other missions and churches active in the Kalenjin-speaking areas.[15]

A translation committee was formed in 1951 with Earl J. Anderson as its chairman. The translation team consisted of Frances J. Mumford of AIM, together with Ezekiel A. Birech, now the retired bishop of AIC in Kenya, as

---

14. Rottland, *Die Suednilotischen Sprachen*, 26–29.

15. Fish and Fish, in *The Kalenjin Heritage: Traditional Religious and Social Practices* (1995), attempt to describe the common religious and social strands that bind the Kalenjin communities together.

well as Erasto A. Sio (AIC) and Daniel A. Salat (AGC). Genesis was published in 1958, Mark in 1960, John in 1963, Matthew in 1965, Luke in 1966, Acts–Revelation in 1968, and the OT in 1969. The launching of the translation took place in Kapsabet with Daniel arap Moi (at that time a minister in the Kenyatta government, but later President of Kenya), as guest of honor. This translation brought together a number of churches active in the Kalenjin area, among them the Africa Inland Mission (which created the Africa Inland Church), the World Gospel Mission (which created the Africa Gospel Church), the Pentecostal Assemblies of God, and the Anglican Church. The translation also brought together those using the Nandi, Kipsigis, Tugen, Terik, Keyo, and Markweta dialects. The translation center was at Kapsabet from where the translation team worked. In an interview on the Kalenjin union translation, one of the translators who was a member of the team at the time, Pastor Daniel A. Salat, stated that the Nandi Bible of 1939 was used as a working draft that was reworked and developed into what became the Kalenjin Bible. In doing this reference was made to both the Revised Standard Version in English and the Swahili Union Version.[16] The intention was to create a translation that members of these six Kalenjin dialects could understand. The resulting new union translation took some time to become established. At present, it is used and fully supported by the members of the Kalenjin community.

At the same time, there were those who held that the earlier practice of translating in the different dialects of Kalenjin would be a more fruitful and better idea than the union translation. Indeed, the need for translation into the various Kalenjin dialects still exists, and recent attempts to revise and reprint the Nandi Bible is a recognition of this fact, as is true also with attempts to translate into the Endo-Marakwet, Sabaot, Sabiny, Pokoot, or even Datooga of Tanzania. On the other hand, political considerations gave the idea of a union Kalenjin Bible viability, so that there was an attempt to prepare a revision of the 1969 Kalenjin Bible, recently completed and now available in two editions for use by the Catholic and Protestant churches in the Kalenjin speaking areas.

This Kalenjin Bible revision project was launched in 2005. Its goal was to make the 1969 Bible more current and intelligible to a majority of speakers of Nandi, Kipsigis, and the other minority dialects of the cluster, such as the Terik, Tugen, Keiyo, and Marakwet. At that time, it seemed pointless to include the Pokoot, the Sabaot, or even the others (such as the Sabiny in Uganda or the Datooga in Tanzania), since all these are developing their own

---

16. Personal conversation with Pastor Daniel Salat at a review meeting of the Kalenjin revision project held in Eldoret on 8 October 2007.

Scripture translations. It was also hoped that the revision would encourage the participation of the Roman Catholic Church, which plays a significant role in the religious life of the Kalenjin peoples. Catholic participation would inevitably call for the inclusion of the Deuterocanonical books, which were not included in the 1969 Protestant translation. The project was based in Eldoret and has included translators from the Catholic Church (Nandi speaker, Father Charles Kirui), as well as from the Africa Gospel Church (Kipsigis speaker, the Rev Samwel Kimeto arap Kikwai), and from the Reformed Church (Keiyo speaker, the Rev Musa Maina). The revision team was expected to update all archaic terms, correct unnatural expressions and forms, and correct any faulty exegesis or translation, making the new revised edition of the Kalenjin Bible accessible to a new generation of contemporary readers and Christians within an interconfessional framework. The Revised 1969 Kalenjin Bible was dedicated and launched on the vibrant Rift Valley town of Eldoret on 22 July 2017. It was produced in two editions, namely a Protestant edition and a Catholic edition containing the Deuterocanonical books.

Figure 12.1. The Rev Daniel Salat, the only surviving translator of the Kalenjin Bible. He is one one of the reviewers of the new revised translation. Photo © Aloo Osotsi Mojola

Figure 12.2. The Rev Musa Maina, the Rev Samuel Kimeto arap Kikwai, and the Rev Father Charles Kirui, revisers of the Kalenjin Bible. Photo © Aloo Osotsi Mojola

The Kipsigis New Testament

The Kipsigis (or Kipsikiis) are a major group in the Kalenjin dialect cluster.[17] Their main urban center is Kericho. They live in a rich and fertile area, where they practice mixed farming – planting tea, maize, and sugar cane – as well as dairy farming. The Kipsigis community has had a missionary presence since the beginning of the twentieth century. Bible translation was a top priority for the early missionaries. Already in 1912 O. H. Scouten of the Lumbwa Industrial Mission had translated the Gospel of Mark into Kipsigis. This was published by BFBS. A. M. Anderson of AIM embarked on a translation of the entire New Testament, starting, interestingly, with Romans, rather than with one of the Gospels as is more often the case. Romans was published in 1929 and was followed by 1 and 2 Timothy in 1930 and 1931, and the Gospels in 1932. Earl J. Anderson took over from where his father left off and revised the already-translated books while translating the rest. By 1953 the entire NT had been completed. Earl Anderson was assisted by Douglas A. Mutai, Jason A. Munai, and Paulo Claroigin.

---

17. More information on Kipsigis history can be found in Mwanzi, *History of the Kipsigis*, and in Toweett, *Oral Traditional History*.

Commenting on this translation, ABS translations officer Dr Eugene Nida wrote on 8 March 1948, "The translation gives evidence of being quite idiomatic and at the same time is faithful to the text. Mr. Anderson's exceptional ability in the language (he is more fluent in its use than English, so I am told) has meant that the translation is of exceptionally good quality." Yet, Dr Nida added, "The syntax of the translation is rather awkward in some places, but this is due to a misunderstanding on the part of Mr. Anderson as to what he could do in the way of representing a Kipsigis sentence structure."[18]

Nida found the orthography used in the translation inadequate and made strong recommendations for certain changes. The translators sought the advice and counsel of Professor A. N. Tucker of School of Oriental and African Studies, but as Dr Nida notes, due to "conservatism" and "scholarly caution" this intervention did not result in any of the desired changes.[19] This NT was eventually published by BFBS in 1953.[20]

The Nandi Bible

The Nandi people comprise a significant and influential component of the Kalenjin community. Their major urban centers are Kapsabet and the southern suburbs of Eldoret. The Nandi are famous for their bravery and warlike spirit, which were shown in their resistance to British colonialism. Koitalel arap Samoei and his brother Kipchomber arap Koilegei are well known for their leadership of the Nandi resistance against the British in the years 1890 to 1906. Missionary work started in Nandi at the beginning of the twentieth century. Although translation work among the Nandi started later than among the Kipsigis, it went much faster and was completed earlier. The first Nandi portion, namely, the Gospel of John, appeared in 1926, followed by Romans in 1929, and Matthew in 1931. It is interesting to note that in both the Kipsigis and Nandi translations, the first portions to appear (i.e. the Epistle to the Romans and the Gospel of John), were heavily theological. The translators of the Nandi portions were missionaries of AIM who included Marie Hansen, Frances and George McCreary, A. M. Anderson, and Signe Kristensen. This team did not, however, go beyond these first portions. A new team led by Stuart M. Bryson of the Church Missionary Society (Australia), who was assisted by Samuel A. Gimnyegei, Reuben A. Seroney, and Elijah A. Chepkwony, revised the earlier

---

18. American Bible Society, Unpublished Historical Essays, No. 16, p. 280.

19. American Bible Society, Unpublished Essays, No. 16, p. 280.

20. American Bible Society, Unpublished Essays, No. 16, p. 280.

portions and translated the remaining books of the New Testament. The NT was completed and published by the Central Press at Sydney, Australia, in 1933. Genesis was translated and published in 1935 and the whole Bible was completed and published by BFBS in 1939.

With the publication of the Kalenjin union version in 1969, both Nandi and Kipsigis translations were superseded and went out of print. The Bible Society of Kenya has reported recent enquiries from church leaders for the reprinting of the 1939 Nandi Bible, but after the BSK declined, these leaders turned elsewhere. As a result, Bible League reprinted the 1939 Nandi Bible. This outcome is, however, predictably unsatisfactory given the changes in the language in the last sixty or more years. A fresh translation would have answered this expressed need and given the Nandi people a Bible in their own idiom. The Bible Society decided, however, to support the revision of the 1969 Kalenjin Bible in the hope that Nandi-speaking Christians will find it satisfactory and adequate for their needs.

The Endo/Marakwet Translation

Bible Translation and Literacy has recently started a translation in the Endo/Marakwet dialect. This is part of the Marakwet cluster which has at least five dialects.[21] The Endo/Marakwet translation project was initiated by Ken Greenlee of SIL and Elijah Yego in 1983, and was carried on for some time by a team consisting of Philemon Kisang', Philip Sang, and Johnstone Chelang'a. The project encountered many difficulties and was considerably slowed down in its progress. It was later reconstituted under Edwin Suter as team leader and translator, and Philip Sang as a member of the translation team. James and Lydia Ziersch (SIL) and Vivian Jeruto have been active in literacy programs. Galatians, Colossians, 1 and 2 Timothy, Titus, Philemon, and James were published in one volume in 2005. Subsequently, the translation of the NT was completed and was officially launched at a colorful ceremony held at the Tot Primary School in Marakwet District on 21 February 2009. The ceremony was graced by three bishops from the area – the Roman Catholic Bishop Cornelius Korir, the Anglican Bishop Stephen Kewasis, and the Africa Inland Church Bishop Patrice Chumba. The two area members of Parliament were also present – the Honorable Lina Jebii Kilimo of Marakwet East and the Honorable Boaz Keino of Marakwet West. The guest of honor for this occasion was the

---

21. As reported in Kipkorir, *People of the Rift Valley*, and in Rottland, *Die Suednilotischen Sprachen*, 22.

Government Minister of Information and Communication, the Honorable Samuel Poghisio, who hails from the neighboring Pokoot district. He is known to be a strong supporter of the Bible cause.

The Sabaot Scriptures

The Sabaot translation was undertaken under the direction of BTL. It was started in 1981 by Alice and Iver Larsen of SIL working jointly with mother-tongue speakers of Sabaot: Francis Kiboi, Kiboki Kigai, Patrick Mang'esoy, Fred Matei, and Christopher Kiplang'at. The Larsens were later replaced by Jim and Henny Leonard. Mark's Gospel was the first portion to be published in this language in 1987. It was followed by the Gospel of Luke in 1990. The selected Epistles of Paul, James, and John were dedicated for public use in December 1992. A trial version of the complete NT was released for reviewing sometime in 1994. The NT was eventually released on 14 December 1997, after a ceremony at Kapsokwony on the lower slopes of Mount Elgon in Sabaot country. The NT has proved popular and is widely used by speakers of the language and has been reprinted. Genesis and Exodus were published in 1993. The addition of Chosefu Chemorion, who completed his doctorate in biblical studies at the University of Stellenbosch in South Africa, no doubt contributed to the quality of this translation. Other translators included Sabila Ng'ania, the project leader, James Kiboki, and Phanice Matony. Anne Musiya and Jenny Jones were actively involved in the literacy program. This project may be said to be the model SIL-BTL project in East Africa and is the first of the SIL-BTL projects to produce a complete Bible. The launching and dedication of the complete printed Bible in Sabaot took place at Kapsokwony town on the slopes of Mount Elgon on 10 June 2012. This was warmly accepted in a ceremony attended by all leading church, cultural, and political leaders from the Sabaot-speaking, as well as the neighboring, communities.

Sabaot and Kupsapiny on the other side of the border in Uganda would have made a perfect match as a joint translation because the two dialects are mutually intelligible. However, an important difference between the Kupsapiny and'" Sabaot translations is the orthography employed. While the Kupsapiny has been conservative, preferring the traditional orthography based on Swahili and Luganda, the Sabaot has been more innovative in its orthography, which better represents the complexities of the spoken language and minimizes ambiguity, thus avoiding faulty and inaccurate readings of the Sabaot text. It is clear that the future of translation in the languages of the Kalenjin cluster will focus less on the idea of developing a union language and more on the nurturing of the local intelligible varieties in the hopes of maximizing intelligibility and use.

Translation into Kupsapiny

Kupsapiny is spoken on the slopes of Mount Elgon in the Sebei District of eastern Uganda. It belongs to the Southern Nilotic language family and is a member of the Kalenjin cluster of dialects spoken mainly in Kenya. Kupsapiny and Sabaot as spoken on the Kenyan side of the border are known to be mutually intelligible. As already noted, a joint translation of these two dialects would have served the people well and would have saved unnecessary duplication of outlay of resources. As it is, however, there are now two ongoing translation projects in these two mutually intelligible dialects, each with its own orthography.

The Rev A. Mathers of BCMS pioneered missionary work in the 1930s among the Kupsapiny who were referred to as Sebei at that time, and still are by some people. Mathers tried to use and popularize the Luganda language and culture as well as its Scriptures. It was Hamilton Paget Wilkes, also of BCMS, who made the first attempt to translate the Scriptures into Kupsapiny (Sebei). He succeeded in translating the Gospel of Mark, but prevailing circumstances led him to believe that the time had not come for publishing it. Already in 1936, as can be seen in the Rev W. J. Mowll's report to BFBS, Archdeacon Mathers had voiced his view that the Sapiny "need literature translated for them. Some few may understand Ganda – but this Bantu tongue is not suitable for them."[22]

It was four decades before this view could be acted upon. The man who took the lead in this direction was Canon John Kissa, a native Kupsapiny speaker. He was the main translator of the New Testament when the Bible translation project was started in the early 1970s. He was assisted in the early stages of the work by Mr William A. M. Cuypers a linguist who had extensive work on the linguistic situation of this language. The Gospel of Luke and the book of Acts were published in 1975. Work on the NT was rather slow but has been completed. After a wait of more than twenty years, the NT was finally launched in July 1996 at a ceremony held at Kapchorwa on the slopes of Mount Elgon. This first Kupsapiny NT was very enthusiastically received. The many years that the Nilotic Kupsapiny speakers have had to struggle under the weight of the unfamiliar Bantu Luganda Bible may be a thing of the past. It has, however, taken time to get the OT started, and this will certainly delay

---

22. See the Archival Records in the Bibliography, BFBS files.

the switch from using Luganda to using the vernacular Kupsapiny Scriptures. Work on a new translation under the auspices of the Bible Society of Uganda is being undertaken with assistance from some members of the translation team that workd on the Kenyan Sabaot Bible. A decision has been made to adapt the orthography used for the Sabaot Bible.

The Pokoot Scriptures

Three other dialects in the Kalenjin cluster already have Scriptures or have ongoing translation projects. Pokoot had its first Scripture portion, Ruth, published in 1936 by AIM at Kijabe, and the Gospel of Mark published by BFBS in the same year. The former was translated by Tom Collins of AIM and the latter by Lawrence and Annette Totty of BCMS. A complete New Testament in Pokoot was translated mainly by Lawrence Totty with the assistance of several people including his wife Annette. A number of "acute difficulties as well as many fluctuations of opinion with regard to orthography"[23] contributed to the slow progress of this translation. It was eventually completed and published by the Trinitarian Bible Society,[24] London, in 1967. The portions of Matthew, Acts, and Romans had been published earlier by BFBS, Nairobi, in 1963.

The Pokoot common-language translation was initiated in 1975 at a meeting of the local churches and the Bible Society of Kenya. At that meeting the churches acknowledged that the orthographic problems as well as issues affecting naturalness and clarity meant that they could not accept the existing Pokoot New Testament. It was neither easy to read nor intelligible for readers in the Pokoot-speaking area. By 1977 the Gospel of Mark in the new orthography, translated by the new team, was published. The complete draft of the NT was finished by 1982, but publication of the corrected text by the Bible Society of Kenya did not take place until 1988, when it was dedicated and launched. Work on the OT progressed well under leadership of Canon Daniel Tumkou of the Anglican Church. The translators who worked together with Canon Tumkou at various times during the life of this project include Ronald Chumum (AIC), Elijah Nyeris (Lutheran), Joseph Murupus (Reformed), Alston Toroitich

---

23. Citation is from the BFBS files on this project, see the Archival Records in the Bibliography.

24. The Trinitarian Bible Society accepts only the Greek Textus Receptus of Erasmus as a base text for NT translation. They are not associated with any of the national Bible Societies that are members of the United Bible Societies.

wero Long'oriaki (Reformed), Francis Nalelio (Anglican), and John Ngimor (Deliverance Church).

Genesis was published in 1991 and Exodus in 1995. Work on the OT and the revision of the 1982 NT was completed in 2005. However, the process of preparing these manuscripts for publication took rather long. Canon Tumkou, the main pillar of this translation project, passed away in 2007 before he could see the fruits of his labor. His labors in the Lord were, however, not in vain for on 15 August 2009, the day for the dedication and launch of the first Bible in the Pokoot language finally arrived. As expected, the Bible received an enthusiastic reception which reverberated with the music of church choirs as well as the dancing and music of the traditional pastoral and semi-nomadic peoples of West and East Pokoot who are the primary users of this language. The occasion was graced by people from all walks of life, including religious leaders and local politicians.

The Datooga of Tanzania

In the mid-1980s, various Tanzanian church leaders were contacted by SIL with a view toward cooperation in Bible translation and literacy work. SIL researchers in Tanzania reported at that time that nineteen languages in Tanzania had a "definite need" for a Bible translation with a further sixty-three languages having a "possible need." Furthermore, in 1987, SIL conducted an initial sociolinguistic survey of Datooga, a Nilotic language of approximately 100,000 speakers in the Mbulu district of Singida region. The research confirmed the need for translation in Datooga, and at the invitation of the Evangelical Lutheran Church of Tanzania Diocese of Mbulu, SIL placed a translation team in the area that was led initially by John and Heidi McCauley. After a short while, toward the end of 1989, they were replaced by Ralph and Anette Schubert.

Earlier attempts by both SIL and the Bible Society of Tanzania to collaborate with the local churches on this language had been frustrated by the unavailability of competent mother-tongue speakers. Communication problems and disagreements, as well as policy differences with the Mbulu Lutheran Diocese, led to the withdrawal of SIL from the Datooga translation project. After some protracted pleading by the Mbulu Lutheran Diocese and discussions with the Bible Society of Tanzania, the project has been revived with Bible Society support. The initial translation team was composed of Elikarim Gayewi, Festo Basso, and Joseph Maho. The persistent efforts of Dr Isaac Malleyeck and his campaigns on behalf of this project, as well as the generous support of the late Dr Ole Halgrim Evsen Olsen of Haydom Lutheran Hospital and his family, have been crucial to the progress of the project. The orthography that SIL had helped develop laid the foundation for subsequent work and it continues to be improved and refined as new problems and challenges are encountered. By 2002 the entire draft of the NT had been completed even as work on the OT has proceeded at a steady pace.

The Gospel of Mark was published as a portion and released for distribution at a dedication and launching service held at the Lutheran Church by Lake Basotu on 7 July 2002. All the 2,000 copies of this Gospel printed by the Bible Society of Tanzania were quickly distributed. The complete NT was enthusiastically accepted by the churches when it was dedicated and launched on 4 October 2009, at a ceremony held at the local Lutheran church on the shores of Lake Basotu, where the work had been based since the beginning. It was a truly joyous and historic event. The ceremony was led by the Lutheran bishop of Singida Central Diocese, the Rev E. Sima, stepping in on behalf of the Mbulu Lutheran Bishop Zebedayo, himself a Datooga, who was out of the country. The Bible Society was represented by the General Secretary, the Rev Dr Mkunga Mtingele, and several of the Bible Society staff. The American Bible Society Global Impact team, based in Philadelphia, sent four guests to witness this unique event. Other visitors included representatives of the Norwegian Lutheran Mission, the Haydom Lutheran Hospital, Mama Kari, the wife of the late Dr Olsen, government officials, and local political leaders. Local choirs and musicians from the various Datooga congregations and churches were well represented and contributed to making the event most exciting and joyful. Work on translation of the Bible is complete and eagerly awaited, perhaps in 2020.

The Bible into Maasai

The Maasai-speaking peoples are to be found in a very wide territory spreading from northern Kenya as far south as the central areas of Tanzania. A language spread this wide that does not have the means to maintain linguistic uniformity or standardization, must contend with significant dialectal variation, a fact which was not seriously taken into account in the preparation of the new common-language translation of the Bible. Moreover, the Maasai are a pastoral and nomadic people. They are very closely tied to their traditional way of life. The development of modern educational institutions in Maasai lands continues to be a challenge. Church planting has also posed similar challenges, both for the Maasai of Kenya and of Tanzania. Some of the challenges involved in the evangelization of the Maasai or in helping the Maasai to see Christianity from their cultural perspective are posed vividly in Father Vincent J. Donovan's classic memoir, *Christianity Rediscovered*, which came out of his struggles to live among the Maasai so they could be evangelized from an incarnational perspective. The dialectical varieties were a complicating factor in communicating or translating the Bible. Some of these dialects include the Purko of Narok, the Matapato of Namanga, the Aitayok of the Serengeti plains, the Parakuyo (or Baraguyu) of Morogoro, the Arusha of the Arusha area, the Kenkere (or Dalalakutu) of Kajiado, and the Kaputiei of the Athi plains.[25] The historical tendency to serve the Samburu, Ilchamus, and the Mukogodo with one Bible translation did not help matters.

The first translation of the entire Bible in Maasai was started in the early 1970s mainly through the initiatives of John Ole Tombo Mpaayei, General Secretary of the Bible Society in East Africa (1961–1971), and of the Kenyan Maasai churches in Kajiado and Narok. The first African to hold the position of Bible Society General Secretary, the Rev Mpaayei was ahead of his time. Already in the 1950s he had obtained his Master's degree from Cambridge University. Now he provided the inspiration and leadership for the common-language translation. Working under his supervision, the translation team that he put together worked steadily on the translation of the Bible. The Gospel according to John was published in 1973, Matthew and Luke in 1976, and the NT in 1983. The first book of the OT to be published was Proverbs in 1987. When the OT was completed and printed together with a revised NT, the complete Bible was dedicated and launched at Namanga on the Kenya-Tanzania border in January 1992. This new Bible had red or maroon covers in line with the aesthetic worldview of the Maasai peoples. The black cover that is common elsewhere was not culturally appropriate for the Maasai. Among the members of the translation team, all of whom came from the Kajiado and Narok area, were Joseph Kasio (Anglican) and William Sankan (AIC) serving as the main translators. Mpaayei (AIC) and L. Takona (AIC) contributed significantly as translators in the initial stages. Thereafter, they made enormous contributions both at the review and administrative levels.

The translation was prepared according to the standards of a union translation, as it was intended for use among all Maasai-speaking peoples in Kenya and Tanzania. An attempt was made to involve, at least on the translation review committee, individuals representing the different Maasai dialect areas

---

25. See the details in Mol, *Maa: A Dictionary*, 99–100, and also Mol, *Maasai Language and Culture*, 241.

of Kenya and Tanzania, from the Samburu in the north to the Parakuyo in the south. However, the dialectal distance between the various Maasai dialects may in the long run call for more than one version or edition of the Bible in Maasai, as it has become clear that one version cannot meet the needs of all the Maasai-speaking peoples. Some leaders are now expressing the need for Scriptures that take into account the Parakuyo (Baraguyu) Maasai dialect of the Morogoro region of Tanzania, as well as the Samburu and Ilchamus Maasai dialects of north-central Kenya.[26]

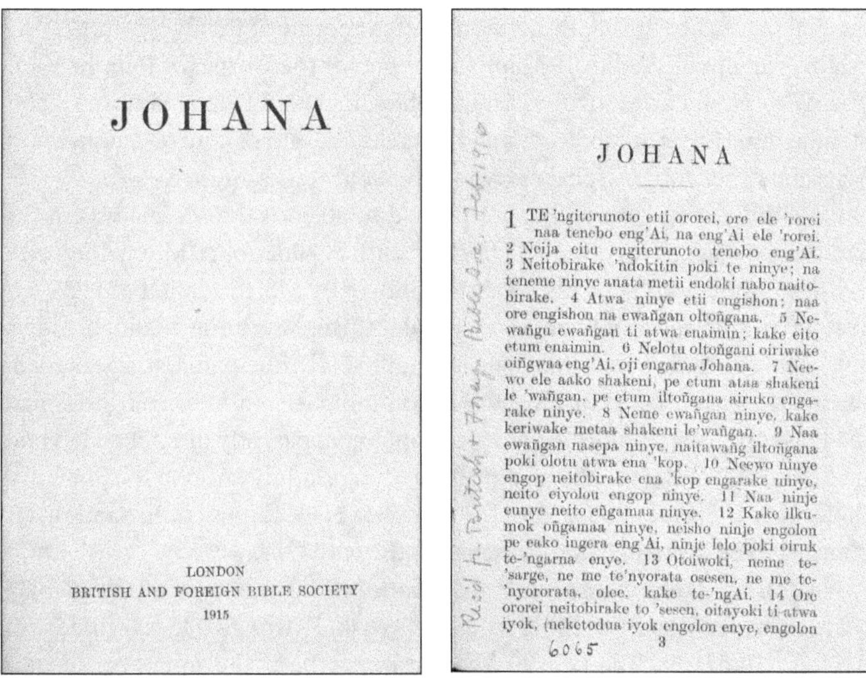

Figure 12.3. Two pages from the Gospel of John in Maasai, first published in 1915. American Bible Society Library and Archives. Used by permission.

This 1992 common-language translation of the Bible was by no means the first attempt to translate the Bible into Maasai. By 1905, A. C. Hollis, a British colonial officer, assisted by Justin Lemenye, Enoch Boi, and others, had the Gospel of Mark translated and printed by BFBS. This had very limited

---

26. An excellent discussion and review of the Maasai communities in East Africa can be found in Spear and Waller, *Being Maasai*. See also the authoritative work of Mol, *Maa: A Dictionary* and *Maasai Language and Culture*, or the very brief but authoritative volume by Sankan, *The Maasai* (1971). On the Maasai language, see Mol, *Lessons in Maa*.

circulation and use, given the low literacy levels among the Maasai community at the time. Moreover, the church in the Maasai-speaking area was not yet very extensive. The second attempt at translating Scripture into Maasai was done under the auspices of the Africa Inland Mission. AIM has been very active in Maasai territory since the beginning of missionary presence in the area and needed the use of the Bible in the vernacular to make any significant gains. This attempt led to the publication of the Gospels of Luke and John, as well as Acts, and 1 Timothy–Philemon being published by BFBS in 1915. Galatians–Philemon was published locally at Kijabe by AIM in 1919 and the NT in 1923 by BFBS, in London, with a reprint of this NT in 1967. The Psalms were published in 1934 and a revision of the Gospel of John in 1947. The AIM missionaries involved in this effort included Bertha Simpson, John Stauffacher, H. Herdman, Ruth and Roy Schaffer, and of course, a number of Maasai mother-tongue speakers who provided vital assistance.

A third attempt at making Scripture available for the Maasai was in the Samburu dialect. It involved an effort by Ruth Schaffer of AIM together with B. Ruby Grindley and C. Edith Webster, both of BCMS, to adapt the 1923 New Testament into the Samburu Maasai dialect. This was quite a laudable idea, given the realization that this dialect is sufficiently intelligible to speakers of the main Maasai dialect to allow use of common Scriptures. In 1961 they had the Gospel of Mark published as a portion, but apparently did not go beyond that. The BTL took over the responsibity of translation work on the Samburu Bible. This continues in earnest. The complete New Testament in Samburu is planned to be dedicated and launched at the end 2019.

A fourth attempt was made by Johannes Hohenberger of the Leipzig Mission to translate the Bible into the Arusha/Kisongo Maasai dialect of northern Tanzania. The Leipzig Mission in northern Tanzania opened new work among the Maasai in 1927, led by Hohenberger. This work led to his mastery of the Arusha Maasai dialect and his eventual translation of the New Testament. This was published in 1964 at Neuendettelsau by the Leipzig Mission. Unfortunately, this translation was never used widely. It eventually went out of print and has been replaced by later Bible Society publications.

It should be noted that although the Catholic Church was not actively involved in actual translation work among the Maasai, the church did, through the bishop, strongly and actively support the translation work of the Bible Society, both morally and financially. Indeed, the Catholic bishop of Ngong, Bishop C. C. Davies, is also the one who gave the imprimatur for the Swahili common-language translation, which he actively supported. The records, however, show that the Catholic Churches prepared Maasai translations of the Sunday readings (lectionary) for use in the Mass. These were prepared between 1960 and 1963 by John Leffers of the Mill Hill Fathers in handwritten and typed copies at Ngong.[27]

A number of Maasai-speaking churches expressed a need for a revision of the 1992 Maasai Bible, indicating a need to produce an adaptation for the Kenyan Maasai and another for the Tanzania Maasai. A revision for the Kenyan Maassai was limited to the Maasai variety spoken in Kajiado and Narok. This was undertaken by the Bible Society of Kenya with a team consisting of Rev David Lekotit and Peter Sentero, and later including Father Anthonu Koikai and Peter Sena. The complete revised Maasai Bible in Kajiado and Narok variety was launched and dedicated in Narok, Kenya, on 11 August 2018. The Samburu and the Parakuyo also need their own Scriptures. Since 2005 a team composed of David Lebarleyia and Timothy Lesimalele have been working on the new Samburu translation planned to replace the existing Maasai Bible. Another effort to translate the Bible into Ilchamus was launched in 2004 under the leadership of Alfer Letiyon who also serves as translator together with David Lekurle. Ilchamus (also called Njembs) is distinct dialect of Maasai and is spoken in the Baringo area of Kenya. Work on the NT is now complete, and dedication and launching is expected in 2019 with the complete Bible as the target.

---

27. See Rijks, *Guide to Catholic Bible Translations*, vol. 2, 218.

13

The Jii Peoples of East Africa

Alur, Acholi, Lango, Kumam, Padhola, and Luo

The Jii Peoples

The Jii peoples belong to the Western Nilotic language family and are sometimes called River Lake Nilotes, in contrast to the Eastern (or Plains) and Southern (or Highland) Nilotes. Their ancestral home is believed to have been in southern Sudan where most Jii peoples still live. Those who left that area over a period of many years found their way to northern Uganda, to Bunyoro in western Uganda, to northeastern Congo, to eastern Uganda, and as far south as south-western Kenya and northern Tanzania. Today they are found as far north as the southern Sudan and extend as far south as the North Mara lake district of Tanzania. Professor Bethwell A. Ogot has written, "They all use the term 'jii' meaning 'people,' hence the name."[1] Among those included under the term *Jii* are:

> the Alur, who live in the Okoro and Padyere counties of West Nile in Uganda and in the Mahagi District in Eastern Congo, where the majority of them live, the Acholi who live for the main in Northern Uganda and on the border of Southern Sudan, the Ocholo (Shilluk) who live along the West Bank of the White Nile from Lake No where they had settled at Wipaco between 1031 and 1058 CE, the Luo who live in the Bahr el Ghazal Province of the South West Sudan who usually refer to themselves as the descendants of Podho, the Shatt or Thuri together with many offshoots in Bahr el Ghazal; the Pari or Lokor in Equatorial Province, the Anywaa (Anuak) who call their country which is

---

1. Ogot, *Jii-Speakers*, 1.

situated along the banks of the rivers in the Southern-East Sudan and West Ethiopia, *Pach Anywaa;* the Naath (Nuer) and Jieng' (Dinka) both living in Southern Sudan; the Padhola who live in Tororo District of Eastern Uganda; the Labwor in Eastern Uganda, the Paluo in Bunyoro, and the Luo who in live in Western Kenya and Northern Tanzania.[2]

Translation into the Languages of Northern Uganda

The evangelization of northern Uganda was not as dependent on Baganda agents and evangelists as was the case in eastern Uganda. Here it was the Bunyoro connection that proved fruitful. Banyoro evangelists and northerners who had become Christian while in Bunyoro took the initiative in spreading Christianity. This is perhaps not surprising, given the historical and cultural links between the two areas going back as far as the Bachwezi and Babito eras. Thus, for example, the Acholi chief Awich Rwotchamo in a Macedonian type of call requested help from Bunyoro in 1903. Similarly, in Lango the local chief Odora made requests for missionaries to be sent to his area.

The Verona Fathers, a Roman Catholic congregation, met with some outstanding success in both northern and eastern Uganda. The years 1910–1913 mark the beginnings of Catholic evangelization in northern Uganda, where the Verona Fathers arrived from the Sudan.[3] They commenced work among the Alur and their Chief Omach on 28 February 1910.[4] Among these missionaries was a young man, Father Pasquale Crazzolara (1884–1976) who distinguished himself by his research in the history and languages of this region and is fondly remembered by scholars and others who have researched the peoples of this region.[5] The Verona Fathers entered Karamoja territory among the Karimojong in 1929 but did not meet the same measure of success as,

---

2. Ogot, *Political and Cultural History*, 3. Professor Ogot's magisterial, *A History of the Luo-Speaking Peoples of Eastern Africa* (2009) offers a more detailed and documented study of the Jii peoples. It crystallizes his research in this area, which began with his trailblazing PhD at the London SOAS in 1967, *History of the Southern Luo.*

3. See Cisternino, *Passion for Africa*, 340–408.

4. Cisternino, 346.

5. See the bibliography for an impressive list of linguistic, anthropological, and cultural works authored by Father Crazaolara over a three-decade period. Professor Bethwell Ogot dedicates *A History of the Luo Speaking Peoples of Eastern Africa* to "Father J.P. Crazzolara, F.S.C. 1884–1976 in recognition of his enormous contribution to the unraveling of the history of the Luo speaking peoples in Eastern Africa." Poet Okot p'Bitek also refers much to the writings and researches of Father Crazzolara, for example, in his *Religion of the Central Luo* (1971).

for example, among the Acholi, Lango or the Teso. They found the Anglican BCMS there but these had met with minimal success, but are appreciated for starting Bible translation work in the Karimojong tongue. John Baur writes,

> The Comboni with their charitable work were more successful but their converts remained mostly nominal Christians . . . A great step forward accompanied the advent of Bishop Sisto Mazzoldi and some of his priests expelled from the Sudan. The diocese of Moroto was erected for them in 1965. The school system became the approved method of evangelization. By 1979 the first priest could be ordained, Fr. Thomas Logyel who was followed by several others. By 1990 nearly half of the Karimojong led a sedentary life and most of them were baptized in the Catholic Church – the greatest number of any nomad tribe in Africa.[6]

The Acholi, Okot p'Bitek and the Hellenization and Christianization of African Gods

The Acholi currently number well over one million and are mainly found in Uganda in the districts of Gulu and Kitgum, formerly the Acholi district. Other Acholi speakers are to be found across the border in southern Sudan. Acholi, a Western Nilotic language, is very closely related to Lango. In fact, some people believe these two languages are mutually intelligible. The evangelization of the Acholi inevitably led to the consideration of translating the Scriptures into vernacular languages. Neither the Luganda nor the Runyoro Scriptures were acceptable to the Acholi people, as the Nilotic Acholi is quite unrelated to these two dominant Ugandan Bantu languages. The Scriptures simply had to be translated into Acholi.

A celebrated Acholi writer, the poet and literary scholar Okot p'Bitek (1931–1982), did much to popularize his language through his literary creations. He wrote first in Acholi and then had his writings translated into English. Among these the most famous was the *Wer pa Lawino*[7] which was translated

---

6. See Baur, *2000 Years of Christianity in Africa*, 486. For a detailed and extensively documented history of the evangelization of southern Sudan and northern Uganda, the area of our interest here, see Cisternino, *Passion for Africa*.

7. *Wer pa Lawino* was published in Nairobi by the East African Publishing House in 1969.

into English as *Song of Lawino*.[8] In this work, Lawino's misunderstanding of the Christian concept of God, a misunderstanding due to the term used to translate the Christian deity, results in her complete inability to understand the Christian faith or accept it.[9]

In Acoli (an alternate spelling of Acholi p'Bitek employs) the Christian God is rendered as the "Hunchback spirit." Lawino asks:

> The Hunchback
> Where did he dig the clay
> For moulding things? . . .
>
> When Skyland was not yet there
> And Earth was not yet moulded
> Nor the Stars
> Nor the Moon,
> When there was nothing,
> Where did the Hunchback live?
>
> Where did the Hunchback
> Dig the clay for moulding things,
> The clay for moulding Skyland
> The clay for moulding Earth
> The clay for moulding Moon
> The clay for moulding the Stars?
> Where is the spot
> Where it was dug,
> On the mouth of which River?
>
> And when the Hunchback
> Was digging the clay
> Where did he stand?"[10]

The Christian God among the Acholi is called *Rubanga*, which also happens to be the name of the spirit that causes tuberculosis of the spine. Thus, *Rubanga* is also the Hunchback Spirit. Okot narrates how this came to be:

---

8. Okot p'Bitek's works of poetry and scholarship include: *Song of Lawino* (1966), *Song of Ocol* (1970), *Two Songs: Song of Prisoner and Song of Malaya* (1971), *African Religions in Western Scholarship* (1970), and *Religion of the Central Luo* (1971).

9. For the full discussion, see Mojola, "Okot p'Bitek and the Translation of Divine Names."

10. Okot p'Bitek, "From the Mouth of Which River?" in *Song of Lawino*, 86–87.

In 1911, Italian Catholic priests put before a group of Acoli elders the question "Who created you?" and because the Luo language does not have an independent concept of create or creation, the question was rendered to mean, "Who moulded you?" But this was still meaningless, because human beings are born of their mothers. The elders told the visitors that they did not know. But, we are told that this reply was unsatisfactory and the missionaries insisted that a satisfactory answer must be given. One of the elders remembered that, although a person may be born normally, when he is afflicted with tuberculosis of the spine, then he loses his normal figure, he gets "moulded." So he said, "Rubanga is the one who moulds people." This is the name of the hostile spirit which the Acoli believe causes the hunch or hump on the back. And instead of exorcising these hostile spirits and sending them among pigs, the representatives of Jesus Christ began to preach that Rubanga was the Holy Father who created the Acoli.[11]

This anecdote helps to show that the Christianization of African deities or spirits was no easy task. Translating names for God into African languages often led to misunderstandings or misinterpretations. In a number of cases among African peoples, the competing Christian groups settled for competing deities as being identical with the supreme God. The African deities identified as identical to the Christian God were subsequently Christianized and given all the attributes and character of the Christian God. This process was applied more or less in all situations where Christians made contact with non-Christians. Okot holds that, "The African deities of the books, clothed with the attributes of the Christian God, are, in the main, creations of the students of African religions. They are all beyond recognition to the ordinary Africans in the countryside."[12] Okot cites Father Crazzolara's reflection on this matter when he writes:

> Based on such assumptions, natives were urged with tiresome questions to make a choice as to which of the Jok among the many had created them. Such questions implied suppositions which probably never occurred to their simple minds; it puzzled them as they are still puzzled at such questions. With hesitation they answered that they did not know, which was more near the

---

11. See Okot p'Bitek, *African Religions*, 62; and *Religion of the Central Luo*, 41–58.
12. Okot p'Bitek, *African Religions*, 88.

truth, but less satisfactory, or they decided that it was Lubanga or Rubanga.[13]

Okot's claim is given credence by some African Christian theologians and Christian students of religion. For example, John S. Mbiti did exactly that. His *Concepts of God in Africa* reads like a Christian text of systematic theology. The first chapter is divided into five sections, the omniscience of God, the omnipresence of God, the omnipotence of God, the transcendence of God, and the immanence of God. Mbiti claims that the African conceptions of God included these absolute categories. Hence the first line of chapter 1 reads: "By attributing omniscience to God, African peoples are placing him in the highest possible position."[14] But in so doing, Mbiti was involved in a process of Hellenizing African deities. Okot in contrast claims that "African peoples may describe their deities as 'strong' but not 'omnipotent'; 'wise', not 'omniscient'; 'old', not 'eternal', 'great' not 'omnipresent'. The Greek metaphysical terms are meaningless in African thinking."[15]

The Ghanaian philosopher, Kwasi Wiredu (1931), who considers Okot to be "the true pioneer of conceptual decolonization in African philosophy,"[16] agrees with Okot that African deities need to be decolonized. The African deities who are Christianized or Hellenized in this way lose their original character as understood through the tenets of African religions. Christianized African deities do not tell us much about the nature of these deities before the time of Christianization or Hellenization.

The Bible into Acholi

The translation of the Bible into Acholi owes much to the work of the Rev Arthur Leonard Kitching, a CMS missionary who took on this onerous task with the assistance of Sira Dongo, a convert from the Madi ethnic group. Kitching developed the Acholi orthography and went on to become a translator. He and Sira Dongo translated the four Gospels which were published by BFBS. The Gospel of Mark was published in 1905, Matthew in 1906, Luke and John in 1907, and the revised Gospels together in 1914. Kitching later became the first bishop of the Diocese of the Upper Nile, which included northern as well as eastern and northwestern Uganda. Another CMS missionary, Philip H. Lees,

---

13. Quoted in Okot p'Bitek, *Religion of the Central Luo*, 44.

14. Mbiti, *Concepts of God in Africa*, 3.

15. Okot p'Bitek, *African Religions*, 88.

16. Wiredu, "On Decolonizing African Religions," 33.

continued where Kitching and his colleague left off. Lees revised the Gospels which were published by BFBS in 1921. BFBS also published Acts, Philemon, James, and Ephesians–Colossians in 1928, all translated by Lees. The Acholi NT published in 1933 by BFBS was a product of the labors of Kitching, Lees, Thomas Lawson Lawrence, and Harold F. Davies.

Apart from the efforts of a team of Comboni Fathers led by Father Giuseppe Rinaldo and Father Umberto Cardani that culminated in the publication of the Gospels and Acts in 1948, little translation work took place after the 1933 New Testament. However, the Roman Catholics had published translations of OT and NT selections as early as 1915 and continued this up until the work of Rinaldo and Cardani. Later, the translation of the Gospels and Acts by Father Vincenzo Pellegrini, also of the Comboni Fathers congregation, was published in 1973 and his NT in 1976, both published at the Gulu Catholic Press.

Work on the Old Testament was held up until the late 1960s when Alipayo O. Latigo, assisted by Edna Mildred Brown of CMS, took up the task of a union translation. When this union experiment failed, Latigo and Brown turned their attention to producing Scriptures in the Acholi tongue. Their focus was to translate the complete Bible. In 1967 they had produced a new translation of the Gospel of John that was reprinted in 1974. The book of Exodus appeared in 1972, the Gospel of Mark in 1974, the book of Genesis in 1975, and the Epistle to the Ephesians in 1988 with reprints in 1991 and 1992. The complete Bible in Acholi appeared in 1986 followed by a reprint in 1988. All these were published by the Bible Society of Uganda.

Translation into Lango

Lango, like Acholi, belongs to the Western Nilotic language family. The case for the Lango Scriptures was similar to that of the Acholi, that is, the Luganda and Runyoro translations could not be understood by the Lango speakers. But the response to this need was slow. Perhaps because of the perceived mutual intelligibility between Lango and Acholi, when the Scriptures were translated into Acholi, it was assumed that these would also satisfy the need for Lango Scriptures. Apparently this was not the case. Since the experiment to have Scriptures in a union Acholi-Lango version had not met with success, the case for the Lango Scriptures was shown to be legitimate.

The Lango Bible was the work of a translation committee that included Reuben Ogwal, A. H. Okada, and Edna Mildred Brown (CMS), as well as a team of reviewers. The Gospel of John was published by the Bible Society in East Africa in Nairobi in 1967, while the Bible Society of Uganda published the Gospel of Mark in 1972, and Exodus in 1974. It was also in 1974 that the Lango New Testament translated by this team first appeared. It was published by the Bible Society of Uganda. Genesis appeared in 1975, while Hosea, Amos, and Micah appeared in 1977. It was a year later, in 1978, that the complete Bible in Lango was published by the Bible Society of Uganda.

It is interesting to note that 1974 saw the publication of two New Testaments in Lango. Not only did the Protestant translation of the NT come out, so did a Roman Catholic version. The Roman Catholic version was published at the Marianum Press at Kisubi, Kampala. It was the work of a team consisting of Germano Agostini, G. Opio, A. Aryang, J. Galeotti, S. T. Agwe, V. J. M. Ouni, and C. Bruno of the Verona Fathers.

The Acholi-Lango Union Version

At the beginning of the 1960s some church leaders thought that, given the closeness between Acholi and Lango, it would be possible to avoid duplication of translation effort by producing one common version of the Scriptures that would be equally intelligible to both groups. Union translations had been tried elsewhere for a number of languages, and had succeeded in some. This attempt was led by Edna Mildred Brown of CMS together with a representative committee of mother-tongue speakers of both Acholi and Lango. The union language form was christened "Lwo." In the translation, where a common word could not be found, alternatives in each language were printed together. The committee succeeded only at producing two books of the Bible, the Gospel of Mark in 1960 and Genesis in 1962, both published by the BFBS. But the project proved unpopular and unworkable. The test portions were apparently not well received, and it was decided to discontinue the experiment in favor of dealing with each language separately on its own terms.

Translation into Alur

Alur is a Western Nilotic language widely spoken in DRC[17] and in Uganda. Of the over one million Alur speakers, there are about twice as many in DRC as there are in Uganda. They mainly occupy the area to the northwest and

---

17. The Democratic Republic of Congo (DRC) has gone under many names during its existence as a unified country – first as the Belgian Congo, then as Congo-Leopoldville, then as Congo-Kinshasa, then as Zaire (from 1971 to 1997), and now as the Democratic Republic of Congo.

northeast of Lake Albert on both sides of the border. Among the main dialects of Alur are the Jokot, Jonam, Mambisa, and Wanyoro.

The main pioneer missionaries in this area were from AIM. It appears, though, that translation efforts were not coordinated between those working in Congo and those working in Uganda. The result was a duplication of effort and an inability to share common valuable experience and solutions to intractable problems. For example, on the Zaire/Congo side of the border the missionary translators found the local name for the deity objectionable and not suitable to be taken as a starting point for the name of God. They concluded that the local deity had more in common with the devil than with the God of the Bible as they understood it. So they borrowed the Swahili name for God *Mungu* for use by the Congo Alur. The current ongoing Alur Bible project in DRC has also settled on the Swahili *Mungu* as suitable for their new translation. In Uganda the traditional concept and name was adopted for use in the Scriptures. This situation is not desirable as it creates problems of religious dialogue and conflict between these closely related traditional Alur communities. After all, the national border is an artificial and recent creation.

The first Scripture portion in Alur was the Gospel of Luke translated by James O. Averill of AIM and published in 1921. Other Scriptures followed, as shown in table 13.1, culminating in the publication of the complete Bible in 1936. A corrected reprint of the Bible (but one that still retained the old orthography) was undertaken by Fred G. Lasse of AIM and a committee and appeared in 1955.

As was the case with Acholi, Catholics had prepared translations of OT and NT selections for liturgical use as early as 1915 and 1917. These first translations by anonymous Comboni Fathers were published at the Mission Press in Khartoum. Over the years, up into the 1980s, more selections were added from the pens of Fathers Francesco Colleoni, Stephen Opira, Danilo Castello, Carlo Cappellotti, and Felice Centis, all members of the Comboni Fathers.

The 1955 reprint of the Alur Bible was apparently done with the DRC as the main focus. Another edition with an orthography revised by the Alur Language Committee under the chairmanship of BeatriceT. King of AIM was published in 1970 by the Bible Society of Zaire, Kinshasa. In the 1980s the BSZ gave support to a new effort to translate the Bible into a modern, common-language, functional equivalence version in the Zaire Alur dialect. This task was led by Miss Millie Coulton of AIM assisted by, among others, Udjuro Mikum and Undiga Umer. A number of obstacles and problems have prevented this effort from being completed. The text of this new translation is in a new orthography, with which the majority of speakers and readers, including those

Table 13.1. Translations of the Bible into Alur

Year	Publication	Translator(s)	Published by
1921	Gospel of Luke, 1 John	James O. Averill of AIM	AIM Press, Kijabe
1922	Gospel of John	James O. Averill of AIM	BFBS, London
1923	Old Testament stories	Lilian M. Halstead of AIM	AIM Press, Kijabe
1927	Gospel of Matthew, Acts, 1 & 2 Thessalonians, Titus	Lilian M. Halstead, Harriet M. Halsey, Sarah Stirton, C. L. Trout of AIM, and Kaveve Daudi	BFBS, London
1928	Gospel of Mark, 1 & 2 Peter	Lilian M. Halstead, Harriet M. Halsey, Sarah Stirton, C. L. Trout of AIM, and Kaveve Daudi	BFBS, London
1933	New Testament	Lillian M. Halstead, Harriet M. Halsey, C. L. Trout and Margaret Moore of AIM, and Samwil Wapol	BFBS, London
1936	Bible	Above texts + Old Testament translated by AIM team (as in the NT above)	BFBS, London
1955	Bible (revised)	Above texts slightly revised by Fred G. Lasse of AIM	BFBS, London

who used the older translation, are not familiar. The instability and insecurity as well as tragic mass killings that have befallen much of eastern DRC in the recent period has had a negative impact on the efforts to complete the work to which Miss Millie Coulton dedicated her life. Sadly, Miss Coulton passed away in retirement in Canada before she was able to complete the work. She made one last attempt when she was in her eighties to visit her co-laborers in the Mahagi area, to revive interest in the work and encourage the remnants of her team, but alas, the time was not right. There has since been a renewed interest in this work and a team supported by the Bible Society of Congo (DRC). The complete Bible was completed, dedicated and launched in 2018.

Meanwhile in Uganda, the Bible Society of Uganda sponsored a new common language interconfessional translation of the Bible in Uganda Alur. Its first publication in 1970 was the Gospel of Mark translated by A. Bedathal and H. Opio with the support of an interconfessional review committee. The complete NT in this interconfessional common-language version of Uganda Alur was published by BSU in 1978, followed by an edition of the New Testament and Psalms in 1979.

Translation into Kumam

Kumam is spoken in the western part of the Teso District of Uganda. It belongs to the Western Nilotic language family and is closely related to Acholi and Lango. The Kumam people number well over 200,000. As early as 1923 Father John Renckens translated NT selections on the life of Jesus. These were published in Rome at St Peter Claver's. These were followed by further Catholic OT and NT selections published locally at the Soroti Catholic Mission. However, despite a felt need for Scriptures in Kumam, local attempts by some Kumam churchmen to satisfy the need for Scriptures in their local vernacular have yet to be satisfied. In spite of an ecumenical effort at translating the Scriptures into Kumam by a team that included M. Ejumu (Anglican), Canon I. Ekadu (Anglican), A. Foster (Anglican), Father C. Rothweiler (Roman Catholic), and others, the only published result has been two selections based on Luke 15, namely, *Lost and Found*, which appeared in 1972, and a Christmas selection which appeared in 1973.

In 2000, BSU set up a project based at their Soroti center to produce the first NT in Kumam. A team consisting of the Rev Boniface Esomu (Anglican) and Father Richard Edonyu (Catholic) completed the New Testament, which was dedicated and launched in March 2007 at Soroti. The same team carried on with Old Testament work that started at the beginning of 2006, and completed, dedicated, and launched it at Kaberamaido, eastern Uganda, in 2013.

Translation into Dhopadhola

Dhopadhola is spoken by over 200,000 people in eastern Uganda in the Tororo District. It belongs to the Western Nilotic language family and is closely related to the southern Luo of Kenya and to the Acholi and Lango of northern Uganda. The Jopadhola have been using the Luganda Bible ever since they were evangelized, and are often referred to by their Bantu nickname of "Badama." The first efforts at translating the Scriptures into Dhopadhola date back to 1950, when a translation of various selections of the Bible was sponsored and published by Scripture Gift Mission as *Words of Wisdom*. It was not, however, until 1976 that an interconfessional translation committee was established and charged with the task of translating the Bible into this language. Father Zakaria Ochwo (Roman Catholic) and the Rev E. Matthew Owori (Anglican) were the two members of this team. The first Scripture publications from these two translators were the Epistle to the Ephesians published in 1977 and the Gospel of Mark published in 1978. Unfortunately, this team broke up bringing work to a standstill. The translation was taken over in the late 1980s by another interconfessional team consisting of Father Pius Oburu, Yesero Makola, and Lamech Obeli. Obeli passed away in March 1986 and his colleagues were not been able to keep up with the required pace. Thus, work on this New Testament was delayed and readers' expectations were frustrated. Martin Odoi (Pentecostal) and Domiciano Oboth (Roman Catholic) were later recruited to finalize work on the New Testament. After some difficulties and persistence, the work was completed and the entire NT in Dhopadhola was dedicated and launched in Tororo in March 2003. Translation work on the OT started in 2004, with the Rev Meibo Nyangwen (Anglican), and the Rev Father Richard Owor (Roman Catholic) as translators. The new Dhopadhola Bible was dedicated and launched in Tororo Uganda in April 2019.

Translation into Dholuo of Kenya

The Luo, who currently number about four million, are the only representatives in Kenya and Tanzania of the Western Nilotic or River-Lake Nilotic branch of this family. Among the Jii speakers, it is the Luo of Kenya who moved furthest from their original homeland, ending up in the south-western corner of Kenya along the shores of Lake Victoria. Some Luo went further south and ended up in the North Mara District of Tanzania. Their arrival in this area has been dated to between 1490 and 1560. They arrived in four waves comprised successively of the Joka-Jok, the Joka-Owiny, the Joka-Omolo, and the Luo-Suba. Bethwell Ogot has described this process in his text *History of the Southern Luo: Migration and Settlement*. Traditionally, the Luo have lived as fishermen and cattle keepers as well as farmers of grains such as millet, sorghum, and maize, as well as cassava, sweet potatoes, and varieties of vegetables. They are patrilineal and practice polygamy[18] and wife inheritance

---

18. For information on the traditional life of the Luo, see Mboya, *Luo: Kitgi gi timbegi*, now a classic, or Ocholla-Ayayo, *Traditional Ideology and Ethics*. For some idea of Luo grammar, see Omondi, *Major Syntactic Structures*. Cohen and Odhiambo, *Siaya: The Historical Anthropology of an African Landscape* (1989), offers a rich and interesting discussion of the contemporary Luo situation.

like most of their neighbors, lifestyle issues that have contributed somewhat to the relatively high incidence of HIV/AIDS among the Luo.

Two dialects or varieties of Luo are generally recognized, namely, the South Nyanza and the Central Nyanza. However, these possess a very high level of mutual intelligibility, a fact which has greatly facilitated the development and promotion of common literature in the Luo language. It is, nonetheless, clear that the South Nyanza variety has usually been favored: it has more publications, and is generally the more dominant of the two varieties. This can be explained simply by noting that it has more speakers and has produced more writers in the language. Moreover, translations of the Bible in Dholuo are usually in this dialect, which has benefitted from translators who were either fluent or mother-tongue speakers of this variety.

The first Christian missionary outreach in Luo land had its beginnings in 1906. The foundations for educational, missionary, and medical work were laid at Maseno, with the aim of reaching both the Luo and Luyia, who are to be found to the south and north of Maseno, respectively. J. J. Willis of CMS arrived there from Uganda. He baptized his first converts, consisting mainly of young men who had been recruited to his Maseno school. Although the Banyole who live in the neighborhood of Maseno were included in Willis's missionary outreach, his linguistic efforts were mostly directed toward the needs of the Nilotic Luo.[19]

Thus, after learning Dholuo, Willis, together with A. E. Pleydell, another CMS missionary, translated and arranged for the publication of the Gospel of Mark in 1911 and the Gospels of Luke and John in 1912 by BFBS. In South Nyanza, A. A. Carscallen of the Seventh-Day Adventist Mission translated the Gospel of Matthew, which was published by BFBS in 1914, while J. F. Clarke of AIM translated the Book of Acts, which was published in 1915. It was left to Pleydell to translate the remaining books and revise some of the earlier ones: Mark, Luke, John, James in 1917; Romans–Philippians and Titus in 1921; and John in 1924. He also coordinated the effort that saw the publication of the Luo NT in 1926 by BFBS.

The first book of the Old Testament did not appear until 1933. This was the work of Grace A. Clarke of SDAM, assisted by William Ogembo, Paul Mboya, and two other mother-tongue speakers named Sila and Apola. However, the final OT translation published in 1953 by BFBS, was mainly the work of Grace Clarke (SDAM), Walter Edwin Owen (CMS), and H. Capen (AIM). This was a good example of interdenominational cooperation and endeavor.

---

19. See Omulokoli, "Historical Development of the Anglican Church."

Canon A. E. Pleydell, one of the key translators of this first Luo Bible, came to East Africa in 1904 in the service of CMS and spent thirty years among the Luo. He was then compelled by deafness to retire and settle in England. Pleydell worked on Isaiah and the Minor Prophets. His version of the Luo Anglican Prayer Book was published by SPCK in 1921 and included many Psalms. In comments made to the Secretary of CMS in London on 9 August 1943, translator Canon Owen stated: "I have long felt reluctant to put the Old Testament into the hands of converts until they had attained a more enlightened background for it. However, other views have prevailed." Commenting on his translation technique he stated:

> One of my rules is to translate a Hebrew figure of speech or idiom by an elegant figure of speech or idiom of the Luo. Failure to translate in the idiom of the people has already resulted in the emergence of a debased pidgin Luo which the people refer to as *dholuo mar Kitabu* ("speech of the Book"). It is a literary crime to publish work so bad.[20]

The same cooperative interdenominational spirit that characterized the first Bible was very much evidenced in the move to do a new common-language translation. The first portion of the new translation, the Gospel of John, appeared in 1962, followed by Matthew in 1963, Mark in 1964, and Luke in 1966. The common-language New Testament appeared in 1968, published by the Bible Society in East Africa. This new effort was the work of A. W. Mayor (CMS), Roy L. Stafford (CMS), H. and A. Capen (AIM), assisted by P. Kusmin (Finnish Lutheran Mission), and a number of native speakers, including Daniel Songa, Daniel Ongile, C. Skoda, and Barack Omolo Iro. The final interconfessional Bible with the Deuterocanonical books appeared in 1977, published by the Bible Society of Kenya. Roy Stafford with Jacob G. Ouko, Nikon Owuor, and J. Ouma, assisted by a committee of reviewers, are to be credited with the actual work of translating the OT and coordinating the effort in the language-speaking area to make the interconfessional Bible available to the churches. This team worked from their center at Ngiya in Siaya. This was the first complete Bible published by the Bible Society of Kenya that contained the Deuterocanonical books. The current policy of BSK is to produce two editions of every translation or Bible, that is, a Protestant edition without Deuterocanonical books and a Catholic edition with the Deuterocanonical books. Indeed, all new projects specifically require that this be so.

---

20. BFBS ESC Minute Cards, Vol. 5, 1943, p. 7.

In translating the Luo Bible, the translators had to grapple with numerous problems, for example how to translate "Holy Spirit." Swahili had settled for *Roho Mtakatifu*, that is, "Spirit Holy" and Luganda had settled for *Omutukuvu*, i.e. the word coined for "holy." The Catholics preferred *Muya Mahagios*, "Holy Breath" (*Muya* means "breath" or "steam" and *Mahagios* is from the Greek word *hagios* meaning "holy"). CMS had popularized the use of *Chuny Maler*, literally "white heart" or "clean heart." After much discussion and compromise, the group settled for *Roho Maler*, borrowing the Swahili word *Roho* for "spirit," which in turn is borrowed from the Arabic and related to the Hebrew *Ruach*. There is, however, still a problem with *Maler* whose common meaning is "clean, white, spotless." Up to now, however, this term has been in the Luo Christian lexicon for nearly a century and has thus been "Christianized," taking on the components of meaning that Christians have associated with it, based on their theological and doctrinal teachings. It is unlikely at this time that an acceptable new term will be coined, except perhaps on an experimental or even a private basis.

These translations of the Bible in Dholuo had an immense impact on the young Luo church. The young Christians for the first time started reading the Bible in their own language. They started interpreting the Bible for themselves and comparing what they were finding and seeing in their Bibles with what their missionary teachers and clergymen had been telling them. The stage was now set for advancing interpretations of Scripture texts based on vernacular translations of Scripture that could question and challenge the missionary hermeneutic. The result was the emergence of a number of new church movements that split from the mother missionary churches. This was part of a new phenomenon, namely, the African Independent Churches (AICs) that were widely reported at the time. The Luo independent churches were among the first to appear on the Kenyan church landscape. Among these were the Johera, the Nomiya Luo Church, and the Legio Maria independent churches.

One of the scholars who was well placed to see and report on these events was David Barrett, then a young Anglican missionary in Luo Nyanza. His research, like that of others, into this phenomenon of African Independent Churches is well documented.[21] These researchers noted that the availability of a complete Bible in a community tended to destabilize the missionary churches. Many independent churches drew heavily from the OT, where they presumably saw many parallels between the OT setting and traditional

---

21. See Barrett, *Schism and Renewal in Africa*. See also Welbourn and Ogot, *Place to Feel at Home*, and Spear and Kimambo, *East African Expressions of Christianity*.

African communities. These churches also encouraged the introduction of many OT practices, such as the prohibitions in Leviticus and the practice of polygamy, among others. These inevitably led to church divisions and the emergence of new churches. Current discussions regarding enculturation and contextualization have been inspired and driven by some of the developments among the AICs.

14

The Sudanic Peoples of the West Nile

Kakwa, Bari, Madi, Kebu, and Lugbara

Translation into the Languages of the West Nile District

The West Nile region of Uganda includes three districts, namely, the Nebbi, the Arua, and the Moyo Districts, and is more linguistically diverse than any other area of the country. All the language families of Uganda are represented in this north-western corner, which shares borders with both the Democratic Republic of the Congo and Sudan. It is the home of several languages belonging to language families not found anywhere else in Uganda or East Africa. Among these are Lugbara, Madi, Kebu, Bari, Luluba, and Mangbetu, all of which belong to the Central Sudanic family of languages; Gungu, which is Bantu; Nubi, which is an Arabic-based creole; Kakwa, which is Eastern Nilotic; and Alur which is Western Nilotic. The Lugbara is the largest ethnic group of the West Nile.

This area, however, is more often than not associated in recent times with its most notorious son, the dictator of Uganda Idi Amin Dada, who held the office of president from 1971 to 1979. Mark Leopold in his book *Inside West Nile: Violence, History and Representation on an African Frontier* observes that the negative image of the district as a marginal place populated by inherently violent people long predated the former dictator.[1] It began before British colonial rule, and even before the Belgian and Ottoman predecessors of the British. From as far back as the late nineteenth century until now Arua (formerly West Nile, formerly the Lado Enclave, formerly southern Equatoria) has been a liminal frontier zone, a border area in much more than the purely

---

1. Leopold, *Inside West Nile*, 3.

politico-juridical sense, and its people continue to experience the violence and marginalization that has characterized their experience since they encountered outsiders from a radically different culture in the form of Arab slave traders in the nineteenth century. The arrival of Arab slavers from the Sudan under Turko-Egyptian hegemony heralded the cataclysms and turbulences that were to hit this area in the future. Many of the region's people were lost through slavery during this era.

European presence in the area began in the mid-nineteenth century. The presence of Emin Pasha and his encounter with Henry Morton Stanley in 1888 brought this area to the attention of the Western press. C. H. Stigand, writing in 1923 in *Equatoria, the Lado Enclave*, noted that "this little territory has perhaps passed through more vicissitudes and has at one time had more interest centered around it, than any part of central Africa."[2] The legacy of Emin Pasha, a German convert to Islam and one-time governor of the Egyptian province of Equatoria that extended over this region, has been described as being,

> . . . both material and ideological; he left behind him an enduring place for the region in European fantasies of Africa, and he also left a considerable number of troops, former slave soldiers who settled in the area forming the core of what became a new "ethnic" category, the "Nubis" or "Nubians", whose numbers later included Emin's namesake,[3] Idi Amin himself. It was Emin's troops, believed by the British to be "the best material for soldiery in Africa" who were used by Captain Lugard of the Imperial British East Africa Company to enable the Buganda kingdom to overcome the neighboring polities and form what in 1900 became the Uganda Protectorate.[4]

Leopold writes further:

> It was probably the story of Emin Pasha's enclave, surrounded by hostile African forces, which inspired Joseph Conrad to begin writing his *Heart of Darkness*. It was also Emin's material legacy, in the form of troops who found the ethno-religious occupational group known as the Nubi, which produced the phenomenon of Idi Amin, perhaps the pre-eminent modern exemplar of Africa

---

2. Quoted in Leopold, *Inside West Nile*, 10.

3. *Emin* is the Turkish version and *Amin* is a transliteration of the Arabic form of this common Muslim name meaning "Faithful."

4. Leopold, *Inside West Nile*, 10.

as a heart of darkness . . . The images of inherent violence and marginality conjured up both by Amin and by Conrad's book are intimately linked to the history of West Nile, both as causes and as effects; however, the processes involved in this also tell us a good deal about European domination in its material and ideological, colonial and postcolonial forms.[5]

This area changed hands several times. It was a property of King Leopold of Belgium from 1885 to 1894 when it came under the administration of the so-called Congo Free State. In 1910 it became a province of Anglo Egyptian Sudan under British control and in 1912 the southern half was absorbed into the Uganda Protectorate. The West Nile, part of what was called the Lado Enclave, was "a playground and a killing ground for white adventurers, the last place in Africa in which unrestricted elephant hunting was possible."[6] John Middleton,[7] Aidan Southall,[8] and other anthropologists of the British school have published ethnographical studies and, in the process, have contributed to popular images of this area. The West Nile has a sizable Islamic minority out of which Idi Amin came. It is, however, predominantly Christian, having been evangelized by the AIM and CMS missions, as well as by the Roman Catholic Verona Fathers. It is thus a religious and ethno-linguistic microcosm of Uganda; a claim no other part of Uganda can make.

The foundation for making translations of the Bible in the languages of the West Nile area was laid at a language conference of missionary societies of the White Nile districts convened under the auspices of the British and Foreign Bible Society at Arua in October 1918. Among the missionaries who attended were Arthur Leonard Kitching (CMS), C. E. Hurlburt (AIM), L. H. Downing (AIM), G. Fred B. Morris (AIM), Harold F. Davies (AIM), and A. Shaw (AIM). Apart from making recommendations on orthographical matters, they made decisions on how to handle certain key terms. For example, they recommended that the following terms should be rendered as shown in table 14.1.[9] These recommendations were intended for new translations in the languages and dialects of the area. It is interesting to note that by and large

---

5. Leopold, 13.

6. Leopold, 11.

7. See Middleton, *Lugbara Religion*.

8. See Southall, *Alur Society*.

9. BSA/E3/3/317. These terms were mostly borrowed terms, and, similar to those in Swahili, they were either from Arabic or were transliterations of the Hebrew or the Greek word.

these were followed, not just in the translations into languages of this area but further afield as well.

Table 14.1. Missionary societies' recommendations to translators working in West Nile languages

English Term	Missionaries' Recommendation	Basis of Recommended Term
prophet	*nebi*	Transliteration of Hebrew
angel	*malaika*	Transliteration of Hebrew
temple	*yekalu*	Transliteration of Hebrew
hell	*gehenna*	Transliteration of Greek
king	*melek*	Transliteration of Hebrew
church	*kanisa*	Transliteration of Hebrew
Messiah	*Masiya*	Transliteration of Hebrew
Satan	*Satani*	Transliteration of Hebrew/Greek
Christ	*Kristo*	Transliteration of Greek
Spirit	*Roho*	Transliteration of Hebrew
wine	*bino* or suitable indigenous term	Transliteration of Latin or translation of phrase "juice of vine"
heaven	A suitable indigenous term	Common term for "sky" or "above"
Devil	A suitable indigenous term	Common term for "false accuser"
Lord	A suitable indigenous term	Common term for ordinary word for "chief"

Translation into Kakwa

The Kakwa are found in the extreme northwest corner of Uganda in the West Nile district. They straddle the borders of Uganda, DRC, and Sudan. Kakwa belongs to the Eastern Nilotic branch of eastern Sudanic languages, as do Karimojong of eastern Uganda and Turkana and Maasai of Kenya. It is closely related to Pojulu, Bari, Ngyepu, Kuku, Nyanggwara, and the Mondari languages of those neighboring countries. *Ethnologue* gives the level of mutual intelligibility within this family of dialects or languages as ranging from 61 percent to 74 percent.[10] The first portion of Scripture in Kakwa was the Gospel

---

10. See Grimes, *Ethnologue*, 14th ed., which gives 74% lexical similarity with Pojulu, 73% with Bari, 72% with Ngyepu and Kuku, 68% with Nyanggwara, and 61% with Mondari.

of Mark, translated by Kenneth Richardson of AIM, together with Yoane Akudri, and published by BFBS in 1930. After a break of over thirty years, the translation of the Scriptures into Kakwa was begun anew by a team comprised mainly of Anglican missionaries working for AIM under the direction of the Rev A. Seton Maclure. It was, however, a translation team consisting of the gifted translator, Joy E. Grindey, together with Rebecca Akuzo and John Dronyi, that saw to the actual work of rendering the Bible into Kakwa. Miss Grindey, a student of modern languages at Oxford University in England, spent many years as an Anglican missionary working under the auspices of the Africa Inland Mission in the West Nile district of Uganda. The Gospel of Luke translated by Grindey and Dronyi was published in 1967 by the Bible Society in East Africa, followed by the Gospel of John in 1969, and the Gospel of Mark translated by Grindey and Akuzo in 1972. The New Testament appeared in 1974 and the Psalms in 1977, the work of the three translators and a committee of reviewers. Both were published by the Bible Society of Uganda. Grindey and her team continued to labor under the difficult political circumstances and vicissitudes of that time, eventually completing the whole Bible, which was published in 1983 by the Bible Society of Uganda.

Translation into Bari

Bari properly belongs to Sudan, where the majority of its speakers are found, but speakers are also found in the northwest corner of Uganda as well as in the northeast corner of DRC. It belongs to the Eastern Nilotic language family and is very closely related to the neighboring Kakwa. The earliest work in this language was carried out by Roman Catholic missionaries in what is now southern Sudan. In 1858 Father Franz Morlang and Xavier Logwit Lo Lado of the Comboni Fathers translated Old and New Testament stories into Bari, leading to the translation of the Gospels in 1860. A prayer book with lectionary readings from the Gospels was prepared by anonymous Comboni Fathers, and published by the Nigrizia Printing Press School in Verona in 1926. This was followed in 1936 by Carlo Muratori's translation of the Acts of the Apostles, also published in Verona. A number of lectionary readings and Bible stories were translated and printed in mimeograph form throughout this period.[11]

The first portion of Scripture to appear in this language in Protestant circles was the Gospel of Mark translated by H. G. Selwyn, a CMS missionary. This was published by BFBS in 1927 and it was followed by Selwyn's Gospel of John

---

11. Rijks, *Guide to Catholic Bible Translations*, vol. 2, 389–391.

in 1930, also published by BFBS. The task of translating the NT into Bari fell to another CMS missionary, P. O'B. Gibson. In 1934 he had the Gospels of Mark and John revised and published by BFBS in a new orthography. Between 1939 and 1946, Gibson translated alone. BFBS published Acts and James–Jude in 1939; Matthew in 1942; and 1 and 2 Corinthians in 1945. From 1946 on, Gibson was joined by O. C. Allison and a number of native speakers including Jebedayo Jeda, Rubena Loro, Nikodemo Göri, Jakaria Lako, Yisaka Wani, and Tadayo Konosu. Luke appeared in 1946, Galatians–Philemon in 1949, Romans in 1951, and the NT in 1954, all published by BFBS.

In 1960, a Roman Catholic translation of selections from the Gospels was published at the Arua Catholic Mission Press, but this was not followed up by further Catholic publications of Scripture at that time. Meanwhile, among the Protestants, Gibson pressed on with work on the OT, but he was only able to translate twenty-two Psalms. The rest of the Psalms were translated by Philippa F. Guillebaud of CMS, assisted by Matatio Lado and Daniele Wani, and were eventually published by BFBS in 1962. In 1964 the book of Genesis translated by this team was published by the Bible Societies in Khartoum. This was followed some years later in 1973 by the book of Isaiah translated by Guillebaud, Elisa Petero, and James Jada, and reviewed by an interconfessional committee. The complete Bari Bible that was published by the Bible Society in the Sudan at Khartoum in 1979 was the culmination of well over a century's worth of translation effort by Roman Catholics and Protestants working separately at first, but then joining together to produce one Bible for all Bari-speaking Christians.

Translation into Madi

Madi is spoken in the West Nile District of Uganda by over 250,000 people in this north-western corner of the country. There are also some 100,000 Madi speakers in the neighboring areas of Sudan. Madi is closely related to the Moru language spoken in Sudan, to Logo and Lendu spoken in DRC, as well as to the neighboring Lugbara of the same district. These languages belong to the East Central branch of the Central Sudanic family of languages. Madi is spoken in a number of dialectal forms including Pandikeri, Lokai, Borulo, Okollo, Ogoko, Moyo, and Oyuwi. Some of these dialects are mutually intelligible with Lugbara. Some are even thought to be closer to Lugbara than to Madi.

Roman Catholic missionaries were the first to prepare an orthography for the language which they used in the catechism they translated. The pioneer in Bible translation here was, however, the veteran translator Hamilton Paget

Wilkes of BCMS. He and his wife opened a station at Moyo among the Madi people in April 1934. Working with a team of local Madi speakers, Paget Wilkes and his wife were able to plunge immediately into translation work. In 1935 their translation of the Gospel of Mark was published by BFBS. This was followed three years later by the publication of Ruth and the Gospel of John. Paget Wilkes reported that the book of Ruth was prepared by his wife who found that it appealed to the Madi women. In a letter to BFBS dated 20 October 1936 he stated that his translation,

> is not altogether a one man translation since my wife is also working on the language and has done quite a lot of Old Testament stories and is now at work on Ruth. She has also looked over my translation of St. John and has made certain suggestions and alterations. In addition to her I have had two competent native assistants and another for reference in special cases. One of these native assistants has first class knowledge of Kakwa, Acholi, Swahili and Nubi as well as Madi so that his help has been most valuable especially as we have had the use of Acholi and Swahili New Testaments to work with.[12]

The couple were not able to complete this work, and it was picked up some years later by Donald R. Fonseca, who attempted a new translation of the Gospel of John. This was published by Missionary Crusaders of Lubbock, Texas, in 1963, but unfortunately, there was no further progress due perhaps to lack of sponsorship or interest.

It was the interconfessional effort of the Roman Catholic and Anglican churches that finally led to the translation of the complete New Testament and Psalms in Madi. This committee prepared a common-language version in current, everyday Madi. The Gospel of Mark came off the press in 1975, while the complete New Testament and Psalms appeared for the first time in Madi in 1977, published by the Bible Society of Uganda.

It should be noted that various OT and NT selections were also translated into Madi by the Roman Catholic translators Father Joe Buffoni, Father John Ferrazin, David Luga, Peter Rokani, Benjamino Bata, and Father Luigi Gabaglio. Further, a team led by Father John Ferrazin translated the book of Genesis, which was published in 1982 by the Moyo Catholic Mission Press.

---

12. BFBS EA languages correspondence files, letter dated 20.10.36.

Translation into Kebu (Ndo)

Kebu is spoken in West Nile District of Uganda and in the neighboring region of DRC. It is a dialect of the Ndo language spoken mainly in DRC, and is a member of the Mangbutu-Efe group of the East Central branch of the Central Sudanic languages.

The first effort in translation work in Kebu was undertaken by Beatrice T. King, an Anglican missionary of the Africa Inland Mission, together with Simasona Yele, Eliakim Obovi, Yoasa Ndona, Onesimos Edrovi, and a team of reviewers. Their effort resulted in the publication of the Gospel of Mark in 1964 by the Bible Society in East Africa.

The next effort was under the direction of Joy Grindey, the Anglican missionary seconded to AIM who had also worked on the Kakwa NT translation. Around 1987 she started working with Hilkiah Ubia, a mother-tongue speaker of Kebu. The entire New Testament was completed and published in 1995 at Nebbi in the West Nile District. This was the first NT in this language of well over 300,000 speakers.

Translation into Lugbara

There are two types of Lugbara spoken in the West Nile district of Uganda, a High Lugbara and a Low Lugbara. Both belong to the East Central branch of the Central Sudanic family of languages. High Lugbara is also known as Terego Lugbara and Low Lugbara is referred to as Aringa Lugbara or as Andre-Lebati or as Kuluba. High Lugbara is considered to have a 71 percent mutual intelligibility level with Low Lugbara. They are really two dialects of the same language.

Translation work has mainly taken place in the High Lugbara dialect through the initiative of missionaries of AIM. It was the Rev C. H. Mount who first took on translation work into Lugbara with his translation of the Gospel of Mark that was published by BFBS in 1922. As can be seen in table 14.2, many different people were involved in translating the different books of the NT which were published by BFBS over an eleven-year period.

The responsibility for finalizing the translation and revision of the New Testament was borne by A. E. Vollor, Florence M. Vollor, Helene Nolting, and Anne Souther. When this team forwarded their copy of the NT in Lugbara to the BFBS they wrote, "We have been, and always are, greatly indebted to the Bible Society, and if this present big undertaking can be added, we and this native Church shall indeed be grateful."[13] The first Lugbara NT was published by BFBS, London, in 1936.

Table 14.2. Translators and timeline of the Lugbara Translation

Year	Publication	Translator(s)
1922	Mark	Rev. C. H. Mount
1926	Luke	Agnes H. Bell
1926	John and 1, 2, 3 John	J. W. Bell and Agnes H. Bell
1926	James	Kate Mather
1928	Matthew	Rev. G. Fred B. Morris
1928	Acts	A. E. Vollor
1929	1 & 2 Corinthians; Romans; 1 & 2 Peter	A. E. Vollor
1933	Galatians to Thessalonians	A. E. Vollor
1933	Mark (revised)	A. E. Vollor

The Rev A. E. Vollor carried on with translation of the OT books. By 1939 he had translated much of the Pentateuch. The Rev G. C. Dusen, Field Director of AIM, and the Rev H. Stamm, Chairman of the Literature Committee, did not feel that any more books of the Bible were needed in Lugbara. They were of the view that the government education policy for the area demanded the use of Swahili and required the teaching and popularizing of Swahili. Undeterred, the Rev Vollor put forward a strong case for translating the whole Bible into Lugbara before BFBS representatives in London, but was unable to continue with the work. His mantle, however, was fully taken up by the Rev A. Seton Maclure and Miss Laura Belle Barr, both of AIM, assisted by an African translation checking committee. This team translated a number of OT portions that were printed locally. At the same time, they promoted literacy throughout the language area.

A new orthography for Lugbara, recommended by Dr A. N. Tucker of the School of Oriental and African Studies in London, was approved and adopted by the Lugbara Language Committee in 1949. In addition to her work on the OT, Miss Barr was given the responsibility of revising the 1936 Lugbara NT, with the help of a committee. The revision took into account the new official orthography of 1949. Canon Maclure assisted also in the NT revision. Thus,

---

13. BFBS ESC Minute Cards, Vol. 5, see 4.12.35, p. 43.

an edition of Romans by Laura Belle Barr was published by BFBS in 1952. Revised editions of the Gospels of John and Luke by a team consisting of M. R. and A. Seton Maclure and Laura Belle Barr, assisted by H. T. Ajule, B. Obetia, N. Yii, Y. Debi, N. Fore, K. Angodubo, M. Adama, and Bartoyomayo, were published by BFBS, London, in 1960. By October 1960 Canon Maclure was able to report from Arua, Uganda, to BFBS, that "the basic work on the translation of the OT and revision of the NT was completed . . . Work is beginning on the preparation of references."[14] Nearly four years later, in February 1964, the relevant BFBS committee "resolved to recommend that the text of the Bible in Lugbara be accepted as conforming to the Rules for Translators" and therefore met the conditions for publication by BFBS.[15] Consequently, the culmination of the labors of A. E. Vollor, Laura Belle Barr, M. R. and A. Seton Maclure, H. T. Ajule, B. Obetia, and N. Yii, as well as others on the translation committee, was the first complete Lugbara Bible. It was published in 1966 by the Bible Society in East Africa and sent to enthusiastic and expectant Lugbara speakers in the northwest corner of Uganda.

Mention should also be made here of the various lectionaries prepared by the Comboni Fathers as early as 1926. Matthew and Mark diglots in Lugbara and English were published in 1960 and 1964, respectively, at the Kisubi Marianum Press, and a translation of the Psalms by Fathers John Ferrazin and Antony Androa was published in 1979 in Vicenza, Italy.

An interconfessional translation project was sponsored and launched by the Bible Society of Uganda, but it did not result in a complete interconfessional Bible. The interconfessional team, headed by Mataya Anguandia (Anglican) including both Catholic and Protestant members, produced the Gospel of Mark and the Epistle to the Ephesians as test portions in 1975 and 1977, respectively. They managed to complete the NT, which was published in 1978 by BSU and was reprinted in 1982. The need to complete this interconfessional translation should be reconsidered by the Bible Society of Uganda as well as by the other stakeholders.

---

14. See the Archival Records in the Bibliography, BFBS files.

15. BSA/E3/3/317 Lugbara 1921–1972.

15

The Cushitic Peoples of Kenya and Tanzania

Iraqw, Somali, Oromo, Borana, Burji, Daasanach, Orma, and Rendille

Peoples of the Horn of Africa

The Cushitic peoples are part of the larger Afro-Asiatic language family that includes Semitic peoples and extends throughout most of the northern parts of Africa including Ethiopia. Most Cushitic speakers live in the Horn of Africa, but our focus is on the translations in north-central and north-eastern Kenya where the majority live, although a number of Cushitic dialects and languages are also found in northern Tanzania. As we will see, this explains why Johann Krapf traveled to the East African coast on his way to evangelize the Oromo-Borana, whom he called the "Galla," deciding this point of entry would be easier than through Ethiopia where he had first gone.

Scriptures into Iraqw

The Iraqw of Tanzania are sometimes referred to as Erokh or Iraku, or by the name of their geographic locale, Mbulu. They belong to the Southern Cushitic language group. They are closely related to the neighboring Gorowa (or Goromo, also called Wathiomi by their Bantu neighbors), Alawa, Burunge, as well as the Mbugu people of the Usambara Mountains, all in Tanzania. Gorowa and Iraqw are mutually intelligible, which accounts for the partnership of the Gorowa in the Iraqw Bible translation project that was at first based at Haydom and later Mbulu, all in the Mbulu District of Tanzania. The project was actually an Iraqw-Gorowa project but was named after the more numerous and larger group. The Iraqw speakers currently number well over half a million people. They live a little to the south of the famous Ngorongoro Crater, between Lake Eyasi and Lake Manyara. They are mainly farmers and cattle keepers.

The first Protestant mission among the Iraqw and Datoga peoples in the Mbulu region was the Swedish Evangelical Lutheran Mission (SEM) which only started its work there around 1938. They came at the invitation of the Datoga chief Gitagno Falla. The first SEM missionaries to arrive at Dongobesh were the Revs Martin Nordfeldt, Herbert Uhlin, and Tore Fryhle. The SEM missionaries did not stay long; they worked in the area only from 1939 to 1950 when they handed over the work to the Norwegian Lutheran Mission (NLM).

The first NLM missionary to arrive in the Mbulu area was a nurse, Gudrun Folleso. She arrived in September 1950 and was received at Dongobesh by the SEM nurse Anna Strøm who stayed on as an NLM missionary. These two nurses were followed by other NLM missionaries who had been forced out of China by the Mao-led communist revolution. They were the Revs Alfred Lien and Finn Espegren, and their families. The Lien family arrived in October 1950 and the Espegrens arrived in December. The NLM accomplished significant work in the Mbulu area. The present Evangelical Lutheran Church of Tanzania (ELCT) Diocese of Mbulu under Bishop Yoram Girgis is a fruit of this witness. The Haydom Lutheran Hospital that opened in January 1955, is another of the lasting fruits of the ministry of this mission.

However, the task of communicating the Christian message in the Iraqw language did not begin with the SEM or NLM. As early as 1916 and 1926 the Holy Ghost Fathers of the Roman Catholic Church translated and published selections of OT and NT stories, the first at St Peter Claver's in Rome and the latter at the Maison-Carrée in Algiers. A Catholic catechism in the Iraqw tongue, the *Katekismo kangw Iraqw*, was published in 1922. And yet, despite these early efforts, the Roman Catholics did not play a significant role in Scripture translation.

The work of translating the Scriptures into Iraqw was pioneered by NLM through the former SEM nurse, Anna Strøm, who worked closely with a team of mother-tongue speakers. This team included Pastor (later Bishop) Bartolomayo Yonathan, Athanasio Quwanga Mathiya, Yonathan Matle, and Filipo Wakari. The first Scripture portion they translated was the Gospel of John, published by BFBS in 1957. By December 1960, Miss Strøm reported from Dongobesh that she and her team had completed translating the New Testament into Iraqw.

Publication of this New Testament, however, was held up as a result of a number of queries that readers raised when the translation was tested. These included the issue of an inadequate orthography which affected the readability of the Strøm text. Questions of translation style, clarity, and naturalness were also raised. It was therefore recommended that a committee be set up to examine the manuscript and make suggestions and proposals regarding the translation. When the Rev John Mpaayei, General Secretary of the Bible Society in East Africa, returned from a visit to the Mbulu country in 1962, he confirmed that the manuscript needed to undergo further scrutiny and correction. A committee consisting of Bartolomayo Yonathan, Peter Goti of Gospel Furthering Fellowship (GFF), the Rev Finn Espergren, and Miss Frøydis Nordbustad of the Norwegian Lutheran Fellowship (NLF) was requested to study this matter. The committee found that the translation not only used the inadequate and unsatisfactory orthography that had been used for all earlier publications in this language, but the translation itself was fairly literal and not natural in style. They eventually decided that the NT manuscript needed to be reworked and thoroughly revised.

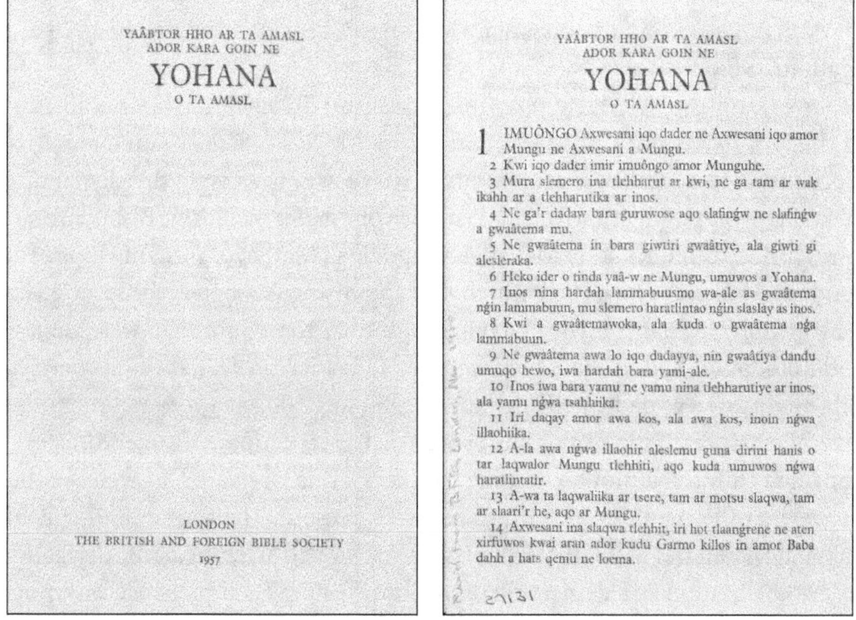

Figure 15.1. The Gospel of John in Iraqw, the title page and first page. American Bible Society Library and Archives. Used by permission.

The responsibility for this task fell to Miss Nordbustad, together with Pastor Yoram Girgis and Yohana D. Baha. Nordbustad, who had arrived in Mbulu country in 1958, had been actively involved in educational and evangelistic work in the diocese. This translation assignment led her to become deeply involved in literacy work. After linguistic training from 1963 to 1964 at the Wycliffe Bible Translators center in England, she was better equipped to do sound linguistic analysis of the Iraqw language and to assist in working out an adequate and acceptable orthography for the language. This linguistic research and analysis led to several publications, including an Iraqw grammar and dictionary, as well as a number of literacy materials. The new Iraqw orthography resulting from this research eventually received the approval of the Iraqw language committee, and all subsequent Scriptures and literacy materials have used it.[1]

Nordbustad and her team did an extensive overhaul of the Strøm NT draft, thoroughly revising and re-translating entire sections, as well as rewriting it using the new orthography. This work really got underway in 1965. Their first publication was the Gospel of Mark, published in 1970 by BFBS, and followed by the Gospel of Luke in 1974, published by the Bible Society of Tanzania, Iringa. The complete NT was published in 1977 by the Norwegian Bible Society and the Bible Society of Tanzania, Dodoma. A reprint appeared in 1979 and again in 1988.

Work on the OT did not commence immediately after the publication of the NT. It was not until 1991 that this work was officially launched. Miss Nordbustad was recalled from retirement in Norway to assist in this demanding task. She worked together with a team of volunteers including Bishop Yoram Girgis, Mary Bura, Kristina Mallange, Magdalena Mathayo, Yotham Girgis, and Ibrahim Mathiya, as well as with Hezekia Kodi and Yohana Nahhato, both of GFF in Gorowa country. The first books of the OT to be published were Genesis and Ruth, published by the Bible Society of Tanzania in 1995. The first complete Bible in Iraqw was dedicated and launched in July 2004 at a very well-attended ceremony at which the Honorable Frederick Tluway Sumaye, Prime Minister of Tanzania (himself a mother-tongue speaker of this language), as well as other members of Parliament from this area were present. The former and current General Secretaries of the Bible Society of Norway led an enthusiastic delegation to this celebration and dedication of the Iraqw Bible. Their presence was much appreciated in recognition of the enormous contribution of the Norwegian churches and the Norwegian Bible Society to this endeavor.

----

1. Besides authoring invaluable linguistic resources on the Iraqw language, Frøydis Nordbustad wrote down and published several folk stories and various literacy materials to promote the reading of Iraqw. Many of these are not dated but probably go back to the late 1960s and early 1970s. For titles and publication details of Nordbustad's impressive output, see the bibliography to this volume.

The Name of God in Iraqw

One of the challenges in translating the Iraqw Bible was the problem of translating the name for God. In the New Testament translation, a decision was made to borrow the Swahili name for God, *Mungu*. The indigenous and traditional Iraqw name for God, *Looa*, was thought to be unsuitable. Some key members of the Iraqw NT translation team justified this choice by pointing out that in Iraqw tradition and usage, *Looa*, the creator of the world and the giver of life, is female. *Looa* is referred to as the mother of all and the source of life. The "femininity" of *Looa* is reflected by the fact that the Iraqw language classifies nouns with three gender markers. The first group includes singular male animates while the second group includes singular female animates. The third group is predominately made up of plurals. Non-animates fall into any of the three groups.

Even though according to the Iraqw world-view, *Looa* the creator God has most of the positive moral attributes ascribed to the Christian God, the translation team felt at the time that *Looa*'s "femininity" was incompatible with the God of the Bible believed to be "masculine" in the Judeo-Christian tradition. The team therefore decided to borrow from the Swahili, the dominant lingua franca in the region. God's name in Swahili, *Mungu*, is not gender specific. The Swahili language only places *Mungu* in the class of persons. *Mungu* or a variant in some languages, *Mulungu*, is a common Bantu term for "God" and is used by many other languages in the region. *Mungu*, or *Mulungu*, is believed to be the creator and sustainer of the world and of all life in it. The concept is more in terms of personhood rather than of gender, because Bantu names and pronouns do not specify gender. However, the Cushitic language Iraqw specifies *Looa* as person and as a feminine being, that is, as mother.

The question that stands out in the case of the Iraqw translation remains this: Why was it necessary to borrow the name of God from the Swahili? Borrowing the name of God from another language or community is uncommon in East Africa. The Alur case we discussed in chapter 13 was an exception and, interestingly, was a decision taken by a mission board. In general, using God's name in the indigenous language and culture has helped to develop a strong point of contact between the new faith and the traditional indigenous faith. It provides continuity and a basis for the contextualization and Christianization of existing forms and beliefs, adding, subtracting, or changing them as necessary. It makes possible an easier transition to the new.

God's name in Swahili, *Mungu*, grafted or transplanted into the Iraqw linguistic religious space, has not succeeded in supplanting the traditional name for God despite years of its presence in the area, and despite the attempt to popularize it in the language, culture, and faith of the Iraqw-speaking Christians. That *Mungu* is male or masculine has not helped, since among the Iraqw the devil is believed to be masculine. The devil is given the name *Neetlangw*. It is he who must be placated through sacrifice. *Neetlangw*, the chief evil being, is the one who demands the blood of cattle, goats, and sheep lest he avenge himself on the people. He is the cause of evil. He is assisted by male spirits referred to as *Gi'i* who are generally understood to be the living dead or the spirits of the forefathers. Some of these are considered to be evil in the Iraqw worldview. Christians have pluralized the proper name *Neetlangw* to stand for evil spirits, *neetlaame*.

Looa, in contrast to *Neetlangw*, is believed to be loving and kind. She is the provider, the protector, the merciful, the giver of life. She is the creator, the giver of children and blessings. She is light. She is the sun. She watches over all and is opposed to darkness. She is the one every Iraqw prays to for protection. She is the one dear to the heart of every Iraqw. She is the one on the lips of every Iraqw, Christian or non-Christian, at a time of danger. The primordial cry in the time of danger is *Ayi ee a Looa!* ("O God, my mother!"). *Ayi* in Iraqw refers only to one's own mother. The borrowed Swahili term *Mungu* has not been contextualized or indigenized. *Mungu* is still "a book affair," a matter of Christian liturgy. He is not in the everyday life of the people. Iraqw Christians do not evince or express strong feelings of closeness and endearment to God's name in Swahili when they are in the context of their own language and culture. The foreign name does not carry as much moral power or force as would the indigenous name within the general Iraqw socio-cultural space.

At a reviewer's seminar for the OT translation that UBS staff organized in Haydom, Mbulu, in 1990, a number of Iraqw Christian leaders and pastors were invited for a consultation on this issue. It was clear that most of them were not happy with the choice of the Swahili *Mungu*. Many strongly pleaded for a change in official church usage from *Mungu* to God's name in Iraqw. One leading Christian woman and teacher at the Waama Lutheran Bible School in Mbulu argued that she had found it very difficult to do evangelism using God's name in Swahili. She claimed that to the contrary it was much easier to evangelize and discuss religious matters with non-Christian Iraqw when God's Iraqw name was used. One Lutheran pastor in the Karatu area of Iraqw country is reported to have rebelled by persisting in the use of *Looa* in his preaching and teaching. Later, at a translation workshop discussion in October 1993 which included some leading Iraqw Lutheran Christians, there was a strong expression of the need to go back to use of *Looa* by the Iraqw Christian churches. Some felt that the portions of the OT that were to be printed, namely,

Genesis and Ruth, should use God's Iraqw name on an experimental basis. The overwhelming feeling was that this experiment would receive an enthusiastic and positive response from the majority of the Iraqw-speaking Christians.

The objections expressed by some of those who did not favor this proposal were mainly two-fold. The first objection, as previously stated, was that *Looa* is believed to be feminine, whereas the Christian God is generally conceived of and presented as masculine. He is the Father of our Lord Jesus Christ. He is depicted in masculine anthropomorphic imagery. How does one overcome this long tradition of usage? How does one deal with the strong masculine and patriarchal imagery of the Judeo-Christian Scriptures? Second, *Looa* has strong associations with the sun. It is even possible that some identify *Looa* with the sun, or think that the sun is *Looa*.[2] This is partly due to the fact that the sun is also called *looa*, but the term *looa* also refers to mirror, clock, and hour. Some Christians think that this association is a negative factor or even a distortion of the biblical monotheistic idea that places God the Creator above every created being, emphasizing his transcendent nature. But not everyone accepts the identification proposition, that is, that the sun and God the Creator are identical.

There is no doubt that the Iraqw see *Looa* as the supreme God. The sun is understood to be only a symbol of the supreme God. It is not itself God but God's eye. This is similar to the Akan of Ghana who speak of God, *Nyame*, as "the Giver of light or sun." They call God "the shining one."[3] It is also similar to the Ankole of Uganda for whom "one of the names or titles for God, Kazooba, means sun (Kazooba) and they believe that His presence in the universe is symbolized by the moving of the sun across the whole earth."[4] The traditional Iraqw, like the traditional Luo, pray facing the sun every morning for blessings and long life.

According to the Kenyan theologian John S. Mbiti,[5] the sun metaphor is common to many African peoples who see the sun as God's "Great Eye." Among these are the Akan, the Balase, the Galla, the Hadya, the Nandi, the Ovambo, and the Sidamo. This is considered symbolic. For many other African peoples, the name or title for God is also used for the sun (e.g. Ashanti [*We*], Chagga [*Ruwa*], Elgeyo [*Asis*], Sonjo [*Riob*], etc.). Mbiti in discussion of this matter reaches this very important conclusion: "I have not come across any

---

2. Hauge, "Loa, the Sun-Deity," 51–57.

3. Mbiti, *Concepts of God in Africa*, 57.

4. Mbiti, 57.

5. Mbiti, 94.

clear indication that the sun is considered to be God or God to be the sun. As our evidence shows, different peoples personify the sun, others take it to be a manifestation of God, and others closely associate it with him."[6]

Thus, we can suggest that the association of *Looa* with the sun is mainly metaphorical and does not necessarily imply the identity of the two.[7] Indeed, many of the peoples referred to above who have a similar usage have not provided a strong justification for borrowing God's name from another distant language group for use by the Iraqw, given the overwhelming psychological resistance to it. To paraphrase Swahili scholar and cultural anthropologist, Farouk Topan, "perhaps feelings of closeness and intimacy evoked by this indigenous term, *Looa*, explains its retention in popular Iraqw usage and practice, even after the appearance of the Swahili or Bantu name *Mungu* and its current common usage in Christian formal liturgy and normal worship."[8]

The idea of God as mother also is not limited to the Iraqw. A number of other African peoples share it. Mbiti notes that, "The southern Nuba who have a matrilineal system of descent refer to God as 'the Great Mother' and speak of him (her) in feminine pronouns."[9] They say "God gave birth to the world, earth,"[10] or that "God as a mother gives birth to, nurtures, cares for, nurses, brings up, protects, etc., her children."[11] The Ovambo of Namibia who are also matrilineal say, "The mother of people is God."[12]

The objection to the use of *Looa* based on the gender argument appears to be the only major obstacle Iraqw church leaders and translators have to deal with, given the strong tradition of Christian male chauvinism and patriarchy. They would do well to remember the remarks of South African theologian, Gabriel Satiloane:

> What we cannot buy in Western theology is its inevitable
> dependence on Western culture, civilization, or whatever you call

---

6. Mbiti, 134. See also Shorter, "African Religions," 428.

7. See also C. B. Johnson, "Some Aspects of Iraqw Religion," 53–56.

8. An adaptation of Topan's statement in, "Swahili as a Religious Language," 336, where in answer to the question, "Why was Mungu not replaced by Allah?" Topan speculates that this is "probably related to the existence of a notion, or concept, of godhood among the Swahili and their neighbours prior to the introduction of Islam in the coast." He adds that "perhaps feelings of closeness and intimacy evoked by this indigeneous term explains its retention even after the appearance of the Arabic Allah."

9. Mbiti, *Concepts of God in Africa*, 92–93.

10. Mbiti, 92–93.

11. Mbiti, 92–93.

12. Mbiti, 92–93.

> it. Its Greek-Roman thought-forms and modes of expression are the "swaddling clothes" that we need to tear open in order to get to Christ. . . . If theology is reflection, in African theology we try to break the seal of Western thought-forms so that we can come face to face with Christ, in him see ourselves and others.[13]

Another theologian Robert Hood agrees with the above when he observes:

> Traditional Christian doctrines and the theological formation of missionary Christianity both display what can be described as the Greco-Roman legacy, which is a primary feature of European and American ethnocentric churches' cultures. This legacy – especially perpetrated in such fundamental doctrines as the Trinity, the two natures of Christ, the work of the Holy Spirit, the concept of sin and salvation, and the division of flesh and spirit – in effect has become a kind of orthodox monoculture that has been universalized as a litmus test for Christianity in the Third World.[14]

It is this influence and theological heritage which has contributed to the rejection of the idea of God as mother or God as female. A metaphor or picture of God may be the product of a certain period, a certain society, or certain circumstances, but the central meaning of that picture may transcend those realities. Thus, a new picture or metaphor may be required to capture the same essential meaning for another period, another society, or other sets of circumstances, if such meaning is to retain validity and relevance.

Such is the problem with the biblical metaphor of fatherhood in capturing the essential nature of the Supreme Being. In the Iraqw worldview, fatherhood is a metaphor for the dark side of existence. Fatherhood is connected with evil, destruction, death, vengeance, darkness. Thus *Neetlangw*, the supreme evil being, is conceived in terms of fatherhood. He is the father of evil. He is *taata Neetlangw*, "father *Neetlangw*." Motherhood, on the other hand, is connected with light. *Looa* is the sun; she is light; she is *Ayi Looa*, "mother *Looa*." In the Iraqw worldview, this is a metaphorical model for describing their conception of the divine. This is the way reality is perceived. This is the truth for the Iraqw. The picture is relative to the Iraqw worldview, as other pictures are relative to their time and place.

This is admittedly an over-simplification of a complex issue – perhaps a mystery relating to the very nature of God. The Iraqw traditional concept

---

13. Setiloane, quoted in Hood, *Must God Remain Greek?*, 124–125.

14. Hood, *Must God Remain Greek?*, 124.

of God as mother encourages believers to re-examine their ways of talking about God and perhaps warns them of the dangers of cultural absolutism and obscurantism or of even some form of imperialism. It permits spiritual seekers to explore and to admit new and positive metaphors or models, satisfying the criteria of intelligibility, acceptability, relevance, correctness, and validity, consistent as well with their view of a just and loving God. As African churches wrestle with these issues, the Iraqw translators will be forced to face these serious theological issues as they seek the best way to render the name of God in the Bible.

The Other Cushites in Northern Tanzania

In late 1995 a team of SIL sociolinguistic researchers, Rachel Sowers and Tracy Tooley, conducted a number of language surveys to determine Bible translation needs in north-central Tanzania. In that same year, an SIL office was established in Dodoma on the premises of Mackay House of the Anglican Diocese of Central Tanganyika. As a result of these concerted efforts, SIL sent translation teams into two new projects. In 1996 Michael and Sibylle Endl started laying the groundwork for translation into Burunge, a Cushitic language in the Kondoa District of Dodoma Region. At the same time, Scott and Susan Lewis commenced work on Mbugu, also called Ma'a, a small Cushitic-Bantu hybrid language spoken in the Usambara Mountains.[15] Other SIL translation teams currently involved in Bible translation in Tanzania include Oliver and Dorothea Stegen, working on Rangi, a Bantu language of 270,000 speakers, and Brian and Karen Anders, working on Wasi, also called Alagwa, a Cushitic language of 40,000 speakers. Both Kirangi and Wasi are spoken in the Kondoa District of Tanzania.

Translation into the Cushitic Languages of Northern Kenya

Another group of Cushitic languages is spoken mainly in and north-eastern Kenya in the area bordering Ethiopia and Somalia. Both East Cushitic and South Cushitic languages are represented in Kenya. Dahalo (also called Sanye, Guo, or Garimani), a language with clicks but unrelated to the Khoisan

---

15. Grimes, *Ethnologue*, 14th ed., 235, describes Mbugu as a "mixed language, Pare-Cushitic. People call themselves 'Va-Ma'a.' A hybrid language; Bantu inflectional (prefix and concord) system with Cushitic vocabulary. Derivational morphemes are Bantu and Cushitic (or non-Bantu). The Bantu influence is from Pare (Shambaa)." See also Whiteley, "Linguistic Hybrids," 95–97, and Goodman, "Strange Case of Mbugu," 243–254.

languages, is the only South Cushitic language spoken in Kenya. It is spoken in the Tana River and Lamu districts of Kenya's Coast Province and has very few speakers. Very little has been written or described about this group in Kenya, and consequently no missionary or translation work has been reported among this people.

The other Cushitic languages spoken in Kenya are members of East Cushitic and are divided into two groups, namely, the Highland and Lowland groups. Burji is the only member of the Highland group; the others belong to the Lowland group. These are Yaaku, Daasanech, Elmolo, Rendille, Boni, the Oromo cluster (which includes Gabra, Borana, Sakuye, Garreh, Ajuran, Orma, Munyo, and Waata), and the Somali cluster (comprised of Leisan, Murulle, Degodia, Harti, Isaaq, Ogaden, Aulihan, Abdwak, and Abdalla). These ethnic groups are predominantly Muslim, but with some Christian minorities among them.

The Cushitic-speaking peoples of Kenya represent new challenges and opportunities for Bible translation work as well as for Christian mission in Kenya today. They live in very harsh and difficult terrain and very few churches have any missionary outreach among these communities. They are generally marginalized in terms of availability of education, literacy, and lack most modern facilities. Translation work among the different groups is only beginning.

The Somali Bible

The Somali people number at least eight million or more in Somalia, Ethiopia, and Kenya. They are united by a common language, the Islamic religion, and a common ethnic origin. Somali is an Eastern Cushitic language. The earliest known Scripture texts in the Somali language were sponsored by the Roman Catholic Church, and were mostly selections from the Bible that were published in Vienna in 1900.[16] A Bible history by the Capuchins was published in 1908 in Freiburg, Germany, and this was followed by further Scripture selections published in Asmara, Eritrea, in 1914 by the Catholic Press.

The first whole book of the Bible translated into Somali was the Gospel of Mark published in 1915, followed by the Gospel of John more than a decade later in 1929, both by BFBS. This version of the Gospel of John was reprinted in 1949. It was the work of P. Ohlssen (Swedish National Evangelical Society) in the Ogaden-Harti dialect of Ethiopia. Ohlssen completed the translation of

---

16. Biblical selections in Reinisch, *Die Somali-Sprache*, 1–73.

the four Gospels and requested their publication by BFBS, but he unfortunately died before this could happen. BFBS noted that, "There is nobody at the present who can continue that translation work."[17] In 1935 a translation of the Gospels edited by anonymous Capuchins, members of the Roman Catholic Mission of Arabia and British Somaliland, was published by the Catholic Mission Press in Aden. This version was used in Aden and Djibouti and was very much appreciated by the American Sudan Interior Mission missionary, W. H. Modricker, working in the south.

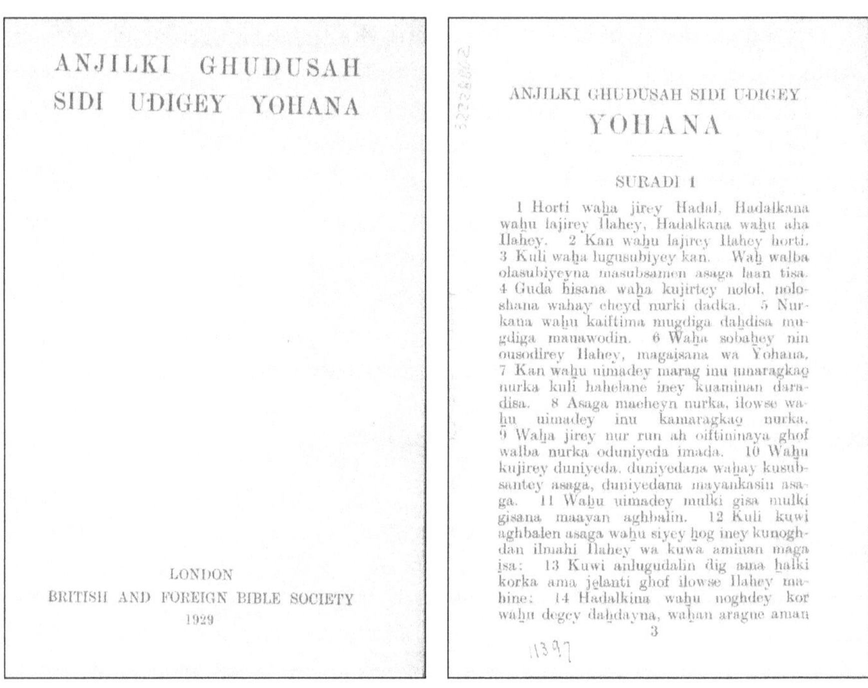

Figure 15.2. The Gospel of John in Somali, the title page and first page. American Bible Society Library and Archives. Used by permission.

Among those who tried their hand at translating the entire New Testament into Somali were G. Nylander of the Swedish Mission and the Rev A. Keene Spitler, who worked on the NT in the northern part of Somalia. Keene Spitler tried several times to get in touch with Modricker in an attempt to propose some collaborative endeavor. Unfortunately, this did not materialize. In the end Keene Spitler was only able to finalize the Gospel of Mark, which was published

---

17. See BFBS – ESC Minute Cards, vol. 7.

in 1971, and the Gospel of John, which came out in 1974, both published by the Bible Society of Ethiopia using Ethiopic script.[18] He was assisted by John Dahir Hassan. The problem of orthography remained a major challenge for the writing of Somali both in the Ethiopic or Roman script because a proper linguistic study had not been done on how to reduce the language to writing accurately.

W. W. Grey of the Anglican Bible Churchmen's Missionary Society (BCMS) in Djibouti collaborated with Modricker also on a translation of the Gospels into Somali. However, they waited for all the Gospels to be translated before printing and they also wanted to know which system of orthography would be adopted by the Somali government. Modricker stayed in Somalia for about two decades and translated a number of OT and NT books but felt they were not ready for publication. In the end, however, it was the work of Modricker and his wife Dorothy, assisted by Adan Jimale Farah, Yusuf Mur'lse, and Yusuf Salad, that eventually resulted in producing the present Somali Bible. The Gospel of Luke was published in 1969 by the Bible Society in East Africa and the first published New Testament appeared in 1972, published by the Bible Society of Kenya. A reprint in a revised orthography appeared in 1976. This was again published by BSK. The books of Genesis, Exodus, and Psalms were published by the World Home Bible League in South Holland, Illinois, in 1977, and the entire Bible in 1979 by BSK. The Society for International Missions (SIM) with the cooperation and support of BSK made further corrections and minor revisions to the Somali 1979 Bible, resulting in a new corrected edition of the Somali Bible which was launched and dedicated on 28 February 2009. This text is now currently in circulation for interested readers from the Somali-speaking communities.

From a Christian perspective distribution figures for the Somali Bible are discouraging to say the least. They provide an indication of the extremely limited extent of Christian presence and Christianization among the Somali. Less than one-tenth of one percent of the Somalis are thought to be Christian; 99.8 percent, or higher, are thought to be Muslim. The problem of readership and distribution will remain a perennial challenge!

---

18. Languages that straddle the borders of Ethiopia and the neighboring countries have faced the challenge of needing to be written in both the Ethiopic script and in the Roman script common in the other countries. In some places Arabic script has also been used for some languages; hence countries like Eritrea, Djibouti, and Sudan, require texts in three scripts – Ethiopic, Roman, and Arabic!

The Oromo Scriptures

The Oromo group excited missionary interest right from the start of the modern missionary era. It will be recalled that Johann Krapf's main dream and desire was to reach the Galla (i.e. the Oromo). In 1839, during his first tour to Ethiopia at Ankobar, Krapf translated and published a draft of the Gospel of John in Galla in 1839, giving credit on the title page to a Galla man named Birkius for his help. Thereafter, he continued to translate the Gospels of Luke, Matthew, Mark, and the Acts of the Apostles, as well as the OT book of Genesis. In addition to Birkius, he was helped in his later translation efforts by an Ethiopian named Debtera Sareb and a Galla person named Roofo. Even after he had to leave the area, Krapf never forgot the Galla, these Oromo-speaking peoples. His passion was such that even after his retirement to Germany he continued to preoccupy himself with the question of Galla scriptures.[19] Krapf's translations, the fruits of his labors, were published in the 1870s, thirty years after his time in Oromo country. BFBS published Exodus in 1877. Apparently, these Scriptures were never used in missionary or evangelistic work among the Oromo peoples. It would appear that his translations did not receive the support or interest necessary to lead to wide publication and distribution. Some of his manuscripts can still be found in archives in Germany and in England in the care of CMS, BFBS, or other missionary agencies.

The Borana Bible

The Borana of Kenya, the only Oromo-speaking group in Kenya with a complete New Testament or complete Bible, had to wait to be evangelized until the coming of the Anglican Bible Churchmen's Missionary Society (BCMS), who received the exclusive right from the colonial government to establish themselves at Marsabit in northern Kenya in 1931. Although John Baur notes that "Their chief work was Bible translation,"[20] it is true that Canon Eric J. Webster and his BCMS teammates evangelized extensively in the area, traveling by camel and donkey. The response to their work was poor and disheartening, as was clearly reflected in their translation work. Even though their first Scripture portion into Borana was the Gospel of Luke, translated by Eric J. Webster, assisted by A. W. Haylett and David Donabo, and published in 1934, the Gospel of Mark only appeared more than thirty years later in 1965. This was the work of Stephen Houghton, a BCMS missionary who started work

---

19. Schaaf, *On Their Way Rejoicing*, 73–74, 76.

20. Baur, *2000 Years of Christianity in Africa*, 476.

at Marsabit in 1960. The Gospel of John, as well the books of Acts, Romans, 1 Corinthians, James, and 1 John were translated and published in a single volume in 1966. The complete NT was finalized and published in 1978.

Work on the OT started in 1979. Houghton, the main translator, was assisted by David Diida, a former schoolteacher from Marsabit, and there was a team of reviewers. With the translation of the OT nearing completion and the revision of the NT also in progress, Stephen Houghton unfortunately died in the April 1983, before seeing the conclusion of his life's work. The translation, however, was finalized by David Diida. The complete Bible, one edition with the Deuterocanonical books and the other without them, was published by the Bible Society of Kenya and launched at a joyful and well-attended ceremony on 19 March 1995, at Marsabit, nearly 385 miles (620 kilometers) northeast of Nairobi. The launching could have actually occurred much earlier if it had not been for certain orthographical problems which were only addressed toward the end of the translation. There was no quick fix for sorting them out and correcting the entire text consistently. After the Swahili and Luo Bibles, the Borana Bible became the third published Bible in a Kenyan language to have an edition with the Deuterocanonical books.

The Burji New Testament

Burji, like Borana, is spoken in both Ethiopia and Kenya. Initiatives to translate into this language have been spearheaded by SIL under the sponsorship of the Lutheran Church in Ethiopia. The translation team, composed of Salle Chota and Debbebe Saafe, assisted by Charlotte Wedekind of SIL, prepared the Gospel of Luke that was published by the Bible Society of Ethiopia in 1981. The NT was completed by 1994 and thereafter published. A problem with this publication, as with other Ethiopia/Kenya cross-border publications, is that, because it is written in the Amharic script, Kenyan Burji speakers will not be able to benefit from this excellent effort as they are unfamiliar with that script. The Bible Societies of Kenya and of Ethiopia were involved in exploratory discussions to have the Burji Scriptures published in both the Amharic and Latin scripts. However this was not successful.

Translation into Daasanach, Orma, and Rendille

Daasanach work is underway due to the initiatives of SIL and Bible Translation and Literacy (BTL). The initial translation team in 1983 was composed of Jim and Sue Ness of SIL as project leaders and technical advisors, and Jackson

Lochua Achinya, James Koriiye Haile, Gosh Kwanyang, and Yergalech Komoi as translators. This was followed by a team consisting of Jim and Sue Ness, as well as James Korie, Yalagalech Komoi, and Benedict Lokono. Genesis was published in 2000, Luke in 2003, and Exodus in 2006. The translation of the New Testament was completed, dedicated and launched the 18 August 2018. Work on the Old Testament began on January 2019.

The Orma translation project was initiated in 1986 by an SIL couple, George and Wendy Payton. Instability in the area has greatly delayed translation progress. Dale and Carole Hoskins were the initial project leaders and technical advisors but gave way to others. The translators include Joseph Diba, Omar Goricha, Sofia Salad, and Mohamud Wachu. The book of Genesis was published in 2000 by the BTL agency in Nairobi, Kenya. Due in instability in the area work has been slow and uncertain.

Translation work among the Rendille was started in 1981 under the leadership of Nicholas and Lynne Swanepoel, Steven and Johanna Pillinger of SIL and a team of mother-tongue speakers, including Laban Eysinkeele, Francis Letiwa Galboran, Judy Amiya, Mohamed Arbele, and Joshua Galimogle. Of the original members, only Laban Eysinkeele and Joshua Galimogle remained part of the team. The Gospel of Mark was published by the BTL agency in Nairobi, Kenya. Copies were received with jubilation at Korr in Marsabit District in August 1994. The book of Acts followed in 2000 while the Gospel of John and 1 and 2 John appeared in 2004. The publication and launch of the New Testament took place on 18 August 2018. Work on the Old Testament is in progress.

16

Concluding Remarks

The survey of the history of Bible translation in the East African countries of Tanzania, Uganda, Kenya, Rwanda, and Burundi shows that much has been accomplished since Johann Krapf and Johannes Rebmann set foot on these shores in 1844. Translations of the complete Bible in both Roman Catholic and Protestant editions, of the New Testament, and of single books have been completed in many languages. The church has thereby been empowered and strengthened, and has consequently grown, and continues to grow. The work yet to be done is nonetheless daunting. The challenge is ever new for the churches and for the Bible Societies to carry on the unfinished task of Bible translation in these nations.

New Technologies

Many of the pioneer translations are either obsolete or are becoming unusable as languages change and adapt to the needs of the present day. Some of the older translations were not well received, as they had a number of problems, and are in need of revision or new translation. Many of them were literal word-for-word or formal equivalence translations that are well established and still widely used in church liturgy and worship. These may need to be complemented by modern, contemporary translations of a functional equivalence or meaning-based variety. This is already happening in many places. The demands for work on languages without a Bible, a New Testament, or even a portion or selection are even greater. How to prioritize these needs, given the limited resources available, is a task that the Bible Societies and the churches need to tackle together.

A number of Bible Societies are exploring new approaches in making the life-giving message of the Scriptures available to the people. Traditionally, this is done by means of the print medium. It was not always so from the beginning. At the beginning was the spoken word. This was passed on orally, by word of mouth from person to person, and from community to community. It was argued, discussed, debated, accepted, believed, and, in some cases, rejected. Eventually, what was most widely accepted was written down by hand, and copied and recopied and passed on. Obviously, the manual writing and transmission of this written text was very slow. Then came the Gutenberg revolution and the mechanical reproduction of the written text in large quantities at a fast speed. Later came the revolution in means of transportation and travel, together with the history-shaking events of European colonialism, Christian world evangelization, and globalization. These, as well as rapid and fast-changing developments in all areas of technology, have made change the order of the day. All things have become new![1]

Although the Bible as we know it has been mainly based on the written text, today new technologies, such as radios, computers, phones and others, have created and multiplied opportunities for carrying on the vision of making the word of life known as widely as possible to the ends of the earth. The limit is no longer the written text. We no longer need to think of God's word only in terms of the book. New images and metaphors of conceptualizing the word of life are emerging and these are calling for new criteria of assessing faithfulness and accuracy in the transmission of the word as it is moved from one medium to another. The new media also pose new demands for flexibility and creativity in how the word is to be shared and used.

The earliest use of the new media in East Africa was the recording of the written text in audio form for use by non-literates or pre-literate populations. A number of agencies have been active in rendering this service, among them, Portable Recording Ministries, Gospel Recordings, and Hosanna's Faith Comes by Hearing (FCBH) program. In Kenya, for example, Portable Recording Ministries was among the first to enter the area. They were able to record New Testaments in Swahili, Gikuyu, Maasai, Luo, Turkana, Pokoot, and Kalenjin, among others. In general, and as a rule, they favored recordings in contemporary, common-language translations except where these were not available. The quality was initially poor but has been steadily improving all the time. Instead of single-voice recordings, multi-voice dramatized recordings are now available, done professionally under strict standards of control. Whereas initially the recordings were analogue, now they tend to be digital, so that instead of having the recordings on cassette, they are mostly available in digital format, for example, FCBH's Talking Bible. More recently these digital

---

1. N. Chanda's book *Bound Together: How Traders, Preachers, Adventurers and Warriors Shaped Globalization* (2007) tells this story in a very captivating and stimulating manner. The East African story is a fine illustration of the process so vividly portrayed by Chanda's global story.

recordings of the Scriptures in various tongues have been made available in a variety of media including CDs mini disks, as well as directly from the internet for use in various electronic devices.

Using the Pauline text of Romans 10:17 as a motto, "Faith comes by hearing and hearing by the Word of God," (NKJV), the America-based Hosanna Ministries has embarked on an ambitious program in collaboration with the Bible Societies to put many African-language Scriptures on tape. In Tanzania this program has several New Testaments in local languages in audio format including Swahili, Maasai, Iraqw, Sukuma, Cigogo, and Ruhaya. In Uganda they have recorded the NT in Luganda, Karimojong, Rukiga-Runyankore, and Dhopadhola, among others. In Kenya FCBH recordings include Gikuyu, Kalenjin, Luo, Kamba, Maasai, Borana, Turkana, Pokoot, Embu-Mbeere, Meru, and Lwisukha-Lwitakho-Lutrichi. The FCBH recordings have proved to be very popular. Unfortunately, only the NT is available despite expressed demand for the entire Bible. None of the books of the OT have been recorded in any of the languages of East Africa.

Some Bible Societies are considering use of film, television, and the multi-media environment made possible by the digital computer revolution. Societies in the technologically developed north have made great strides in tapping and applying this revolution to Scripture use, adaptation, reproduction, and distribution. African examples of adapting Scripture text to drama and video production are two attempts by Jean-Claude Loba-Mkole, a Congolese biblical scholar and theologian, and Edward Kabuye, a Ugandan dramatist and musician, namely, *Mwana wa Mungu Aliteswa* ("The Son of God was made to suffer") and *Leo Mwokozi amezaliwa* ("Today the Savior is born"). As Loba-Mkole himself describes them:

> *Mwana wa Mungu aliteswa* is a drama that uses the African art of storytelling in terms of narrations combined with drums, songs and dances. It is an Easter drama that narrates the story about the suffering, death and resurrection of Jesus Christ. It is furthermore an audio-visual exegesis of the Gospel of Mark 14–16. . . . *Leo Mwokozi amezaliwa* points out that the event of the Saviour's birth is relevant for today, a hope for the present time, . . . taking the Gospel from the printed medium and communicat[ing] it or interact[ing] with it through another medium, namely an African audio-visual dramatization.[2]

---

2. Loba-Mkole, *Triple Heritage*, 136–139. See also the discussion of these issues by K. J. Noss, "Communicating Scriptures," 152–164.

Loba-Mkole's exegetical interpretation of these texts together with Kabuye's dramatic and musical interpretation of them has made for a lively and dramatic audio-visual rendering of these biblical stories.

The new technologies are multi-sensory intensive; they do not limit themselves to the use of just one sense, e.g. sight or hearing or touch (e.g. Braille). They are often active and participatory. It could be argued that compared with the printed page or the book the new technologies of the word, or the new media, are closer to the world of the traditional African village society with its storytellers, griots, singers, drummers, and dancers. The traditional African in the rural village can now move straight into the modern and postmodern world fully exploiting the new technologies. It is not necessary to pass through all the previous technological stages or the sequential progressions through history that have brought them about. The dependence of all these media on the translated texts or on scripts adapted from translated and written texts cannot, however, be bypassed. Translation occupies a special place in the entire process.

African church leaders need to ponder the implications of the new technologies. They need to plan carefully and strategically for their full exploitation in the service of the gospel. These technologies are already here and will not wait to be invited. Yet they profoundly affect how reality is perceived, how it is understood and interpreted, how truth is to be understood, and how the word is to be understood. The church is not fully prepared for this. The African church is still theologically unsophisticated and less developed technologically and may not have begun to think through the implications of this phenomenon. And therein lies the danger if a viable and sustainable conceptualization of the word and its multi-forms is not worked out.

The role and place of the written text is basic and will continue to be with us. Yet many people in rural and pre-literate communities have not experienced the word in its written form. They have encountered it in its oral form and will continue to do so. The technological revolutions are complicating this simple situation by widening the options and by making obsolete the primacy of the older forms. The new forms are, to be sure, more powerful, more appealing, and more tempting.

Does this mean that Bible translation as we know it has no future? Certainly not. Yet the understanding of translation and the uses to which it is being put or will be put are changing. The translation task in Africa is unfinished. The majority of Africa's more than 3,000 languages (*Ethnologue* 17th edition) do not yet have the Bible, the New Testament, or even a portion of Scripture translated into them. According to the *UBS Global Scripture Access Report* of

2014, by the end of 2012 only 189 languages in Africa had a complete Bible, only 343 had a New Testament, and only 216 had only one book of the Bible. Many of them have not been reduced to writing. Church leaders, Bible Society representatives, missiologists, and missionaries never lose an opportunity to remind us that the peoples and cultures represented by these languages urgently need the word of God in their own words and thought-forms, expressed in their own native genius.

To accomplish this task, personnel and resources need to be committed to meet the continued challenge of Bible translation in Africa. A number of questions need to be asked about how this is going to be done, by what means, by what technologies, and to what end. What results or consequences for the transformation of peoples and cultures or even for the transformation of the original source text and message are to be expected? A key challenge is to understand better where we have come from in order to focus better on where we are going.

Translation and the Churches

As we have shown in this account, Bible translation is inextricably connected to mission history and church growth. Invariably, the first Scripture translations into any of the languages we have discussed were done by the pioneer missionaries and their successors, and later by the churches they helped establish. Scripture translations that are a result of pure private interest or unconnected to a mission agency or a local church are rare in East Africa. The Bible Societies have taken good account of this fact and hence see themselves as handmaidens to the churches and their evangelistic, pastoral, and apologetic mission.

Translation projects are thus essentially a responsibility of participating churches. The Bible Societies come in as partners to offer technical, linguistic, and exegetical help – which often includes the training of personnel and the provision of essential resources such the original source texts, reference materials, and other translators' helps, as well as providing quality control of the manuscripts before publication. The publication and distribution of the published Scriptures, at often highly subsidized prices, is the responsibility of the Bible Societies. The resulting published translations of the Bible are, however, seen as belonging to the churches in their language areas, even though the Bible Society may hold the copyright of the particular translations of the Bible, on behalf of the churches.

Additionally, it is evident that the early translations of the Holy Scriptures were almost always credited to the pioneer missionaries behind the translation endeavors. Rarely was there mention of the contribution of mother-tongue speakers. This invisibility of collaborators and co-translators tends to give the impression that missionary-translators worked single-handedly. The reality, of course, is much different. We know that, without the collaboration and contribution of the mother-tongue speakers of the languages concerned, very little would have been achieved and the quality would have been compromised. Thus, while many of those who contributed to this effort remain mostly anonymous, or in cases where they are mentioned they are identified merely as informants, helpers, or assistants, it is clear and now acknowledged that these local participants played significant and indispensable roles in the actual translation process in their own languages.

The problem in many cases was that local participants and collaborators were generally not treated as equals, and hence were rarely given a decision-making role in these matters. This perhaps explains why they were not given their due credit for their contributions. This is a phenomenon that is as evident in church planting as it is in translation work. Wilson Niwagila, in *From the Catacomb to a Self-Governing Church*, as we noted in chapter five, takes up this issue in his discussion of the founding of the Lutheran church in Bukoba. He observes, for example, that even though the church in Buhaya was started in the early 1890s largely by the Bahaya themselves as a spill-over from the Uganda mission, these local initiatives have been completely ignored by some who prefer to see the beginning of the church in Buhaya as coinciding with the arrival of the German missionaries of the Bethel Mission in 1910.

Even in the case of the Bethel Mission, this problem of not recognizing the local input is inherently present. Niwagila cites the case of Wilhelm Rascher of Bethel Mission who was sent from Usambara to Bukoba together with four African colleagues, namely, Jonah, Neaman, Isaac, and Thoma, from the Usambara congregation, an offshoot of the Bethel Mission. Niwagila comments as follows: "These four Africans are mentioned by Rascher and the missionaries in Usambara as being helpers. The pride of the missionaries has always prevented them from seeing that the Africans who took part in missionary activities were also missionaries. Without these people, missionary work could not have been successful."[3] He adds, referring to the use of single names: "The names given are only Christian names, which is also an indication that the African names were very much ignored by the missionaries." He concludes:

---

3. Niwagila, *From the Catacombs*, 132.

"It is my great conviction that these four men were commissioned by God and their congregations to work in Bukoba as missionaries."[4]

In the current phase of the history of Bible translation, first language or mother tongue speakers of the language of translation are normally given priority in any program of translating Scriptures in that language. Moreover, local churches are often actively involved in the identification and choice of suitable and acceptable translators who satisfy the relevant criteria. This norm is sometimes difficult to realize in situations where there is no established Christian community, or where the level of literacy and education is so low that finding qualified translators is an insurmountable problem. SIL and BTL are mostly involved in situations of this nature. In such situations, a missionary translation model which respects and gives credit to the mother-tongue speaker's input and contribution has an important place and role on the basis of partnership in mission. However, in the case of the Bible Societies, the present ongoing translation projects in East Africa are mostly carried out by mother-tongue speakers who receive technical help and resources from the Bible Societies.

Translation Methods

During the missionary period, two types of translations could be distinguished: those whose source or base text was the original biblical source languages – that is, Hebrew, Aramaic, and Greek – and those whose source or base text was a version, or versions, in the missionary's mother tongue or in some cases a version in a lingua franca such as Swahili. For example, in Upare the German missionaries of the Bethel Mission insisted on using the original source biblical languages for translating into Chasu, whereas the German missionaries of the SDAM, assisted a local team of Chasu Christians, produced their translations into Chasu based on the Zanzibar Swahili Version, which the missionaries reworked and improved using Bible versions in major Western languages such English, French, German or Portuguese. Or in the case of the first Iraqw translation, Anna Strøm's four African colleagues worked from the Swahili text, while she herself worked from the Swedish, Norwegian, English, Italian, and Swahili versions. It is not clear whether the source or base text used made any difference to the quality of the translation. Perhaps what mattered most was the clarity of the translation as well as the intelligibility and natural flow of the translated text when read aloud to the intended audience.

---

4. Niwagila, 132.

Further, the emphasis in current ongoing translations is on the functional equivalence model rather than on the formal correspondence model. The former places a premium on naturalness and intelligibility, as well as on the accurate communication of the meanings of the original text. This is in stark contrast to the emphasis placed on capturing the form and syntactic patterns of the original text as well as the preference given to word-for-word correspondence characteristic of the formal correspondence approach. This change of emphasis is mainly due to the efforts of Dr Eugene A. Nida of the American Bible Society, who developed this approach in the 1960s and promoted it vigorously as he trained translators around the world.

On the whole, missionary translations tended to be of a formal correspondence variety, although some were of a functional equivalence variety. This latter case was the exception rather than the rule. Moreover, some pioneer missionary translators embarked on their translation enterprise after only brief exposure to the language and when they were still ignorant of the complexities of the receptor-language culture. To achieve mother tongue or first language competence in any language and to master it to the extent of exploiting its resources, figures, and idioms, is certainly a life-time enterprise which requires years of complete immersion in the culture in all its diversity and depth. This observation is not intended to belittle the thankless yet remarkable missionary achievement in Bible translation. There is hardly any doubt to the perceptive observer that these missionary translations were the single most important tool indispensable for their pioneering work in Christian mission. The phenomenal church growth on the mission field and the mushrooming of indigenous churches owe much to Bible translation, production, and distribution. Dr David Barrett's studies and publications on the growth and expansion of the church in Africa – and especially on the rise of the indigenous independent churches – are sufficient to confirm this observation.[5]

Translations by mother-tongue speakers also fall into the two above-mentioned categories, (i.e. those based on the original source language texts, and those based on versions in major languages or lingua francas). At the present time, a majority of ongoing translations are of the second variety, that is, they are based on versions in major languages. It is probable that with the present-day spread and increased investment in theological and biblical studies and education, translations of the first variety are likely to increase. Again, while translations of the functional equivalence variety have been popular

---

5. For more on this, see Barrett et al., *Kenya Churches Handbook*, and Barrett, *Schism and Renewal in Africa*.

and have been encouraged in Bible Society circles in recent times, more and more users and church leaders are indicating a preference for more literal and liturgical translations. A situation is developing that allows for users to have access to different types of translations. Thus, users may have a preference for one type of translation or another, or even for a variety of translations depending on the function or occasion of use. This is in line with views of translation currently supported by the Bible Societies. They see the need to consider the nature of the audience and the needs of the audience as well as the intended function of the translation. Now Bible Societies are free to support translations for children, translations for evangelism, translations for liturgical purposes, and even literary translations as well.[6]

Such translations done by first-language speakers of African languages working directly from the original source languages, equipped with modern exegetical, linguistic, and text-critical tools, represent the expected norm and ideal toward which the African churches must strive. At the present time, only a minority of translations even partially fulfill this ideal. The majority are still far behind. Nonetheless, the human capacity to communicate and to process information helps to explain how even through imperfect translations the message of the translator has been retrieved. There is in reality no perfect communication. Human communication happens in the context of noises, distractions, and interruptions. The listener or reader brings to bear their own imperfections in deciphering or making out what has been communicated. The process is complex. It is a miracle of grace that God still uses imperfect human vessels and processes as instruments for the communication of the divine word and the extension of his kingdom. It could be argued that the vernacular and local situations provide the ideal context for maximizing degrees of understanding in communication. Use of a second or even third language leads to greater challenges in communication and results in lower levels of understanding or comprehension.

Translation and Language Policy

In East Africa and especially in the coastal parts of Kenya and most parts of Tanzania, the dominance of Swahili means that many people in these parts do not read the Scriptures in their mother tongue. They receive God's word through use of this lingua franca which has been given the status of a national and official language in both Kenya and Tanzania. The dominant relationship of

---

6. For more about diversity of approaches to Bible translation, see Wilt, ed., *Bible Translation.*

Swahili vis-à-vis the other indigenous languages and dialects is a challenge for language planners and those interested in developing the numerous vernaculars spoken in these nations. This relationship has placed these other languages at risk. Indeed, some are already in danger of possible extinction. The roots of this crisis are found in the ninteenth and twentieth centuries. Swahili, which had its home base along the coastal areas of Kenya and Tanzania, spread widely into the interior during this period, especially in the areas bordering the old caravan and trade routes. The Arab slave trade and its widespread nature in the interior of East and Central Africa certainly laid the basis for the further spread and consolidation of Swahili. In comparison to Kenya, the interior of Tanzania was more deeply penetrated by these traders, who needed a lingua franca, a function for which Swahili was well suited. Moreover, Swahili was given strong support and was widely promoted and extended throughout these territories by both the German and British colonial administrations as part of their educational policy and in their actual administrative practice. The new Christian churches that were being planted by missionaries also played their role as agents for the promotion of this lingua franca in their mission activities. This was at the expense of the other indigenous languages and dialects.

Thus, for example, in Tanzania during the post-independence period, it was easy for President Julius Nyerere's administration to consolidate and extend this language policy, which was not only politically and ideologically expedient, but economically and administratively the most efficient and effective means for the realization of the government's goals and political agenda. During Nyerere's administration, Swahili became entrenched as the main language for governmental and official business, primary and post-primary education, adult education, mass media, for use in parliament, and as the main language of business and commerce throughout the country. English was marginalized for use in secondary and tertiary education by a minority, whose mastery of it is today increasingly threatened. The other indigenous languages were weakened and impoverished by being denied official recognition or by not being granted any official instruments favoring their development and growth. This situation was tellingly reflected in the Bible Society's structure of Scripture translation, production, and distribution. For example, a recent visit to the main Bible warehouse of the Bible Society of Tanzania at Kitunda, Dar es Salaam, revealed that vernacular Scriptures were moving very slowly. Of the Scriptures distributed by the Bible Society of Tanzania, more than 95 percent are Swahili Scriptures. Scriptures in vernacular languages together with English Scriptures form only a small proportion of the Society's Scripture distribution record.

These data illustrate the effectiveness of Tanzania's language policy and the hegemony and near monopoly of Swahili over all social and cultural discourse in everyday life. Perhaps this is more evident in the urban communities, but this situation is also encroaching onto the realities of village life to varying degrees. The universal use of Swahili as the medium of communication in all primary schools throughout the United Republic of Tanzania is perhaps the main vehicle for overturning the tables of language use in the villages, especially among the youth. The use of Swahili in Kenya and Uganda as well as in Rwanda and Burundi, not to mention the eastern parts of DRC, is also increasing and slowly following in Tanzania's footsteps, especially in the urban areas where Swahili takes on the role of an inter-ethnic medium of discourse.

The above notwithstanding, it can still be said that the indigenous languages continue to predominate in the villages, insofar as they are the vehicle for the transmission of local cultures and practices, values, and musical expression. They provide the basis for cultural and ethnic self-identification and they constitute a rich source of cultural pride and expression for East African ethnic cultures. Without the former, East African national cultures would have no foundation on which to build. There is no way that they can be conserved in Swahili or in some other foreign language. Swahili has its own coastal heritage and cultural expression different from these other indigenous expressions. These languages individually represent the subconscious world of every community; yet the national cultures which are in the process of being created and consolidated are simply synthesizing these various strands.

Are the indigenous languages and dialects experiencing a slow process of language death? This may possibly be the case for some languages. Such languages as Chasu, spoken on the slopes of Pare Mountains, or the Chagga dialects, spoken on the slopes of Mount Kilimanjaro, are facing this danger. Any visitor to these areas will be surprised to hear more Swahili spoken there than the local dialects. Zaramo on the Tanzanian coast is another such language, given its violent suffocation by the merciless cultural mix and the fast invasion of its language and territorial space in the ubiquitous Swahili-ized world, and the ethnic melting pot of Dar es Salaam in whose environs Zaramo finds itself. It is not yet obvious, however, that the death knells for Zaramo are soon to be heard. Languages do not die and disappear without a struggle among a population that is still reproducing itself culturally. The dynamic and vigorous Zaramo musical and religious cultural heritage will ensure that this struggle is prolonged. How about other languages far away from the front line? The coastal languages of Kenya and Tanzania are more or less in the same boat as

Zaramo – under serious threat from Swahili language and culture as well as Islamic religion.

Some East African languages have disappeared from the scene and will remain only in the history books. Among these we may mention such languages as El Molo, Kwad'za and the various Okiek dialects (also known as Dorobo). The reasons for this phenomenon are not unrelated to Swahili-ization, globalization, or other national language policies. The causes are complex and are no doubt connected to the sociocultural dynamics of the El Molo, Kwad'za, and Okiek communities, that is, their cultural, economic, and traditional value systems in the context of their precarious ecology and life-patterns as well as in the context of the national economies and political situations of the East African area.

However, the extinction of many endangered languages and dialects is not a foregone conclusion. Many remain resistant to the threats they face and they are likely to be with us for some generations to come. And doubtless they touch deeper chords and arouse deeper emotions for their mother-tongue or indigenous speakers than Swahili ever will. This alone justifies their preservation and use for the communication of the gospel for the millions who will continue to claim them as their mother tongues. A low demand for Scripture in these languages is a measure of other variables and factors and not necessarily the values placed upon these languages and dialects by their speakers. Encouraging the use of these local vernaculars empowers the people and communities who use them. It anchors the message communicated and understands it on the basis of home-grown metaphors, figures, symbols, signs, rhythms, agenda, and *raisons d'être*. Encouraging the use of the local vernaculars facilitates the process of enculturation, indigenization, and identification with the new. The local empowers and frees. It provides the soil and ground for domesticating the foreign and owning it.

Swahili will naturally continue to predominate at the national level as well as throughout the broader east and central African region. Similarly, English will continue for some time to be the main medium of communication on the international level. And so most enlightened non-urban East Africans will need to be proficient in at least three languages: their rural mother tongues such as Ruhaya, Cigogo, Kinyakyusa, Kisukuma, Iraqw, Maasai, Gikuyu, Dholuo, Kalenjin, Borana, Turkana, Luganda, Runyankore, Acholi, Lugbara, among others; the national language Swahili; and the international language, English. Hence Scriptures will continue to be needed to satisfy demand in these three areas – the rural mother tongue at the primary level, Swahili at the secondary and national level, and English or French at the tertiary and international level.

Therefore, current efforts in Bible translation to operate in all three areas are not in vain. If anything, more needs to be done than is already being done in the on-going efforts in Bible translation in the nations of East Africa.

Conclusion

It is the translation of the Bible into the ancient language of Ge'ez in the fifth to sixth centuries CE that established the Ethiopic script, literacy, and writing in Ethiopia from ancient times to this day. The old scrolls of the biblical text and its interpretation, found in the ancient Ethiopian monasteries in places such as Gondar, Lalibela, and Axum are testimony to this fact. Bible translation has been arguably the major force in the development and growth of East African languages. The need for Bible translation led to the development of nearly all the existing orthographies of East African languages. These became the basis for subsequent literacy programs that contributed to the emerging and growing shift from an oral culture to a literate culture. The Bible inadvertently became the first book in nearly all the East African languages, with the exception of Swahili. The pioneer Christians in many East African language communities were referred to as *wasomi* "readers." Christianity being a religion of the book necessarily needed such readers to facilitate its growth and spread. Bible translation thus became the engine of alphabetization or the culture of literacy. East African languages that possess the Bible as well as other literature are generally more vibrant and proudly spoken by first speakers than languages that do not have the Bible. The story that we have narrated here is thus a recognition and celebration of the story of the vernacularization of the Bible in East African languages. This has in turn contributed to other developments in the local languages and cultures. What Johann Krapf and Johannes Rebmann started in 1844 has grown beyond their wildest dreams. To God be the praise and glory. *Soli Deo Gloria!*

Appendix A

Perspectives from Kenya

Table A.1. Main languages and dialects of Kenya[1]

I. Nilotic Languages		
1. Luo[2]		
[2–10] *Kalenjin Language and Dialect Cluster*		
	[2–6] *Nandi-Marakweta Branch*	
	2. Nandi	
	3. Kipsigis	
	4. Keiyo	
	5. Tugen	
	6. Marakweta Cluster	[Endo, Borokot, Almo, Kiptari, Sengwer-Cherang'any, Markweta]
	[7–8] *Kalenjin Elgon Branch*	
	7. Sabaot Cluster	[Kony, Pok, Bong'om]
	8. Terik	
	[9] *Kalenjin Okiek Branch*	
	9. Okiek	[Sogoo, Kinare]
	[10] *Kalenjin Pokoot Branch*	
	10. Pokoot	
11. Omotik – almost extinct		
12. Teso		

---

1. The content of this table is based primarily on Bernd Heine and Wilhelm J. G. Mohlig, *Language and Dialect Atlas of Kenya* (Berlin: Verlag, 1980); other sources were also consulted.

2. Although linguists continue to debate the difference between the categories of "language" and "dialect," for the purposes of this table numbered items are usually considered distinct languages and unnumbered items are most often understood to be dialects of the language listed to their left in the table.

13. Turkana		
14. *Maasai Dialect Cluster*	[Loitokitok, Dalalekutuk, Damat, Kaputiei, Keekonyokie, Matapato, Loitai, Loodokilani, Purko, Sikirari, Siria, Uas-Nkishu]	
15. Ilchamus (Njembs)		
16. Samburu (Sampur)		
II. Cushitic Languages		
17. Yaaku		
18. Burji		
19. Daasanach		
20. El Molo		
21. Rendille		
22. Boni		
23. Sanye (Dahalo)		
[24–28] *Oromo Language Cluster ("Galla," "Borana")*		
	24. Gabra	
	25. Borana	
	26. Sakuye	
	27. Garreh	
	28. Ajuran	
29. Orma (Wardai)		
30. Munyo		
31. Waata		
32. *Somali Dialect Cluster*	[Leisan, Murulle, Degodia, Harti, Isaaq, Ogaden, Aulihan, Abdwak, Abdalla]	
III. Bantu Languages		
33. Malakote (Ilwana)		
34. *Pokomo Dialect Cluster*	[Malalulu, Zubaki, Ndura-Ndera, Malachini]	
[35–44] *Mijikenda Language Cluster*		
	35. Rabai	
	36. Duruma	
	37. Digo	
	38. Giriama	
	39. Kauma	

	40. Chonyi	
	41. Jibana	
	42. Kambe	
	43. Ribe	
	44. Chwaka	
45. *Swahili Dialect Cluster (Kenyan Coastal Group)*	[Tikuu (Bajuni), Siyu, Pate, Amu, Mvita, Jomvu, Shirazi (Chifundi), Vumba]	
46. Kidawida (Taita)		
47. Sagalla		
48. Taveta		
49. Kuria		
50. Gusii		
51. Suba		
[52–58] *Luyia Language Cluster*		
	52. Bukusu	
	53. Logooli, Tachoni	
	54. Samia, Nyala (B), Khayo	
	55. Wanga, Marama, Kisa, Tsotso, Marachi (Central Oluluyia)	
	56. Nyole	
	57. Isukha, Idakho, Tiriki	
	58. Nyala (K)	
	59. Kabras	
[60–64] *Meru Language Cluster*		
	60. Igembe, Tigania, Imenti, Miutini	
	61. Igoji	
	62. Nithi (Mwimbi-Muthambi)	
	63. Tharaka	
	64. Chuka	
65. Embu-Mbeere		
66. *Kamba Dialect Cluster*	[Masaku, South Kitui, North Kitui, Mumoni]	
67. *Gikuyu Dialect Cluster*	[Mathira, Nyeri, Muranga, Kiambu, Ndia, Gichugu]	

Table A.2. Scripture publications in Languages of Kenya

A. Languages with a Complete Bible				
Language (listed alphabetically)	**First Portion**	**First New Testament**	**First Bible**	**Key Subsequent or Ongoing Translation Work**
1. Borana	1934	1978	1995	
2. Dholuo	1911	1926	1957	second Bible (interconfessional) 1975
3. Gigikuyu	1903	1926	1951	second Bible (interconfessional common language) 2009
4. Kalenjin	1958	1968	1969	revised Bible (interconfessional) 2017
5. Kidawida	1904	1922	1998	common language
6. Kiembu-Kimbeere	1998	2003	2012	Interconfessional common language Bible
7. Kigiryama	1892	1901	1908	Second Bible translation (common language) in progress; NT 2004, Bible 2019
8. Kikamba	1850	1920	1956	Second Bible (interconfessional common language) 2011
9. Kimiiru	1921	1952	1964	Second Bible (interconfessional common language) 2010
10. Lubukusu	1985	1992	2010	
11. Lukakamega/ Lutirichi	2000	2005	2014	
12. Lulogooli	1911	1925	1951	Second Bible (common language) 2009
13. Lunyole	1915	1936	2002	
14. Maasai	1905	1923	1992	Revised Bible dedicated 2018
15. Nandi	1926	1933	1939	
16. Oluluyia (central)	2001	2005	2016	Interconfessional translation.
17. Oluluyia (union)	1954	1968	1975	
18. Pokoot	1936	1967	2009	second NT (common language) 1988; 2009 Bible was also common language

Language (listed alphabetically)	First Portion	First New Testament	First Bible	Key Subsequent or Ongoing Translation Work
19. Sabaot	1987	1997	2012	
20. Somali	1915	1972	1979	
21. Swahili (common language)	1975	1977	1996	
22. Swahili (Mombasa)	1878	1909	1914	
23. Swahili (union)	1934	1950	1952	Revised Swahili Union Bible 2006
24. Turkana	1972	1986	2000	
B. Languages with a New Testament but No Bible				
25. Burji	1981	1994		
26. Daasanach	none	2014		
27. Digo	1993	2007		
28. Duruma	1848*	1999*		*first common language Portion 1989; 1999 NT was common language
29. Igikuria	1969	1996		
30. Kipokomo	1894	1902*		*second NT (common language) 2004
31. Kipsigis	1912	1953		
32. Kisagalla	1892	1994		
33. Kitaveta	1892	1906		
34. Marakwet	1998	2009		
35. Oluhanga	1914	1939		
36. Orma	none	2014		
37. Rendille	1994	2018		
38. Suba	none	2011		
39. Tharaka	1934	2001	2019	
C. Languages with a Portion but No New Testament or Bible				
40. Ribe	1878			

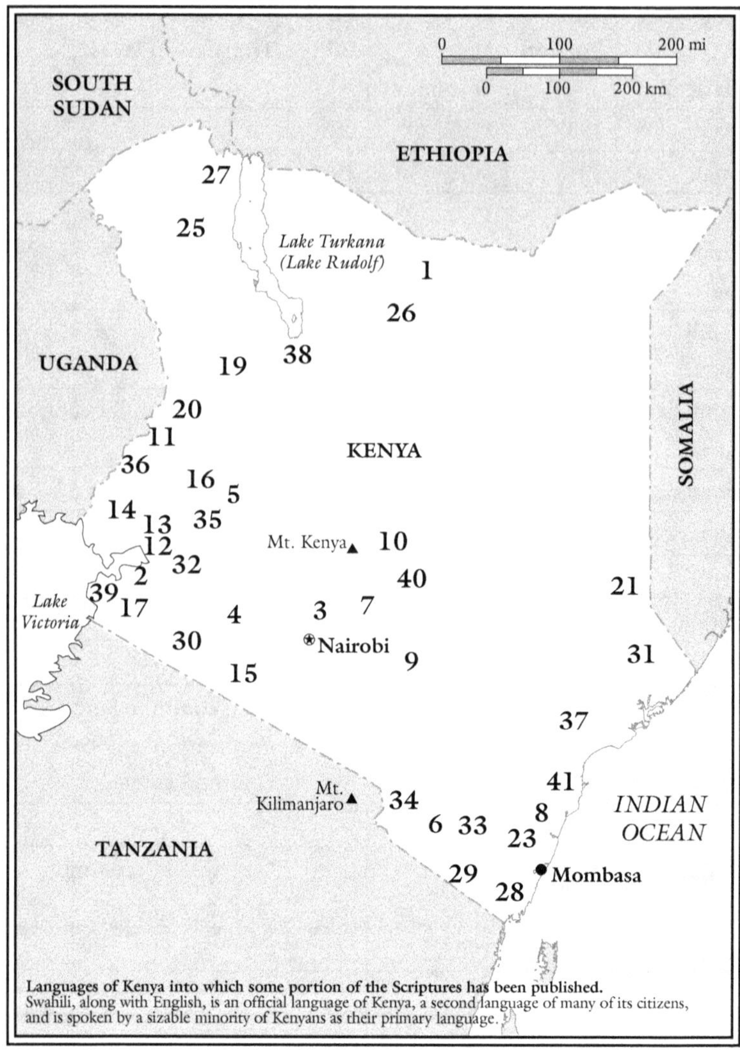

Map A. Languages and Dialects of Kenya. American Bible Society Library and Archives. Used by permission.

Map A works together with table A.2. The numbers on the map correspond to the numbers in the table.

A Historical Overview of Bible Work in Kenya

In his outline of the history of Bible work in Kenya, the Chairman of the Board of the Bible Society of Kenya, the Rev Canon Wycliff Balongo, divided the work into six overlapping periods. The following outline is taken from the Society's 2004 report[3]:

Figure A.1. Bible Society Kenya Bible House, Nairobi. Photo © Aloo Osotsi Mojola

The Period of Voluntary Work: 1844 to 1869

This period marks the beginning of the work and was signaled by the arrival of Johann Ludwig Krapf in 1844. Work was carried out by volunteer missionaries, rather than organized in any formal manner. Krapf's translations of the New Testament in Mombasa Swahili (Kimvita) (unpublished), the Gospel of Luke into Kiduruma (1848), the Gospel of Mark into Kikamba (1850), among others were accomplished during this period.

---

3. The original reports used throughout the appendicies can be found through the various Bible Societies.

The Period of Agency Work by the British and Foreign Bible Societies and the American Bible Society: 1870 to 1958

The BFBS and the ABS carried out work in East Africa through agencies and missionaries from their own countries. Several Scriptures were translated during this period, including the Swahili, Gikuyu Dholuo, Nandi, and Kikamba Bibles. The period was characterized by competing and overlapping missions in Bible work that was finally organized and administered by the United Bible Societies, which was formed in 1946. Kenya had no centralized system of keeping and distributing Scriptures. Scriptures were sent to missionaries to distribute as part of their work. The Bible House on Mfangano Street (then Jeevanjee Street) was opened on July 16, 1958 by the then chief secretary of Kenya, the Hon. W. F. Coutts and dedicated by the Moderator of the Presbyterian Church of East Africa, the Rev. Robert MacPherson. Scriptures produced during this period include the Bible in Mombasa Swahili (NT 1909, Bible 1914), Swahili Union Bible (NT 1934, Bible 1952), Gikuyu Bible (NT 1926, Bible 1951), Dholuo Bible (NT 1926, Bible 1957) Giriama Bible (NT 1901, Bible 1908) Logooli Bible (NT 1925, Bible 1951), Kikamba Bible (NT 1920, Bible 1956), Nandi Bible (NT 1933, Bible 1939), Kipsigis New Testament (1953), Kidabida New Testament (1922), among others.

The Modern Bible Society Work: 1959 to 1970

With the opening of Bible House, Bible work in Kenya found a home. Missionary work was coordinated through the BFBS agency housed at Bible House on Jevanjee Street (now Mfangano Street). The Rev. John Mpaayei was appointed the first African executive secretary of the Bible Society in East Africa in 1961. His work extended beyond Kenyato Uganda, Tanzania, and the Indian Ocean islands of Madagascar, Mauritius, and Seychelles. He succeeded the Rev. Frank Frederick Bedford who had followed the Rev. L. V. D. Ashley. The Rev. Mpaayei like his British predecessors was responsible directly to BFBS who were responsible for Bible work in this region as in all the former British colonies. On March 10, 1964, the Kenya Council of the Bible Society was formed under the chairmanship of the Rev. John Gatu, now a retired former Moderator of the Presbyterian Church of East Africa. Much local initiative went into setting up the work under the leadership of local Christians. A constitution was drawn up, discussed, and lodged with the national Registrar of Societies. The Bible Society of Kenya was formally registered in 1970, with the first Annual General Meeting held that year on November 21. The newly formed Bible Society of Kenya was inaugurated on November 28 at the All

Saints Anglican Cathedral with Mr. Peter K. Thande as the Society's first council chairman. Scriptures translated during this period include the Kimeru Bible (1964), Kalenjin Bible (1969) the Oluluyia New Testament (1968), and the Pokoot New Testament (1967).

First Transition: 1971 to 1980

After registration in 1970, the Bible Society of Kenya applied for associate membership in the United Bible Societies. This was granted in October 1972. The Rev. David Gitari became the first general secretary of BSK in June 1971, taking over on September 9. The Society applied for full membership of the UBS and this was granted in September 1977. BSK went through a period of instability and uncertainty trying to find its bearing as a full member of the UBS. The last Council of BSK was held on November 23, 1972. The new board of governors was formed December 8, 1972. Some of the challenges facing BSK during this period includedsetting up viable management structures, putting in place financial and accounting systems, and establishing relevant and viable BSK programs and committees to manage them. BSK was challenged to think more concretely with the African context and realities in mind, looking for ways to raise the historically low local contributions by individuals and churches (which stood at 2.3% in 1972), and addressing the challenge to serve RomanCatholics with the Scriptures. This commitment was put to the test when Catholics placed an order for 160,000 Bibles and 240,000 New Testaments, a quantity greater than BSK could supply to all the other churches in its territory combined.

In February 1975, BSK expanded the office space of its Bible House on Mfangano Street by adding two additional floors to meet the expanded demand for more offices and storage space. After four years of service to BSK, the Rev. David Gitari resigned as general secretary and was consecrated bishop of the Anglican Diocese of Mount Kenya East on November 30, 1975. He was succeeded by the Rev. Johana Mbogori of the Methodist Church on November 3, 1975.When the Rev. Mbogori was consecrated bishop on October 16, 1979, he was succeeded by Pastor Joseph Musembi on May 1, 1980.

At a meeting of BSK's board held on December 9, 1977, three immediate tasks were identified: to achieve self-sufficiency, to undertake meaningful market research in order to assure effective distribution, and to revive, build, and encourage the formation of Bible Society branches and auxiliaries within BSK's domain.

Scriptures translated during this period included the Oluluyia Bible (1975), the Dholuo common language Bible (1975), and the Somali Bible (1979).

Dependent Autonomous Bible Society: 1981 to 1996

The years from1981 to 1996 were characterized by much growth in the BSK programs. There was, however, little effort made to harness local resources, a goal that had been identified in the previous period. At that time, financial resources were readily available in UBS. All that was needed was to identify feasible programs and UBS would invariably fund such programs. On January 13, 1981, it was reported that BSK had been allocated a plot of land in Madaraka Estate. A new Bible House was eventually built on this plot and consecrated in 2001. Pastor Musembi retired from his position as general secretary on December 31, 1986. He was succeeded by Dr. Otieno Mare Munala in April 1987. BSK faced many management, distribution, and staff challenges in those years. Dr. Munala retired on August 3, 1992, and was succeeded by the Rev. Henry Kathii on March 4, 1993. The problem of getting sufficient, timely stocks of Scriptures through the UBS hampered BSK's ability to serve its constituency, and continued to do so until the turn of the millennium. Although technically autonomous, BSK remained dependentupon UBS for its management, financing, and general direction for its operations.

Scriptures translatedand published during this period included the Ekegusii Bible (1988), Turkana New Testament (1986), Pokoot New Testament (1988), Maasai Bible (1992), Borana Bible (1995) Sagalla New Testament (1994), Igikuria New Testament (1996), and Lubukusu New Testament (1992).

Second Transition: 1997 to 2004

The board meeting of July 12, 1996, resolved to build Bible House on the Madaraka plot, sell the old Bible House on Mfangano Street, and raise additional finances from the UBS for the building project. This was approved by the UBS in September 1998. The old Bible House was sold to the Pentecostal Evangelistic Fellowship of Africa (PEFA). UBS loaned BSK additional finances in May 2000. Construction of the new Bible House was completed at a total cost of 87 million Kenya shillings, and was opened and dedicated by His Excellency the President of Kenya, the Hon. Daniel Arap Moi on November 21, 2001. During this period, the board approved new strategic plans designed to catapult the Society to self-supporting status. This prepared the Bible Society to move into the next period as a fully autonomous society.

Scriptures translated during this period include the Biblia Habari Njema (1996), the new Kikamba New Testament (2003), Kiembu-Kimbeere New Testament (2003), Lunyole Bible (2001), and the Igikuria new Kidabida Bible (1998).

A Supporting Bible Society: 2004 to the Present

This period found BSK in its modern and spacious Bible House on Langata Road in Madaraka. In 2004 BSK was able to balance its budget from from operations efficiencies and income from sales and local giving. The level of Bible distribution was greatly increased, with yearly Bible distribution reaching 300,000. From 2005, BSK no longer needed support from UBS, and for the first time in 2007, it budgeted to contribute to UBS from its operation. In 2006, Bishop Henry Kathii, who had overseen the transition, retired as general secretary, assuming a new position as Bishop of the Anglican Diocese of Embu. His successor, Mrs. Elizabeth Muriuki, who had previously served as the business manager and then as finance and management manager since 2000, took over as the new general secretary of the Bible Society on September 1, 2006. Mrs. Muriuki hopes to continue to raise the ministry and administrative achievements of the Bible Society to new heights, making BSK a well-endowed institution that uses its financial and people resources wisely in service to the Bible Cause internationally.[4]

---

4. Reported by The Rev Canon Dr Wycliff Balongo, Chairman of the Board, Bible Society of Kenya (2001–2004). Adapted by the author.

Author's Interview with Mrs Elizabeth Muriuki, General Secretary of the Bible Society of Kenya

Bible House, Nairobi, 30 July 2007

Figure A.2. Mrs Elizabeth Muriuki. Photo © Aloo Osotsi Mojola

Mrs Elizabeth Wanjiru Muriuki was born at Banana Hill, Kiambu, near Nairobi. She received a Bachelor of Commerce degree in accounting from the University of Nairobi in 1992. In July 2000, she joined the Bible Society of Kenya as business manager. She was promoted to the position of Finance and Administration manager in 2002. She continued in this position until July 2006, when she was appointed to the position of general secretary of the Bible Society of Kenya.

AUTHOR: What brought you to Bible work and specifically to the Bible Society of Kenya?

MRS MURIUKI: I always had a desire to serve in a Christian organization. When I saw an advertizement for the position of business manager of the Bible Society of Kenya, I believed that was my job. I prayed about it, applied for it, and eventually got the job. I joined the Bible Society in July 2000 and [have] very much enjoyed my work as well as the working environment . . . [At] the University of Nairobi, [I] used Bible study materials prepared by the Fellowship of Christian Unions in partnership with the Bible Society of Kenya . . . I found these guides to beof much benefit and value for my Christian growth and development.

AUTHOR: Did you associate the Bible Society with mother-tongue Scriptures? Was there any special Scripture that provided that link?

MRS MURIUKI: Interestingly, I did not. Although I was a regular user of the Gikuyu Bible, the Bible in my own mother tongue, I did not associate it with the Bible Society. I first [learned] about Bible translation and the role of the Bible Society in translating Bibles [into] local languages through a meeting with Mr Timothy Kamau who was at the time . . . involved in the revision of the 1952 Swahili Union Version.

AUTHOR: Having now worked with the Bible Society and having gained a better understanding of Bible work, to what extent do you appreciate the work of Bible Society?

MRS MURIUKI: [Serving] with the Bible Society has given me much appreciation for the work and ministry of the Society . . . I now appreciate that the churches are mostly dependent on the Bible Society for meeting their Scripture needs. Many Bibles that the Society provides cannot be found anywhere else. The Bible Society is the custodian and sole provider of most vernacular Scriptures in Kenya, such as the Gikuyu, Luo, Kikamba, Kalenjin, Gusii, Luyia, Meru, Maasai, and Swahili, among others. [This] ministry of the Bible Society [is] indispensable to the work of the churches in preaching, evangelizing, or encouraging believers to read the Bible . . . in their own languages. I have also [come to value] the work of translation. I believe it is important for people to speak in their own mother tongues. Reading the Bible in one's own language helps one to understand [its] message more clearly and deeply, and also to identify with it. I have very high regard for the Faith Comes by Hearing (FCBH) program whose main task is to bring the word of God to people who cannot or do not want to read. FCBH's main agenda is to help people hear the word of God in their own language through recorded Scriptures. This is done through special programs organized by the Bible Society in partnership with the churches.

AUTHOR: How do you view Bible translation? What is the place of Bible translation in the work of the Bible Society?

MRS MURIUKI: Translation is the backbone of Bible Society work. It is translation that has given us all the Bible versions we have . . . Kenya has many languages and not all of them have the Bible. It is important that all these people be reached with the word of God in their own languages. Having a translation of the Bible also allows the preparation of audio Scriptures . . . for reaching those who cannot read or who prefer non-print media.

At the present time there is a big need in the area of revisions of the old missionary translations and the provision of study Bibles in these languages. The Society has already started responding to needs in this area. For example, the Society partnered with the Bible Society of Tanzania to revise the 1952 Swahili Union Version . . . The Swahili language has undergone much change since this version was published. Some . . . expressions and sentences needed review and possible correction or restructuring in line with current usage, and also in line with the demands for accuracy and faithfulness to the original texts. A project to revise the Maasai Bible is being considered for 2009, while a project to revise the old Kalenjin Bible is already underway. This project is interconfessional and fully supported by all the churches including the Catholic Church . . . As an example of work on study Bibles, the Bible Society of Kenya together with the Bible Society of Tanzania sponsored and supported the preparation of a new study Bible based on a new contemporary translation of the Bible, *Biblia Habari Njema*. This Swahili Study Bible prepared by local Swahili speakers . . . is particularly sensitive to their cultural, social, religious, and historical contexts. It is being printed and is eagerly awaited. At the beginning of 2008, another project is envisaged to prepare the Gikuyu Study Bible based on the new contemporary translation and along the same lines as the Swahili.

AUTHOR: Kenya has many languages, how do you prioritize among them?

MRS MURIUKI: The question of prioritization is crucial. This applies not just to the need for new translations but also to emerging needs for revisions and Study Bibles. The Bible Society responds to this question by listening carefully to the partner churches. Market surveys and research of the needs is another important factor. Close consultation withpartners in the Forum of Bible Agencies active in Kenya such as the Bible Translation and Literacy agency is important. According to [a Memo of Understanding between the two organizations], BSK is expected to deal [mainly with] the major languages of Kenya and their Scripture needs while BTL is expected to deal mainly with the smaller languages and their needs . . . Cooperation and collaboration with such Bible agencies as the Bible League and the International Bible Society has not been very successful. But efforts are being made to improve the situation. Relations with the other Bible agencies stress the principle of complementarity. It is important to avoid duplication, unhealthy competition, and [wasted] resources, given that we are serving the same master and reaching the same people. Since prioritization also depends on availability of funds for the projects identified, the Bible Society makes every effort to look for support from partners, sponsors, or donors.

AUTHOR: How do you view your present role as the CEO of the BSK? What is your vision for the work?

MRS MURIUKI: My role is to champion and strengthen the Society's mission, "to make available and to promote use of Scriptures in languages people understand best, at prices they can afford to pay and in suitable formats." I believe that much has already been done, but that much still needs to be done. The provision of Scriptures in our country will contribute to satisfying the Society's vision of "a people whose lives are changed through Scriptures." The society therefore needs to continue its mandate of engaging in our core activities of "sharing the Good News of Jesus Christ by translating, producing, distributing, and encouraging use of the Holy Scriptures."

My vision for the Bible Society is to see a society that is professionally run to a level competitive with the other best-run professional bodies in the country. I look forward to seeing this society strengthen her ability to meet the Scripture needs of Kenya, using [its own] internal resources, but also [to] increasingly support other societies outside Kenya financially and morally. I see a society that serves all the Christian churches in Kenya . . . with their essential Scripture needs.

Author's Interview with the Rt Rev Henry Nyaga Kathii, former General Secretary of the Bible Society of Kenya

At his home in Kithegi, Embu, Kenya, 22 July 2007

Figure A.3. Rev Henry Nyaga Kathii. Photo © Aloo Osotsi Mojola

The Rt Rev Henry Kathii was born on 21 November 1949, and educated at Kangaru High School in Embu before going on to attend the University of Nairobi where he earned a Bachelor of Commerce degree in in 1975. He later earnedr an MA in leadership from the Azusa Pacific University in California (2002) and a Bachelor of Theology degree from the University of South Africa in Pretoria (2005).

Before joining the Bible Society of Kenya in 1993, Kathii held positions of leadership in Scripture Union, Kenya (1975–1977), Maridadi Fabrics (1977–1981), Embu District Cooperative Union (1981–1986), Kenya Planters Cooperative Union (1986–1989), Kenya Students' Christian Fellowship (1989–1990), and National Council of Churches of Kenya (1990–1993). Ordained into the priesthood in the Anglican Church of Kenya in 1989, he currently serves as Bishop of the Diocese of Embu.

With decades of managerial and leadership experience to his credit, the Rev Kathii received the call to join the Bible Society of Kenya and to serve as its general secretary, a position he held until August 2006. In this position, he oversaw the total operations of the Society, an interdenominational organization with a mission to provide scriptures to all people in Kenya in a language that they understand best in suitable formats and at a price they can afford.

AUTHOR: What brought you to the Bible Society of Kenya?

REV KATHII: In 1986, I had been approached with a view to applying to take up the position of the General Secretary then. I could not do this as I had just taken up the appointment with the KPCU . . . After some time, the Lord used friends to confirm to me that I needed to apply to serve with the Bible Society of Kenya. I had been a member of the Society, and therefore was aware of its central ministry in the service of the church. I applied and after rather rigorous interviews, I was appointed the General Secretary in March 1993.

AUTHOR: Did you enjoy the work at the Bible Society of Kenya?
REV KATHII: I enjoyed fulfilling the four pillars of the Bible work, viz., translation, production, distribution, and use of Scriptures. I enjoyed the administration of the programs, the facilitation of the translation work, where I was able to incorporate the translation staff to become full time staff of the BSK and general development of the Bible Society to become a church ministry that is professionally managed to achieve its objectives. I sincerely miss the work and the people I had grown to love and serve with.

AUTHOR: What were your main challenges when you joined?
REV KATHII: I had three main challenges when I joined the Bible Society. [First,] working structures and systems of the BSK were not enabling enough for the work to go on efficiently and effectively. [Second,] the environment in which the BSK work was being carried out was not conducive. Mfangano Street [was a congested], dirty neighborhood and was not attracting the right kind of customers and supporters because of insecurity. It was necessary for us to move to the plot we had on Langata Road. [And third,] BSK was having difficulties in meeting the Bible needs in Kenya because of the heavy subsidy the UBS had to give to the Society. This restricted the number and variety of Scriptures we could order for [such a] huge market. It also meant that we could not [hire] the staff we felt were needed to carry out the ministry. I therefore saw sustainability as a great challenge.

AUTHOR: What were your most gratifying accomplishments or achievements?
REV KATHII: I see the main accomplishments as follows: Integration of the translation program with the rest of the Bible Society work, and reduction of the time it takes to complete a translation project; setting and improvement of operation systems and procedures; relocation of the BSK offices from Mfangano Street to Langata Road; appointment and [development] of professional staff; increase in the diversity of Scripture formats for the market, including setting up of effective distribution channels; setting up programs and systems that made the BSK self-supporting and moving on to becoming a supporting Bible society.

AUTHOR: What were your achievements in the area of translation? Are there any more challenges to address in this area?

Rev Kathii: We were able to attract better academically and theologically qualified translation staff to the BSK. This reduced the time it took to see a translation carried out to launching . . . Main challenges in translation in Kenya remain [achieving a] balance between the ministry needs of the small language groups and the economic and commercial viability of translating Bibles for such groups.

Author: What do you see as the future role of the Bible Society in Kenya?
Rev Kathii: The future of the Bible Society consists of completing present translation projects, and embarking on revisions of the older versions. BSK must also work toward producing materials that help people to interact with the Bible, including Bible concordances, Study Bibles, Bible commentaries, and so on. The Bible Society will also need to look at ministry to children and prepare Scripture materials that meet the needs of the children in different languages.

Author's Interview with The Rt Rev John Akhura Muhambi Bishop of Kakamega Central Diocese, African Church of the Holy Spirit and Bible Translator with the Lwisukha-Lwitakho-Lutirichi project

At the Mukumu Catholic Church, 4 April 2007

Figure A.4. Rev John Akhura Muhambi. Photo © Aloo Osotsi Mojola

John Akhura Muhambi was born in 1956 in Shivagala Village, in the Kakamega District of Kenya's Western Province. He studied at a technical institute and graduated as a grade 1 artisan in building. He worked for a number of construction firms before responding to God's call in 1982 to leave Nairobi and to give his life to church work, serving the rural areas.

Christian by faith, John Akhura had been baptized and raised in the African Church of the Holy Spirit (ACHS), an African instituted church. This church, with roots in the Quaker mission to Africa, has a long and interesting history. Today it is a member of many ecumenical bodies, including the Bible Society of Kenya.

The Rev Akhura is an ordained minister in ACHS and currently serves as the Bishop of Kakamega Central Diocese. He earned an advanced certificate in church administration from the Nairobi Ecumenical Study Institute under the sponsorship of NCCK and has a Bachelor of Divinity degree from St Paul's United Theological University, Limuru. In addition, he received a post-graduate certificate from the Ecumenical Institute in Bosey, Switzerland, where he majored in Peace Studies. He also had an opportunity to study at the World Council of Churches' graduate school in Bosey, where he explored the perspectives of various religious traditions, including those of the Eastern Orthodox Church and of Islam. The Rev Akhura has participated in many national and international activities and has been invited to present papers at conferences organized by NCCK, AACC, WCC, and UNICEF on such issues as the problem of refugees in Africa, the question of traditional medicine and healing, African culture versus the Christian faith from an Independent Church's perspective, and issues concerning women and youth in Africa.

The Rev Akhura brings this rich background into his Bible translation work. Most recently he served on a team of three translators tasked with preparing the Lukakamega-Lutirichi Bible translation, a project which was moving into its final stages at the time of this interview.

Author: How did you join the translation project?
Rev Akhura: In 1995, the then general secretary of the Bible Society of Kenya, the Rev Kathii, visited St Paul's Theological College, where I was a third-year student, [and gave a] talk about translation. After graduating, I got a scholarship to study ecumenism in Switzerland at the Faculty of Theology, University of Geneva, at their campus in the canton of Vaud, at Bossey. After my studies at the end of 1996, I came back to Kenya to find a letter from the Bible Society inviting me to be part of the committee to help start a translation in the Lwisukha-Lwitakho-Lutirichi dialects of Luyia. Since I had done well in biblical studies at Limuru University, I was appointed by the Bible Society of Kenya as a translator and the first coordinator of the project on 1 June 1977.

Author: What made you decide to accept the invitation?
Rev. Akhura: [First,] I [took into] consideration the fact that my people have never had a Bible in their own language. Second, I thought this was a very noble assignment, being one of the first scholars in my community to put down a document in written form. Third, I thought this would be an opportunity to help my people to know and understand their mother tongue, especially the young generation.

Author: Which Luyia Bible were you using in your church? Were they happy with it? If not, what were their concerns?
Rev Akhura: Our community is divided into three groups that use three different Bibles. The Catholics use the Oluluyia Bible, most of the Protestant churches use the Lulogooli Bible, while the Church of God uses the Lunyole Bible. Our community has had difficulty understanding these foreign dialects, the Logooli, Lunyole, and the Luluyia based on the Wanga-Marama-Kisa-Tsotso dialects. [Consequently,] they need a Bible in their own dialects.

Author: Why do you think this Bible that brings together three dialects of Luyia is needed?
Rev Akhura: This Bible is essential to our people for [enabling] them to understand clearly and naturally the word of God in their own language.

Author: From your experience, do you find translation work easy?
Rev Akhura: For the time I have been alive on this earth, I have never come across a job that is so challenging as Bible translation.

Author: What are some of the challenges as a translator?
Rev Akhura: From a historical point of view, [it is rare for] a Bible translation project here in East Africa [to last] for more than ten years with the same group of translators remaining intact. We have seen many projects which started more than twenty years ago still struggling. The Lukakamega-Lutirichi project will be the first project to finish after only ten years.

In many of our translation projects, [some of the] translators die before finishing. Others [become frustrated and overwhelmed] . . . as a result of much thinking when dealing with difficult verses. All these are caused by [the high] expectations of the churches and other stakeholders which results in too much stress.

Author: Can you give examples of some difficult terms to translate that you encountered and how you dealt with them?
Rev Akhura: Sometimes people mistake translators to be preparing a dictionary that could preserve their language. Others expect to see translation coming straight from English versions, which is not [our practice]. Others would wish to see some of their [own traditions'] doctrines enshrined in the translation. We have noted that translation of sensitive concepts also affects the outcome of the translation. Matters relating to sex and sexual taboos, among others, always pose a problem in translation. We are a community who share many concepts and customs with the Jewish community. So, just as they use euphemistic expressions, we also have done the same. We [did] this after much consultation with the churches and reviewers.

Author: How hast the New Testament, which was launched on the 2 April 2005, been accepted? Did all the churches accept it? Have they sent any feedback? Do you think a complete Bible will be well received?
Rev Akhura: Our New Testament was received with mixed reactions. A [segment] of the people were very happy to have a New Testament of their

own. Others who are very conservative took time to accept it. I want to thank the Catholic Church for being in the forefront in the circulation of the first New Testament. Other churches, like the Salvation Army, believe that the word can only be heard well in Swahili, while the new Pentecostal ministries [prefer] English, [and still] others [are hanging onto] Luwanga and Lulogooli. Time will tell. As for me, I believe the future rests with the new translation.

We have received many reactions from people who have some questions on the orthography used and the spelling of certain words. On the whole, it was clear that those who pride themselves in being Vakakamega-Vatirichi have really appreciated what we have done so far.

At first, the mainline churches were not comfortable with me as a member of an African instituted church translating the Bible. However, they accepted me after learning that I am an ecumenist who has done studies in Catholic theology in Rome, then Orthodox theology at Chambezy in Switzerland, Reformed theology at the University of Geneva (also in Basel) and at the John Knox Centre in Geneva, Lutheran theology in Germany, Monasticism in Taizé under Brother Roger in Cluny, France, as well as Islam in Paris.

Having tasted a small bit of the Bible, people from this area are eagerly waiting for the complete Bibleand I hope and believe this will [inspire] scholars from this region to start developing this beautiful language linguistically.

Appendix B

Perspectives from Tanzania

Table B.1. Main languages and dialects of Tanzania[1]

I. Khoisan Languages	
1. Sandawe[2]	
2. Hadza	
II. Nilotic Languages	
3. Luo	
4. Maasai	[Arusha, Kisongo, Parakuyo (Baraguyu/Kwavi)]
5. Datooga	[Bajuta, Gisamjanga, Barabaiga, Isimijega (of East Datooga), Rotigenga, Buradiga, Biyenjiida (of West Datooga)]
III. Cushitic Languages (Southern)	
6. Mbugu (Ma'a)	
7. Kw'adza (almost extinct)	
8. Asa	
9. Iraqw	
10. Gorowa	
11. Burunge	
12. Alagwa (Wasi)	

---

1. The contents of this table are based on Edgar C. Polome and C. P. Hill, eds., *Language in Tanzania* (Oxford: Oxford University Press, 1980); Bernd Heine and Derek Nurse, eds., *A Linguistic Geography of Africa* (Cambridge: Cambridge University Press, 2008); and other sources, as well as the author's own experience and work in translation in Tanzania with the BST and UBS since 1984.

2. Although linguists continue to debate the difference between the categories "language" and "dialect," for the purposes of this table numbered items are usually considered distinct languages and unnumbered items are most often understood to be dialects of the language listed to their left in the table.

IV. Bantu Languages	
A. North Coast	
13. Digo	
14. Segeju (Dhaiso)	
15. Shambala	
16. Bondei	
17. Zigula	
18. Nghwele	
19. Doe	
20. Kwere	
21. Ngulu	
22. Swahili	[Vumba, Mtang'ata, Mrima, Pemba, Tumbatu, Hadimu, Makunduchi (Kae), Unguja, Mafia, Ngao, Mwani]
23. Sagala	
24. Rugulu	
25. Zalamo	
26. Vidunda	
27. Kutu	
28. Kami	
B. South Coast	
29. Ndengereko	
30. Rufiji	
31. Matumbi	
32. Ngindo	
33. Mwera	
34. Machinga	
35. Yao	
36. Makua	
37. Maviha	
38. Makonde	
39. Hehe	
40. Mbunga	

41. Ndamba	
42. Pogolo	
43. Ngindo	
44. Ngoni	
45. Bena	
46. Pangwa	
47. Ndendeule	
48. Matengo	
49.Mpoto	
50. Manda	
51. Kisi	
52. Kinga	
53. Nyakyusa	
54. Ndali	
55. Safwa	
56.Lambya	
57. Wanji	
58. Malila	
59. Sangu	
60. Mwanga	
61. Nyiha	
62. Bungu	
D. Central Region	
63. Kimbu	
64. Nyamwezi	
65. Konongo	
66. Nyaturu (Remi)	
67. Nilamba	
68. Isanzu	
69. Langi	
70. Mbugwe	
71. Gogo	
72. Kagulu	

E. Western (Lakes Tanganyika and Rukwa)	
73. Ha	
74. Jiji	
75. Vinza	
76. Tongwe	
77. Holoholo	
78. Bende	
79. Pimbwe	
80. Fipa	
81.Rungi	
82. Mambwe-Lungu	
83. Mwanga	
84. Rungwa	
F. Lacustrine (Lake Victoria)	
85. Nyambo	
86. Rwanda	
87. Haya	
88. Zinza	
89. Rundi	
90.Shubi	
91.Hangaza	
92.Sumbwa	
93.Sukuma	
94.Kerewe	
95.Kara	
96.Kwaya	
97.Sizaki	
98.Suba	
99.Ikizu	
100. Zanaki	
101.Ikoma	
102.Agurimi	
103.Kuria	

104.Jita	
105.Ganda	
G. Northern (Arusha and Kilimanjaro Area)	
106.Rwa (Meru)	
107. Chagga	[Siha, Machame and Kibosho (in Hai or Western Chaggaland), Mochi and Vunjo (in Vunjo or Central Chaggaland), Rombo (in Rombo or eastern Chaggaland)]
108. Ngasa	
109. Kahe	
110. Taveta	
111. Gweno	
112. Asu	
113. Sonjo (Temi)	

Table B.2. Scripture publications in languages of Tanzania

A. Languages with a Complete Bible				
Language (listed alphabetically)	**First Portion**	**First New Testament**	**First Bible**	**Key Subsequent or Ongoing Translation Work**
1. Cigogo	1886	1899	1962	second common language Bible 2002
2. Dholuo	1911	1926	1953	second common language interconfessional Bible 1975
3. Kinyakyusa			1996	
4. Kisukuma	1895	1925	1960	second common language interconfessional Bible expected 2014
5. Ichinamwanga	1903	1930	1982	
6. Iraqw	1957	1977	2004	
7. Maasai	1905	1923	1992	revised Bible in progress

Language (listed alphabetically)	First Portion	First New Testament		Key Subsequent or Ongoing Translation Work
8. Ruhaya	1920	1930	2001	
9. Swahili (common language)	1975	1977	1996	interconfessional, also 1996
10. Swahili (Union)	1934	1950	1952	revised Bible (interconfessional) 2006
11. Swahili (Zanzibar)	1868	1879	1891	
B. Languages with a New Testament but No Bible				
12. Chasu	1910	1922		
13. Chikaguru	1885	2010		
14. Chimanda	1913	1937		
15. Datooga	2002	2009		complete Bible expected 2016
16. Ecijita	1934	1943		
17. Ekibena		1914		
18. Ichifipa		1988		
19. Ichimambwa–Ichilungu	1893	1901		
20. Igikuria	1969	1996		complete interconfessional Bible in progress
21. Kichagga–Kimachame	1932	2000		complete Bible expected 2016
22. Kichagga–Kimochi	1892	1939		second NT 1999; complete Bible expected 2016
23. Kichagga–Kivunjo	1996	1999		complete Bible expected 2015
24. Kihehe	2000	2009		complete interconfessional Bible in progress
25. Kikerewe		1946		
26. Kikinga		1961		

Language (listed alphabetically)	First Portion	First New Testament		Key Subsequent or Ongoing Translation Work
27. Kinilamba	1940	1967		second NT 2010; completeBible in progress
28. Kinyakyusa–Kingonde	1895	1908		
29. Kinyamwezi	1897	1909		
30. Kirwa (Kimeru)		1964		
31. Kishambala	1896	1908		
32. Kitaveta	1892	1906		
33. Kizaramo	1967	1975		
34. Shinyiha	1904	1913		
C. Languages with a Portion but No New Testament or Bible				
35. Chimpoto	1913			
36. Giha	1960			Bible project now in progress; NT expected 2016
37. Ikizanaki	1948			
38. Kibondei	1887			
39. Kihangaza	1938			
40. Kingoni	1891			
41. Kinyaturu (Kiremi)	1956			NT dedicated 2010
42. Kivwanji	1985			
43. Kizigula	1906			
44. Kizinza	1930			

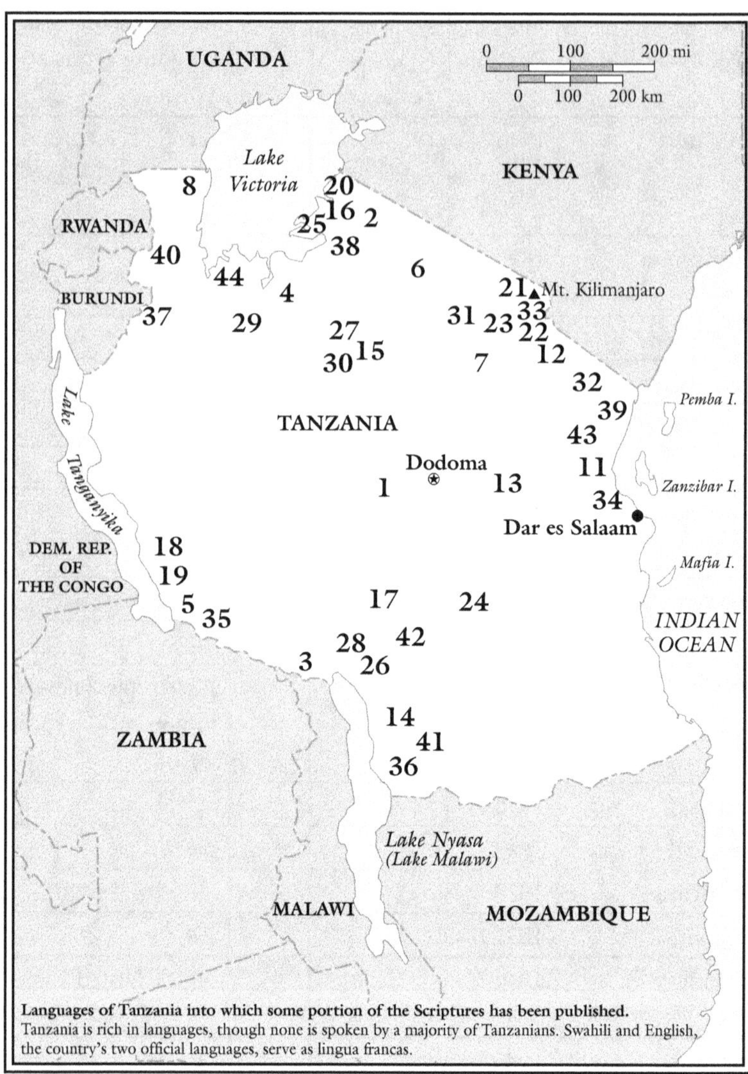

Map B. Languages and Dialects of Tanzania. American Bible Society. Used by permission.

Map B works together with table B.2. The numbers in the table correspond to the numbers on the map.

A Historical Overview of Bible Work in Tanzania.

Figure B.1. Expansion of the Bible Society of Tanzania Bible House in Dodoma, Tanzania. Photo © Aloo Osotsi Mojola

The following is adapted from the Bible Society of Tanzania's report.

The history of the Bible Society of Tanzania is embedded in the history of Christian missionary work in East Africa and in the activities of the British and Foreign Bible Society who worked through and with them. Their first involvement in Tanzania was the publishing of the translations of the Universities Mission to Central Africa, starting first with the Psalms in 1871 and the Gospel of John in 1875. A complete New Testament (revised) was published in 1883. Another revised edition was published in 1892. Thereafter many translations followed including a Swahili Union Bible NT in 1934 and the full Bible in 1952.

More formalized Bible Society work in Tanzania started when a depot was established in 1965 with its head office in Iringa under the leadership of the Rev Rodden Ngota as its executive secretary. In 1970, Tanzania was registered with UBS as a Bible Society office instead of as a depot. When the government announced that the capital of the country would shift to Dodoma from Dar es Salaam, the Bible Society of Tanzania relocated its head office from Iringa to Dodoma. In 1973, the office building in Dodoma was bought at a cost of only 90,000 Tanzania shillings and in August 1974 the Society moved to Dodoma at its present location at the junction of Makumbusho and 9th Street.

In 1978, the Bible Society of Tanzania became an associate member of the United Bible Societies. This was the year when the Rev Rodden Ngota stepped down and Emmanuel Kibira (now deceased) was promoted from executive secretary to general secretary. Ten years later, the Bible Society of Tanzania became a full member of the United Bible Societies at that body's World Assembly in Budapest, Hungary, on 22 September 1988.

List of BST leaders

The Rev Rodden Ngota (executive secretary, 1965–1978) laid the foundations of the Society in Tanzania and oversaw its relocation from the Iringa depot to the Dodoma Bible Society office.

Mr Emmanuel B. Kibira (general secretary, 1978–1989) is remembered for building relationships with the churches and increasing distribution. Mr Kibira came to Bible Society work after retiring from the government as director of adult education, and prior to that as a member of Parliament and an inspector of education. He laid the plans for the expansion of Bible House and the warehouse but did not implement them. However, he did oversee the building of staff houses.

The Rev Albert Mongi (general secretary, 1990–2005) strengthened the infrastructure of the Society, extending what his predecessors had already done by expanding and renovating the Dodoma Bible House (completed 1997) and building a new warehouse at Kitunda, Dar es Salaam. The latter was dedicated on 12 July 1995. The Rev Mongialso increased the Society's fleet of delivery vehicles – acquiring Land Rovers and a big lorry to better serve its far-flung clientele.

The Rev Dr Mkunga H. P. Mtingele was installed as general secretary, in September 2005 until his retirement in December 2018. Mr Alfred Kimonge, who was then the Society's Business Manager, took over as General Secretary from January 2019.

Key Milestones and Achievements

The move to Dodoma from Iringa was a milestone in the ministry of the Bible Society of Tanzania because it allowed BST to more efficiently serve the Tanzanian population from a central location.

During the leadership of Emmanuel Kibira, thirty auxiliaries were established. BST became the leading distributor of the New Testament in Africa. BST was also awarded a certificate of merit by the UBS for their exemplary distribution record. BST's work was also recognized by the Roman Catholic Church who have made a commitment to contribute annually towards Bible Society work. Between 1990 and 1996, BST undertook construction of a warehouse for Scripture in Dar es Salaam – the biggest such facility in Africa – and the extension and renovation of a modern Bible House in Dodoma. Translation and publication of the interconfessional *Biblia Habari Njema* cooperatively sponsored by the Bible Society of Kenya and the Bible Society of Tanzania on 24 March 1996, is another key milestone.[3]

---

3. Reported by the Rev Dr Mkunga H. P. Mtingele, General Secretary Bible Society of Tanzania. Adapted by the author.

Author's Interview with The Rev Canon Dr Mkunga Mtingele, General Secretary of the Bible Society of Tanzania

Dodoma, Tanzania, 2 July 2007

Figure B.2. Rev Mkunga Mtingele. Photo © Aloo Osotsi Mojola

The Rev Canon Dr Mkunga Mtingele was born in 1949 at the Lukwika village in what is now Nanyumbu District (Mtwara Region), southern Tanzania. Mtingele studied law at the University of Dar es Salaam and graduated with a first degree in law (LLB. Hons.) in 1977. He was then employed in the Attorney-General's chambers, Ministry of Justice, and worked as State Attorney in Dodoma and Arusha for nearly a decade. In 1986 he was asked by the House of Bishops of his church, the Anglican Church of Tanzania, to serve as its Deputy General Secretary, a position he accepted.

Mtingele was in the UK from 1989 to 1991 studying for a postgraduate degree in theological studies at St John's College, Nottingham. He was appointed General Secretary of the Anglican Church of Tanzania in June 1991. In 1995 he obtained an MA in theological studies with the Open University of UK in collaboration with St John's College. Continuing his studies, he received a PhD in management in 2005, again with the Open University of UK, St John's College. Upon his return to Tanzania, the Rev Mtingele joined the Bible Society of Tanzania as General Secretary in September 2005.

AUTHOR: What brought you to the Bible Society of Tanzania?

REV DR MTINGELE: I have been a life member of the Bible Society since 1988 and one of [its] trustees since 1995. My desire was to contribute to the Bible cause. I felt my experiences as a lawyer for the government and as an administrator for the Anglican Church would be needed by the Bible Society . . . Having served the Anglican Church in Tanzania for nineteen years, I was keen to serve the wider church, i.e. all the churches of Tanzania, both Protestant and

Catholic. My prayer is to see that every person in Tanzania has a Bible – or at least a New Testament – in a language they can understand.

AUTHOR: What do you see as the major role of the Bible Society?
REV DR MTINGELE: I see the Bible Society as a servant of the churches, an instrument to assist the churches make sure the Holy Scriptures are available and accessible to all who need them. I am committed to working closely with and for the churches. To this end, I see the need for the Bible Society to listen carefully and respond sensitively to the needs of the churches.

AUTHOR: What is your vision of the Bible Society?
REV DR MTINGELE: I want to see the Bible Society of Tanzania [become] one of strongest Bible societies in Africa. To reach this goal I want BST to be widely known and recognized by everybody in Tanzania. Further, through effective ministry and quality service of the word, the Society should be widely appreciated, valued, and loved by all who support and benefit from this service. The Society should not only be fully "owned" by member churches (as well as by individuals) and fully supported by them, but should be *seen* to be so. My vision is to achieve the goal of a strong self-supporting Bible society that can in turn support [still struggling] societies in the region. This can only come about if the Society is fully supported and owned by the churches and individuals. To achieve [this], the Bible Society should cultivate a strong and genuine relationship with the churches, not only with the church leaders but with individuals at the grassroots level.

We have challenges, however. Our distribution of Scriptures and the amount of local support are far below the national potential. This is unacceptable . . . The structure of BST is a contributory factor. All our distribution staff are based in Dodoma. They go to their respective distribution areas or zones thrice a year . . . I would have liked to see that distributors are based and operate from their distribution zones. This will not only enhance distribution of Scriptures, but will also create awareness.

I want to see a structure that will support our vision and mission and to have staff that will be able to support the structure and implement what we have agreed to do in the strategic plan . . . [Such changes] can only be achieved through transformational leadership. By this I mean leadership that transforms those I lead in BST to [become] a much stronger team and organization. It also means leadership that also transforms [me] as a leader – a leadership that values the contribution of those I work with and those who "own" the Society, namely, churches and individuals . . . I am therefore ready and willing to learn from those I lead and from others. This is what I practice and it is a continuous process.

The location of the Bible House in Dodoma (a designated capital of the country with a population of [only] 500,000 people) is not a strategically ideal location to have a Bible House. There are inherent advantages and disadvantages with this set up. Dar es Salaam [is] a commercial city of about four million people, where most of government activities take place. It is easily accessible and has more facilities than Dodoma. Our intention is to [establish] a strong presence in Dar es Salaam.

Author: What do you see as the place of translation in Tanzania?
Rev Dr Mtingele: The key role of Swahili, [Tanzania's majority language], is undeniable . . . It is the main language of government, civil society, the media, education, Christian evangelism, liturgy, relationship, and so on. There are, however, people deep in villages who do not understand Swahili as well as their mother tongue. There are also many people who understand Swahili but prefer to read or hear God's word in their own languages.

I see translation as a tool for evangelism. Translation also contributes to the preservation of languages and of the cultures embedded in those languages, both of which are under threat of extinction. Translation should not be restricted to new translation. Revision of [previously] translated work becomes an important part of translation. Languages are dynamic; new words are born and others become redundant. The Bible Society should not [overlook] this reality.

Author: How do you prioritize among the 130 languages?
Rev Dr Mtingele: As [an instrument] or servant of the churches, prioritization depends solely on the needs of the churches and requests to the Bible Society. It does not pay to dictate. The Bible Society can only respond to the needs and requests of communities and churches. Proper research is therefore required to establish the needs of users. Having fewer projects . . . allows for a proper focus on quality. Quality is essential and non-negotiable.

With [so many] languages it [would] be unrealistic to say that BST can carry out translation work in all languages. We need the assistance of others to supplement our efforts. Already we have other partners in this such [organizations] as SIL, PBT, and word for the World. These should be seen as fully partners and we should work in consultation with each other. I want to see transparency and honesty as we work with each other, as well as respect and appreciation for one another's contributions.

Author's Interview with The Rev Albert Mongi, former General Secretary of Bible Society of Tanzania

Uhuru Hostel, Moshi, Tanzania, 6 June 2007

Figure B.3. Rev Albert Mongi. Photo © Aloo Osotsi Mojola

The Rev Albert Mongi was born in 1939 in Marangu, Kilimanjaro. He is the fifth-born in a family of eight sons and three daughters. He earned a BS in forestry at the University of Washington, USA, (1965), before pursuing theological and pastoral training at the Lutheran Bible Institute, Seattle/Issaquah, Washington, USA (BS in Biblical studies, 1985) and at Concordia Theological Seminary, Fort Wayne, Indiana, USA (M.Div. in pastoral ministry, 1987).

After leaving university, the Rev Mongi first worked at Tanga as Regional Director in Agriculture, Forestry, Veterinary Services (1970–1971), and subsequently as Chief Conservation Officer, Tanzania National Parks (TANAPA, 1971–1974), and then as Conservation Advisor, United Nations Environmental Program (1974–1981) before accepting the call to serve as the General Secretary of the Bible Society of Tanzania (1990–2005). Since 2006, the Rev Mongi worked as the Chaplaincy Coordinator for Institutions of Higher Learning of the Evangelical Lutheran Church of Tanzania, Northern Diocese until his death in April 2018.

AUTHOR: What brought you to the Bible Society?

REV MONGI: As a pastor, my calling is to get the word to as many people as possible. After completion of seminary training, I was sent forth to proclaim the gospel of Jesus Christ. After some time in parish work, my bishop, Dr Erasto Kweka, requested me to consider joining the Bible Society as the general secretary. Emmanuel Kibira, then [general secretary], was retiring. This was providential after finishing biblical studies at the Lutheran Bible Institute and obtaining a Masters in Divinity degree in pastoral ministries at Concordia Theological Seminary.

After about two and a half years in the parish, Bishop Kweka, approached me with an "ultimatum": the church wanted me to join the Bible Society of

Tanzania to work in Dodoma at the Society's national headquarters. . . . [The bishop gave me time to] think about it, but it did not take long for me and my family to agree that it must be God's calling. So, I agreed. And I have not had occasion to regret my wholehearted readiness to go to Dodoma . . . My interest in the BS, however, was not [exactly] new since I had had discussions with the UBS regional translation coordinator, Dr Eugene Bunkowski, in Nairobi when I was working for the United Nations. Also, I [previously learned] something about translation from Dr Renju, a fellow Tanzanian who had worked as a translator for the Swahili Habari Njema Bible based in Nairobi.

AUTHOR: What was your vision for the Bible Society?
REV MONGI: At the beginning I did not know much about the mission, vision, and ethos of the Bible Society. My concern was for rural pastors who had a one-reference-book library, the Bible. In Tanzania this was the Swahili Union Version. It was without any concordance, thematic references, or any other readers' helps. The type of binding on most of our Bibles was the kind that cannot withstand the rigors of daily use. My desire was to see the Bible Society provide pastors Bibles with concordances, chapter introductions, section headings, and plenty of other helps for the reader.

When I was trained in the USA, I had several versions of the Bible in English, yet most of the pastors and evangelists [in Tanzania] had only the Swahili Bible, and lacked a Bible in the vernacular – in their own mother tongue. And this despite the fact that the people whom they were serving spoke [not only] Swahili, but their mother tongues as well. So, it was my hope that the Bible Society would have a program through which [Scriptures] could be made available in the mother tongues, especially in the areas where the church was vibrant and the vernacular was cherished.

My third hope was that there would be Scriptures for the young people in their own language, idiom, and level . . . It was my wish that during my stay at the Bible Society that the Bible or parts of the Bible would be made available for different age groups of people.

AUTHOR: What was your vision for Bible translation in Tanzania?
REV MONGI: I saw my contribution to Bible translation in the wider context of the mission of the Bible Society, namely, availing God's word to the people of Tanzania in various languages, languages they spoke and understood in their everyday lives, in formats that were appropriate to them, and in a product mix that made sense. My vision was to address key areas of concern: improve the one-book-library scenario; reassess the available versions of the Bible; . . .

promote revisions . . . ; [undertake new] translations in popular languages; [address the Scripture needs of] young people; and look for resources to subsidize these Scripture [activities]. In order to bring this about I resolved to work closely with the churches.

When talking about vision, how do you tackle it? [One needs] resources – the means for realizing this vision and bringing about fruitful activities. So . . . my work concentrated on helping the churches to realize that the Bible Society was a servant of the churches and needed their full support if it was to succeed. This was a formidable undertaking, [and] very frustrating. The churches did not need to be convinced that the vision of the Bible Society was worthy. It was obvious to them. It was frustrating that the churches' involvement in providing budgetary means and support to the Bible Society . . . did not match their conviction.

But I must, however, express my gratitude that the churches spared their scarce resources in terms of qualified personnel – trained translators, pastors, reviewers, etc. – in order to realize our translations. My agony was that [globally] the Bible Society [movement seemed to be] relegating to low priority the concept of its being a missionary organization, in favor of adopting a business approach [focused primarily on] the production and management process of Scripture [development].

My vision for the national Bible society can be likened to a village well that will always have water for any person seeking water. Even if you cannot [draw] a tankerul from the well, at least you can [draw] a bucketful . . . But this scenario has disappeared and some Bible societies have become purely money generators and some don't even handle Scriptures.

AUTHOR: How did you plan and proceed to make your vision come true?
REV MONGI: To make the vision come true depended on the leadership structure in place. At BST it was vested in the Board and its various committees – under the very persistent advice and monitoring of the UBS Africa Regional Center in Nairobi which translated the global mission, vision, and ethos of the UBS into reality and requested the Board to see how the local or national society would implement it. So it was providential that the UBS concern for translation programs and Scriptures for youth was very much in line with my hope.

AUTHOR: How did you establish priorities among languages? Were you influenced by national governmental policy, church policy, or your own insights?
REV MONGI: Tanzania is a very pluralistic society with about 132 language groups, but it is fortunate that the country has [Swahili as its] so-called national

language. But it is not universally spoken. If you go deep, deep into Uhehe, e.g. Boma Ngombe, where we went to introduce the Gospel of Matthew . . . people spoke to us in Kihehe. There are many distinct language groupings that jealously guard their ethnic identity. There is no way I could establish priorities. UBS had guidelines to be followed, e.g. the Chiang Mai goals, the Addis Ababa Declaration, the Mississauga goals. It was difficult to translate those into action, but at least they guided our priorities. I advised the Board [of BST] at various committees to be pragmatic in that there was no sense in doing a translation where people would not appreciate it. It was safer to invest in vernacular translations where large sections of the speakers looked forward to having translations in their mother tongue, for example, among the Maasai or Wasukuma or Wahaya or Wairaiqw or Wadatooga or Wahehe where the mother tongue is held in high regard and used in everyday life. Appreciation did not come about spontaneously. We talked about the translations – the Haya, the Chagga, the Sukuma – and did a lot of publicity . . .explaining why the vernacular was important, and in the process, promoted and encouraged the use of these languages in the churches and in homes.

Author: How did you see Swahili in Tanzania in terms of Bible Society policy and goals?

Rev Mongi: Swahili is still the most widely spoken language in Tanzania . . . With the effects of globalization of communication, many foreign or borrowed expressions are becoming the norm and widely acceptable. Even expressions which would have previously caused people to raise eyebrows, no longer have the same effect.

Swahili is . . . increasingly becoming the national language. For serious or formal conversation, there is the standard Swahili [regulated by] Baraza la Kiswahili Tanzania (BAKITA or the Kiswahili Council of Tanzania) which helps to establish national norms to be taken into account when new words are being incorporated and to recommend rules to govern the standard usage. Swahili is, however, like a tree with many branches. Some branches . . . reach out to incorporate the influences of the local vernaculars into the national vocabulary while others reach out to the lower strata of society . . . For example, Swahili in schools is standard but outside the classroom students use their own lingo.

Yes, many people speak Swahili but they often resort to the vernacular, to their mother tongue. I myself speak Swahili in Moshi, Kichagga in Marangu, and at Masoka I use a mixture of English and Swahili. Because of this diversity . . . we need several different translations. For young people, the contemporary

Biblia Habari Njema is what they like. For older people, I am almost forced to use the Swahili Union Version. If I am speaking with older pastors they prefer the Roehl translation . . . The English Standard Version (ESV) is becoming popular at the university level – that is what I promote at Masoka.

AUTHOR: Now that you are out of Bible Society through retirement, and on a new assignment, do you see the Bible Society contribution differently?
REV MONGI: Something I very much wished [we could have brought about was] greater involvement with the grassroots in financing Scriptures for the people. I was very much impressed by the structure of the Bible Society in India where the auxiliaries are financed by the grassroots. The grassroots is also fully involved in promoting the desired goals of the Society. They support translation projects, the development of Scriptures in desired formats, and even promoting the mission, vision, and ethos of Bible Society . . . So if I were to do it over again, I would spend more time in selected auxiliary areas, at the grassroots, with ordinary Christians.

Because of inadequate resources at the UBS and at the local Bible Society, the quality of book production was not good. We sacrificed quality for quantity. So, I would really go for quality – good binding, presentation of the page, and fonts mindful of a majority of readers . . . Quantity does not always satisfy the need . . . A Bible should last many years. I bought mine in 1978 and I still use it every Sunday

AUTHOR: So what do you see as your key contributions to the Bible Society of Tanzania that made a real difference to its present and future ministry?
REV MONGI: This is a difficult question. However, I take what people have said to me as an assessment of our efforts. For example, in Dodoma one person told me, "I really appreciate your coming to the Bible Society. We appreciate the way you stopped the sewage which one had to walk through in coming to the Bible Society offices and also in removing the garbage dump in front Bible House." In retrospect, I agree that was a significant contribution I made because we built a sewer connection to the main sewage [line] and effectively stopped garbage disposal in front of Bible House. I also extended the Bible Society building to adequately accommodate the [space requirements for] administration, translation, and warehousing, as well as the Bible shop.

Other examples come from people who have seen the Bible Society warehouse at Kitunda in Dar es Salaam. This warehouse provides adequate storage for incoming Scriptures for the whole of Tanzania and for our neighboring countries [Rwanda, Burundi, Malawi, Zambia, and DRC]. Mr

Million Belete, the former UBS Africa Regional Secretary said to me, "The Bible Society of Tanzania will never forget you for what you have done – having the vision and building this warehouse." Another comment was made by Monseigneur Kangalawe at the Catholic Secretariat in Dar es Salaam. When I visited the secretariat as I was leaving the Bible Society as General Secretary, he said, "When you first visited us and talked about the work and needs of the Bible Society we thought, who are you to remind us? But as the years have gone by, we have been part of your vision and now take the Bible as our basic tool for everyone in the Catholic Church. You can retire with a sense of gratitude that God allowed you to do what you have done over these years."

Personally, I think my greatest contribution stemmed from my original desire to make available a Bible with a concordance and readers' helps. I especially think of the children's Bible and the family Bible with extensive picture illustrations suitable for all age groups.

AUTHOR: Anything else that you would like to add?

REV MONGI: I would like to express profound gratitude to God for the opportunity he gave me to be involved in making the word of God available in various formats. I am very grateful for [BST's] involvement in making available special Scriptures to prisoners – with an estimated [average] literacy [level] said to be [only slightly] above third grade – in cooperation with the Lutheran Braille Workers of America. I want to thank the UBS for the wide exposure I received as a member of Africa Regional Executive Committee and the Africa Area Board . . . My gratitude goes to many people in the fellowship, the Bible Society of India, the British and Foreign Bible Society, the Germany Bible Society, and the very dedicated commitment of my colleagues at the Bible Society [of Tanzania], including those working in translation, distribution, and administration, at all levels. I am indebted to Dr Mojola with whom I worked for eleven years at the Bible Society in Dodoma and with whom we pioneered many translation projects whose real usefulness will attest itself in the course of time.

Author's Interview with The Rev Canon Naphtali Petro Lusinde, Cigogo Bible Translator

Dodoma, Tanzania, 1 July 2007

Figure B.4. Rev Naphtali Petro Lusinde. Photo © Aloo Osotsi Mojola

The Rev Canon Naphtali Petro Lusinde was born in 1921 in the village of Kilombo, in the Dodoma Region of Tanzania. His father, Petro Lusinde Malecela, was a school teacher who later became a priest in the Anglican Church. Naphtali's grandfather, Malecela Mawula, was one of the first local evangelists in the Dodoma area to work with the first Anglican missionaries.

After graduating from Dodoma Boys' Central School in 1938, Naphtali received a call to Christian ministry in 1951 and decided to join the Anglican Church as an evangelist. Upon completing his initial training, he was sent to Kigwe Chikola in Dodoma to work as an evangelist. In 1953, he went for further training at St Philip's Theological College, Kongwa, Dodoma. Upon finishing his training, he was ordained a priest. Over the years, the Rev Lusinde has served as a parish priest in Arusha, Tengeru, Magugu, Mbulu, Babati, Dongobeshi, and Mpwapwa, and elsewhere.

In 1962–1963, the Rev Lusinde received theological training at Moore Theological College in Sydney, Australia. On his return he was appointed to lead in three key areas of the Diocese of Central Tanganyika: as Archdeacon of Mpwapwa and Kongwa, as Diocesan Administrative Secretary, and as Diocesan Education Secretary. In 1974, he was appointed Diocesan Director of Evangelism under Bishop Yohana Madinda. From 1978 to 1985, he served as Dean of the Dodoma Cathedral of the Holy Spirit.

In addition to these extensive church responsibilities, Canon Lusinde has demonstrated a strong commitment to civic service. He has worked as Chairman of the Board of several schools and has served as Chairman of the Education Committee of the Dodoma municipality. He was also a member of the Dodoma City Council, inspector of prisons in the Dodoma Region, and a member of various development committees.

In 1986, the Rev Lusinde was appointed by the bishop of the diocese of Central Tanganyika and seconded to the Bible Society to head the translation team responsible for the Cigogo Bible project, a task he joyfully committed himself to for the fifteen years it took to complete. The Cigogo Bible was published and dedicated on 2 November 2002.

AUTHOR: What brought you to Bible translation?

REV LUSINDE: Since childhood I loved learning more of God's word . . . In my twenties, I loved very much to teach other people God's word and to explain it to them. My father and grandfather were both teachers and preachers of God's word and I desired very much to follow in their footsteps. I also loved to write booklets that explained God's word to people. So, when I was requested by Bishop Madinda to consider being a translator of the new Cigogo Bible in present day speech, I did not hesitate to accept this call.

AUTHOR: What was your vision for the Cigogo Bible Translation?

REV LUSINDE: I very much wanted to see people reading God's word in their own language and fully understanding. The word of God would thereby work in their lives and transform their lives, enabling them to walk in obedience to this word.

AUTHOR: Why was Cigogo necessary for this? Wasn't Swahili sufficient?

REV LUSINDE: No, Swahili is not sufficient. There are many Wagogo people, especially in the rural areas who do not understand Swahili well or who cannot speak it well. In any case, it is important that a people use their own language given to them by God and that they enjoy and benefit from its use . . . It was necessary to translate a new Bible in contemporary Cigogo to replace the old and outdated Cigogo translation. Although it was printed in 1960, it was actually in very old Cigogo. The New Testament of this Bible came out in 1899. That was why I was keen to be involved in this new translation.

AUTHOR: Now that the new Bible is out, how are the Wagogo responding to it?

REV LUSINDE: It was very well accepted. People are very happy to hear it read in churches or in their homes. Unfortunately, the sales of this Bible have not been very encouraging. There are a number of factors for this. [For one thing], our people are not used to buying books or reading books. Yes, they have bought this new Bible, but not insufficient numbers . . . Second, we have a new, younger generation who are more used to Swahili and are not keen to buy and use their Cigogo Bible. They need to be encouraged to love and to use their own tongue. The older generation . . . love the language. They love to hear it. Some can read it, but some cannot afford to buy it.

AUTHOR: So are people buying?
REV LUSINDE: Yes, they are buying, but they need to be encouraged to buy even more. The bishop, pastors, and evangelists need to encourage all Christians to buy and own a copy of this Bible for their own use and for use in their homes and for sharing it with others. We need to encourage this especially in the rural areas.

AUTHOR: Do you think there is need for further translation of the Bible in the languages of Tanzania?
REV LUSINDE: Certainly there is much need. There are many languages in Tanzania and many people who do not have God's word in their own mother tongue. This is very important. Of course, Swahili is there and many can hear God's word through Swahili. But there are many others who will hear it even better in their own tongues.

Appendix C

Perspectives from Uganda

Table C.1. Main languages and dialects of Uganda[1]

I. Sudanic Languages
A. Central Sudanic
1.Lugbara
2.Madi
3.Kebu (Ndo)
4.Luluba
5.Mangbetu
II. Nilotic Languages
A. Western Nilotic (River-Lake Nilotes)
6.Acholi
7.Alur
8.Dhopadhola
9.Kumam
10.Lango
B. Eastern Nilotic (Plains Nilotes)
11.Ateso
12.Karamojong
13.Kakwa
14.Mening
15.Nyangi

---

1. The content of this table is primarily based on the online version of *Ethnologue* (see bibliography), though other sources were consulted. The list above is however an edited version of the *Ethnologue* 14th edition. Please note however that the various *Ethnologue* editions list some languages such Bukusu, Thur, Ndrulo, Kuku, Amba not usually recognized by other language workers in Uganda.

16.Ik
17.Soo
C. Southern Nilotic (Highland Nilotes)
18.Kupsapiny
19.Pokoot
III. Bantu Languages
A. Western Bantu
20. Rukiga
21. Runyankole
22. Runyarwanda
23. Rutooro
24. Runyoro
25. Ruruli
26. Lukonjo
27. Rwamba
28. Rubwisi (Lubwisi or Talinga-Bwisi)
29.Rugungu
27. Rwamba
B. Eastern Bantu
30. Luganda
31. Lusoga
32. Lumasaaba (Lugisu)
33. Lugwere
34. Lunyoli
35. Lusamia/Lugwe (Luluyia)
IV. Arabic-based Creole
36.Nubi

Table C.2. Scripture publications in languages of Uganda

A. Languages with a Complete Bible				
Language (listed alphabetically)	**First Portion**	**First New Testament**	**First Bible**	**Key Subsequent or Ongoing Translation Work**
1. Acholi	1905	1933	1986	Bible revision in progress
2. Alur	1921	1933	1936	second Bible (common language) expected 2021
3. Ateso	1910	1930	1961	
4. Kakwa	1967	1974	1983	
5. Karamojong	1932	1974, 1997	2011	second NT 1997
6. Kumam	none	2007	2013	
7. Lango	1967	1974	1979	
8. Luganda	1887	1893	1896, 1968, 2015	second Bible (common language interconfessional) 2003; revision of 1896 Bible complete, publication 2015
9. Lugbara	1922	1936	1966	
10. Runyankole-Rukiga	1907/ 1957	1962	1964, 1989	second Bible (common language interconfessional) 1989
11. Runyoro-Rutooro	1900	1905	1912, 2010	second Bible (common language) 2010
B. Languages with a New Testament but No Bible				
12. Dhopadhola	1977	2003	2019	complete interconfesional Bible in two editions.
13. Kebu	1964	1995		
14. Kupsapiny	1975	1996		complete Bible in progress
15. Lumasaaba	1904	1977	2016	complete interconfessional Bible in two editions.
16. Lusoga	1896	1999	2015	complete interconfessional Bible in two editions..
17. Madi	1935	1977		
C. Languages with a Portion but No New Testament or Bible				
18. Lukonjo	1914			

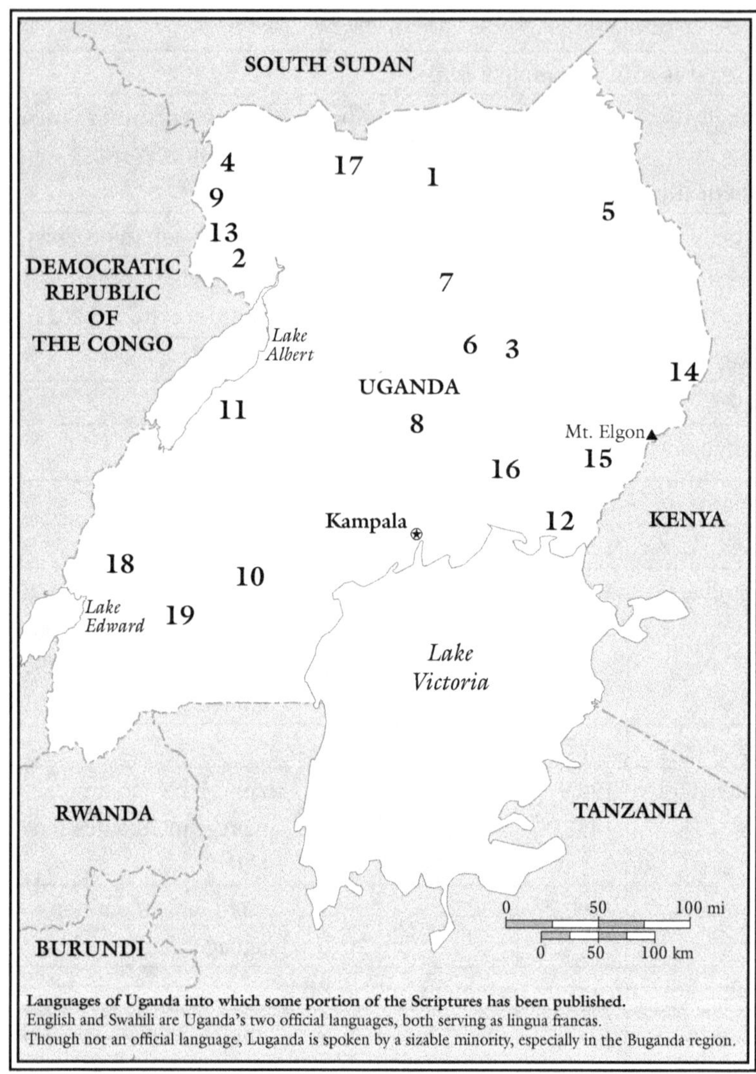

Map C. Languages and Dialects of Uganda. American Bible Society Library and Archives. Used by permission.

Map C works together with table C.2. The numbers in the table correspond to the numbers on the map.

A Historical Overview of Bible Work in Uganda

Figure C.1 Bible Society of Uganda Bible House, Kampala. Photo © Aloo Osotsi Mojola

The following is adapted from a report by the Bible Society of Uganda.

From 1849 on, Uganda was included in the general work of the British and Foreign Bible Society who played a significant role in the early years of the missionary penetration of theAfrican continent that began on the coast of the Indian Ocean. From 1896 to 1916, Bible Society workin the region operated through the Egyptian Agency of BFBS at which time the Bible Society in East Africa was established, initially as a "Joint Sub-Agency."

In the early 1960s, the Bible Society in East Africa was extended, first by the appointment of an indigenous staff for Kenya, the Rev John Mpayeei, followed by two additional appointments, for Tanganyika and Uganda (in 1964). The Rev Asa Byara, a man of great stature and initiative (from Tooro Kingdom), laid the foundation for the inauguration of the Bible Society of Uganda on November 24, 1968, as a national office run under an advisory council with the Hon. Serwano Kulubya (former mayor of Kampala) as its first chairman. Mr Kulubya was followed as BSU's chairman by Dr Dunstan Nsubuga (then Bishop of Namirembe Diocese), with Mr John Kyeyune serving as Treasurer.

On April 24, 1972, the advisory council adoptedthe constitution and bylaws that paved the way for the recognition of the Bible Society of Uganda as an associate member of the United Bible Societies in 1974. The 1970s were difficult years, not only for the Bible Society but for Uganda as a whole, but in spite of these circumstances distribution and financial contributions from Bible Society members increased.

At the end of 1970, the Rev Asa Byara passed away suddenly and Mr Michael Kalule, BSU's business manager, served as acting executive secretary until 1974 when now-retired Bishop Yokana Mukasa was appointed executive secretary. Later, when the Bible Society of Uganda attained associate member status, Bishop Musaka was invited to continue his leadership role as general secretary.

Under Bishop Mukasa's leadership the interdenominational character of the Bible Society was established. It will be remembered that the mid-sixties saw the exposure of the Roman Catholic laity to Scripture through policy changes made at the Second Vatican Council. The visit of Pope Paul VI to Africa in 1969 helped to enhance cooperation between the Bible Society movement and the Roman Catholic Church. A deeper and more consistent cooperation between the Bible Society ministry and all Christian denominations and congregations, however, remains a challenge.

When the Rev Mukasa became Bishop of Mityana in 1977, Bishop Akisoferi M. Wesonga assumed leadership as general secretary; when he in turn was made Bishop of Mbale Diocese in 1981 the Rev Canon Benezeri Kisembo (now Bishop) took over as general secretary, holding the position until 1987 when Mr Jeroham Kaddu became the first layman appointed as substantive general secretary. When Mr Kaddu retired, the Rev Canon Benezeri Kisembo was transferred from his position as a UBS translations advisor to serve another tenure as general secretary from July 1996 to December 1999, when he stepped down to serve as Bishop of Rwenzori Diocese. He was succeeded by Mr Henry Kalule who was installed in 2000 and successfully led BSU till his retirement in 2009. Simon Peter Mukhama succeeded him as the General Secretary.[2]

---

2. Reported by Bishop Benezeri Kisembo, Rwenzori Diocese, Anglican Church of Uganda, former General Secretary of the Bible Society of Uganda. Adapted by the author.

Author's Interview with Mr Henry Kalule, Former General Secretary of the Bible Society of Uganda

Bible House, Kampala, Uganda, 24 July 2007

Figure C.2. Henry Kalule.
Photo © Aloo Osotsi Mojola

Henry Kalule was born in 1957 of Muslim parents, in a small town just east of Kampala. He enrolled in Makerere University in 1977 and graduated in 1980 with an honors degree in economics. He later received an MBA degree from Maastricht School of Management. Henry married his wife, Peninnah, in January 1982 and the couple have been blessed with five children. On leaving Makerere University, Henry was appointed as an economist with the Ministry of Planning and Economic Development, but a year later was called to serve his church. He served the Seventh-Day Adventist Church as secretary/treasurer of a diocese and later was advanced to assistant treasurer of the archdiocese.

In November 1999, Mr Kalule joined the Bible Society of Uganda as General Secretary, having served on its board for five years. He no longer serves the Bible Society. He is currently involved in running his own business. He served as the chairman of the executive board of the inter-religious Council of Uganda, and continues to serve the SDA Church on different boards, including school boards and the Adventist Relief Agency (ADRA).

AUTHOR: What brought you to the Bible Society of Uganda?

MR KALULE: My Association with the Bible Society dates way back [to] 1982 when I joined the Society as a life member. My motivation was to make a contribution to [a] cause I felt was noble because it was vital in the fulfillment of God's commission. In 1999 Canon Kisembo, the General Secretary of the Bible Society of Uganda, was called to serve as Bishop of the Rwenzori Diocese and the hunt for a replacement started.

It was when Canon Kisembo called me . . . and requested me to express an interest in serving the Bible Society that it dawned on me that the Lord may be calling me to the ministry on another dimension altogether.

AUTHOR: Do you enjoy the work at the Bible Society of Uganda?

MR KALULE: The work is challenging and there is something enjoyable about challenge. You have something new every morning to tackle and there is never anything like routine. The beauty of the Bible Society is the fellowship arrangement, [the assurance] of mutual support. With every challenge there is help around the corner.

AUTHOR: What were your main challenges when you joined?

MR KALULE: I can point out the following as the major challenges that I encountered: How to meet the growing demand for the Scriptures in light of limited funds; bringing to the organization a new way of looking at things and blending our management with modern business principles; and attracting and motivating staff to meet the challenges.

AUTHOR: What were your accomplishments or achievements?

MR KALULE: I see the main accomplishments as follows. [First,] improved stock levels with the right mix of slow- and fast-moving [inventory], enabling us to meet demand for the Scriptures as well as improving on our funding options. [Second,] good progress in improving the welfare of the staff and the establishment of a provident fund for retirement of staff. [Third,] we have managed to attract substantial donor funds for our extra programs, especially in the area of HIV intervention and adult literacy. [And fourth,] integrating the translation function into the other activities of the Bible Society and [maintaining] translators as full-time staff of the Bible Society of Uganda.

AUTHOR: In your view what is the place of Bible translation in the Bible Society and in the church?

MR KALULE: Given the context in which the Bible Society of Uganda is operating, with many indigenous languages, the importance of translation cannot be overemphasized. It justifies the existence of the Bible Society. Any organization could probably engage in production and distribution, but there are very few that can manage translation. As for the church, with half the population hardly exposed to any formal education, what other language can it use to teach the people the way of God other than vernaculars? So to both the church and the Bible Society, Bible translation is central to all activities.

AUTHOR: What were your achievements in this area? Are there any more challenges in this area?

MR KALULE: Much progress is being done in this area. New translations have been started as [earlier] ones are concluded. We have also improved on the time [it takes] to complete a translation, mainly because the Bible Society has taken full responsibilities [for] the translators. Old translations are being revised and improved on. We have also been able to enhance our collaboration with the churches [by promoting] inter-confessional translations.

AUTHOR: What do you see as the future of the Bible Society in Uganda? And its role?

MR KALULE: The future of the Bible Society consists in having the Bible translated into major language groups and taking on strategies that ensure promotion of Bible engagement. In the future we shall have to consider product enhancement by providing Bibles with study notes and concordances. With 60 percent of our population below eighteen years, we have to look at [this] age group with keen interest.

AUTHOR: If you were to do it all over again, would you do anything differently?

MR KALULE: What we have done in the past has been done in a particular way because it was being done in a specific context and environment. The context and environment keep on changing and if we were to do the same things again, we would probably employ different techniques.

Author's Interview with Bishop Benezeri Kisembo, former General Secretary of the Bible Society of Uganda

Fort Portal, Uganda, 25 July 2007

Figure C.3. Bishop Benezeri Kisembo. Photo © Aloo Osotsi Mojola

Bishop Benezeri Tibenderana Kisembo was born in Kiburara, Kabarole, on the slopes of the Ruwenzori Mountains in western Uganda in 1944. Kisembo attended the University of East Africa, Makerere University College, Kampala, where he earned his BA in religious studies in 1970. In 1971 he married his wife, Lovey, a fellow religion student at Makerere University. He continued his education, earning his MA in religious studies at Makerere University in 1977 and an MTh from Aberdeen University, Scotland, in 1990. Kisembo was ordained deacon in the Anglican Church of Uganda in 1978, priest in December 1979, and was appointed canon in January 1985. His wife Lovey was ordained deacon in 1977 and priest in 1989.

The Rev Kisembo was a lecturer at the Department of Religious Studies and Philosophy, Makerere University, from 1973 to 1981. The following year he joined the Bible Society of Uganda where he served as the distribution and promotion officer and acting general secretary before being invited to serve as general secretary, a position he held until 1987. From February 1987 to January 1988, he worked as the assistant to the BSU translation consultant. After completing his studies at Aberdeen University, the Rev Kisembo was appointed as the translation manager for the BSU. Shortly afterward, he accepted a position as UBS translation advisor-in-training responsible for work in Uganda. In July 1996 he was invited to resume his former duties as general secretary of the Bible Society of Uganda. In January 2000 he left this leadership role to assume the role of Bishop of the Ruwenzori Diocese of the Church of Uganda. He is currently retired and resides in Kampala, Uganda.

Author: So what brought you to the Bible Society of Uganda?

Rev Kisembo: I was teaching biblical studies at the Makerere University at the time, and so when I was invited to lead the ministry of the Society that publishes the Scriptures . . . I was happy to accept the invitation. The circumstances indicated that God was calling me to be involved in Bible translation, publishing, and distribution. Although it was prestigious to teach at the university . . . I still felt strongly that I should leave. It was three years after my ordination and I thought that the church needed my services through the Bible Society ministry. At that time, the country was in dire shortage of the Holy Scriptures. Access to the Scriptures during those tragic Idi Amin years was almost impossible. As the head of the Bible Society ministry, it was my job to help get Scriptures for the people of Uganda.

Author: Can you talk more about some of these challenges?

Rev Kisembo: The initial challenge for me was to start work as a distribution officer. I had been invited to work as general secretary, but some UBS people wanted me to work first as a distribution officer, arguing that I had no relevant Bible Society experience. So, I worked as a distribution officer as well as acting general secretary. Later on, I was interviewed for the position of general secretary and [was] formally offered this position.

The second challenge . . . was the acute shortage of Scriptures. This was mainly due to the runaway inflation of the Uganda currency . . . The money that came from the sale of Scriptures could not be sent back to [our suppliers to] acquire more Scriptures. We were a blocked-cash country. So I remember with a lot of sadness that I had to ration Bibles. I had to limit how many Bibles [individual customers] could take from the Bible House. Some people used the Bible as merchandise to be sold on the black market at a profit, taking advantage of the serious shortages to make money from the Bible.

The breakthrough came after I made the plight known to the United Bible Societies fellowship. The British and Foreign Bible Societies through the UBS fellowship answered our cry by sending two plane loads of Scriptures. They brought in 100,000 Bibles: 50,000 Luganda Bibles and 50,000 English Bibles. These were in greatest demand.

During this same period, the country had a lot of insecurity. Nowhere was safe. There was a guerrilla war in the country. There was fighting in the bush, in the rural areas. Many areas of the country were no-go areas, for example, the Luwero area in the north. [In 1985,] western Uganda was completely cut off for almost half a year.

The other ongoing challenge for the Society was staffing. Finding [suitable] people to work for the Bible Society was not easy. This was compounded by the challenge of working with budgets . . . and implementing budget plans in a highly unstable inflationary financial climate and in insecure and difficult times.

The other big challenge was the need to mobilize local support through local fundraising and through Scripture distribution. This was complicated by the factors mentioned above.

Finally, the greatest challenge in my view was having no property of our own. UBS policy at the time did not allow us to buy property. We had to rent offices, our own storage facilities, and staff accommodation as well. This was very expensive . . . the Bible Society . . . finally allowed me to use our blocked cash to purchase a house to serve as residential facility for the general secretary.

The next issue was the arrival of lots of Scriptures but no storage. We had Scriptures stored in as many as five different places. Our stock movement and management were not made easy due to the number of places we had to visit, etc. [The UBS finally agreed] to support us in purchasing a building that could serve as our Bible House. We moved to purchase a plot on Bombo Roadin Kampala, working together with the then Chair of the Executive Committee, the late John Kyeyune. After [an unsuccessful attempt to acquire a house on McKinnon Road, the decision was made to focus instead] on building the present Bible House on the Bombo Road plot.

Author: What were your accomplishments and achievements?
Rev Kisembo: During my time at Bible House one of my contributions was the introduction and establishment of Bible Society branches throughout the country. . . . By the time I left at the end of 1999, I [had] established two strong centers, at Fort Portal and at Iganga. These became centers of Scripture distribution to the neighboring areas. We started work at Ndeba in the Mukono area and moved on to set [up] centers at Mbale, Soroti, Kabale, and Luwero. I still believe strongly that these centers are important. [The] Bible Society should not just be [solely] in Kampala but should be stationed among the people who need the Bible in their own language.

It is important for every language to have a Scripture center that is easy to access. For some areas this is very expensive to create. You need someone committed to the Bible Society to offer storage and [a means] to facilitate the safe distribution and management of Scriptures. This would in addition stir up and [retain] support from the people, [knowing] that the Scriptures are available within their own area . . . and other Scriptures could also be distributed from those points, for example, the English language Scriptures, but the Scriptures in the main language spoken in the area should be available as well.

The other part is property ownership. When I joined Bible Society there were no fixed assets for the Society. When I left Bible Society there were many fixed assets, for example, the general secretary's house and the Bible House itself. We also had a plot that had been donated by Mr Christopher M. S. Kisosonkole's family. [It is situated] in Ntinda near Kyamboga and is yet to be developed.

I was also involved in Bible translation, as you know. I look back with satisfaction on this period. During my time many languages received Scriptures, others started to translate Scriptures in their own languages. Significant among these was the Karimojong Bible now completed, the Lusoga NT completed and the OT ongoing, the Kumam NT recently launched and the OT ongoing, and the Lusamia-Lugwe NT nearing completion. I found others going on – some of these have been completed, e.g. the Rukiga-Runyankole and the Luganda interconfessional common-language Bibles. Others are yet to be completed, such as the interconfessional Runyoro-Rutooro common language Bible.

During my time we were very actively involved in preparing and promoting the New Reader Portions in English as well as in [several] vernacular languages. I loved this [program] very much and would wish to see this continued . . . Now there is an educational policy in our country to use the vernacular languages in the first three to four years of primary school. These New Reader Portions are of great help as they assist in developing literacy and reading in the local languages.

Author: In your opinion what is the place of translation in the Bible Society and in the church?

Rev Kisembo: Translation is so very dear to my heart, that after a number of years working as the general secretary I found myself making a decision to switch from being a general secretary to becoming a UBS translation advisor. As I see it, the translation of the word of God in languages people use and understand is fundamental to the task of Christian mission. I have experienced the joy and excitement of seeing people receive for the first time Scriptures in their own languages. Having a Bible in their own languages . . . offered local readers an experience that cannot easily be described.

Bible translation is indeed a key area of the mission of the church and of Bible society ministry. Hence the need for the best qualified translators so as to ensure translations that are as accurate and as meaningful as possible, translations that allow readers to get as close as possible to the meaning of the original . . . text. I am hoping that I can be of some further use to translation when I retire, be it on a national or international level.

AUTHOR: What was your specific contribution to translation as General Secretary of the Bible Society of Uganda and in your short stint as a translation consultant in the Bible Society?

REV KISEMBO: During my time as general secretary and as translation advisor, I had lots of enthusiasm for translation work and often accompanied the TCs and translators to translation conferences and workshops. I participated in these as much as I could because the Bible hasbeen the fascination of my life.

AUTHOR: What do you see as the future of the Bible Society in your country?

REV KISEMBO: As someone retired from active involvement . . . I must confess that I have left my successor to go on with the work. Occasionally, I visit Bible House and I cannot say I am up to date with current plans and developments in the Bible Society of Uganda. My hope is that the Bible Society can work toward sustainability through property ownership, distribution of what is published, support from members and churches. Like many voluntary organizations this calls for hard work and effort from those in the service of the Society. I also think that there is need for the staff to be frugal in the utilization of resources, and a need to prove to the church and the public at large that what is available is being put to good use.

I know there are pressures on the Society. . . . There are insufficient local contributions and also in some cases, a low demand for the Scriptures, and so my appeal would be for vigorous marketing. People need the Scriptures but do not know how to get them or where to get them. There is need to do more promotion of our Bibles *before* publication [in order to] to boost distribution.

Finally, here in the Anglican Diocese of Rwenzori we have offered a plot to the Bible Society for use as a depot, or as a fundraising resource. The plot could also be [used] to develop a residential property for generating income for the Society.

AUTHOR: If you were to do it again what would you differently?

REV KISEMBO: A number of things I would do differently. For instance, [I'd examine] the perceived need to decentralize Bible Society services by establishing centers away from the Kampala headquarters. A thorough market survey to determine priorities and likely success would need to done. During my time [we] met the needs of the various areas mainly using my contacts and people I could trust in those parts. Now the situation is stable. So a business survey [could now be undertaken] to see which approaches would benefit the Society most. Another [priority I'd set] would be to capitalize on income generating projects. This would call for a [careful discernment] in the recruitment of staff. We would need staff who would benefit the Society with their ministry skills, experience, and drive. We would need people with training in business and marketing skills.

Circumstances have changed so much even as the UBS too has changed, especially in its attitude toward national Bible societies. National boards and their chief executives need a freer hand to make decisions based on their knowledge of local situations, without undue pressure from the UBS. Often we at BSU had national plans that UBS did not give much weight to. We had to abandon some of these because they were [not] approved by UBS. The [national] societies need more autonomy and a freer hand to make decisions that promote the cause of the Bible in their contexts without undue interference from UBS officials who know [little] about the national context.

Author: Can you give some idea of the history of Bible Society in Uganda?
Rev Kisembo: The British and Foreign Bible Society after many years finally handed over work to the Bible Society in East Africa, which [continued to work] under its supervision.Between 1963 and 1965 the Bible Society in East Africa decentralized its activities by establishing national offices in the three countries of East Africa. The first executive secretary for Uganda was the Rev Asa Byara [who moved from Fort Royal] to Kampala to assume the new responsibilities. He [had taken] over from Mr John Mpaayei who had been the executive secretary for the whole of East Africa.

In 1968, Uganda became a national office under Rev Byara. In 1970 Asa Byara died suddenly. Michael Kalule, his accountant, [was appointed] acting secretary, and remained in this position until 1974, when Yokana Mukasa became executive secretary. He retired [in 1977] to become Bishop of Mityana Diocese. He was succeeded by Rev Akisoferi Wesonga who also retired on becoming a bishop in 1981. In 1981 I succeeded Bishop Wesonga as general secretaryuntil 2000. Mr Jeroham Kaddu took over as general secretary in the years 1987–1996 during my stint as a translation advisor. In 2000 I became Bishop of Rwenzori Diocese [and] Henry Kalule became my successor and remains in that position to date. The Bible Society of Uganda became an associate member of UBS in 1975 and a full member in 1986.

Author's Interview with the Rev Dr Francis Xavier Mbaziira, Luganda Bible Translator

Bible House, Kampala, 24 July 2007

Figure C.4. Rev Francis Xavier Mbaziira. Photo © Aloo Osotsi Mojola

The Rev Father Francis Xavier Mbaziira was born in 1935 at Kyakasalaga-Bugere, in the Rakai District of Uganda. He studied at the Bukalasa Minor Seminary (1949–1955) and the Katigondo Major Seminary (1956–1959) as part of his priestly formation. For his university education he attended the Pontifical Urbaniana University Propaganda Fide in Rome from 1959 to 1964. It was here that he earned his BA, MA, and PhD degrees in biblical theology.

Father Mbaziira returned to Uganda in 1965 and was posted for priestly ministry to various parishes before being assigned teaching duties at the Katiggondo Major Seminary (1966–1967 and 1968–1970); Makerere University, Kampala (1967–1968); and the Uganda Martyrs College (1970–1972). From 1972 onwards, he was assigned to the Luganda Bible translation project.

AUTHOR: What brought you to the Luganda Bible translation project?

FATHER MBAZIIRA: [Following] Vatican II the church was keen to be involved in Bible translation. The *Verbum Dei* document had urged the church to render the word in indigenous languages. As part of fulfilling this mandate, the [Catholic and Anglican churches] in Uganda met at Rubaga in Kampala and agreed to collaborate in translating the Luganda Bible, among others. The Catholic Church appointed two Catholic priests for this task and requested them to avail themselves for translator training at Rubaga Social Center in 1972 in preparation for [this work]. I was [one of] the two. The other was the late Monseigneur Mpuga. He was involved in the Luganda translation review committee. The project began in November in 1972. The Anglican translator was the Rev Christopher Ssenyongo. Our translation office was at the Bible

Society office on Siad Barre Avenue in Kampala. I had to leave Masaka and relocate to Kampala, where I [found residence] at the Naguru Catholic Church parish. I worked on a full-time basis. After finishing the Gospel of Mark and publishing it as a portion, the Rev Ssenyonjo left the project to become bishop. He was succeeded by the Rev Kephas Mwanje [Anglican]. The consultant to the project at the time was Miss Jill Smith.

AUTHOR: Since the Baganda had the 1896 translation, why did they need another translation?

FATHER MBAZIIRA: The reasons for a new translation were clear. Pilkington's translation was in 1896 more than one-hundred years old. It had become archaic, it was literal, it was inaccurate and unnatural at many points, and it was not interconfessional. It was, however, generally quite good, but difficult to understand. For example, at Mark 10:17 of Pilkington, the meaning is completely lost since the language has changed. Many of the words mean something different. In that text, for example, it says *Bwe yali ng'agenda mu kkubo, omu n'ajja gy'ali ng'addukana, n'amufukaamirira*, which could mean "while he was going on the way, he had diarrhea," which is not the intended meaning. For ecumenical reasons, Christians were awakened to the need for joint work. The acceptance of the Catholic Church to work with others was a golden opportunity. *Verbum Dei* encouraged collaboration.

AUTHOR: What was your vision for the new Luganda Bible? What kind of Bible did you want to see?

FATHER MBAZIIRA: We wanted to see a Bible that speaks the language of the people in dignified but clear, understandable language, a text that is readable, attractive, and that does not [require] users to check [meanings in] dictionaries or ask older people. We had the model of the GNT. We wanted something like the GNT but in Luganda. I feel we achieved our objective, judging by what people say. They read it, they understand it, they appreciate it. I have listened to Catholic readers of this Bible, to Anglican readers and others, and the feedback is the same, it is encouraging. [One fellow priest, however, reported wanting] a literal translation, but felt that this translation was nevertheless good to read and easy to understand, [though] not for him. He wanted something closer to the original. For us, however, we wanted something that communicates to the common person, to the youth, and to the average reader. And we succeeded in doing just that.

Author: What were the main challenges as you were making this new translation?

Father Mbaziira: The main challenge was personnel. We were fortunate that I was able to stay on the team throughout. The turnover was quite high. I collaborated with eight or nine translators in all. This [frequent turnover] tended to break continuity and [failed] to provide stability to the project and the team.

The other challenge was the problem of insecurity. The years of Idi Amin were tragic years. Many innocent people were killed. The economy was in tatters. The high rate of inflation rendered our money useless. Working under those conditions was not easy. At one point my car was robbed at gun point and the manuscript of the book of Psalms that I had with me was taken and lost. The book was eventually found but burnt beyond recognition. Traveling or getting around was not easy. It was not easy for translators to meet regularly.

A third challenge was connected again with the personnel issue. The churches appointed translators who were not . . . adequately trained. So I was often forced to assist [the new translators] – to train them, to teach them, and to go through their work. My church withdrew me from the project as a way to show [their] dissatisfaction. During my time away, [others] did such poor work that I was requested to come back again. A delegation was sent to my bishop, requesting him to reassign me to the project. My bishop agreed to reassign me. On rejoining the team . . . we rechecked the work done during my absence. We had to revise and correct quite a bit of [it]. We had to retranslate, for example, the books of Samuel up to those of Chronicles.

The other challenge was from the Seventh-Day Adventist church. When we finished the Gospel of Mark the SDA leader, Rev Kyambadde, wrote a critique in which he thought the translation was not genuine since it was not literal and warned us, citing a text from Revelation that talked of the serious danger of changing, adding to, or omitting any text from the Bible. I had to explain that a meaning-based translation is not . . . the same thing as adding, changing, or removing from the Bible. After explaining what we were doing, we got the support of the church. [In terms of resolving differences,] some team members thought we could solve issues through voting, but we found that it was much better to explain, to understand, and to convince others.

Author: What was your main translation technique? Were you influenced by other major translations?

Father Mbaziira: I would say that the translation that influenced us most was the GNT (aka TEV). This was our model, while the RSV was our base text. The focus was *meaning* rather than *words*.

Author: Your translation is interconfessional. Is this a good thing? Did you experience any challenges producing this kind of Bible?

Father Mbaziira: For us as translators we had no problem with this. The problem was mostly on the side of reviewers and church members who were more familiar with the older versions, such as the King James or the old Luganda Bible. They expected us to follow their old favored translations. Our translation seemed to differ. It *was* different. We focused on the meaning. For example, we did not say, "The Lord is my shepherd," i.e. *musumba wange*. In Ganda culture a shepherd is an employee. He is usually a poor fellow working for someone else. So we focused on the idea of someone who takes care of me rather than someone who takes care of my sheep. Thus, we said, "The Lord takes care of me" or "shepherds me." We removed the ambiguity and made it clearer.

Author: Are you happy with this Bible that you translated? Would you have done it differently if you were to do it again?

Father Mbaziira: I am quite happy with it. I do not think I would have done it differently. But there are a few places where a revision would be called for. For example, when Moses is asking for God's name and he is told "I am that I am has sent me" – the Luganda translation is not quite clear. It is rather literal and ungrammatical.

Author: What are the main responses from readers? How about the sales – are people buying it in sufficient numbers?

Father Mbaziira: The demand for the Luganda Bible currently exceeds its availability. We do not have enough copies and many people are asking for it. Currently, I am involved in popularizing and promoting the use of the Bible in the Catholic Church in the Luganda-speaking areas of this country. My dilemma is that I encourage use of the new Luganda translation but am discouraged by the lack of availability in the market. What is needed now is perhaps to think of preparing a Luganda study Bible based on this new translation. This would be timely now that people have read this text and have basically shown that they accept it and love it. A study Bible would be a good follow-up.

Appendix D

Perspectives from the Region

Reflections on Translation and Revision from Timothy G. Kamau, a Reviser of the Swahili Union Version Bible

In August 2007, I had the opportunity to talk at Bible House in Nairobi to one of the revisers of the 1952 Swahili Union Version, Mr Timothy G. Kamau. The following are his recollections, written for this book, of how he and his colleagues went about the awesome task of revising one of East Africa's most important and historically influential translations.

Figure D.1. Timothy G. Kamau

The revision of the Swahili Union Version (SUV) started on April 1, 1999. The revision was jointly done by the three Bible Societies of Kenya, Uganda, and Tanzania, which comprise the Swahili Bible constituency. Uganda, however, did not assigna technical person to the revision team. Therefore, the team was comprised of only two people – Dean Rev Wilson Lugakingira of the Evangelical Lutheran Church of Tanzania's north-western diocese and myself, from the Anglican Church of Kenya. Besides our denominational affiliations, we two revisers were different in several other ways. The elderly Rev Lugakingira, a highly respected clergy in the See, is a New Testament (Greek) and Hebrew scholar and a daily user of the SUV Bible. Younger than my colleague, I am a Swahili scholar specializing in linguistics.

There were times when the literalisms in the biblical languages posed disagreements in our grammatical Swahili renderings. The same occurred in some lexical items like *ilhali* that seemed to be unacceptable to the Tanzania Swahili speech community. At times my colleague and I found ourselves on a collision course with part of the clergy. A case at hand is the change on the word *kumsulibisha* ("to crucify him"), and all its derivations to *kumsulubisha* in line with the current Swahili usage. Some SUV readers, too, were hesitant to see the Bible revised and some openly stated they wanted it retained as it was. The Bible Societies addressed this concern immediately by assuring their constituencies that the SUV, as it is, would remain on the market for conservative readers and traditionalists. It also was clear that the clergy and Bible users in general had not been made aware as to how the revision would likely affect liturgy. Consequently, at times we revisers were called upon to play the role of public relations for the revision.

The revision team encountered several handicaps in changing words like *ghadhabika* ("to be enraged, to be furious"), and *tahayarika* ("to feel ashamed"), and their derivations that were deemed archaic. This is because there were instances where the suggested replacements occurred side by side with these forms. Consequently, some of these forms still persist. Other targeted words that were prominent in the liturgy include: *umbu* that was replaced with *dada* (both meaning "sister"), *chuo* replaced by *kitabu* ("book"), *mkono wa kuume* ("right hand side") by *mkono wa kulia* (lit. "hand for eating"), and many other similar pairs of synonymous words or expressions.

The Rev Lugakingira and I worked in our respective countries with frequent rotational team meetings to discuss the proposed changes. This meant that when an issue that required reference to the original Greek or Hebrew text arose, the Rev Lugakingira was called upon to look into it. However, there were interlinear translations for the biblical texts available for quick references. These proved helpful because SUV is a literal translation. Working in different stations far apart as such proved to be a great challenge for the revision team. Our team meetings were never sufficient to exhaust everything.

We began the task by revising the Old Testament at Genesis, dividing the work onwards. Each reviser read an alternate book noting areas that needed to be revised according to a set of criteria [originally suggested in Eugene Nida and Jan de Waard's book *Functional Equivalence*]:

- Where literal rendering would give an entirely wrong meaning.
- When a borrowed term gives "zero" meaning or if it is entirely meaningless.
- When a literal rendering leads to obscurity in meaning.

- When a literal rendering leads to bad grammar style in the receptor language.
- When a literal rendering leads to ambiguity not in the source text.
- When the style and syntax of the source language is too complex and difficult.

The procedure was that each of the revisers would read his given book noting areas that require revision and take the lead in discussing it during the subsequent team meetings. The first such team meeting that served as the launch of the project was held on 8–9 April 1999, at the United Bible Societies Offices in Nairobi. It was attended by the general secretaries of Kenya, Uganda, and Tanzania, Dr Aloo Mojola (UBS Regional Translation Coordinator and translation consultant assigned to this project), as well as by the two SUV revisers.

The revision process began with our identifying numerous changes, mainly at the word level. It was felt that some of the words were archaic and they needed to be revised to the current language use. Words like *mwivi, wevi,* (singular and plural meaning "thief"), *watumwa* (in the context of servant), *kuume* (for "the right side"), and *hata* (as applied to "until") were replaced with *mwizi, wezi,* (singular and plural meaning "thief"), *watumishi* (pl. "servants"), *kulia* (right hand side), and *hadi* ("until") in the specified contexts. Other words like *marago* for "camp" (Lev 6:11) were replaced with *kambi* (modern equivalent of *marago*). We cannot also fail to note the change of *kunya* (originally meaning "to rain" but now means "to defecate") to *kunyesha* (which means "to rain").

Beyond the word level, compound nouns like *kondoo mume* ("male sheep," Lev 5:16) were regarded as incorrect and were replaced with *kondoo dume* ("male sheep"). Similarly, *mtoto mwanamume* ("male child," Judg 13:7) was replaced with *mtoto wa kiume* ("male child") for obvious cultural reasons. The hyphenation for words like *mwana-kondoo* ("lamb") and like compound words was dropped. Similarly, the spaces in *o-rejeshi-* (the grammatical relative pronoun) and constructions like *ye yote, lo lote, ko kote* were changed to *yeyote, lolote,* and *kokote.*

In cases of archaic tenses like **nalisikia** ("I heard") in Gen 3:10 and **nalidhani** ("I thought") Judges 15:2, the revision team resolved to use the conventional past tense *nilisikia* ("I heard") and *nilidhani* ("I thought"), respectively. The other tense that was seen to be archaic was that of *kuifikilia* ("to reach it") in Josh 16:3 and *itakapokujilia* ("when it get to you") in 1 Sam 16:16, to the more common forms of *kuifikia* and *itakapokujia,* respectively.

Sayings like *kifulifuli hata nchi* ("face downwards on the ground") in 2 Sam 24:20 were replaced with *kifudifudi hadi chini* (same as above). Other idioms that that do not capture the intended meaning in Swahili were also revised. A good example is 1 Sam 24:3 where we read *Sauli aliingia ndani ili kuifunika miguu* ("Saul entered inside in order to cover his feet") which is an obscure literal translation of the Hebrew idiom "to cover his feet." This was made more vivid by saying that *Sauli alienda haja* ("Saul went to relieve himself").

Our major hurdle in citing the areas needing corrections was the requirement that we write on a separate sheet that would later on be typed by a keyboarder. Editing what had been typed took quite some time, time which could otherwise have gone into actual revision. The revisers then discussed these changes before passing them on to the keyboarder for entering into the Bible typescript. It was not until we entered the final stages of our work that we, the revisers, started using computers ourselves. We used them mostly for checking our revisions.

The United Bible Societies translation consultant for the revision project was Dr Aloo Mojola who was based at Dodoma. The team also benefited from the advice of another translation consultant, Dr Peter Renju, who was based at the UBS Nairobi offices, where I also worked. The Rev Lugakingira worked from the Evangelical Lutheran Church of Tanzania's northwestern diocesan offices in Bukoba and later on from his residence at Kashura, in the suburbs of Bukoba. Given the participants' multiple commitments, this meant that the revisers only rarely were able to work directly with the consultant, meaning much of the consulting had to be done by phone.

The first team meeting was held in Dodoma in May–June 1999 under the tutelage of Dr Mojola. He took time from his busy schedule to attend to the issues raised by the revisers. Similar subsequent fortnightly meetings were held in Nairobi and Bukoba. A two-day reviewers' meeting involving close to twenty SUV Bible revision reviewers drawn from both Kenya and Tanzania was held at the Kurasini Catholic Center in Dar es Salaam in April 2001. This was the only reviewers' meeting to be held and only the first five books drafted were reviewed. The keyboarders for the SUV revision project included Mrs Margaret Thiong'o during the initial stages, Ms Assumpta Kimathi who did the bulk of it, and Ms Piera Marigu in the final stages. The Bible was typeset by Mr Stephen Mwangi. The entire SUV Bible revision processtook slightly over three and a half years ending on December 31, 2002.

This revision period could have been greatly reduced had the revisers been introduced to using computers in 1999 when we began our work. Another thing that could have helped would have been to put in place a secretariat to handlethe logistics since the project involved more than one country.

The revised SUV has reader-friendly helps that will provide necessary help to lay readers and the clergy alike. These include the introductions to the Bible and to individual biblical books together with a summary of the book's content. There are also section headings within the text. The Revised SUV also includes a chart of weights, measures, and currencies, as well as maps of Bible lands. All in all, it is hoped that the SUV Revised Edition will be more updated in terms of the current Swahili usage than its predecessor – thus, more user friendly to its dynamic users. Those that regard the SUV Bible as the "KJV of the Swahili Bible" should now see a "Swahili NKJV" in the revised SUV.

In conclusion, it's worth noting that we as revisers were careful not to change the nature of the text. In fact, the overall changes introduced needed to be limited to between 20 and 30 percent; anything more, we felt, would constitute a new translation. Because no translation or revision is ever perfect and because languages continue to change and grow, I want to repeat to all speakers of Swahili a challenge and invitation I extended to those who attended the celebration in Nairobi to launch the revision: Please read the Revised SUV and let us know how you feel about it. We sincerely welcome any suggestions you may have on how the translation could be further improved so that God's word will speak clearly and powerfully to all who need God's saving message.

Author's Interview with Dr Peter Masumbuko Renju, former UBS Translation Consultant and Bible Translator

Moshi, Tanzania, 10 October 2007

Figure D.2. Dr Peter Masumbuko Renju. Photo © Aloo Osotsi Mojola

Dr Peter Masumbuko Renju was born in 1936 in Kirua-Moshi, Tanzania. He studied philosophy at the Kibosho Seminary at Kilema, Kilimanjaro. In Rome, he obtained a Masters in theology at the Universitas Urbaniana and a Masters in Sacred Scriptures at the Pontifical Biblical Institute. He received his PhD at the University of Utrecht in the Netherlands in 1986.

Dr Renju worked for many years as an ordained Catholic priest. From 1966 to 1972, he taught at the Kibosho Philosophicum (Tanzania Episcopal Conference) as a lecturer of the Old and New Testament. From 1973 to 1976, he served on behalf of the Tanzania Episcopal Conference as a translator, and as the project coordinator, for the Swahili common language Bible project which produced the Biblia Habari Njema (NT 1977, the complete Bible 1995). From 1974 to 1975 he worked as Assistant to the Catholic Chaplain at St Paul's Catholic Chaplaincy of Nairobi University.

From 1976 to 2001, Dr Renju worked as a translation consultant for the United Bible Societies and was actively involved in training and supervising translators of the various African Bible societies, among them those of Malawi, Angola, Mozambique, Uganda, Tanzania, Kenya, Seychelles, and Madagascar. After retiring in 2002, Dr Renju has continued to serve the UBS fellowship by consulting from time to time on various assignments. Most recently he assisted in the preparation of the Greek-Swahili Interlinear New Testament published in 2008.

AUTHOR: What brought you to Bible translation work?

DR RENJU: The Catholic Church in Tanzania had grown rather . . . weary of the existing Bible translation of the Union Version, first because it did not cover [the church's] interests.[1] Second, the language used in this translation was generally unacceptable, especially with regard to its lexicon, which includes archaic words that no longer communicated meaning in modern Swahili . . . The Catholic Church in Tanzania requested UBS to initiate a new translation [that] would take into consideration the above problems. In 1972, the Tanzania Episcopal Conference agreed to release me from my lecturing position . . . for the newly-set-up interconfessional Bible Society project to translate the Bible in contemporary Swahili.

AUTHOR: As the principal translator of *Biblia Habari Njema*, do you think there was a real need for this? Wasn't the Swahili Union Version enough?
DR RENJU: No, [the SUV was not enough]. There was indeed a need for a new type of translation. There was also the need of having an ecumenical translation . . . Special consideration was to be taken in favor of the growth of the language to cover extensive areas of East Africa. It was observed also that the time had arrived [for] people who have this language as their own day-to-day language of communication [to] be given a chance to decide what style of language was to be used. Most early translations were made by missionaries with the help of some speakers in the area where they worked. It is relevant to note here that the Swahili language has developed very fast since the independence of the countries of East Africa that use this language.

AUTHOR: How did you proceed with this translation?
DR RENJU: We began by laying down principles of translation and the goal of communication. Principles used elsewhere in the Bible Societies' translation projects were studied and relevant approved approaches were adopted, [such as] . . . the principles for common language translations espoused by Dr Eugene Nida. We took into consideration that the Swahili language . . . was not homogenous and that care was to be taken to make sure the translation used a lexicon that is acceptable to the majority of speakers. To achieve this, a team of translators as well as a review committee was established representing various sectors of the community – youth, mature people, as well as Bible scholars and scholars in the Swahili language. As for the source language, at least one translator with knowledge of the original biblical languages . . . was chosen to serve full time.

---

1. Author's note: The Catholic canon of Scripture, besides the sixty-six books of the Protocanon, includes a number of books not typically found in Protestant or Jewish Bibles and which Catholics refer to as the Deuterocanon ("second list").

AUTHOR: What kind of language was used in this translation?

DR RENJU: The common language, the type used in the day-to-day communication of people in Tanzania and Kenya in particular, but [which is] also easily understood by Swahili-speakers in the rest of East Africa [more] generally.

AUTHOR: Did you follow any particular theory of translation?

DR RENJU: The Committee was guided first by the principle that the Bible contains a message that people were expected to understand. Hence the principle of . . . dynamic [equivalence] translation, that is, translation that readily communicates the meaning of the original without the need of an interpreter. In other words, this translation was to avoid obscure words and expressions no longer [used by] ordinary Swahili speakers.

AUTHOR: What Bible translations, if any, influenced your work?

DR RENJU: This is a difficult question . . . The committee, including myself, was [leery of settling upon] "models" for fear of building on a foundation of others and not the original "foundation" (1 Cor 3:12–13). The original was to be followed. However, [one translation that was used for checking purposes] was the Good News Bible. Translators and reviewers were constantly reminded of this. Hence, the value of principles of translation, especially as outlined by Eugene Nida and Charles Taber [in *The Theory and Practice of Translation*].

AUTHOR: With whom did you work?

DR RENJU: First were the translators whose work was drafting. These were selected from the two East African countries of Kenya and Tanzania [and were] Cosmas Haule from Tanzania and Jared Mwanjala from Kenya, among others.

AUTHOR: How long did the work take?

DR RENJU: Work started in earnest in 1970. The NT was published 1977 and the Bible in 1995.

AUTHOR: How was it received among the people?

DR RENJU: In general, it was very well received. I remember at the inauguration of the publication of the New Testament in 1975, the general secretary of the Bible Society of Tanzania, the late Immanuel Kibira, a copy in his hand, announced to the people gathered *Hivi ndivyo Maandiko Matakatifu yanavyosema kwa lugha yetu ya siku hizi!* ("This is how the Scriptures speak in our language today!"). On more than two occasions I have heard a Catholic priest encouraging children who were preparing for Holy Communion, to have a Bible in their hands for the celebration and added, "Not any Bible, but *Biblia Habari Njema kwa Watu Wote*" (i.e. the new contemporary translation in Swahili). It was very well received, especially among Catholics and by youths of different denominations.

AUTHOR: How about the Swahili Study Bible of which you were also the principal editor? What were the challenges in producing this?

DR RENJU: Here we faced enormous challenges. First was the question of how far can one go? In general, the committee, which again was composed of people from Kenya, Tanzania, and Uganda, [and included] some Bible scholars, felt that we should [only provide notes that addressed] problems of understanding the original in its context. Even with this guideline [in place], there [persists] the [more cautious] feeling from certain quarters [that] "no additions, no subtractions, and no changes" [should be made] with regard to the Scriptures. Luckily, more and more people appreciate the problems involved and the production of a study Bible (the first in Swahili, I think) will be appreciated.

AUTHOR: I understand you are also finalizing the *Greek-Swahili Interlinear New Testament* as well as the Greek-Swahili dictionary. What are the challenges in producing such works?

DR RENJU: The first challenge goes with the name itself, "Interlinear" Swahili. The production of this type of translation will be, I think, the first of its kind in our language . . . In the introduction to this publication we indicate why this translation [is needed] and what is its goal, as well as [who we envisioned as its] target users. It is, in brief, a scholarly publication that will be used by translators who want to see the nuances of meaning . . . in the original Greek [in order] to see if these can be meaningfully represented in the target language.

Many major languages of the world have produced such translations, and because Swahili is recognized . . . as one of the major languages of Africa, this alone would warrant a venture of this kind. Translators [working] in different languages within the Swahili-speaking world will be able to appreciate the choices of tense and aspect in the original and [thereby determine] how they can produce the same correctly in *their* languages for *their* people. Others, preachers and exegetes, will have before them a text that can help them to appreciate the meaning in the original language for their people. For translators this will be an indispensable publication.

Now with regard to the *Kamusi ya Kigiriki ya Agano Jipya* ("Dictionary of New Testament Greek"), this also targets scholars and translators. The model here is Barclay Newman's *Greek-EnglishDictionary of the New Testament*. Both the *Greek-Swahili Interlinear NT* and the *Kamusi ya Kigiriki ya Agano Jipya* will be indispensable, I think, for serious study of the New Testament.

Appendix E

History and Achievements of Bible Translation and Literacy in Kenya

Bible Translation and Literacy (BTL) in Kenya

Figure E.1. Headquarters for BTL (Kenya), SIL, and WBT Africa. Photo © Aloo Osotsi Mojola

The following is adapted from a report by Bible Translation and Literacy in Kenya.

In 1977, the Summer Institute of Linguistics (SIL) began carrying out sociolinguistics surveys to determine the translation needs in Kenya. This was done in association with the Bible Society of Kenya (BSK) and the Department of Linguistics and African Languages of the University of Nairobi. The surveys revealed that several small language groups in Kenya which lacked a written system were nonetheless in need of Scriptures. These languages posed a unique challenge that BSK was not prepared to address. It was therefore necessary to start an organization to give priority to this challenge.

While it would have been possible for SIL, a linguistics-based mission organization with a long history of working with primarily oral minority languages, to have begun a branch in Kenya to deal with this situation, it was decided on the encouragement of the SIL Africa Director to establish a new organization for this purpose. This organization, known as Bible Translation and Literacy (BTL), was registered in Kenya on 4 March 1981, as a charitable Christian organization.

With the assistance of SIL, a team called the "Kenya Working Group" was constituted and two language projects, Sabaot and Rendille, were begun in 1981. A local person was appointed as the chief executive officer, that is, as general secretary, in November 1983. However, BTL's operations continued to be managed by the Kenya Working Group, which was essentially an SIL team, until January 1987 when BTL assumed responsibility for translation work in Kenya. BTL became an affiliate of WBTI in May 1996.The following table lists some of the highlights of the still-unfolding story of BTL (Kenya):

Table E.1. Ministry highlights of BLT (Kenya) from 1977 to present

1977	SIL commenced work in Kenya with a socio-linguistic survey of the country.
1981	On 4 March 1981, Bible Translation and Literacy – Kenya was registered with the government as "a company limited by guarantee and not having share capital."
	Translation work commenced on the Sabaot and Rendille languages.
1982	WBT and BTL signed the first cooperative agreement.
1983	Endo and Daasanach language programs commenced.
	Construction of the East African Translation Center was completed.
	In November 1983 the first CEO, the Rev Canon Micah Amukobole was appointed.

1985	Pokomo language program commenced.
1986	Orma language program commenced.
1987	Duruma and Digo language programs commenced.
	Literacy work in Borana language commenced (translation of whole Bible in Borana had been completed in 1985 by BSK).
1988	Tharaka language program commenced.
	The Project planning document "Goals for the 1990s" was adopted by the BTL Board.
1989	Giriama language program commenced.
	Malakote language program commenced.
1991	BTL was registered as an NGO with the Office of the President, Kenya.
1992	Suba language program commenced.
1993	Ilwana (Malakote) program suspended due to persistent insecurity.
1994	Ruiru Center started operating and providing services.
1995	Aweer (Boni) language program was commenced.
	"Goals for the 1990s" document was revised.
1996	BTL became an affiliate of WBTI.
1997	BTL published the New Testament in Sabaot.
2000	Direct secondment to BTL of WO members began.
	Duruma NT published.
2001	Tharaka NT published.
	UNESCO recognition of the literacy activities of BTL.
2004	Ilchamus project commenced.
	Giriama NT published.
2005	Samburu project commenced.
	Centre for Literacy and Language Development commenced work
	Pokomo NT published.
	Tharaka OT started.
2007	Digo NT published.
2008	Giriama OT started.
	Pokomo OT started.
2009	Marakwet NT published.

2010	Digo OT started.
	Duruma OT started.
2011	Suba NT published.
2012	Sabaot Bible published.
	Marakwet OT started.
2013	Start-up projects started in Chonyi, Tugen and Upper Pokomo language communities.
2014	Start-up projects started in Chuka and Taveta language communities.
	Daasanach NT published.
	Orma NT published.

Bibliography

Archival Records

Documents listed here are from the British and Foreign Bible Society Archives at Cambridge University Library, West Road, Cambridge, CB3 9DR, catalogue A-E1 and A-E2. Online catalogue of materials available at the BFBS collection at the Cambridge University Library can be viewed at the following URL: http:/janus.lib.cam.ac.uk. ESC refers to Editorial sub-committee minutes; LSC refers to Library sub-committee minutes.

BFBS- ESC Minute Cards, vols. 4 and 5
BSA/E3 Records of Editorial/Translations Department
BSA/E3/3/1 Correspondence incoming 1832–1908
BSA/E3/1/4 Editorial correspondence incoming 1858–1897
BSA/E3/2 Correspondence outgoing 1832–1908
BSA/E3/3 Correspondence language files 1908–onwards
BSA/E3/3/30 Chasu 1909–1968
BSA/E3/3/50 Bena 1914–1965
BSA/E3/3/189 Ha Nov 1952–Oct 1965
BSA/E3/3/191 Hanga Aug 1913–Apr 1942
BSA/E3/3/194 Haya 1918–1972
BSA/E3/3/223 Jita July1953–Nov 1961 and June 1968
BSA/E3/3/231 Kaguru March 1965–June 1973
BSA/E3/3/233 Kakwa Aug 1964–July1971
BSA/E3/3/235 Kalenjin 1956–1977
BSA/E3/3/236 Kamba 1909–1974
BSA/E3/3/241 Karamojong 1955–1974
BSA/E3/3/246 Kavirondo, includes Ragoli Aug 1913–Nov 1946
BSA/E3/3/247 Kebu Mar 1954–Apr 1964
BSA/E3/3/253 Kikuyu 1909–1972
BSA/E3/3/257 Kipsigis (Lumbwa) May 1912–Mar 1939
BSA/E3/3259 Kisii 1955–1976
BSA/E3/3/317 Lugbara 1921–1972
BSA/E3/3/316 Luganda 1908–1973
BSA/E3/3/320 Luo 1909–1976
BSA/E3/3/321 Lusoga Dec 1910–Jan 1911

BSA/E3/3/324 Luyia 1946–1977

BSA/E3/3/328 Makua April 1923–Oct 1946 and Sept 1961–Feb 1964

BSA/E3/3/359 Maasai 1914–1970

BSA/E3/3/374 Meru-Kenya 1918–1974

BSA/E3/3/375 Meru-Tanzania Feb 1957–Feb 1966

BSA/E3/3/409 Namwanga (Inamwanga) 1912–1979

BSA/E3/3/410 Nandi-Kipsigis 1912–1955

BSA/E3/3/428 Ngwana Congo Swahili

BSA/E3/3/433 Nkole (incl Konjo) Apr 1909–Dec 1955

BSA/E3/3/434 Nkore-Kiga 1956–1977

BSA/E3/3 Nyakyusa-Ngonde 1952–1971

BSA/E3/3/448 Nyamwezi Mar 1909–June 1971

BSA/E3/3/454 Nyoro 1911–1977

BSA/E3/3/479 Pokomo Mar 1909–May1936

BSA/E3/3/490 Ragoli May 1859–May 1969

BSA/E3/3/498 Ruanda 1913–1973

BSA/E3/3/500 Rundi June 1952–Sept 1973

BSA/E3/3/512 Sebei July 1969–Nov 1972

BSA/E3/3/519 Shambala July 1910–June 1963

BSA/E3/3/531 Somali 1910–1977

BSA/E3/3/543 Sukuma 1910–1974

BSA/E3/3/545 Swahili Jan 1909–Aug 1974

BSA/E3/3/546 Swahili popular June 1964–Aug 1974

BSA/E3/3/552 Taita (Dabida and Sagalla) 1910–1966

BSA/E3/3/563 Teso June 1909–1966

BSA/E3/3/588 Turkana May 1935–Mar 1975

BSA/E3/3/623 Zaramo Jan 1966–May 1974

BSA/E3/3/629 East African languages (correspondence with W. J. W. Roome, Agent, tour reports, etc. Jan 1917–Mar 1952: 8 files

BSA/D3/3/18 1931–1969: 9 files (Kenya).

BSA/D3/3/18/1 papers regarding versions in Swahili 1931–1940

BSA/D3/3/18/2 papers regarding versions in Swahili 1941–1951

BSA/D3/3/18//3 papers regarding versions in Luyia (Hanga and Luo) 1932–1950

BSA/D3/3/18/4 papers regarding versions in Kamba, Kipsigis, and Nandi 1932–1950

BSA/D3/3/18/5 papers of versions in Kikuyu 1933–1950

BSA/D3/3/18/6 miscellaneous correspondence and papers regarding staff 1949–1969

BSA/D3/3/18/7 papers regarding the Kenya Council of the Bible Society and the Bible Society in East Africa 1948–1967

BSA/D3/3/18/8 correspondence regarding Roman Catholic use of the Swahili Bible 1962–1965

BSA/D3/3/18/9 correspondence regarding the resolution of the Council for Cooperation in Nairobi 1931 and the gift for support of colportage in East Africa 1934–1940

BSA/D3/3/29 Tanganyika 1930–1956: 2 files

BSA/D3/3/29/1 papers regarding versions in Gogo and Nyakyusa Ngonde

BSA/D3/3/29/2 papers regarding versions in Kijita and Luhaya (Haya) 1930–1950

BSA/D3/3/30 Uganda 1933–1968: 2 files

BSA/D3/3/30/1 miscellaneous correspondence, David Cohen's account of the Uganda tour, and papers regarding the Teso Bible 1951–1968

BSA/D3/3/30/2 papers regarding versions in Karamojong, Luganda, and Lugbara 1933–1950

Books, Articles, Chapters

Abdulaziz, Mohammed H. "Tanzania's National Language Policy and the Rise of Swahili Political Culture." In *Language Use and Social Change: Problems of Multilingualism with Special Reference to Eastern Africa*, edited by Wilfred Whiteley, 160–178. London: Oxford University Press, 1971.

———. *Muyaka: 19th Century Swahili Poetry.* Nairobi: Kenya Literature Bureau, 1979.

Abungu, George H. O. "City-states of the East African Coast and Their Maritime Contacts." In *Transformations in Africa: Essays on Africa's Later Past*, edited by Graham Connah, 204–218. London: Leicester University Press, 1998.

Abuto, Paul Asaka. *A Traditional History of the Abakuria: 1400–1914.* Nairobi: Kenya Literature Bureau, 1980.

Ali, Tariq. *The Clash of Fundamentalisms: Crusades, Jihads and Modernity.* London: Verso, 2002.

Allen, James de Vere. *Swahili Origins: Swahili Culture and the Shungwaya Phenomenon.* London: James Currey, 1993.

American Bible Society. "Historical Essays." Unpublished. New York: American Bible Society Library and Archives.

Anderson, David M., and Richard Rathbone, eds. *Africa's Urban Past.* Oxford: James Currey, 2000.

Anderson, David M., and Vigdis Broch-Due, eds. *The Poor Are Not Us: Poverty and Pastoralism.* East African Studies. Oxford: James Currey; Nairobi: East Africa Educational Publishing; Athens: Ohio University Press, 1999.

Anderson-Morshead, A. E. *The History of the Universities' Mission to Central Africa.* Vol. 1., 1859–1909. London: UMCA, 1956.

Anderson, William B. *The Church in East Africa 1840–1974.* Dodoma: Central Tanganyika Press, 1977.

Angogo, Rachel M. "Dialect Problems and Bible Translation." *The Bible Translator* 33, no. 1 (1982):127–134.

———. "Standard Swahili: Its History and Development." MA diss. University of Texas, Austin, 1978.

———. *Unity in Diversity: A Linguistic Survey of the Abaluyia of Western Kenya.* Vienna: Afro-Pub, 1983.

Apter, David E. *The Political Kingdom in Uganda.* Princeton: Princeton University Press, 1961.

Arnaud, Gerard, and Henri Lecomte. *Musiques de toutes les Afriques.* Paris: Fayard, 2006.

Asante, Molefi Kete. *The History of Africa: The Quest for Eternal Harmony.* New York and London: Routledge, 2007.

Asaka Abuto, Paul. *A Traditional History of the Abakuria: 1400–1914.* Nairobi: Kenya Literature Bureau, 1980.

Askew, Kelly M. *Performing the Nation: Swahili Music and Cultural Politics in Tanzania.* Chicago: University of Chicago Press, 2002.

Ayot, Henry Okello. *A History of the Luo-Abasuba of Western Kenya: from AD 1760–1940.* Nairobi: Kenya Literature Bureau, 1979.

Banham, Martin, ed. *A History of Theatre in Africa.* Cambridge: Cambridge University Press, 2003.

Barnard, Alan. *Hunters and Herders of Southern Africa: A Comparative Ethnography of the Khoisan Peoples.* Cambridge: Cambridge University Press, 1992.

Barrett, David B. *African Initiatives in Religion.* Nairobi: East African Publishing House, 1971.

———. *Schism and Renewal in Africa: An Analysis of Six Thousand Contemporary Religious Movements.* Nairobi: Oxford University Press, 1968.

———. "The Spread of the Bible and the Growth of the Church in Africa." *UBS Bulletin* 128/129 (1982/1984): 5–18.

Barrett, David B., George K. Mambo, Janice Mclaughlin, and Malcom J. McVeigh, eds. *Kenya Churches Handbook: The Development of Kenyan Christianity 1498–1973.* Kisumu, Kenya: Evangel Publishers, 1973.

Bart, Francois, Milline Jethro Mbonile, and Francois Devenne, eds. *Kilimanjaro: Mountain, Memory, Modernity.* Dar es Salaam: Mkuki na Nyota Publishers, 2006.

Bassnett, Susan. *Translation Studies.* New York: Routledge, 1991.

Bastin, Yvonne. "The Interlacustrine Zone (Zone J)." In *The Bantu Languages,* edited by Derek Nurse and Gérard Philippson, 501–528. London: Routledge, 2003.

Baur, John. *The Catholic Church in Kenya: A Centenary History.* Nairobi: St Paul Publications Africa, 1990.

———. *2000 Years of Christianity in Africa: An African History, 62–1992.* Nairobi: Paulines Publications, 1994.

Bedford, Francis J. *The Bible in East Africa.* London: British and Foreign Bible Society, 1954.

Bediako, Kwame. *Christianity in Africa: The Renewal of a Non-Western Religion.* New York: Orbis Books, 1995.

Beidelman, T. O. *Moral Imagination in Kaguru Modes of Thought*. Bloomington: Indiana University Press, 1986.

Berry, John A., and Carol Pott Berry. *Genocide in Rwanda: A Collective Memory*. Washington, DC: Howard University Press, 1999.

Bierman, John. *Dark Safari: The Life Behind the Legend of Henry Morton Stanley*. New York: Alfred Knopf, 1990.

Binns, H. K. *Swahili-English Dictionary: Being Dr Krapf's Original Swahili-English Dictionary Revised and Rearranged*. London: SPCK, 1925.

Blood, A. G. *The History of the Universities' Mission to Central Africa*. Vol. 2, 1907–1932. London: UMCA, 1957.

———. *The History of the Universities' Mission to Central Africa*. Vol. 3, 1933–1957. London: UMCA, 1962.

Brock, Beverley. "The Nyiha (of Mbozi)." In *Tanzania before 1900*, edited by Andrew Roberts, 59–81. Nairobi: East African Publishing House, 1968.

Burke, David G. "Text and Context." *Current Trends in Scripture Translation UBS Bulletin* 194/195 (2002): 299–332.

Byaruhanga-Akiiki, A. B. T. *Religion in Bunyoro*. Nairobi: Kenya Literature Bureau, 1982.

Cagnolo, C. *The Agikuyu: Their Customs, Traditions and Folklore*. New edition edited by Hilary Wambugu, James Mwangi Ngarariga, and Peter Muriithi Kariuki. Nairobi: Wisdom Graphics Place, 2006.

Cancel, Robert, and Winifred Woodhull, eds. *African Diasporas: Ancestors, Migrations and Boundaries*. Trenton, NJ: Africa World Press, 2008.

Casad, Eugene H. *Dialect Intelligibility Testing*. Dallas: Summer Institute of Linguistics, 1974.

Casco, Jose Arturo Saavedra. *Utenzi, War Poems, and the German Conquest of East Africa: Swahili Poetry as Historical Resource*. Trenton, NJ: Africa World Press, 2007.

Chanda, Nayan. *Bound Together: How Traders, Preachers, Adventurers and Warriors Shaped Globalization*. New Haven, CT: Yale University Press, 2007.

Chebet, Susan, and Ton Dietz. *Climbing the Cliff: A History of the Keiyo*. Eldoret: Moi University Press, 2000.

Chesaina, Ciarunji. *Oral Literature of the Embu and Mbeere*. Nairobi: East African Educational Publishers, 1997.

Chubwa, P. *Waha: Historia na Maendeleo*. Tabora, Tanzania: TMP Book Department, 1979.

Church, Joe E. *An Autobiographical Account of the East African Revival*. Exeter: Paternoster Press, 1981.

Cisternino, Mario. *Passion for Africa: Missionary and Imperial Papers on the Evangelisation of Uganda and Sudan, 1848–1923*. Kampala, Uganda: Fountain Publishers, 2004.

Church Missionary Society. *CMS Missions in East Africa*. London: Christian Missionary Society Publications, 1913.

Coetzee, P. H., and A. P. J. Roux, eds. *Philosophy from Africa: A Text with Readings*. Cape Town: Oxford University Press, 2002.

Cohen, David William, and E. S. Atieno Odhiambo. *Siaya: The Historical Anthropology of an African Landscape*. Oxford: James Currey, 1989.

Coldham, Geraldine E. *A Bibliography of Scriptures in African Languages*. Vols. 1 and 2. London: British and Foreign Bible Society, 1966.

Connah, Graham. *African Civilizations: An Archaeological Perspective*. Cambridge: Cambridge University Press, 1987.

————, ed. *Transformation in Africa: Essays on Africa's Later Past*. London: Leicester University Press, 1998.

Conteh-Morgan, John. "Francophone Africa South of the Sahara." In *A History of Theatre in Africa*, edited by Martin Banham, 85–137. Cambridge: Cambridge University Press, 2003.

Crazzolara, Joseph Pasquale. *The Lwoo*. 3 vols. Verona: Istituto Missioni Africane, 1951–1954.

————. *Outlines of a Nuer Grammar*. Vienna: Missionsdruckerei St. Gabriel, 1933.

————. *A Study of the Acholi Language: Grammar and Vocabulary*. 2nd ed. London: Oxford University Press, 1955.

————. *A Study of the Logbara (Ma'adi) Language: Grammar and Vocabulary*. London: Oxford University Press, 1960.

————. *A Study of the Pokot (Suk) Language: Grammar and Vocabulary*. Bologna: EMI, 1958.

————. *Zur Gesellschaft und Religion der Nueer*. Vienna: Missionsdruckerei St. Gabriel, 1953.

Criper, Clive, and Peter Ladefoged. "Linguistic Complexity in Uganda." In *Language Use and Social Change: Problems of Multilingualism with Special Reference to Eastern Africa*, edited by Wilfred Whiteley, 145–159. London: Oxford University Press, 1971.

de Waard, Jan, and Eugene A. Nida. *From One Language to Another: Functional Equivalence in Bible Translating*. Nashville: Nelson, 1986.

Dimmendaal, Gerrit Jan. *The Turkana Language*. Dordrecht: Foris Publications, 1983.

Donovan, Vincent J. *Christianity Rediscovered*. Maryknoll, NY: Orbis Books, 1978.

Doyle, Shane. *Crisis and Decline in Bunyoro: Population and Environment in Western Uganda, 1860–1955*. Oxford: James Currey, 2006.

Dundas, Charles. *Asili na Habari za Wachagga*. London: Sheldon Press, 1932.

————. *Kilimanjaro and Its People: A History of the Wachagga*. London: Witherby, 1924.

Eber, Jochen. *Johann Ludwig Krapf: Ein schwaebischer Pionier in Ostafrika*. Basel, Switzerland: Verlag Arte Media, 2006.

Ehret, Christopher. *The Civilizations of Africa: A History to 1800*. Oxford: James Currey, 2002.

———. *The Historical Reconstruction of Southern Cushitic Phonology and Vocabulary*. Berlin: Verlag, 1980.

Fage, J. D., with William Tordoff. *A History of Africa*. 4th ed. London: Routledge, 2002.

Faupel, J. F. *African Holocaust: The Story of the Uganda Martyrs*. London: Geoffrey Chapman, 1962.

Feierman, Steven. "The Shambaa." In *Tanzania before 1900*, edited by Andrew Roberts, 1–15. Nairobi: East African Publishing House, 1968.

———. *The Shambaa Kingdom: A History*. Madison: University of Wisconsin Press, 1974.

Fjose, Olav. *Sifa Kwa Bwana: Historia ya KKKT: Sinodi ya Mbulu, 1939–1989*. Nairobi: Acme Press, 1993.

Fish, Burnette C., and Gerald W. Fish. *The Kalenjin Heritage: Traditional Religious and Social Practices*. Kericho, Kenya: Africa Gospel Church; Marion, IN: World Gospel Mission, 1995.

Fortes, M., and E. E. Evans-Pritchard, eds. *African Political Systems*. Oxford: Oxford University Press, 1940.

Frankl, P. J. L., and Yahya Ali Omar. "The Word of 'God' in Swahili: Further Considerations." *Journal of Religion in Africa* 25, no. 2 (1995): 202–211.

———. "The Idea of 'the Holy' in Swahili." *Journal of Religion in Africa* 29, no. 1 (1999): 109–114.

Freeman-Grenville, G. S. P. *The East African Coast: Select Documents from the First Century to the Early Nineteenth Century*. London: Oxford University Press, 1962.

Gall, Sandy. *The Bushmen of Southern Africa: Slaughter of the Innocent*. London: Pimlico Random House, 2002.

Gatwa, Tharcisse. *Rwanda—Eglises: Victimes ou Coupables? Les Eglises et l'idéologie ethnique au Rwanda 1900–1994*. Yaoundé: Editions CLE, 2001.

Gentzler, Edwin. *Contemporary Translation Theories*. London: Routledge, 1993.

Ghaidan, Usam. *Lamu: A Study of the Swahili Town*. Nairobi: Kenya Literature Bureau, 1992.

Gilbert, Erik. *Dhows and the Colonial Economy of Zanzibar, 1860–1970*. Oxford: James Currey; Nairobi: East African Educational Publishers, 2004.

Goodman, Morris. "The Strange Case of Mbugu (Tanzania)." In *Pidginization and Creolization of Languages*, edited by Dell Hymes, 243–254. Cambridge: Cambridge University Press, 1971.

Gordon, Jr., Raymond G., ed. *Ethnologue: Languages of the World*. 15th ed. Dallas: SIL International, 2005. Online version: http://www.ethnologue.com/15/.

Grimes, Barbara F., ed. *Ethnologue: Languages of the World*. 12th ed. Dallas: SIL International, 1992.

———, ed. *Ethnologue: Languages of the World*. 14th ed. Dallas: SIL International, 2000.

Greenberg, Joseph H. *The Languages of Africa*. Bloomington: Indiana University Press, 1963.

Guillebaud, Meg. *Rwanda: The Land God Forgot?: Revival, Genocide and Hope*. Grand Rapids, MI: Monarch Books, 2002.

Gusman, Alessandro. "Being a *Mulokole:* Physical and Spiritual Salvation from the East African Revival to the Contemporary Pentecostalism." In *Rwenzori: Histories of an African Mountain*, edited by Cecilia Pennacini and Hermann Wittenberg, 318–340. Kampala: Fountain, 2008.

Guthrie, Malcolm. *The Classification of the Bantu Languages*. Oxford: Oxford University Press, 1948.

Gutkind, Peter C. W. *The Royal Capital of Buganda: A Study of Internal Conflict and External Ambiguity*. The Hague: Mouton, 1963.

Gutt, Ernst-August. *Translation and Relevance: Cognition and Context*. Oxford: Blackwell, 1991.

Gwassa, G. C. K. "The German Intervention and African Resistance in Tanzania." In *A History of Tanzania*, edited by Isaria N. Kimambo and A. J. Temu, 85–122. Nairobi: East African Publishing House, 1969.

Hansen, Holger Bernt. *Mission, Church and State in a Colonial Setting: Uganda, 1890–1925*. Nairobi: Heinemann, 1984.

Harries, Lyndon P. *Grammar of Mwera*. Johannesburg: Witwatersrand University Press, 1950.

Hastings, Adrian. *The Church in Africa, 1450–1950*. Oxford: Clarendon, 1994.

Hauge, Hans-Egil. "Loa, the Sun-Deity of the Iraqw People." *Temenos* 7 (1971): 51–57.

Heine, Bernd, and Derek Nurse, eds. *African Languages: An Introduction*. Cambridge: Cambridge University Press, 2000.

———, eds. *A Linguistic Geography of Africa*. Cambridge: Cambridge University Press, 2008.

Heine, Bernd, and Wilhelm J. G. Mohlig. *Language and Dialect Atlas of Kenya*. Berlin: Verlag, 1980.

Henschel, Johannes. *Alles Begann in Bagamoyo: 100 Jahre Kirche in Ostafrika*. Aachen, Germany: Missio Actuell Verlag, 1983.

Hess, Mahlon M. *Pilgrimage of Faith: Tanzania Mennonite Church, 1934–83*. Musoma and Tarime, Tanzania: Tanzania Mennonite Church; Salunga, PA: Eastern Mennonite Board of Missions and Charities, 1985.

Himbaza, Innocent. *Transmettre la Bible: Une Critique exegetique de la traduction de l'AT: le cas du Rwanda*. Vatican City: Urbaniana University Press, 2001.

Hinnells, John R., ed. *A Handbook of Living Religions*. Harmondsworth: Penguin Books, 1984.

Hodgson, Dorothy L., ed. *Rethinking Pastoralism in Africa*. Oxford: James Currey, 2000.

Hodgson, Robert, and Paul A. Soukoup, eds. *From One Medium to Another: Communicating the Bible Through Multimedia*. Kansas City: Sheed and Ward, 1997.

Hombert, Jean-Marie, and Larry M. Hyman, eds. *Bantu Historical Linguistics: Theoretical and Empirical Perspectives*. Stanford, CA: CSLI, 1999.

Hood, Robert E. *Must God Remain Greek?: Afro Cultures and God Talk*. Minneapolis: Fortress, 1990.

Hymes, Dell H., ed. *Language in Culture and Society: A Reader in Linguistics and Anthropology*. New York: Harper & Row, 1964.

———, ed. *Pidginization and Creolization of Languages*. Cambridge: Cambridge University Press, 1971.

Iliffe, John. *A Modern History of Tanganyika*. London: Cambridge University Press, 1979.

Insoll, Timothy. *The Archaeology of Islam in Sub-Saharan Africa*. Cambridge: Cambridge University Press, 2003.

Isichei, Elizabeth. *A History of Christianity in Africa: From Antiquity to the Present*. London: SPCK, 1995.

Itebete, P. A. N. "Language Standardization in Western Kenya: the Luluyia Experiment." In *Language in Kenya*, edited by Wilfred Whiteley, 87–114. Nairobi: Oxford University Press, 1974.

Jaesche, Ernst. *Bruno Gutmann: His Life, His Thoughts and His Work*. Erlangen, Germany: Verlag der Ev.-Luth. Mission, 1985.

Jesson, Alan F., and Mario Cignoni, eds. *The Impact of the Word on the World: The Bible from Print to Computer*. Rome: United Bible Societies, 2000.

Johnson, C. B. "Some Aspects of Iraqw Religion." *Tanzania Notes and Records* 65 (1966): 53–56.

Johnson, Frederick. Preface to *A Standard Swahili-English Dictionary*. Nairobi: Oxford University Press, 1939.

Johnston, W. P. *My African Reminiscences, 1875–1895*. London: UMCA, 1925.

Jørgensen, Jan J. *Uganda: A Modern History*. New York: St. Martin's Press, 1981.

Kabwegyere, Tarsis B. *The Politics of State Formation and Destruction in Uganda*. Kampala: Fountain Publishers, 1995.

Kagame, Alexis. *Un abrege de l'histoire du Rwanda de 1853–1972*. 2 vols. Butare, Rwanda: Collection Muntu, 1975.

———. *Les organizations socio-familiales de l'ancien Rwanda*. Brussels: Collection des Memoires d l'Academie Royale des Science d'Outre-Mer, 1954.

———. *La philosophie bantu comparée*. Paris: Presence Africaine, 1976.

———. *La philosophie bantu rwandaise de l'être*. Brussels: Collection des Memoires d l'Academie Royale des Science d'Outre-Mer, 1956.

Kamera, W. D. *Hadithi za Wairaqw wa Tanzania*. Dar es Salaam: East African Literature Bureau, 1978.

Kamusi ya Kiingereza-Kiswahili. Dar es Salaam: University of Dar es Salaam, 1996.

Kamusi ya Kiswahili-Kiingereza. Dar es Salaam: University of Dar es Salaam, 2001.

Kamusi ya Kiswahili Sanifu. Dar es Salaam: University of Dar es Salaam, 1981.

Kanyoro, Musimbi. "Indigenizing Translation." *The Bible Translator* 42, no. 2A (1991): 47–56.

Karibwije, Daniel. *Uganda Districts Information Handbook: Expanded Edition 2011–2012*. Kampala: Fountain, 2011.

Karugire, Samwiri R. *A Political History of Uganda*. Nairobi: Heinemann Educational Books, 1980.

Katamba, Francis. "Bantu Nominal Morphology." In *The Bantu Languages*, edited by Derek Nurse and Gérard Philippson, 103–120. London: Routledge, 2003

Keane, Fergal. *Season of Blood: A Rwandan Journey*. London: Penguin, 1995.

Kee, Howard C., ed. *The Bible in the Twenty-first Century: Symposium Papers*. Philadelphia: Trinity Press International, 1993.

Kenyatta, Jomo. *Facing Mount Kenya: The Tribal Life of the Gikuyu*. London: Secker and Warburg, 1938.

Kibira, Josiah M. *Church, Clan and World*. Uppsala: Almqvist and Wiksell, 1974.

Kiessling, Roland, Maarten Mous, and Derek Nurse. "The Tanzanian Rift Valley Area." In *A Linguistic Geography of Africa*, edited by Bernd Heine and Derek Nurse, 186–227. Cambridge: Cambridge University Press, 2008.

Kilaini, Method M. P. *The Catholic Evangelization of Kagera in North-West Tanzania: The Pioneer Period, 1892–1912*. Rome: Pontifical Gregorian University Press, 1990.

Kimambo, Isaria N. "The Impact of Christianity among the Zaramo: A Case Study of Maneromango Lutheran Church." In *East African Expressions of Christianity*, edited by Thomas Spear and Isaria N. Kimambo, 63–82. Oxford: James Currey, 1999.

————. "The Pare." In *Tanzania before 1900*, edited by Andrew Roberts, 16–36. Nairobi: East African Publishing House, 1968.

————. *Penetration and Protest in Tanzania: The Impact of the World Economy on the Pare, 1860–1960*. London: James Currey, 1991.

Kimambo, Isaria N., and A. J. Temu, eds. *A History of Tanzania*. Nairobi: East African Publishing House, 1969.

Kinoti, Hannah, W. "Christology in the East African Revival Movement." In *Jesus in African Christianity*, edited by J. N. K. Mugambi and Laurent Magesa, 60–78. Nairobi: Initiatives, 1989.

Kipkorir, Benjamin E. *People of the Rift Valley: Kalenjin*. London: Evans Brothers, 1985.

Kipkorir, Benjamin E., and F. B. Welbourn. *The Marakwet of Kenya: A Preliminary Study*. Nairobi: East Africa Literature Bureau, 1973.

Kirkeby, Willy A. *English-Swahili Dictionary*. Dar es Salaam: Kakepela Publishing, 2000.

Kisanji, Teofilo. *Historia Fupi ya Kanisa la Kimoravian Tanganyika Magharibi*. Tabora: TMP Press, Kipalapala, n.d.

Kitching, Arthur Leonard. *On the Backwaters of the Nile: Studies of Some Child Races of Central Africa*. New York: Scribner's Sons, 1912.

Knappert, Jan. *Four Centuries of Swahili Verse: A Literary History and Anthology*. London: Heinemann, 1979.

Knox, Elizabeth. Signal on the Mountain: The Gospel in Africa's Uplands, before the First World War. Canberra: Acorn Press, 1991.

Krapf, Johann. *A Dictionary of the Swahili Language*. London: Trübner and Co., 1882
———. *Outline of the Elements of the Kisuáheli Language with Special Reference to the Kiníka Dialect*. Tübingen: Lud. Fried. Fues, 1850.
———. *Reisen in Ostafrika (1858)*. Published in English as *Travels Researches and Missionary Labours During an Eighteen Years' Residence in Eastern Africa (Missionary Researches and Travels)*. London: Frank Cass Publishers, 1968.
Lane, Charles R. *Pastures Lost: Barabaig Economy, Resource Tenure and the Alienation of their Land in Tanzania*. Nairobi: Initiatives Publishers, 1996.
Larson, Mildred L. "Indigenizing the Translation Process: The SIL Perspective." *The Bible Translator* 42, no. 2A (1991): 34–41.
Latourette, Kenneth. *A History of the Expansion of Christianity*. Vol. 4. New York: Harper and Brothers, 1941.
———. *A History of the Expansion of Christianity*. Vol. 5. New York: Harper and Brothers, 1943.
———. *A History of the Expansion of Christianity*. Vol. 6. New York: Harper and Brothers, 1944.
Legum, Colin, and Geoffrey Mmari. *Mwalimu: The Influence of Nyerere*. London: James Currey; Trenton, NJ: Africa World Press, 1995.
Lema, Anza A. "Chagga Religion and Missionary Christianity on Kilimanjaro: The Initial Phase, 1893–1916." In *East African Expressions of Christianity*, edited by Thomas Spear and Isaria N. Kimambo, 39–62. Oxford: James Currey, 1999.
Lemarchand, René. *Burundi: Ethnic Conflict and Genocide*. Cambridge: Cambridge University Press, 1994.
Leopold, Mark. *Inside West Nile: Violence, History and Representation on an African Frontier*. Oxford: James Currey; Kampala: Fountain Publishers, 2005.
Loba-Mkole, Jean-Claude. *Interacting with Scriptures in Africa*. Nairobi: Acton Publishers, 2005.
———. *Triple Heritage: Gospels in Intercultural Mediations*. Pretoria: Sapientia Publishers; Kinshasa: CERIL, 2005.
Lynch, Gabrielle. *I Say to You: Ethnic Politics and Kalenjin in Kenya*. Chicago: University of Chicago Press, 2011.
Maddox, Gregory H. "The Church and Cigogo: Father Stephen Mlundi and Christianity in Central Tanzania." In, *East African Expressions of Christianity*, edited by Thomas Spear and Isaria N. Kimambo, 150–166. Oxford: James Currey, 1999.
Mafeje, Archie. *Kingdoms of the Great Lakes Region: Ethnography of African Social Formations*. Kampala: Fountain Publishers, 1998.
Mahimbi, Evaristo M. *Utenzi wa Yusufu*. Ndanda, Tanzania: Ndanda Mission Press, 1975.
Maho, Jouni. "A Classification of the Bantu Languages: An Update of Guthrie's Referential System." In *The Bantu Languages*, edited by Derek Nurse and Gérard Philippson, 639–651. London: Routledge, 2003

Masele, Balla F. Y. P. "The Linguistic History of Sisuumbwa, Kisukuma and Kinyamwezi in Bantu Zone F." PhD diss., Memorial University of Newfoundland, 2001.

Maxon, Robert M. *East Africa: An Introductory History*. Nairobi: Heinemann, 1989.

Mazrui, Alamin M., and Ibrahim Noor Shariff. *The Swahili: Idiom and Identity of an African People*. Trenton, NJ: Africa World Press, 1994.

Mazrui, Ali A. *The Africans: A Triple Heritage*. Boston: Little, Brown, and Co., 1986

Mazrui, Ali A., and Alamin M. Mazrui. *The Power of Babel: Language and Governance in the African Experience*. Oxford: James Currey, 1998.

———. *Swahili State and Society: The Political Economy of an African Language*. Nairobi: East African Educational Publishers, 1995.

Mazrui, Ali A., and Pio Zirimu. "The Secularization of an Afro-Islamic Language: Church, State and Marketplace in the Spread of Kiswahili." *Journal of Islamic Studies* 1, no. 1 (1990): 24–53.

Mbaabu, Ireri. *Historia ya Usanifishaji wa KisSwahili*. Nairobi: Longman Kenya, Ltd., 1991.

Mbiti, John S. *African Religions and Philosophy*. Nairobi: Heinemann, 1969.

———. *The Bible and Theology in African Christianity*. Nairobi: Oxford University Press, 1986.

———. *Concepts of God in Africa*. London: SPCK, 1970.

———. *New Testament Eschatology in an African Background*. London: Oxford University Press, 1971.

Mbogoni, Lawrence E. Y. *The Cross and the Crescent: Religion and Politics in Tanzania from the 1880s to the 1990s*. Dar es Salaam: Mkuki na Nyota Publishers, 2004.

Mboya, Paulo. *Luo: Kitgi gi timbegi: A Handbook of Luo Customs*. Kisumu, Kenya: Anyange Press, 1938, 1983.

Melvern, Linda R. *A People Betrayed: The Role of the West in Rwanda's Genocide*. London: Zed Books, 2000.

Meyer, Theodor. *Wa-Konde: Maisha, Mila na Desturi za Wanyakyusa*. Mbeya: Motheco Publications, 1993.

Middleton, John. *Lugbara Religion: Ritual and Authority among an East African People*. London: Oxford University Press, 1960.

———. *The World of the Swahili: An African Mercanitle Civilization*. New Haven: Yale University Press, 1992.

Millroth, Berta. *Lyuba: The Traditional Religion of the Sukuma*. Uppsala: Almqvist and Wiksells, 1965.

Mnyampala, Mathias E. *The Gogo: History, Customs and Traditions*. Translated and edited by Gregory H. Maddox. Armonk, and London: M. E. Sharpe, 1995. First published as *Historia, Mila na Desturi za Wagogo*. Nairobi: East African Literature Bureau, 1954.

———. *Utenzi wa Enjili Takaatifu*. Ndanda, Tanzania: Ndanda Mission Press, 1963, 1967.

———. *Utenzi wa Zaburi*. Ndanda, Tanzania: Ndanda Mission Press, 1965.

Mojola, Aloo Osotsi. "Ngũgĩ wa Thiongo's 'Epistemological Break' and Sacred Scripture Translation in African Languages: Two Sides of the Same Coin." In *African Diasporas*, edited by Robert Cancel and Winifred Woodhull, 358–374. Trenton, NJ: Africa World Press, 2008.

———. "Okot p'Bitek and the Translation of Divine Names Across Languages and Cultures – a Case of 'Contested Terrains and Constructed Categories.'" Paper presented at the annual meeting of the African Literature Conference, Alexandria, Egypt, 2003.

———. "Post-colonial Translation Theory and the Swahili Bible in East Africa – Some Critical Observations." In Postcoloniality, Tranlations, and the Bible in Africa, edited by Musa W. Dube and R. S. Wafula, 26–56. Eugene, OR: Wipf & Stock, 2004.

Mol, Frans. *Lessons in Maa: A Grammar of Maasai Language*. Narok, Kenya: Maasai Centre Lemek, 1995.

———. *Maa: A Dictionary of the Maasai Language and Folklore, English-Maasai*. Nairobi: Marketing and Publishing, 1979.

———. *Masaai Language and Culture: Dictionary*. Narok, Kenya: Maasai Centre Lemek, 1996.

Moon, Karen. *Kilwa Kisiwani: Ancient Port City on the East African Coast*. Dar es Salaam: Tanzania Printers, 2005.

Mugambi, J. N. K. *From Liberation to Reconstruction: African Christian Theology after the Cold War*. Nairobi: East African Educational Publishers, 1995.

Mugambi, J. N. K., and Laurent Magesa, eds. *Jesus in African Christianity*. Nairobi: Initiatives, 1989.

Mugo, E. N. *Kikuyu People: A Brief Outline of Their Customs and Traditions*. Nairobi: Kenya Literature Bureau, 1982.

Muriuki, Godfrey. *A History of the Kikuyu: 1500–1900*. Nairobi: Oxford University Press, 1974.

Mutaka, Philip. "The Kinande Bilingual Dictionary: A Tool for Learning about the Nande/Konzo Traditional Culture." In *Rwenzori: Histories of an African Mountain*, edited by Cecilia Pennacini and Hermann Wittenberg, 153–168. Kampala: Fountain, 2008.

Mwangudza, John. *Mijikenda*. London: Evans Brothers, 1983.

Mwaniki, Henry Stanley Kabeca. *Chuka Historical Texts*. Nakuru, Kenya: Media Document Supplies, 2004.

———. *The Living History of Embu and Mbeere to 1906*. Nairobi: Kenya Literature Bureau, 1973.

Mwanzi, Henry A. *A History of the Kipsigis*. Nairobi: Kenya Literature Bureau, 1977.

Mwangudza, John. *Mijikenda*. London: Evans Brothers, 1978.

Ndarubagiye, Leonce. *Burundi: The Origins of the Hutu-Tutsi Conflict*. Nairobi: Leonce Ndarubagiye, 1996.

Ndoleriire, Oswold K. "Language Use and Attitudes in the Rwenzori Region." In *Rwenzori: Histories and Cultures of an African Mountain*, edited by Cecilia Pennacini and Hermann Wittenberg, 143–153. Kampala: Fountain, 2008.

Neill, Stephen. *A History of Christian Missions*. 2nd ed. London: Penguin Books, 1986.

Newman, Barclay M. *Greek-English Dictionary of the New Testament*. Stuttgart: United Bible Societies, 1971.

Newman, James L. *The Peopling of Africa: A Geographic Interpretation*. New Haven: Yale University Press, 1995.

Ngũgĩ wa Thiong'o. *Decolonising the Mind: The Politics of Language and African Literature*. London: James Currey, 1986.

———. *Devil on the Cross*. African Writers Series 200. Nairobi: Heinemann Educational Books, 1982.

———. *A Grain of Wheat*. African Writers Series 36. London: Heinemann Educational Books, 1967.

Nida, Eugene A., ed. *The Book of a Thousand Tongues*. 2nd ed. London: United Bible Societies, 1972.

———. *Toward a Science of Translating*. Leiden: Brill, 1964.

———. "Trends in Bible Translating within the United Bible Societies." *The Bible Translator* 42 no. 2A (1991): 2–5.

Nida, Eugene A., and Charles R. Taber. *The Theory and Practice of Translation*. Leiden: Brill, 1969.

Nida, Eugene A., and Jan de Waard. *From One Language to Another: Functional Equivalence in Translating*. Nashville: Nelson, 1986.

Nida, Eugene A., and William Reyburn. *Meaning Across Cultures*. Maryknoll, NY: Orbis Books, 1981.

Niwagila, Wilson B. *From the Catacombs to a Self-governing Church: A Case Study of the African Initiative and the Participation of the Foreign Missions in the Mission History of the North-western Diocese of the Evangelical Lutheran Church in Tanzania, 1890–1965*. Hamburg: Verlag an der Lottbek, 1991.

Nord, Christiane. *Translating as a Purposeful Activity*. Manchester: St. Jerome, 1997.

Nordbustad, Frøydis. *English-Iraqw Dictionary for Beginners*. Mbulu, Tanzania: Iraqw Language Committee, Christian Literature Center, n.d.

———. *Historia Fupi ya Lugha ya Kiiraqw*. Mbulu, Tanzania: Iraqw Language Committee, Christian Literature Center, n.d.

———. *Iraqw-English Dictionary for Beginners*. Mbulu, Tanzania: Iraqw Language Committee, Christian Literature Center, n.d.

———. *Iraqw for Beginners*. Mbulu, Tanzania: Iraqw Language Committee, Christian Literature Center, 1983.

———. *Iraqw Grammar*. Mbulu, Tanzania: Iraqw Language Committee, Christian Literature Center, 1985.

Noss, Kathleen Jenabu. "Communicating Scriptures through African Performing Arts." In *Interacting with Scriptures in Africa*, edited by Ernst R. Wendland and Jean-Claude Loba-Mkole, 152–164. Nairobi: Acton Publishers, 2005.

Noss, Philip A., ed. *Current Trends in Scripture Translation*. UBS Bulletin 194/195. Ann Arbor: United Bible Societies, 2002.

———. "Mwalimu Julius Nyerere's Scripture Translation in Kiswahili Tenzi Verse." In *African Diasporas*, edited by Robert Cancel and Winifred Woodhull, 390–409. Trenton, NJ: Africa World Press, 2008.

Noss, Philip A., and Peter M. Renju. "The Tenzi of Mwalimu Nyerere: Scripture Translation in Poetic Form." In *Biblical Texts and African Audiences*, edited by Ernst R. Wendland and Jean-Claude Loba-Mkole, 19–34. Nairobi: Acton Publishers, 2004.

Novelli, Bruno. *Aspects of Karimojong Ethnosociology*. Verona: Comboni Missionaries, 1988.

———. *A Grammar of the Karimojong Language*. Berlin: Reimer, 1985.

———. *Karimojong Traditional Religion: A Contribution*. Kampala: Comboni Missionaries, 1999.

Nthamburi, Zablon, ed. *From Mission to Church: A Handbook of Christianity in East Africa*. Nairobi: Uzima Press, 1991.

Nurse, Derek. "Towards a Historical Classification of East African Bantu Languages." In *Bantu Historical Linguistics*, edited by Jean-Marie Hombert and Lary M. Hyman, 1–42. Stanford, CA: CSLI, 1999.

Nurse, Derek, and Gérard Philippson, eds. *The Bantu Languages*. London: Routledge, 2003.

Nurse, Derek, and Thomas Spear. *The Swahili: Reconstructing the History and Language of an African Society, 800–1500*. Philadelphia: University of Pennsylvania Press, 1985.

Nyaga, Daniel. *Customs and Traditions of the Meru*. Nairobi: East African Educational Publishers, 1997.

Nyerere, Julius K., trans. *Juliasi Kaizari*. [Translation of *Julius Caesar* by William Shakespeare.] Dar es Salaam: Oxford University Press, 1969.

———, trans. *Mabepari wa Venisi*. [Translation of *The Merchant of Venice* by William Shakespeare.] Dar es Salaam: Oxford University Press, 1969.

———, trans. *Utenzi wa Enjili: Kadiri ya Utungo wa Luka* [Translation of the Gospel of Luke.] Ndanda, Tanzania: Benedictine Publications, 1996.

———, trans. *Utenzi wa Enjili: Kadiri ya Utungo wa Marko* [Translation of the Gospel of Mark.] Ndanda, Tanzania: Benedictine Publications, 1996.

———, trans. *Utenzi wa Enjili: Kadiri ya Utungo wa Matayo* [Translation of the Gospel of Matthew.] Ndanda, Tanzania: Benedictine Publications, 1996.

———, trans. *Utenzi wa Enjili: Kadiri ya Utungo wa Yohana* [Translation of the Gospel of John.] Ndanda, Tanzania: Benedictine Publications, 1996.

————, trans. *Utenzi wa Matendo ya Mitume* [Translation of the Acts of the Apostles.] Ndanda, Tanzania: Benedictine Publications, 1996.

Nzita, Richard, and Mbaga Niwampa. *Peoples and Cultures of Uganda*. Kampala: Fountain Publishers, 1993.

Oberg, K. "The Kingdom of Ankole in Uganda." In *African Political Systems*, edited by M. Fortes and E. E. Evans-Pritchard, 121–164. Oxford: Oxford University Press, 1940.

Ochieng, W. R. *A Modern History of Kenya, 1895–1980*. Nairobi: Evan Brothers, 1989.

Ocholla-Ayayo, A. B. C. *Traditional Ideology and Ethics among the Southern Luo*. Uppsala: Scandinavian Institute of African Studies, 1976.

Oded, Arye. *Religion and Politics in Uganda: A Study of Islam and Judaism*. Nairobi: East African Educational Publishers, 1995.

Odden, David. "Rufiji-Ruvuma (N10, P10–20)." In *The Bantu Languages*, edited by Derek Nurse and Gérard Philippson, 529–545. London: Routledge, 2003.

Ogot, Bethwell A. *A History of the Luo-Speaking Peoples of Eastern Africa*. Kisumu, Kenya: Anyange Press, 2009.

————. *History of the Southern Luo: Migration and Settlement*. Nairobi: East African Publishing House, 1967.

————. *The Jii-Speakers: Economic Adaptation and Change*. Kisumu: Anyange Press, 1996.

————. *A Political and Cultural History of the Jii-Speaking Peoples of Eastern Africa*. Kisumu: Anyange Press, 2004.

Ogot, Bethwell A., and J. A. Kieran. *Zamani: A Survey of East African History*. Nairobi: East African Publishing House, 1968.

Okot p'Bitek. *African Religions in Western Scholarship*. Nairobi: Kenya Literature Bureau, 1970.

————. *Religion of the Central Luo*. Nairobi: Kenya Literature Bureau, 1971.

————. *Song of Lawino*. Nairobi: East African Publishing House, 1966.

————. *Song of Ocol*. Nairobi: East African Publishing House, 1970.

————. *Two Songs: Song of Prisoner and Song of Malaya*. Nairobi: East African Publishing House, 1971.

Oliver, Roland A. *The Missionary Factor in East Africa*. 2nd ed. London: Longmans Green, 1970.

Olson, Howard S. *Jifunze Kiyunani cha Agano Jipya*. Dodoma, Tanzania: Central Tanganyika Press, 1972, 1985.

Olson, Steve. *Mapping Human History: Unravelling the Mystery of Adam and Eve*. London: Bloomsbury, 2003.

Omari, Cuthbert K. "The Making of an Independent Church: The Case of the African Missionary Evangelical Church among the Meru of Tanzania." In *East African Expressions of Christianity*, edited by Thomas Spear and Isaria N. Kimambo, 196–212. Oxford: James Currey, 1999.

Omondi, Lucia Ndong'a. *The Major Syntactic Structures of Dholuo*. Berlin: Reimer, 1982.

Omulokoli, Watson A. O. "The Contribution of George L. Pilkington to Christian work in Uganda, 1890–1897." Unpublished paper, 1995.

———. "The Historical Development of the Anglican Church among the Abaluyia, 1905–1955." PhD diss., University of Aberdeen, Scotland, 1981.

———. "The Legacy of Dr Johann Ludwig Krapf." Typescript, 1991.

Osborn, H. H. *Fire in the Hills: The Revival which Spread from Rwanda*. Crowborough: Highland Books, 1991.

Osogo, John. *A History of the Baluyia*. London: Oxford University Press, 1966.

———. *Nabongo Mumia*. Nairobi: Kenya Literature Bureau, 1967.

Pakenham, Thomas. *The Scramble for Africa*. London: Abacus Books, 1991.

Panter-Brick, Catherine, Robert H. Layton, and Peter Rowley-Conway, eds. *Hunter Gatherers: An Interdisciplinary Perspective*. Cambridge: Cambridge University Press, 2001.

Pennacini, Cecilia. "The Rwenzori Ethnic 'Puzzle.'" In *Rwenzori: Histories of an African Mountain*, edited by Cecilia Pennacini and Hermann Wittenberg, 59–97. Kampala: Fountain, 2008.

Pennacini, Cecilia, and Hermann Wittenberg, eds. *Rwenzori: Histories and Cultures of an African Mountain*. Kampala: Fountain Publishers, 2008.

Perrott, D. V. *Teach Yourself Swahili*. London: English Universities Press, 1969. Originally published in 1951.

Philippson, Gérard, and Marie-Laure Montlahuc. "Kilimanjaro Bantu (E60 and E74)." In *The Bantu Languages*, edited by Derek Nurse and Gérard Philippson, 475–500. London: Routledge, 2003.

Pirouet, Louise. *Black Evangelists: The Spread of Christianity in Uganda, 1891–1914*. London: Collings, 1978.

Polome, Edgar C. "Part 1: Languages of Tanzania." In *Language in Tanzania*, edited by Edgar C. Polome and C. P. Hill, 3–102. Oxford: Oxford University Press, 1980.

———. *Swahili Language Handbook*. Washington, DC: Centre for Applied Linguistics, 1967.

Polome, Edgar C., and C. P. Hill, eds. *Language in Tanzania*. Oxford: Oxford University Press, 1980.

Pottier, Johan. *Reimagining Rwanda: Conflict, Survival and Disinformation in the Late Twentieth Century*. Cambridge: Cambridge University Press, 2002.

Prunier, Gérard. *The Rwanda Crisis, 1959–1994: History of a Genocide*. London: Hurst, 1995.

Raum, Johannes. *Versuch einer Grammatik der Dschaggasprache: Moschi-Dialekt*. Reprint ed. Farnbough: Gregg, 1964. Originally published Berlin: Reimer, 1909.

Ray, Benjamin. *Myth, Ritual and Kingship in Buganda*. New York: Oxford University Press, 1991.

Reader, John. *Kilimanjaro*. London: Elm Tree Books, 1982.

Redmayne, Alison. "The Hehe." In *Tanzania before 1900*, edited by Andrew Roberts, 37–58. Nairobi: East African Publishing House, 1968.

Reid, Richard, and Henri Medard. "Merchants, Missions and the Remaking of the Urban Environment in Buganda c. 1840–90." In *Africa's Urban's Past*, edited by David M. Anderson and Richard Rathbone, 98–108. Oxford: James Currey, 2000.

Reinisch, Leo. *Die Somali Sprache.* Vol. 1. Vienna: A. Hölder, 1900.

Renju, Peter M. "The Passover Lamb." *The Bible Translator* 52, no. 2 (2001): 229–234.

Renju, Peter, and Joseph Donders. *Mbinu za Kujifunza.* Tabora, Tanzania: Tanganyika Mission Press, 1974.

Report of the Committee for the Standardisation of the Swahili Language. Dar es Salaam: Government Printer, 1925.

Richards, C. G. *Ludwig Krapf: Missionary, Explorer and Africanist.* Nairobi: East African Literature Bureau, 1973.

Rigby, Peter. *Cattle and Kinship among the Gogo: A Semi-Pastoral Society of Central Tanzania.* Ithaca, NY: Cornell University Press, 1967.

Rijks, Piet. *A Guide to Catholic Bible Translations.* Vol. 2, *Africa.* Stuttgart: World Catholic Federation for the Biblical Apostolate, 1989.

Robert, Shabaan. *Pambo la Lugha.* Nairobi: Oxford University Press, 1966.

Roberts, Andrew. "The Nyamwezi." In *Tanzania before 1900*, edited by Andrew Roberts, 117–150. Nairobi: East African Publishing House, 1968.

———, ed. *Tanzania before 1900.* Nairobi: East African Publishing House, 1968.

———. *Uganda's Great Rift Valley.* Kampala: Andrew Roberts, 2007.

Robertson, Edwin H. *Taking the Word to the World: 50 Years of the United Bible Societies.* Nashville: Nelson, 1996.

Romero, Patricia W. *Lamu: History, Society, and Family in an East African Port City.* Princeton, NJ: Wiener, 1997.

Roscoe, J. *The Baganda: An Account of Their Native Customs and Beliefs.* London: Macmillan, 1911.

Rottland, Franz. *Die Suednilotischen Sprachen: Beschreibung, Vergleichung und Rekonstruktion.* Berlin: Reimer, 1982.

Rwabwoogo, Mugisha Odrek. *Uganda Districts Information Handbook.* Kampala: Fountain Publishers, 1995/96.

Sahlberg, Carl-Erik. *From Krapf to Rugambwa: A Church History of Tanzania.* Nairobi: Evangel Publishing House, 1986.

Sankan, S. S. *The Maasai.* Nairobi: East African Literature Bureau, 1971.

Sanneh, Lamin. "Gospel and Culture: The Ramifying Effects of Scriptural Translation." In *Bible Translation and the Spread of the Church*, edited by Philip C. Stine, 1–23. Leiden: Brill, 1990.

———. *Translating the Message: The Missionary Impact of Culture.* Maryknoll, NY: Orbis Books, 1989.

Schaaf, Ype. *On Their Way Rejoicing: The History and Role of the Bible in Africa.* Carlisle: Paternoster, 1994.

Scriptures of the World. Reading: United Bible Societies, 1995.

Shaw, R. Daniel. *Transculturation: The Cultural Factor in Translation and other Communication Tasks.* Pasadena, CA: William Carey Library, 1988.

Sheriff, Abdul. *Slaves, Spices and Ivory in Zanzibar: Integration of an East African Commercial Empire into the World Economy, 1770–1873.* London: James Currey, 1987.

Sheriff, Abdul, and Ed Ferguson, eds. *Zanzibar under Colonial Rule.* Nairobi: Heinemann Kenya; London: James Currey, 1991.

Shorter, Aylward. "African Religions." In *A Handbook of Living Religions,* edited by John R. Hinnells, 425–438. Harmondsworth: Penguin Books, 1984.

Sim, Stuart. *Fundamentalist World: The New Dark Age of Dogma.* Cambridge, UK: Icon Books, 2004.

Smith, Andrew B., Candy Malherbe, Mat Guenther, and Penny Berens. *The Bushmen of Southern Africa: A Foraging Society in Transition.* Cape Town: David Philip; Athens: Ohio University Press, 2000.

Smith, L., P. Rose, G. Wahida, and S. Wahida, eds. *Fifty Years in the Archaeology of Africa: Themes in Archaeological Theory and Practice.* Nairobi: British Institute in East Africa, 2004.

Smythe, Kathleen R. "The Creation of a Catholic Fipa Society: Conversion in Nkansi District, Ufipa." In *East African Expressions of Christianity,* edited by Thomas Spear and Isaria N. Kimambo, 129–149. Oxford: James Currey, 1999.

Southall, Aidan. *Alur Society: A Study in Processes and Types of Domination.* Cambridge: W. Heffer and Sons, 1953.

Spear, Thomas T. *The Kaya Complex: A History of the Mijikenda Peoples of the Kenya Coast to 1900.* Nairobi: Kenya Literature Bureau, 1978.

Spear, Thomas, and Isaria N. Kimambo. *East African Expressions of Christianity.* Oxford: James Currey, 1999.

Spear, Thomas, and Richard Waller, eds. *Being Maasai: Ethnicity and Identity in East Africa.* Nairobi: East African Educational Publishers, 1993.

Stacey, Tom. "The Snows of Rwenzururu and the Kingdom." In *Rwenzori: Histories of an African Mountain,* edited by Cecilia Pennacini and Hermann Wittenberg, 7–17. Kampala: Fountain, 2008.

Steer, Roger. *The Story of the Bible Society: 200 Years of Making the Bible Heard.* Oxford: Monarch, 2004.

Steere, Edward. *Handbook of the Swahili Language as Spoken in Zanzibar.* London, Bell and Daldy, 1870. A recent reprinting as published by Asian Educational Services, New Delhi, 1999.

Steinhart, Edward I. *Conflict and Collaboration in the Kingdoms of Western Uganda.* Kampala: Fountain Publishers, 1999.

Stine, Philip C., ed. *Bible Translation and the Spread of the Church.* Leiden: Brill, 1990.

Strandes, Justus. *The Portuguese Period in East Africa*. Nairobi: Kenya Literature Bureau, 1961. First published as *Die Portugiesenzeit von Deutsch-und Englisch-Ostafrika* (Berlin: Reimer, 1899).

Sundkler, Bengt, and Christopher Steed. *A History of the Church in Africa*. Cambridge: Cambridge University Press, 2000.

Sutton, John E. G., ed. *The Growth of Farming Communities in Africa from the Equator Southwards*. Nairobi: The British Institute in East Africa, 1996.

———. *A Thousand Years of East Africa*. Nairobi: British Institute in Eastern Africa, 1990.

Swantz, Marja-Liisa. *Ritual and Symbol in Transitional Zaramo Society: With Special Reference to Women*. Uppsala: Scandinavian Institute of African Studies, 1986.

Taylor, John V. *The Growth of the Church in Buganda*. London: SCM, 1958.

Topan, Farouk. "Swahili as a Religious Language." *Journal of Religion in Africa* 22 no. 4 (1992): 331–349.

Tourigny, Yves. *So Abundant a Harvest: The Catholic Church in Uganda, 1879–1979*. London: Darton Longman & Todd, 1979.

Toweett, Taaitta. *Oral Traditional History of the Kipsigis*. Nairobi: Kenya Literature Bureau, 1979.

———. *A Study of Kalenjin Linguistics*. Nairobi: Kenya Literature Bureau, 1979.

Tuma, Tom, and Phares Mutibwa. *A Century of Christianity in Uganda*. Nairobi: Uzima Press, 1978.

Twaddle, Michael. *Kakungulu and the Creation of Uganda, 1868–1928*. London: James Currey, 1993.

van der Jagt, Krijn. *Symbolic Structures of Turkana Religion*. Assen/Maastricht, Netherlands: Van Gorcum, 1989.

von Sicard, S. *The Lutheran Church on the Coast of Tanzania, 1887–1914: With Special Reference to the Evangelical Lutheran Church in Tanzania, Synod of Uzaramo-Ulugulu*. Uppsala: Almqvist and Wiksells, 1970.

Wallis, Andrew. *Silent Accomplice: The Untold Story of the France's Role in Rwandan Genocide*. London: I. B. Tauris, 2006.

Walls, Andrew F. *The Cross-Cultural Process in Christian History*. New York: Orbis Books, 2002.

———. *The Missionary Movement in Christian History*. Maryknoll, NY: Orbis Books, 1996.

———. "The Legacy of David Livingstone." *International Bulletin of Mission Research* 11, no. 3 (July 1987): 125–129.

Wanjohi, Gerald Joseph. *Under One Roof: Gikuyu Proverbs Consolidated*. Nairobi: Paulines Publications, 2001.

———. *The Wisdom and Philosophy of the Gikuyu Proverbs: The Kihooto World-View*. Nairobi: Paulines Publications, 1997.

Ward, Kevin. "A History of Christianity in Uganda." In *From Mission to Church*, edited by Zablon Nthamburi, 81–112. Nairobi: Uzima Press, 1991.

————. "'Tukutendereza Yesu': The Balokole Revival Movement in Uganda." In *From Mission to Church*, edited by Zablon Nthamburi, 113–144. Nairobi: Uzima Press, 1991.

Watt, Nigel. *Burundi: Biography of a Small African Country*. London: Hurst, 2008.

Welbourn, F. B., and B. A. Ogot. *A Place to Feel at Home*. Nairobi: Oxford University Press, 1966.

Welmers, William E. *African Language Structures*. Berkeley: University of California Press, 1973.

Wendland, Ernst R., and Jean-Claude Loba-Mkole, eds. *Biblical Texts and African Audiences*. Nairobi: Acton Publishers, 2004.

————, eds. *Interacting with Scriptures in Africa*. Nairobi: Acton Publishers, 2005.

Were, Gideon S. *A History of the Abaluyia of Western Kenya, c. 1500–1930*. Nairobi: East African Publishing House, 1967.

Were, Gideon S., and Derek A. Wilson. *East Africa through a Thousand Years: A History of the Years AD 1000 to the Present Day*. London: Evans Brothers, 1984.

Whiteley, Wilfred H., ed. *Language in Kenya*. Nairobi: Oxford University Press, 1974.

————, ed. *Language Use and Social Change, Problems of Multilingualism with Special Reference to Eastern Africa*. London: Oxford University Press, 1971.

————. "Linguistic Hybrids." *African Studies* 19 (1960): 95–97.

————. *Swahili: The Rise of a National Language*. London: Methuen, 1969.

Willis, Roy G. "The Fipa." In *Tanzania before 1900*, edited by Andrew Roberts, 82–95. Nairobi: East African Publishing House, 1968.

Wilt, Timothy, ed. *Bible Translation: Frames of Reference*. Manchester: St Jerome, 2003.

Wiredu, Kwasi. "On Decolonizing African Religions." In, *Philosophy from Africa*, edited by P. H. Coetzee and A. P. J. Roux, 109–130. Cape Town: Oxford University Press, 2002

World Translations Progress Report and Supplement. Reading: United Bible Societies, 1996.

Wright, Marcia. *German Missions in Tanganyika, 1891–1941*. Oxford: Clarendon, 1971.

Wrigley, C. C. *Kingship and State: The Buganda Dynasty*. Cambridge: Cambridge University Press, 1966.

Yorke, Gosnell, and Peter Renju, eds. *Bible Translation and African Languages*. Nairobi: Acton Publishers, 2004.

Index of Languages and Dialects

Nations where the language or dialect are primarily spoken are indicated as follows: (K) Kenya; (T) Tanzania; (U) Uganda; (R) Rwanda; (B) Burundi. Language families, branches and clusters are in bold.

Index of Names